STATE OF THREAT

STATE OF THREAT

The Challenges to Aotearoa New Zealand's National Security

Edited by Wil Hoverd
& Deidre Ann McDonald

MASSEY UNIVERSITY PRESS

Contents

Foreword / *Tony Lynch* **7**

Preface / *Bethan Greener* **9**

Introduction: Understanding global and domestic security threats / *Wil Hoverd & Deidre Ann McDonald* **11**

Part 1: Offshore threats and opportunities

1. US-China Great-Power Competition: Risks, opportunities and strategic options for New Zealand / *Reuben Steff* **33**

2. Conventional warfare today: What has the Russian invasion of Ukraine taught us? / *Terry Johanson* **46**

3. Retaining a national security workforce: Army personnel shortages in a mobile neoliberal society / *Nina Harding* **59**

4. Maritime trade security threats: Protecting New Zealand's economic lifeline to the world / *Stephen Hoadley* **70**

5. Supply chain disruptions and deep uncertainty: Implications for New Zealand in a post-Covid environment / *Germana Nicklin* **84**

Part 2: Intelligence and domestic security

6. Out of sight and out of mind: The absolute importance of submarine cables to New Zealand / *Phil Holdstock & John Moremon* **97**

7. Outlaw motorcycle gangs and the illegal drug trade: What national security risks do they pose? / *Chris Wilkins, Marta Rychert, Jose Romeo, Thomas Graydon-Guy & Robin van der Sanden* **109**

8. Biosecurity intelligence in Aotearoa: Adapting to changing national and international conditions / *Madeline Marshall* **122**

9. Does AI dream of protecting sheep? The role of artificial intelligence in national biosecurity / *Jodie Chapell & Deidre Ann McDonald* **134**

Part 3: Governance and extremism

10. Accountability and oversight: Democratic control over New Zealand's secret intelligence activities / *Damien Rogers* **149**

11. Leading New Zealand's security system: Ministerial responsibility for national security and intelligence / *Wil Hoverd* **161**

12. As safe now as we were then: Countering terrorism in New Zealand 1968–2030 / *John Battersby* **174**

13. Behind the floral aesthetic: Women in right-wing extremism / *Donna Carson* **185**

Part 4: Future security challenges

14. Russia's invasion of Ukraine: What is the strategic challenge for New Zealand? / *Justyna Eska-Mikołajewska* **199**

15. Digital currencies: Their potential role in New Zealand's economic statecraft / *José Miguel Alonso-Trabanco* **211**

16. The future of the 'good citizen': A perspective from the Polish frontline / *Marcin Lasoń* **221**

17. Self-determination or territorial integrity? Mixed messages from the Ukraine war / *Rouben Azizian* **231**

Conclusion: Constructing resilience and hope / *Deidre Ann McDonald & Wil Hoverd* **243**

Notes **247**

Bibliography **282**

About the contributors **309**

Acknowledgements **315**

Index **316**

Foreword

This latest contribution to Massey University Press's defence and security series arrives against the backdrop of an unprecedented release of national security documents, including Aotearoa New Zealand's first National Security Strategy — *Secure Together Tō Tātou Korowai Manaaki*. As such, it is a welcome contemporary addition to scholarship on New Zealand's place in the world, on the threats and risks we face as a nation, bringing together a distinctive New Zealand voice and perspective to matters of national security.

It comes at a time when New Zealand faces a fundamentally more challenging security outlook, through an ever more unpredictable and complex global environment. The National Security Survey (2023) found that 80 per cent of New Zealanders felt the world had become a more dangerous place over this last year.

New Zealand is not immune from global trends. In recent years, terrorist events, cyberattacks, transnational organised crime and disinformation have all impacted our communities directly, and are stark reminders that we are exposed to a range of national security risks.

We also learnt from this survey that New Zealanders have an appetite to learn more about national security, to be kept informed and updated on developments and, for many, to be part of conversations about New Zealand's security plans into the future. A clear message is that the more informed New Zealanders are about national security, the better we are able to take decisions about our resilience and wellbeing.

The report of the Royal Commission of Inquiry into the terrorist attack on Christchurch mosques on 15 March 2019 delivered a powerful message about the importance of a public discourse on national security. It challenged the government to develop a conversation with New Zealanders about the national security challenges we face — expressing the hope that by engaging in frank debate everyone would understand their roles and responsibilities in keeping New Zealand safe, secure and cohesive. These objectives lie at the heart of the National Security Strategy.

State of Threat picks up many of the core national security issues identified in the strategy, building our understanding on issues spanning strategic competition and the rules-based order, transnational organised crime, economic security, maritime security, terrorism and violent extremism, and much more. A consistent theme from the contributors to *State of Threat* is that these issues merit and deserve informed debate. And yet our national security conversation has not evolved at the same pace as global events.

We all have a role to play. Not least because few, if any, national security issues lie solely within the capacity of government or any one player alone to resolve. Increasingly, whole of society action is necessary — whether to address the existential threat of climate change, or the effects of disinformation, or terrorism and violent extremism.

My congratulations to Massey University, to the Centre for Defence and Security Studies, and to all the contributors to *State of Threat*, for this important contribution. We are so much the richer for this discourse. As readers, you will be informed, challenged and engaged, and I would encourage you to continue this national security debate in and across your communities, drawing on the breadth of material contained in this volume — and elsewhere!

It is appropriate to conclude this foreword with a whakataukī that encapsulates the essence of our public conversation on national security.

Mā te whakatū ka mōhio
Mā te mōhio ka mārama
Mā te mārama ka mātau
Mā te mātau ka ora

Through discussion comes understanding
Through understanding comes enlightenment
Through enlightenment comes wisdom
Through wisdom comes wellbeing

Tony Lynch
Chair, CDSS Strategic Advisory Board

Preface

Security and defence matters are not typically a part of New Zealanders' daily concerns. Even in election years such as this one, foreign, security and defence issues do not often feature in national conversations. This absence has consequences. It means that such issues remain the concern of a few professionals (bureaucrats, politicians, academics, journalists) and a handful of interested civilians with strong opinions. As such, debates on these topics have not been and are not yet representative.

This is compounded by a lack of diversity in the professional security sector. Yet we know that having access to diverse views increases problem-solving capacity, deepens understanding, and thus aids resilience and agility in responding to challenges. Getting more people interested in these issues — especially in times of increasing complexity and where, as noted in the foreword, national security is not just the task of governments — is extremely important. That is where this book comes in.

State of Threat is aimed at both the already engaged and the yet to be engaged, with the aim of increasing levels of general understanding about our contemporary security situation. It encompasses a range of views on security topics and arrives just after an unprecedented release of national security documents, including the first ever National Security Strategy — *Secure Together Tō Tātou Korowai Manaaki* — and the comprehensive 2023 Defence Policy Review. As such, this book represents a snapshot in time in which its commentators were formulating their own views on security matters in the absence of these documents. Although the authors may bemoan the timing, it provides an overview of the types of issues that concerned a wider range of individuals *before* their views could potentially have been influenced by official statements.

What is clear, is that many of these views align with those official views outlined in the security strategy and the review — particularly in recognising the broad sweep of challenges currently facing the New Zealand security sector and the need for wide-ranging engagement.

The authors include established academics from New Zealand and abroad, new and exciting early career doctoral candidates, and those who have worked for government agencies or who have spent careers critiquing them. At times, the authors disagree with one another. How to understand the Russian invasion of Ukraine and its consequences, for example, are handled differently by different authors, and hence they also arrive at different options for action.

But it is not just difference of interpretation about the motivation or resultant effects of such events that is represented. There are also disagreements about how to interpret what constitutes the security landscape, what the greatest challenges are, or what our security priorities should be in more general terms. Some authors focus on issues of social cohesion or threats to New Zealand's economic or societal security, while others emphasise how international developments have exceptionally broad and deep-reaching impacts and thus prioritise these sites of investigation.

In some ways, the range of views is reminiscent of military planning. What is seen as the greatest threat is not often the most likely. Making decisions in these complex times requires a balance of consideration, and making informed decisions means gathering in broad views as well as engaging New Zealanders as active citizens in the national security space. This is perhaps the greatest challenge, given the allergic response of most New Zealanders when it comes to talking about hard security concerns.

The diverse views presented are the core strength of this text. Readers will find themselves cleaving to some assertions and dismissing others. The book provides useful data about some of the issues and events 'out there' in the world, and it also provides different approaches to how we might go about understanding what these mean for New Zealand security. This matters more than ever as New Zealand sits in a turbulent global environment, one that it is tightly tied to through trade and other commitments, with domestic cohesion also under strain. Bringing more New Zealanders into national security discussions is therefore perhaps the most important challenge for security community today.

Professor Bethan Greener
Head of School of People, Environment and Planning
Massey University

Introduction

UNDERSTANDING GLOBAL AND DOMESTIC SECURITY THREATS

Wil Hoverd & Deidre Ann McDonald

In Aotearoa New Zealand we consider national security to be located at the intersection of domestic and international security. Since 2018, significant change has occurred in this space. Once benign, today the language around domestic and international events, trends and conflict reflects a greater sense of threat, making Aotearoa seem less secure than it was.[1]

In stating this, however, it is important to pause and think: when it comes to discussing the threats facing any country, there is always potential for the fourth estate and expert commentators to engage in self-interest or hyperbole.[2] Few experts discussing New Zealand's national security offer evidence for their claims, however.[3] In a post-truth world, where experts have been replaced by self-interest, spin, mis- and disinformation and fake news, what can we really know about the claims that our national security environment is becoming less secure?

National security is a constantly evolving concept, constructed and interpreted through language, policy, emotion, empirical evidence and the 'only-sometimes-revealed' lived reality of violence and power.[4] Inherent in this is the idea that the voices speaking about national security matter; in constructing the discussion, they influence and inform our emotional state and determine whether we feel secure or threatened.

State of Threat: The challenges to Aotearoa New Zealand's national security presents the editors' view that national security is fluid, dynamic, and constructed through the discourses devoted to the security interactions occurring between New Zealand's domestic and international environments.

The most authoritative voice on national security in this country is that of the government, because the government implements legitimate democratic power to plan any responses to threat. National security is overseen by the Department of the Prime Minister and Cabinet (DPMC), which reports to the prime minister (who is also minister for national security).[5] It is generally accepted that national security policy is bipartisan;[6] as such, the directors-general of the country's two intelligence agencies regularly brief both the prime minister and the leader of the opposition.[7]

The government communicates about national security through the enactment of policy and the prioritisation of funding for the various national security agencies. Due to the apolitical nature of the public service and the hidden nature of classified information, the government's national security voice is often carefully curated; occasional ministerial and chief executive speeches to small, elite audiences provide the most regular insight into the executive's thinking about national security.[8] This communication is clearest when it responds to an issue about which there is public awareness; at other times the messaging can be shrouded, informed by classified material, intelligence concerns and perhaps Five Eyes priorities.[9] Occasionally, in times of crisis, the prime minister will speak directly to the nation — as Dame Jacinda Ardern did immediately after the Christchurch terror attack in 2019.

Sitting beneath the speeches from the executive (the prime minister, ministers and chief executives) is a significant amount of policy, funding and legislative change concerning the governance and implementation of security. So, when we think about the construction of national security in Aotearoa, we must first look to the language of the state, which has the intelligence collection functions, is informed by its international partnerships, and has the executive power to implement national security and legitimate violence.

In August 2023, the government released its first National Security Strategy, which claims that 'New Zealand faces a fundamentally more challenging security outlook.'[10] The strategy employs phrases such as: 'we live in an era of disruption', 'we live in a contested world', 'pressure is likely to grow for countries like New Zealand' and 'threats are reaching New Zealanders more directly'.[11] Consequently, when the government communicates the existence of a threat, we must treat this information with the authority it deserves, since this voice matters the most. Unlike in an authoritarian nation, however, in New Zealand when we construct a view of national security, we are free to consider alternatives, history and ambiguity and to develop critiques unrestricted by the constraints and priorities of government. Most authors in this book do exactly that.

Academic experts also construct the language of national security. For a number of reasons, these voices seem to have receded into the background of the public space.[12] These experts are constantly involved in rigorous assessment and systematic review of data associated with wide-ranging topics of security; as critics and consciences of society, they are mandated to speak a form of 'truth'.[13] Their authority is based upon empiricism, teaching and subject-matter knowledge. They are trained both to deconstruct and reconstruct how we think about national security and threat in Aotearoa. Their experience informs the contributions in this volume, the purpose of which is to present a diverse set of contemporary academic essays intended for New Zealanders.

So far, we have briefly considered three social groups that together hold a form of hegemonic monopoly over the language, governance and construction of national security in Aotearoa. Unfortunately, all are privileged elites who offer prioritised discourses that contain the inherent bias associated with their hegemony (wealth, education, whiteness, heteronormativity and maleness). The fourth social group that must and can engage in and influence the construction of national security is the public, in all its forms.

This country has a long and unresolved colonial history of violence towards Māori.[14] The New Zealand Muslim community has said it feels explicit bias from the state.[15] The 2022 protest in Parliament grounds involved a range of people who felt the state did not represent their views or value them. Together, these examples should make us feel very uncomfortable. Ideally, inclusive discussions that embrace all members of our society should decrease social conflict and make us feel more secure, especially since the implementation of national security is almost always done to those who do not represent the 'nation', in order to secure the nation.[16]

The voice of the public has the power to create substantial change, particularly in terms of diversifying and democratising the voices and viewpoints constructing our security landscape. Elections provide one opportunity for the public to exercise their voice.[17] But while aspects like economic security, policing and law and order are common electoral concerns, matters of defence and security tend not to be. (Debate and protest about the nuclear-free policy is one obvious exception to this.)[18]

Engagement in questions about what it means to feel secure or threatened is essential to both community and national wellbeing. The public needs to understand the various threats to Aotearoa, the prevalence of these, and which ones should be prioritised. They must be able to recognise when security commentators are engaging in hyperbole. Informed voices must be able to contribute to discussions about who we want to be as a nation in terms of both domestic and international security.

NEW ZEALAND'S THREAT ENVIRONMENT 2018–23

Since 2018 our threat environment has changed from benign to threatening. We make this argument to foreground the contemporary essays contained in the volume. But before we shift to those essays, it is necessary to provide a brief history of Aotearoa's national security environment and the major changes that have occurred globally, regionally and domestically from 2018 to 2023. Three key factors have altered the threatscape during this period.

It can be argued that in 2018, national security matters were relatively benign, as most threats had become diffuse and complex rather than imminent threats with single points of origin from terrorist groups or nation states.

In 2018 US President Barack Obama had just left office and Donald Trump had begun his presidency of the United States of America. The world was economically prosperous with strong, interlaced trade relationships occurring across the European Union (EU), Russia, China and the US. New Zealand's 2008 free trade agreement with the People's Republic of China was coming into full force by 2019, and China was now our largest trading partner.[19] By the end of 2018, the Islamic State in the Levant (ISIL) had been declared defeated, terminating the primary initiator of global terrorism.

New Zealand Defence Force (NZDF) commitments to Afghanistan (where eight New Zealand soldiers had been killed over the 20-year deployment), Camp Taji in Iraq and the broader Western Operation Against ISIL were winding down, particularly after the battle for Mosul, although the official investigation into early New Zealand Special Air Service (SAS) actions in Afghanistan was just commencing.[20] Questions were arising about the whereabouts of ISIL captive Red Cross nurse Louise Akavi and the possibility of repatriation for the 'bumbling jihadi' Mark Taylor (both still unresolved today).[21]

Domestically, the Ardern Government had been in office for a year, and Aotearoa appeared to have avoided the terrorist threat of ISIL that had beleaguered Australia and other Western nations.[22] After almost 20 years, Western concerns about globally organised Islamic-inspired domestic terrorism had largely receded.[23]

In terms of regional security challenges, the Labour-New Zealand First coalition government was attempting to revitalise its engagement with the South Pacific under the Pacific Reset Policy.[24] This policy recognised that the region was experiencing stressors from climate change and lack of infrastructure and investment; as well, with Russia and China showing interest in nations such as Fiji, strategic competition had entered the region.[25] Refugee quotas (particularly after the Syrian and Iraq conflicts) were a matter of contention between Australia and New Zealand, specifically concerning the illegal detentions that had occurred at Manus Island until 2017.[26] The matter of '501 deportees' (New Zealand and Pasifika citizens) repatriated from Australia to Aotearoa and the Pacific region was beginning to cause tension between the two nations.[27] As well, the prevalence of Transnational Organised Crime across the Pacific region became a heightened concern, as did ongoing concerns about the prevalence and violence of gangs in Aotearoa.[28]

In 2018, when it came to domestic threats, the Hon Andrew Little (minister for the Government Communications Security Bureau and New Zealand Security Intelligence Service) stated that the two greatest national security threats to Aotearoa were cyberthreats and terrorism, both of which would originate from malicious actors.[29] Yet we know that threats do not only come from such sources: earthquakes, floods, cyclones, sea-level rise and fires are all matters for constant vigilance.

The NZDF has recognised the challenge of climate change,[30] and we can safely say that it is an existential threat globally and specifically in terms of sea-level rise in the South Pacific. In their respective essays, Reuben Steff, Germana Nicklin, Phil Holdstock and John Moremon, Nina Harding, and Jodie Chapell and Deidre McDonald all touch on issues associated with climate change.

Other notable security events have stemmed from non-malicious actors, such as the incursion of the cattle disease *Mycoplasma bovis* in 2017, which cost the country an estimated NZ$886 million;[31] and the December 2019 Whakaari White Island eruption, which killed 22 people and seriously injured another 25. Nevertheless, the malicious-actor definition remains helpful if we want to think about the argument that Aotearoa is more threatened today than in 2018.

One place where that linguistic distinction has been made is by the DPMC itself, which shifted its primary national security definition from an 'all hazards, all risks' approach to 'malicious threats' in 2022,[32] and then in the 2023 National Security Strategy, the phrasing changes to: 'National security is about protecting New Zealand from threats that would do us harm.'[33]

The question then arises: has the threat environment changed, or are there exogenous factors for the language shift?

We consider three key factors to have influenced the alteration of New Zealand's security focus from benign to threatening since 2018. These are the Christchurch terror attack; the Covid-19 pandemic and global recession; and the return of great-power competition (GPC).

The terror attack and the potential of great power competition engage directly with the problem of malicious threats, while the pandemic and global recession form an ideological, social and economic background of increased amorphous insecurity for the population. These security crises inform the essays in this volume. Before introducing the chapters themselves, it is useful to examine how these events have impacted national security.

THE CHRISTCHURCH TERROR ATTACK FUNDAMENTALLY changed the structure of New Zealand's national security environment. On 15 March 2019 a gunman attacked two mosques in Christchurch while worshippers were at prayer, killing 51 people and injuring another 40. The horror, destruction and loss of life resulting from the attack itself was unprecedented in New Zealand. This act of terror represented a failure of the security system to identify and prevent it. More than that, it suggested that the government's focus on Islamic jihadi terrorism had created a situation in which those in the Muslim community were viewed as suspects rather than potential victims.

The mosque attacks demonstrated the power of the right wing to act against multiculturalism, which for some replicates the colonial violence against indigenous peoples and immigrant others.[34] It also showed the public that we are not immune to terrorism, that terrorism could come from anywhere, and that perhaps our nation was not the egalitarian country we imagined it to be. This despicable event has prompted extensive reflection, academic research, a royal commission of inquiry and national security reform. It is not the purpose of this introduction to review those individual responses (although each is referenced for the interested reader). The attack instigated several transformations to New Zealand's national security:

1. A systematic revision of the counterterrorism national security functions[35]
2. Development of a nuanced understanding of violent extremism[36]
3. The understanding that social cohesion in our population is a national security priority[37]
4. The initiation of the Jacinda Ardern-led international Christchurch Call to eliminate terrorist and violent extremism content online,[38] and
5. Reviews of legislation around firearms, hate speech and the Intelligence Security Act 2017.[39]

This slew of sector changes increased national security workstreams, which today suggest an increase in capability across the various initiatives. It has also normalised the increased production of government language and resourcing devoted to mitigating future violent extremist threats. But what are these threats?

There remains future risk from ISIL and Al Qaeda. However, it is generally considered that the main unidentified threat actors in this space today are non-affiliated individuals, described as 'self-initiated terrorists' (replacing the term 'lone wolf', as they are inevitably connected somewhere online) who have fragmented ideologies and utilise low-technology attacks such as improvised explosive devices, knives, firearms and vehicles. The 6 September 2021 LynnMall terrorist fits this model: he was carefully described as acting alone and using a knife picked up in the supermarket in which the attack took place.[40]

On 15 March 2019, New Zealanders learned that our geographic isolation does not secure us from the threat of terrorism; on 6 September 2021 we became aware that this threat is continually present.

FROM JANUARY 2020, THE DEADLY Covid-19 pandemic began to spread through the world. In response to this threat, in March 2020 New Zealand closed its borders and implemented lockdowns in a four-level alert system to control community transmission. The government's elimination policy was in response to the virus's high fatality rate, its potential for long-term harm and its easy transmissibility. A system of controlled border entry was initiated, initially managed by private security companies, but in June 2020 the NZDF was deployed to run these managed isolation and quarantine (MIQ) facilities.[41]

As the pandemic continued, the virus mutated, and with the introduction of vaccines the government's elimination policy became increasingly untenable. Public support for lockdowns waned, especially when Auckland lockdowns were prolonged to buy time to vaccinate the broader population. The implementation of a vaccine mandate culminated in a significant protest in the grounds of Parliament House, Wellington, from 6 February to 2 March 2022, which ended in a violent dispersal of protestors by a nationally mobilised force of the New Zealand Police. From February 2022, the borders were gradually reopened, and all Covid restrictions were lifted on 14 August 2023.

Three ongoing national security concerns arose during the pandemic: the impact of the MIQ deployment on the NZDF; the effect of the Wellington protest on social cohesion; and the continuing impact on supply chain security, along with the resulting economic recession.

AS EARLY AS AUGUST 2021, RNZ political editor Jane Patterson observed that the ability of the NZDF to respond to a major disaster was significantly reduced because so many army personnel were deployed to Operation Protect — staffing the MIQ facilities.[42] As well, Lauran Walters reported, 'rising attrition rates, and personnel satisfaction surveys, reveal issues with culture, morale, opportunities for career development, and pay — issues that have been driven, and compounded, by Operation Protect'.[43]

A 'workforce crisis' was argued to exist around pay rates, though this was mitigated somewhat by the government's announcement of an extra injection of funding in May 2023.[44] Charlotte Cook suggested it could take the NZDF at least two years to rejuvenate its workforce and capabilities as a result. In 2022, attrition rates in the NZDF sat at 16 per cent for the civilian workforce and 15.6 per cent for the regular forces, with a 29.8 per cent staff turnover in the previous two years.[45]

When Cyclone Gabrielle struck in 2023, the NZDF was unable to implement its preferred response, as predicted. Because of an acute shortage of technical and tradespeople, it had to retire its P3 Orion aircraft early, and three naval patrol boats remained tied up at Devonport Naval Base.[46] Chief of Defence Force Air Marshal Kevin Short suggested that it would take four to ten years to fully rejuvenate various NZDF capabilities.[47]

New Zealand now finds itself in a position where its small military cannot function effectively; and in the face of an ageing population and full employment, the country is struggling to attract new recruits. For the foreseeable future, the NZDF will be operating at reduced capability. This is a vulnerability in terms of being able to secure ourselves and our region. It becomes a threat, however, if New Zealand needs to be an active participant in the GPC, as discussed by Dr Reuben Steff and Terry Johanson in their respective chapters.

AT THE PEAK OF THE 2022 Wellington occupation of the grounds of Parliament House, reporters noted 'there were approximately 3000 protesters, 2000 vehicles in surrounding streets and 300 structures illegally erected in and around Parliament'.[48] It lasted 24 days and more than 300 people were arrested. Dispersal of the protestors involved the largest deployment of riot police since the 1981 Springbok tour protests.[49]

The protest's origins lay in widespread dissatisfaction with the government's Covid-19 policy and vaccine mandates.[50] Protestors came from a variety of backgrounds with a range of motivations: early images showed some waving Tino Rangatiratanga flags and others wearing Trump supporter gear. The protest was complex and confounding, and, over a two-week period, slowly escalated from a legitimate traditional protest to violence. Police control was escalated in response.

The demonstration drew on a long history of protest on Parliament grounds, as people with perceived legitimate grievances engaged in the proper exercise of free speech. But these grievances were interspersed with conspiracy theory, intense vitriol against then Prime Minister Jacinda Ardern and a tendency to violence. The scale of the event suggests that care is required in the production of reductionist views regarding protest, or 'othering' the phenomenon using descriptors such as 'it's just the alt right' or 'it's just the anti-vaxxers'. The protest evidenced a divided, perhaps polarised, New Zealand that is not socially cohesive and in which certain groups feel they have been 'othered' by the state.

Six issues for national security that were evident at the protest are ongoing. First, the protest highlighted the vitriol directed at Prime Minister Ardern, which had moved beyond speech to genuine threats to her safety and that of her family.[51] Much of this was severely misogynistic and some was extremely violent in nature. Several of the individuals who threatened the prime minister have since been prosecuted. Misogyny, which is arguably endemic in New Zealand, creates generational and social insecurity for all women.

Second, links were made between the Wellington protest and the 6 January 2021 protest and attack on the US Senate[52] and a similar anti-mandate protest occurring in Ottawa, Canada, and certain groups and individuals wished to exacerbate those links.

Third is the distinct online environment that New Zealanders are engaged in, which encourages the spread of disinformation about vaccines and the role of government.[53]

The fourth is that conspiracy theories can be used to amplify and/or motivate protest action and anti-government dissent.[54]

Fifth is the realisation that the intelligence and policing capabilities of the state in combination with the political will of the executive are not well equipped to disperse and engage democratically with a protest such as this.[55]

And sixth, it appears the acceptance of adversarial ideas is becoming harder, and social groups are forming silos from which it is easier to cancel and silence other views than engage with them, learn from them and perhaps influence them.

While the unifying trigger of the vaccine mandate has now receded, the division and online environment associated with the protest have not, and the threat of another anti-government protest remains. New Zealanders today are not immune to a permissible online environment where individuals can become subject to and receptive of dis- and misinformation, extremism, misogyny and violence.

THE COVID-19 LOCKDOWNS WERE CHARACTERISED by supermarket shortages as consumers placed higher demand on certain products, and at times our domestic and international supply chains were stretched to breaking point. As workforces were sent home, jobs and businesses were lost[56] and the supply of some non-essential goods and services became problematic. Among other industries, tourism, A2 milk formula and international student enrolments collapsed overnight.[57]

China's Covid-19 border closure meant that much of the world's shipping transiting through Shanghai experienced significant delays.[58] Elsewhere, the supply of goods was impacted by increased restrictions and compliance in other jurisdictions. Shortages of supply increased costs for producers, suppliers and consumers; in response, governments increased the money supply and certain subsidies, and lowered interest rates.[59] In New Zealand, housing prices shot to levels unaffordable for most first-home buyers.[60]

Globally, the supply chain shortage played out in the context of the 2020 Brexit withdrawal of the UK from the EU, and a trade war between the US and China that had begun in 2018 with the US placing tariffs on Chinese goods and companies.[61] This economic conflict had already impacted our neighbour, Australia, after China restricted its steel exports to the nation.[62]

Since 2022, the Russia-Ukraine war has had further impact on global grain, natural gas and fertiliser supplies, among other goods.[63] The economic sanctions against Russia have resulted in economic changes whereby Western nations have commenced sourcing products from closer, more expensive but trusted sources. Some have argued that a global economic decoupling is occurring.[64] Certainly, there is some bifurcation taking place between the West, China and Russia that is leading to pressure on economic globalisation.

Across the world, fears of recession have grown as inflation occurs as a product of reduced supply of goods, low interest rates and the increased monetary supply made available by many governments. In her chapter, Dr Germana Nicklin discusses her research on the outcomes for national security that have arisen from this environment of supply chain disruption.

Today, New Zealanders are facing economic hardship from recession and inflation in a way many cannot recall experiencing before. Inflation is sustained.[65] Wage growth has not matched inflation. Prices for goods and services — notably for food and fuel — are increasing. Industry is struggling to pass on the increased expenses caused by inflation. Across the Western world, reserve banks are increasing interest rates to curb inflation and manufacture recessionary environments. Many New Zealanders are finding their mortgage payments increasing as they refix loans; and house prices are falling, leading to negative equity for some.

The resulting economic experience for Aotearoa is one of sustained insecurity. While a recession and shortage of goods and services might not be threatening in and of itself, it heightens anxiety and perhaps creates domestic and international situations where concerns about shortages create the potential for conflict. Associate Professor Stephen Hoadley looks at this potential in his chapter, devoted to the pressures on New Zealand's maritime environment.

THE RETURN OF GPC AND its ramifications, the decline of the multilateral order, and exploring what the threat of war might mean for New Zealand, are the focus of parts one and four of this volume. The National Security Strategy notes that if this 'intensifies, New Zealand may face a less predictable more contested international system that is less aligned with our values'.[66] This threat was triggered by the 2022 illegal invasion of Ukraine by the Russian Federation and concerns about a Chinese invasion of Taiwan after the visit of US politician Nancy Pelosi to Taipei.[67]

China has been undergoing a rapid militarisation over the last few years, significantly growing its military capabilities. In response to Pelosi's visit, it engaged in ballistic missile launches over Taiwan and air and naval operations on the edge of the island's territorial waters.[68] This aggressive response was based on the Chinese view that Taiwan is still part of China. However, the US is committed to assisting Taiwan to resist an attack. China's aggressive military response suggests that war is possible.[69]

Events like the Ukraine war, Putin's nuclear sabre-rattling, the rise of authoritarian regimes, the failure of multilateral institutions such as the UN Security Council and tensions over Taiwan have brought the possibility of contemporary warfare, nuclear conflict and grey-zone or hybrid conflict to the centre of global affairs. The tension is pushing China and Russia closer together and creating tacit Chinese support for the invasion of Ukraine.

Any prospect of war between the US and NATO and one or other of these nations is a matter of deep existential concern. It is leading to militarisation across the Western world (see Professor Marcin Lasoń in this volume), questions about the role of the NZDF (see Terry Johanson), how New Zealand acts in the international environment (Dr Justyna Eska-Mikołajewska writes of this), and how New Zealand balances its trade relationship with China and its Five Eye (FVEY) intelligence and defence relationships with its Western partners (see Reuben Steff's chapter). Together, these writers exhibit distinct unease about the possibility of conflict. Regardless of New Zealand's response, other players in our region are also being pulled into this tension and their involvement should be a matter of concern.

Australia, our only military ally, has entered the AUKUS agreement with the US and the UK, which enables the sharing of military technology and the development of interoperability between the three militaries.[70] This also involves our neighbour committing to the eventual purchase of nuclear-powered submarines to support its navy. China has suggested that it views AUKUS as encirclement and therefore a provocation.[71]

New Zealand's defence minister, Andrew Little, has recently suggested that New Zealand might consider joining AUKUS as a Pillar 2 member, giving us access to technology and joint operations among other perceived benefits.[72] Ideally, any commitment to joining AUKUS first entails conversation with the public, as it commits New Zealand to a certain future.

Although China may view AUKUS as a provocation, it continues to actively exert influence in the Pacific region, engaging in what some have called 'debt trap diplomacy' and a commitment to building a base in Solomon Islands.[73] And FVEY intelligence agencies are increasingly worried about foreign interference occurring in their domestic environments, where China coerces or weaponises its diaspora to gain access to information or influence certain political and community discourses. As the relationship between the West, China and Russia degrades, New Zealanders need to consider how this growing threat will impact our national security.

THE FOUR PARTS OF THIS BOOK each examine a relevant security issue or theme. **Part 1: Offshore threats and opportunities** begins by looking at offshore threats to New Zealand's security, before moving to consider some domestic security challenges and opportunities.

The opening chapter begins with an analysis of the great-power competition (GPC) being enacted between the US and China and how this might impact on the Pacific region. Dr Reuben Steff begins by sharing a sobering statistic, demonstrating that rapid geopolitical shifts in power often result in war. He warns that conflict in the Pacific is 'no longer inconceivable'. Given that China is our largest trading partner and the US is an important partner, the question arises, with whom would the government stand? Would Wellington have to make a choice, or could we retain a balance? These are some of the geopolitical challenges confronting New Zealand's foreign policy. Dr Steff walks the reader through three questions he considers are relevant to our strategic approach and examines the risks and benefits inherent in each. He contributes to the public debates that must continue about the US-China GPC that may call on the government to choose sides in the Pacific region.

Chapter 2 brings the war in Ukraine closer to home. Massey University lecturer Terry Johanson examines lessons that have emerged from the invasion and asks what New Zealand can learn about contemporary conventional warfare. He investigates characteristics of Russia's war against Ukraine and contrasts these with the most likely scenario this country's defence force could face, which he describes as 'defeating Chinese aggression in the Indo-Pacific region'. The challenge, according to Johanson, is to determine where the NZDF should focus its military efforts, given its current financial and human resource limitations. This chapter offers some options to apply lessons from the Ukraine war and discusses the implications of each one. Unlike Professor Lasoń in a subsequent chapter, Johanson argues that focusing on New Zealand's immediate defence environment is the strategic approach.

Dr Nina Harding's sobering discussion about the NZDF's workforce shortages follows. In Chapter 3 Dr Harding examines why people join the New Zealand Army and why they leave. Her research indicates that soldiers want not only to put their skills into service for their country but also to have opportunities for self-development; if those opportunities are not provided, soldiers resign. This point is particularly salient in relation to workforce retention following the MIQ experience. There is a paradox here, however: while long-term retention of soldiers is vital to national security, retaining them is 'incompatible with a neoliberal nation-state' where individual economic security is prioritised and rewarded.

Maritime trade security follows in Chapter 4, by Associate Professor Stephen Hoadley, who reiterates the importance of trade for New Zealand's economic and social security. Hoadley situates his discussion within the strategically relevant maritime space. This chapter sheds light on the importance of maritime security for island states and explains some of the contemporary challenges, including the high attrition rates of navy personnel.

Chapter 5 considers the significance of supply chains and, in particular, the uncertainty caused by their disruption. Dr Germana Nicklin argues that GPC, climate change and resource insecurities can all influence supply chain stability as much as the more obvious disrupters of pandemic proportion. She examines some of New Zealand's supply chain vulnerabilities in detail and considers options for strengthening our preparedness and resilience. The chapter demonstrates that this future-focused work is not optional; it is our pathway towards supply chain resilience.

Part 2: Intelligence and domestic security continues the theme of regional security but moves to consider New Zealand's economic, social and environmental security across a range of topics, from deep-sea submarine cables to the illicit domestic drug trade, the role and function of intelligence gathering for biosecurity purposes, and some of the complexities associated with using artificial intelligence.

In Chapter 6, Phil Holdstock and Dr John Moremon explain the 'absolute importance' of submarine cables to global economic security. This global network of copper and fibre-optic cables exists underground and under oceans and carries almost all the world's electronic communications. New Zealand is dependent on this infrastructure for access to the internet, banking, business, news and more. The authors suggest the cables are not usually considered as a security risk because they are out of sight, and argue that they are more vulnerable than we realise. They outline some of the main threats to this essential communications infrastructure, from human interference to natural disasters. Protection of these cables is particularly vital for a geographically isolated country like New Zealand.

The theme of hidden economic risks continues in Chapter 7, which focuses on illegal trading in outlaw motorcycle gangs. Associate Professor Chris Wilkins, Dr Marta Rychert, Dr Jose Romeo, Thomas Graydon-Guy and Robin van der Sanden expose the growing membership of gangs in New Zealand and the sophistication with which these gangs run their criminal networks. The authors expand our knowledge of gangs' international involvement in illegal drug trading and explain some of the reasons for the lack of available information about gang-related violence. Of particular concern are the social impacts of organised crime, the methamphetamine trade, and gang intimidation in rural areas.

The next two chapters focus on intelligence gathering. In Chapter 8 Dr Madeline Marshall explains the operational aspects of intelligence gathering for biosecurity purposes and describes the process of monitoring overseas threats to New Zealand's biosecurity. She illustrates the importance of gathering offshore data for anticipating pest and disease pathways and showcases the fusion of intelligence and biosecurity disciplines.

Chapter 9 follows her detailed explanation with a discussion about the role of artificial intelligence (AI) in biosecurity. Dr Jodie Chapell and Deidre McDonald argue that AI is a valuable tool for identifying biosecurity threats, but that limitations in the use of this technology require careful consideration. An underlying message is that AI cannot replace human knowledge-sharing or place-based understandings of biosecurity threats in New Zealand. The authors caution that more work is required to ensure transparency, the minimisation of potential harm, and the maximisation of benefits for all kinds of security outcomes.

Part 3: Governance and extremism turns the spotlight on other issues of national intelligence and opens up a debate about the democratic principles of transparency and oversight, and how threats are communicated and understood by the public. It then shifts to the ever-present threats of domestic terrorism and extremism. The contributors unpack some misconceptions about our safety and ask the provocative question, 'What exactly does a terrorist look like?'

In Chapter 10 Associate Professor Damien Rogers argues in favour of more openness and accountability from government about how it manages its 'secret intelligence activities'. The chapter encourages deeper thinking about the role of democracy vis-à-vis those intelligence activities. The author offers some options for democratically driven reform in this area to increase accountability for government and ministerial actions.

In Chapter 11, Associate Professor Wil Hoverd takes readers into the world of national security speeches and the evolution of national security roles and functions within government, with a particular focus on the minister of national security. He analyses how the definition of national security has changed over time and provides examples of how this has been framed for public consumption. His chapter echoes the need for more public awareness of matters of security and suggests the time has come to stop calling for broader conversations about national security and actually start having them.

In Chapter 12 Dr John Battersby begins a conversation that spans the remainder of this section with a piece on the history of terrorism in New Zealand. He provides a troubling reminder that our current terrorism threat level (which is sitting at 'low') is the same as it was on the day of the mosque attacks in Christchurch. Dr Battersby notes that terrorism has been present in New Zealand in various forms for decades; however, the very nature of terrorism makes it difficult to detect, and even more so when the manifestations and motivations are divergent, and where law enforcement agencies, like the NZDF, struggle with finite human resources. He argues that missed opportunities to learn from recent history present an ongoing problem, because counterterrorism preparedness requires (at the very least) a solid understanding of past trends.

The next offering continues this theme of missed opportunities. Chapter 13 explores an overlooked topic: the role and identity politics of women in extremist groups. PhD candidate Donna Carson looks at the influence of gender bias when identifying what an 'extremist' looks like. Carson tells us that women involved with right-wing extremism (RWE) rely on gender stereotypes to hide behind a 'cloak of plausible deniability'. These women appear feminine, are often wives and mothers and tend to live within traditional (Western) nuclear families, yet some have also masterminded extremist actions. The chapter identifies women as powerful actors within RWE movements, and stresses that New Zealand is not immune to their influence.

Part 4: Future security challenges pulls together key conceptual threads from earlier chapters as the contributors look to options for the future. Here, the volume circles back to Russia's invasion of Ukraine and impacts for the territorial sovereignty of small states, with a particular focus on the self-determination of populations.

In Chapter 14 Dr Justyna Eska-Mikołajewska considers Russia's invasion of Ukraine. She argues that the war's impact on global and regional security highlights the importance of stability in the international system, and questions whether this invasion poses a foreign policy challenge for New Zealand despite our geographical isolation. She points out this nation's vulnerabilities in the face of such disruption and ponders how New Zealand can maintain its position as 'a balanced international actor promoting a rules-based order'. The author considers that, despite Russia's invasion of Ukraine changing the international balance of power, New Zealand can retain a strategic independence and support a rules-based order at the same time.

PhD candidate José Miguel Alonso-Trabanco then raises the topical issue of digital currencies and explains the importance of these 'game-changing' currencies for national security. In Chapter 15 he discusses recent examples of these technologies and some of the risks, including illicit activity. He also highlights some non-apparent opportunities for New Zealand that are arising from digital currencies. According to Alonso-Trabanco, digital currencies have disruptive potential, both for good and for bad, and they cannot be ignored.

In Chapter 16 Professor Marcin Lasoń provides a Polish perspective on the Ukraine war and applies the lens of a 'good citizen' to his analysis of Russia's territorial invasion. He urges readers to consider what could happen here if New Zealand were to find itself in Ukraine's position. This forward-thinking chapter offers some Polish experiences as illustration. Professor Lasoń reinforces the view set out in the previous chapters: that New Zealand can no longer rely on its geographical isolation as a measure of protection or a guarantee of continuous territorial sovereignty. There is a recurring theme of threats to the rules-based order from Russia's invasion, and in particular a threat to the sovereignty of small states. Unlike Dr Eska-Mikołajewska, however, Professor Lasoń argues in favour of New Zealand acting 'unequivocally' on the side of the West, in part because of the strategic importance of being seen to do so. The chapter concludes with a call for the government to act not only in its own interests but also in the interests of international military cooperation.

The Ukraine war is also the topic of the final chapter, and again the gaze is turned towards home. In Chapter 17 Professor Rouben Azizian argues against a 'West versus Russia' view of this conflict and calls for a more nuanced framing of self-determination and territorial integrity issues. He critically analyses the ways in which Russia's war against Ukraine has altered global relations and focuses on potential consequences for Pacific Island nations and New Zealand. Professor Azizian likens the Ukrainians' struggle for self-determination with local, indigenous struggles for recognition. This chapter illustrates that tensions between territorial integrity and self-determination are likely to increase due to the existence of authoritarian regimes and increased global geopolitical rivalry. The author suggests New Zealand's approach to domestic and international politics must include consistent and informed consideration of the tension between sovereignty and self-determination.

This introduction has highlighted the contributions to this volume and situated the essays within recent global and domestic security challenges. We are told that New Zealand feels more threatened than in 2018; these essays allow the reader to judge for themselves the state of threat for Aotearoa.

Part 1

OFFSHORE THREATS AND OPPORTUNITIES

The New Zealand people deserve to know what's going on, what is at stake, and the pros and cons of various options.

1.

US-CHINA GREAT-POWER COMPETITION

**| Risks, opportunities and strategic
options for New Zealand**

Reuben Steff

A great-power competition (GPC) is under way in the Indo-Pacific and throughout its sub-regions, including the South Pacific where Aotearoa New Zealand is situated. This contest pits the United States superpower against China, a rising and partially revisionist near-superpower. In 12 of 16 cases over the last 500 years, rapid shifts in power have resulted in war.[1] A conflict in the Indo-Pacific is no longer inconceivable, with both Washington and Beijing preparing for one while jockeying for advantage.

This competition has economic and strategic implications for New Zealand. On the one hand, New Zealand is a near-ally of the US and a military ally of Australia. On the other, China is New Zealand's largest trading partner. New Zealand, therefore, has tried to ensure it does not antagonise either state to the degree that they punish New Zealand. Yet, as the US-China rivalry intensifies and the Indo-Pacific becomes increasingly militarised, Wellington is finding it harder to balance its relations with the US and Australia on one side, and China on the other.

What are New Zealand's strategic options going forward, and what are the risks and benefits of the different options? In light of the US-China great-power competition (GPC) in the Indo-Pacific, and its importance to New Zealand's future security, a systematic debate over these issues needs urgently to be presented before the New Zealand public as the country diligently plots the best path forward.

A GPC IS DEFINED AS 'a permanent, compulsory, comprehensive, and exclusive contest for supremacy in a region or domain among those states considered to be the major players in the international system'.[2] Their reoccurrence and intensification are a persistent feature of human history, since no country has ever been able to stay on top as others 'balance' (by establishing alliances and directing their resources towards expanding their military forces) against them. This creates a cycle of tension and competition, sometimes leading to conflict. War may even occur when neither side wants it, when one becomes convinced that the other seeks conquest and opts to strike first out of fear the other is planning to do the same.[3]

Great powers are the most powerful countries. They usually have large territories, large populations and significant natural resources (or access to them). This allows them to develop and build large and diversified portfolios of political, economic, military and technological capabilities. They can also marshal non-material capabilities or 'soft power': the ability to attract or influence others by engendering respect for national values, culture and success.[4] Collectively, their capabilities allow them to project power and influence beyond their borders to carve out spheres of influence (co-opting or crushing states that oppose them in the process) in order to secure economic resources while denying or impeding competitors' access to these.[5] They may then seek global supremacy.

Smaller states can be significant players in their own regions, but it is the great powers that ultimately set the scene of international politics. In recent decades the ability of larger states to impose their will on smaller ones has been reduced due to the creation of a rules-based international system (discussed below). Smaller states may also be courted by great powers and can leverage this to their advantage. Outright alignment has risks, however, and can come at a price as larger states expect their smaller partners to support their strategic interests.

Since 1945 there have been two GPCs. The first was the Cold War (1945–91) between the democratic United States and authoritarian Soviet Union. Both created exclusive blocs comprised of military, diplomatic and economic allies that had little to do with the other. US strategy facilitated this global separation through a strategy of containment of the Soviet Union designed to prevent the spread of communism.[6] As Figure 1 shows, New Zealand sided in this with the United States. Underpinned by the 1951 Australia, New Zealand and United States (ANZUS) Treaty, close military, intelligence and foreign policy connections were established, and New Zealand participated in distant wars (such as the Korean War and Vietnam War) on the side of US-led forces.

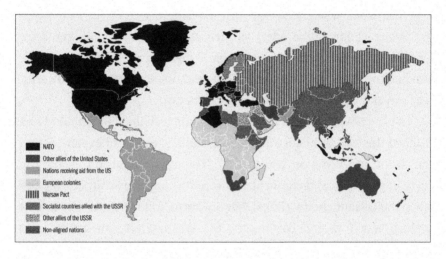

Figure 1: Map of Cold War alliances (the Soviet-Chinese alliance expired in 1979)

As the US and Soviets sought global supremacy, their interests clashed, leading them to conduct military interventions, experience intense crises (for example the Cuban Missile Crisis in 1962), initiate proxy wars, and support coups in the developing world to support their preferred elites.

In 1985 New Zealand chose to give up its alliance with Washington as it no longer felt a significant threat from the communist world, and prioritised a domestic social and political 'nuclear free' movement over continuing to allow potentially nuclear-powered US vessels into New Zealand ports.[7]

It is important to recognise that after 1945 the US led the charge to establish an international rules-based order comprising multilateral institutions (including the United Nations, World Trade Organization and International Monetary Fund), laws and norms. Embedded in this are liberal democratic values and support for human rights that reflect New

Zealand's own domestic values. Ever since, this system has gone some way to ensure small nations like New Zealand are not exploited or bullied by more powerful states. It has also facilitated economic development and New Zealand's access to global markets. The international rules-based order also allows for collective action in response to aggression by states and to global problems like climate change and humanitarian emergencies. Throughout the Cold War, and since, New Zealand has been highly supportive of this order, and Wellington has repeatedly asserted that it seeks to prevent the order from being undermined.

The Cold War ended with the US side's 'victory' in 1991 when the Soviet Union broke apart as their state-run economies could no longer compete with their much more dynamic capitalist competitors. Washington emerged from the Cold War in an extremely powerful position and an era of US global primacy began.

As the Soviet Union's power waned, some claimed humankind had reached the 'end of history'.[8] Liberal democracies would expand across the world and bring an end to GPC. This was a delusion. Below the surface, geopolitical tectonic plates were shifting. This shift accelerated when the US launched a 'Global War on Terror' following the 9/11 attacks against New York and Washington DC. Washington sent hundreds of thousands of troops into Afghanistan and Iraq to fight terrorist groups. The subsequent seven-year combat mission in Iraq and 20-year mission in Afghanistan is now broadly recognised as a profound strategic blunder. It led to civil wars and the emergence of new terrorist groups, like the Islamic State, that filled the power vacuum left by the US's toppling of the Saddam Hussein regime in Iraq and the chaos unleashed throughout Syria in the wake of uprisings there in 2011.

THE US'S MIDDLE EASTERN WARS expended US resources and distracted Washington, giving space for China to rise swiftly, unencumbered economically (a rise the US encouraged until 2017 through a policy of US-China engagement) and militarily. China began to assert itself by militarising the South China Sea, eliminating democracy in Hong Kong, intensifying repression at home and pushing its influence out across the globe. These manoeuvres have been complemented by a massive military modernisation enterprise.[9] For example, between 2014 and 2018, China's shipyards rolled out more naval vessels than the navies of the entire

British, Indian, Spanish, Taiwanese and German fleets combined (it now has the largest navy in the world by number of ships). It is also engaged in a nuclear breakout to expand the number of its nuclear weapons from approximately 200 to at least 1000 by the end of 2030, and its military spending grew 10-fold between 1990 and 2020.[10]

To demonstrate how China has risen in economic and military power relative to the US, Table 1 shows the changes in US and China Gross Domestic Product (GDP), and in their respective defence budgets from 1991 to 2022.

Table 1: China/US GDP and defence budget growth 1991/2022 (USD)[11]

Country	GDP 1991 (trillions)	GDP 2022 (trillions)	Defence budget 1991 (billions)	Defence budget 2022 (billions)
China	0.383	17.88	23.3	229
US	6.16	25.46	551.9	742

China might overtake the US economically by 2030, although, as of August 2023, China's economy appears to be significantly slowing and deflation is occurring; a return to high levels of growth in the near-term are far from certain.[12] Beijing is acquiring the military power to challenge US influence in parts of the Indo-Pacific. China has also threatened to invade Taiwan in the coming years (it considers the island to be a rogue territory); the US, Australia and Japan have said they reserve the right to defend the island should China try this.

Meanwhile Russia, the successor to the Soviet Union, has resurged into some former Soviet areas by conducting military interventions in Georgia in 2008, annexing Crimea in 2014, and launching a full-scale invasion of Ukraine in February 2022.

A new GPC is now under way between the US, its allies and partners and a looser near-alliance between China, Russia and Iran. This was formalised in the Trump administration's 2017 National Security Strategy, which declared, 'after being dismissed as a phenomenon of an earlier century, great power competition [has] returned'.[13] This document shifted Washington's focus to prioritise the challenge of China and Russia, with the Indo-Pacific region the strategic centre of gravity. Figure 2 shows the nations in this mega-region.

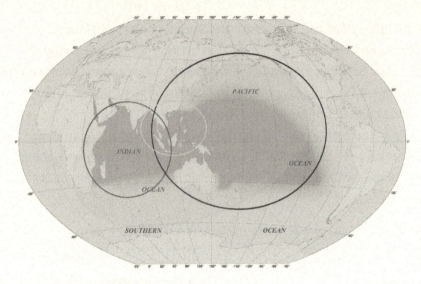

Figure 2: Map of the Indo-Pacific region

In 2017 the US initiated a neo-containment strategy against China. This approach differs from the comprehensive version of containment used against the Soviet Union during the Cold War, since China is now a key trading partner for many countries, including the US. Nonetheless, there are some areas of intense competition where Washington is trying to exclude and contain China's rise and influence. Economically, this involves an ongoing trade war against Beijing and extension of trade restrictions to high technologies (such as semiconductors, artificial intelligence and quantum computing), as Washington has sought to organise the 'techno-democracies' against the 'techno-autocracies'.[14]

Washington also encouraged its allies and partners to ban China's global telecommunications company, Huawei, from building their 5G internet networks, declaring their concern that the Chinese government will use it to spy, thus giving Beijing immense influence over the countries that use it.

The outcome is that we now see a global split: many nations in Latin America, Africa and Asia have acquired Chinese 5G and much of the developed world has opted for US-preferred 5G suppliers, like South Korea's Samsung. The US, Japan and the Netherlands are also cutting off exports of the most sophisticated semiconductors to China. These are critical, as they will drive the next generation of military and civilian technologies and China does not yet have the capability to manufacture its own advanced semiconductors.

The US and China are effectively carving out spheres of technological influence internationally that, in the future, may fully separate from one another if they depend on technologies from exclusive suppliers and technologies that will be used according to different value systems (surveillance and population control favoured by techno-autocracies; transparency and freedom in techno-democracies).

Militarily, the US is reconfiguring its forces to fight in the Indo-Pacific, acquiring new basing rights in the region (for example in Australia and the Philippines), selling advanced military arms to partners and allies, re-engaging island states in the South Pacific that straddle vital sea lines of communication (including agreeing to help Papua New Guinea develop a defence force),[15] and deepening and expanding its network of allies (and encouraging its allies to increase cooperation between themselves).

THERE ARE THREE NOTABLE DIFFERENCES between the Cold War GPC and the current one. First, the current world system is much more globalised: states today are more interconnected and, to a degree, interdependent on one another than they were in 1990.[16] As nations' economies have integrated more with one another, interconnected economic supply chains (for example where parts of many digital products are made in multiple countries), people-to-people ties and investment between countries have increased dramatically.

As such, war between the US and China would roil international markets, significantly reduce (and potentially outright sever) trade, political and people-to-people ties, and likely induce a global economic depression. This could prevent Washington and Beijing from going to war in the first place. Moreover, the thicket of rules, norms and institutions of the international rules-based system may also moderate US-China competition. Nothing is guaranteed, however, since, repeatedly throughout history, states that are interdependent with others have still chosen to go to war.

The second difference is that China has not established an alliance to compete with the US and its allies. It has a treaty with North Korea, but Pyongyang adds little to China's global heft. China's ties with Russia have grown immensely in recent years, leading to the announcement of a 'no limits' partnership just weeks before Russia's invasion of

Ukraine.[17] However, they do not have a military treaty between them; beyond providing diplomatic support and offering an economic lifeline to Russia's sanctions-hit economy (by continuing to purchase Russian goods), Beijing has been unwilling to provide tangible military support to assist Moscow's fight in Ukraine.

A third difference is that China does not offer a convincing ideological alternative to liberal democracy. But the consequences of this should not be overstated — China's state-run capitalist model, and the infrastructure investments and technologies it is willing to export that allow surveillance and control of populations, are compelling to many leaders, especially in the global south where many non-democracies exist.

GIVEN NEW ZEALAND'S REMOTENESS, it is reasonable to ask why we should care about the new GPC. Unfortunately, GPCs are global competitions that have implications for every nation. Consider the South Pacific — a region New Zealand and Australia consider their sphere of influence. If a power like China were to absorb the Pacific Islands into its sphere of influence, New Zealand and Australia's strategic depth would shrink significantly, and in a crisis a strategically placed Chinese military position in the Pacific could reduce Australia, New Zealand and the US's commercial and military freedom to move through the region. Indeed, the New Zealand government's *Defence Policy and Strategy Statement* has now officially declared: 'The Chinese Government in particular has sought to grow its political, economic, and security influence in the Pacific at the expense of more traditional partners such as New Zealand and Australia.'[18]

The last time the South Pacific was seriously contested by great powers was during the Second World War (1939–45). In this conflict Japan occupied parts of the South Pacific, threatened the free transit of cargo and bombed Australia. Only the US's entry into the war, after Japan struck Pearl Harbor in December 1941, saved Australia and New Zealand from eventual Japanese invasion. In recent decades the region has been free from external competition. This is now changing as China increases its diplomatic presence, its economic ties, its aid contributions and its infrastructure developments in the South Pacific. It is also increasing its security and military cooperation.[19]

Solomon Islands is a case in point. In recent years, China's influence there has grown markedly, leading Prime Minister Manasseh Sogavare to sign a security agreement with China.[20] Subsequently, a Chinese state company was awarded a deal in March 2023 to redevelop the port in Honiara. An upgraded port could be converted towards military purposes in the future, providing China with a permanent military position in the South Pacific.

The South Pacific therefore risks becoming a 'shatterbelt' — an area divided internally where great powers actively compete for advantage.[21] In this context, China could pull parts of the South Pacific beyond just the Solomons into its sphere of influence. China is also seeking to militarily dominate the South China Sea further to the north in contravention of international law.[22] These military activities are a major challenge to the rules-based international system that is vital to New Zealand's long-term security.

A second major implication is that both the US and China offer New Zealand economic and technological inducements. Our small economy and population and limited domestic manufacturing base mean that we need to trade with others to remain a first-world nation. On our own, we cannot produce most high-tech goods or weaponry for our military, and many products and inputs that we need for our agriculture, health and transport sectors come from abroad.

New Zealand therefore faces a dilemma: our security ties, values and broad foreign policy interests align us with Australia and the United States, and we are part of the Five Eyes intelligence-sharing arrangement alongside the US, UK, Australia and Canada. Since 2010, most of our military arms have come from the US, and our naval forces now conduct regular joint operations with Washington-led forces in the Pacific.[23] Yet over 30 per cent of our exports go to China; despite repeated encouragement from the New Zealand government to local businesses to 'diversify' away from China, few inroads have been made.[24] Our economic dependence on China actually increased during the Covid-19 years, from 2020 to 2022.[25]

Finally, the US and Beijing have both exploited developments in innovative technologies, energy prices, climate change, counter-terrorism efforts, refugee movements, space exploration, the Olympics and Covid-19 to try to gain advantages.[26] For example, with the objective of undermining the other's global image, each claimed the other was the original source of the Covid-19 outbreak and spent billions providing assistance to other countries.[27] Another example is in space (a frontier that will be increasingly important to economic and military power in coming decades), where both China and the US are competing to build the first Moon-based scientific base and seeking support from other countries.[28]

The areas noted above are of importance to New Zealand, and the manner in which the great powers look to leverage or manipulate them for their own interests ends up affecting New Zealand as well. For example, geopolitical competition can impede global cooperation to address issues such as climate change that, if left unabated, affects New Zealand's ecosystems and economy.

IN RECENT YEARS NEW ZEALAND has attempted to balance its relations with Washington and Beijing through an asymmetric hedging strategy.[29] In other words, it aims to 'cultivate a middle position that forestalls or avoids having to choose one side [the US or China] at the obvious expense of another'.[30] New Zealand's hedge is asymmetric because it has largely aligned itself strategically with the US and economically with China. Pursuing this strategy was not difficult while US-China relations were amicable. Now that their rivalry is intensifying, however, New Zealand's strategy is becoming more difficult to maintain. The chapter now considers three options: New Zealand's existing asymmetric hedging strategy, tight US alignment and armed neutrality.[31]

OPTION 1: ASYMMETRIC HEDGE

New Zealand's existing strategy is an asymmetric hedge, through which Wellington aligns itself with Washington and its other Five Eyes partners (FVEYs) on many aspects of security and military cooperation, while maintaining a margin of difference so as not to invite China's ire. Since New Zealand is much more dependent on the US and China than they are on it, each has immense potential leverage to try to influence New Zealand's foreign, military and economic policies in a manner that supports their own interests at the expense of the other.

To balance, New Zealand maintains a semblance of ambiguity through the absence of an operative New Zealand-US security treaty (New Zealand only has a security treaty with Australia). This distinguishes Wellington from the other FVEY partners, all of which have security treaties with Washington. The diplomatic pillar of New Zealand's hedge involves a messaging strategy that repeatedly stresses Wellington's 'independent' foreign policy in which it takes its own positions on major international issues. By showing Beijing that New Zealand is not fully allied with the US, high levels of trade are sustained with China underpinned by a free trade agreement (FTA) signed in 2008 (and upgraded in January 2021). This FTA has led two-way trade to triple from approximately NZ$10 billion in 2008 to $38.5 billion in the year ending June 2022.[32] China receives $20.84 billion in New Zealand exports compared with Australia, in second place, at $11.3 billion.[33]

As long as neither Washington nor Beijing imposes serious costs on Wellington for sustaining positive ties with the other, it allows Wellington to benefit from both. However, the dilemma remains while the US and China are engaged in a GPC. The response by the US and Australia to China's rise places pressure on New Zealand to show commitment to the FVEYs; for example, New Zealand might join the AUKUS security pact and/or be expected to contribute military forces in the event of a US-China conflict. In the event of conflict, New Zealand could face trade repercussions from China. Norway, Sweden, Australia and South Korea have all borne the brunt of Chinese economic retaliation, and trade restrictions could be applied to New Zealand too. If Wellington joined a US-led war against China, trade ties would likely collapse.

OPTION 2: TIGHT US ALIGNMENT

The second option available to New Zealand is a tight US alignment that could involve New Zealand joining the AUKUS trilateral security pact announced by US, UK and Australian leaders in September 2021 to deepen security cooperation. Pillar I of this agreement will see the US and UK provide Australia with nuclear submarines over the next 20 years.[34] Pillar II involves an agreement to share artificial intelligence, cyber technologies, undersea capabilities, hypersonic weaponry, electronic warfare and information between members. The US offered to allow New Zealand to join Pillar II in March 2023.[35]

Why should New Zealand consider it? Because without access to the aforementioned technologies, the New Zealand military may not be able to operate credibly alongside the US, Australian and UK militaries in the future. Other strategic, security and intelligence ties will deteriorate. Furthermore, these technologies are critical components of the modern economy and will become more so in the years ahead.[36]

A second idea is for New Zealand to establish a new security treaty with the US. Why? First, New Zealand's remote geographic location means its economy is dependent on the US Navy to protect trade routes in the event of conflict. Second, New Zealand's ties to the US and other FVEY nations are cultural, social, familial and linguistic. Common material interests can wax and wane over time, but common values and the common commitment to upholding the rules-based system provide a deep, fundamental platform for partnership.

Third, seamless intelligence-sharing and links between our science and technology agencies (with separate FVEY navy, army and air force programmes) already exist.[37] A security treaty with Washington would add an additional and fortifying connection.

Finally, the combined power of FVEYs nations is formidable. As the international environment becomes more threatening and complex, it is imperative for Wellington to remain on the right side of history — the right side of the power balance that is most likely to define that history. At present, that remains the US and its Western and Asia allies.

OPTION 3: ARMED NEUTRALITY

Should New Zealand seek neutrality? This third option risks New Zealand eventually being dropped from the FVEYs and other security/ military arrangements with Canberra and Washington. If New Zealand goes in this direction, it could engage a strategy of armed neutrality and self-reliance. It would bulk up its military and state capabilities to deal with emergencies at home, towards its national frontiers, and to respond to military or humanitarian contingencies in the South Pacific (climate change makes this region extremely vulnerable to intensifying weather events).

Switzerland provides a model: it is not formally part of NATO and has a significant agricultural industry, demonstrating how this can coexist alongside a high-tech sector — something New Zealand would ideally want as it would be vital to a shift to armed neutrality. An independent military capability starts with a strong economy.

Switzerland's economy, standing at US$800 billion in 2021, allows it to spend just 0.7 per cent of GDP or $5.7 billion on its military. With this, it maintains 24,000 active troops, several frontline air squadrons and more for relatively small expenditure.[38] By comparison, New Zealand's economy in 2021 was US$250 billion, with a $3.39 billion military budget in 2021, requiring 1.4 per cent of GDP. New Zealand maintains 9300 active troops. Switzerland also has mandatory military conscription for every able-bodied male (females can volunteer for any position) and the army is interwoven with Switzerland's society.

In theory, New Zealand could learn from Switzerland. It would expand its military budget and engage a strategy of self-reliance to enhance resilience, ultimately providing a basis for a truly independent foreign policy. However, New Zealanders are already facing cost-of-living concerns. An ideological dedication to low taxes by Labour and National governments also means New Zealand remains in first gear when it comes to the state's capacity to fund its military, welfare and health system and broader infrastructure. If New Zealand wants more, it needs to pay for it.

THE DECISIONS AOTEAROA NEW ZEALAND makes with respect to the US-China GPC in the near-term will reverberate throughout the coming years and have significant implications for the prosperity and security of the nation. New Zealand is in a precarious position. Its broader Indo-Pacific region is militarising and its military has been neglected and is not fit for purpose. Its closest partners are gearing up to deter war — and if necessary to fight one; they want New Zealand on their side. Meanwhile China, the country's largest trade partner, expects New Zealand to keep its head down and, in that way, exerts influence.

The New Zealand people deserve to know what's going on, what is at stake, and the pros and cons of various options. They will benefit from an informed and systematic debate over the US-China GPC that maximises New Zealand's chance of choosing the best path forward. Additional research is required to consider how the country can maximise its agency and utilise diplomacy creatively to forge a common destiny for the nations of the Indo-Pacific. Simultaneously, Aotearoa must prepare for the worst by also taking prudent steps to improve its deterrence, defence and national resilience.

2.

CONVENTIONAL WARFARE TODAY

What has the Russian invasion of Ukraine taught us?

Terry Johanson

The Russian invasion of Ukraine in February 2022 heralded the 'return of conventional warfare to Europe'.[1] This 'special military operation' was considered different from Russia's annexation of Crimea in 2014 as the 2022 Ukraine conflict displayed all the characteristics of traditional interstate warfare. The use of 'little green men'[2] in Russia's Crimean campaign was aligned more to the concepts of 'grey-zone' or hybrid warfare as the conflict was portrayed as an internal separatist uprising of ethnic Russians dissatisfied with their treatment by Ukraine's central government.[3] By contrast, the goal of the 2022 invasion was an overt application of military force to impose change in Ukrainian national leadership by using Russian state military forces inside Ukraine's sovereign territory. This clearly signalled Russian intent for the matter to be settled conventionally.[4]

The obvious difference in size between the Russian and Ukrainian military forces did not reflect the military capabilities able to be employed by each side, unlike previous irregular conflicts in Afghanistan, Syria and post-Saddam Iraq. In those conflicts, state military forces held uncontested air supremacy and possessed a distinct advantage in long-range weapon systems over their non-state opponents. In Ukraine, both sides have the capacity to conduct offensive and defensive air operations, and air defence systems have returned as a key protective measure for important assets. Intensive artillery duels and images of soldiers manning trench systems suggest a more traditional type of combat.[5]

An examination of the lessons emerging from the Russian invasion of Ukraine indicates that this suggestion of a return to a more traditional practice of warfare does not fully appreciate changes in the character of warfare in the contemporary environment. The choice of the term 'character' here is deliberate as it speaks to the way warfare is conducted that is heavily influenced by the technology and thinking of the time.[6] This differs from the 'nature' of war, which is an enduring contestation of wills between human beings for objectives arising from human wants, needs and emotions.[7] The reality that war will be initiated by humans to achieve human ends will not change, regardless of whether the application of violent force is undertaken by people or machines. Therefore, the presence of advanced warfighting technologies, enhanced capacity to control information and greater use of human-machine teaming within the military environment may change the way warfare is conducted, but does not alter war's essential nature.

To appreciate the character of contemporary conventional warfare, therefore, an examination of the 2022 Ukrainian conflict is merited. The aim of this chapter is to investigate the conflict's characteristics as they relate to the paradigms of conventional warfare. To provide relevance to New Zealand's national security discourse, the character of warfare in Ukraine will be contrasted against the characteristics of the most likely conflict in which the New Zealand Defence Force's conventional military capabilities would be deployed: that is, defeating Chinese aggression in the Indo-Pacific region.

A COMMON UNDERSTANDING OF THE term 'conventional warfare' is violent armed conflict between the military organisations of state actors for the achievement of political ends.[8] These conflicts are executed using recognised military capabilities such as tanks, artillery pieces, infantry weapon systems, combat aircraft and naval combat vessels. The aim of conventional warfare is to degrade the will and/or physical military capability of an adversary, to influence their behaviour to be consistent with desired objectives.[9] Traditionally, the military instrument of national power was used as a last resort only after the diplomatic and economic instruments had failed. In this sense, describing warfare as 'conventional' indicates that the conflict represents the accepted, or traditional, way that war is pursued.

In trying to identify whether warfare is conventional or not, it is important to understand why the military force is being applied. The traditional role of state military forces is to deter or defeat external military aggression from other state actors.[10] In the contemporary era, this military role has been broadened to include the use of force against non-state actors and for the protection of vulnerable civilian populations, as well as non-combat support to humanitarian and disaster relief operations.[11]

Emile Simpson proposes two distinct applications of armed force within the context of contemporary conflict. In the first, armed force is used within a military environment to establish the 'military conditions for a political solution'.[12] The second use of military force directly seeks a political outcome without the achievement of preliminary military objectives.[13] Simpson posits that the first application aligns with the traditional concept of war, while the political focus of the second application pushes it beyond the traditional scope. However, he also suggests that the difference between these applications of armed force is not clearly defined.[14] Simpson's proposition of the murkiness of the use of force in contemporary conflict is clearly illustrated in the Russian invasion of Ukraine in 2022.

Although there is a clear use of conventional military capabilities between the state military forces of Russia and Ukraine, there is also the deliberate application of military influence outside of the opponent's military apparatus that is more in line with Russia's hybrid warfare concept.[15] The conflict in Ukraine also contains a greater use of new technologies such as combat drones, hypersonic missiles and sophisticated anti-armoured weapons that impact the character of the warfare. And the use of social and mass media to influence national and international audiences extends the impacts of this conflict beyond an exclusive military domain.

In the case of Ukraine, the operational theatre contains not only state military combatants but also private military contractors, volunteer foreign fighters, civilian non-combatants, non-governmental organisations and volunteer aid workers. This greater congestion within the conflict zone of actors whose rights and protection are not clearly described under the traditional principles of the laws of armed conflict, makes the practice of conventional warfare more complex and provokes greater interest from countries that are not direct parties to the conflict. Greater external interest in the war provides an opportunity for Russia and Ukraine to contest the area of public opinion and garner support or sympathy for their cause.

The reach of this warfare in the information space is unbounded due to the ubiquity of mobile phones and computers and the globalisation of digital communications networks. Broader discussion of the information warfare supporting the operations in Ukraine is beyond the scope of this chapter; the focus of the remaining sections will be on the characteristics of the conventional warfare seen in the campaign so far.

RUSSIA'S MILITARY BUILD-UP AGAINST UKRAINE began a year before the invasion, in March 2021, when large numbers of conventional troops were added to its existing forces on Ukraine's border.[16] This build-up was designed to perform three functions:

1. To put pressure on Western governments to re-engage in the Minsk II agreements;[17]
2. To pre-position equipment around Ukraine to allow for a rapid mobilisation of forces when the time for the invasion came; and
3. To provide an opportunity for Moscow to assess the reaction of Ukraine's international partners.[18]

As it was, Ukraine's international partners dismissed the credibility of the Russian threat because they did not observe the key military capabilities necessary for an invasion. Additionally, the anticipated political shaping of the information environment within Russia to generate popular support for an invasion of Ukraine had not occurred.[19] This dismissal demonstrated to the Russian leadership that their key capabilities could be deployed to forward forces faster than international partners could react; therefore, they could invade Ukraine without significant international interference.[20]

In July 2021 Russia's Federal Security Service (FSB) was tasked with planning the occupation of Ukraine.[21] FSB planning relied on extensive surveys carried out in Ukraine, which painted a picture of a largely politically apathetic civil society that distrusted its leaders, was primarily concerned with the economy, and thought an escalation of the war between Russia and Ukraine unlikely.[22] Additionally, Russian military leadership was confident that after spending more than a decade modernising its forces, they could defeat the Ukrainian armed forces in the field. At the outbreak of the war General Valery Gerasimov stated, 'I command the second most powerful army in the world', and proposed that Russia had achieved conventional military parity with the United States.[23] Russia therefore developed a strategy for an invasion of Ukraine based on the FSB's assessment from the Ukrainian survey data and their faith in the ability of the Russian armed forces.

Russia's strategic objectives for its invasion were to remove Ukraine leadership to eliminate the barrier for support of the occupation; seize heating, electrical and finance infrastructure to control the apathetic population; defeat the Ukrainian military on the battlefield; and act swiftly to render the international community response irrelevant.[24]

To support the achievement of these objectives the Russian military was tasked with:

- degrading Ukraine's defence by destroying air, maritime and air defence forces;
- defeating Ukrainian ground forces by pinning them in Donbas;
- diffusing Ukraine's will and capacity to resist by eliminating their political and military leadership and occupying critical centres of political and economic power; and
- deceiving the Ukrainian government as to the time, location, scope and scale of Russia's invasion.[25]

The Russian invasion commenced with missile and air strikes to disrupt Ukrainian integrated air defence systems and command and control architecture. These strikes were supported by the insertion of special operations forces to secure key objectives and critical infrastructure. This initial phase was quickly followed by a land-force penetration on multiple fronts focused on the encirclement and seizure of the capital, Kyiv.[26] Supporting attacks were made from Donbas and Crimea to hold Ukrainian forces in those regions, thereby reducing their ability to strengthen Kyiv's defences.[27] Secondary objectives for Russian forces, in all areas, were to secure key nodes of energy infrastructure. The final element of the Russian invasion was the creation of two amphibious task groups to conduct landings from the Black Sea ahead of advancing Russian ground forces on the Kherson-Mykolaiv-Odesa axis.[28] Russia's Black Sea fleet was also used to support the strike campaign and isolate Ukraine by blockading its southern coast.[29]

The Russian plan largely followed a conventional template established in the major interstate conflicts of the late twentieth and early twenty-first centuries. The 1991 Gulf War and the 2003 US invasion of Iraq followed a similar pattern: preliminary shaping of the opposing forces by air and missile strikes to disrupt integrated air defence and command and control systems; use of media and military deception to enhance destabilisation of the adversary's defensive plan; the presentation of multiple land axes of attack to disperse defensive resources; and the rapid advance of highly mobile combined-arms task groups to seize key operational objectives and establish the conditions for military success.[30] Likewise, Ukraine's response has been conventional. Ukraine chose to actively resist Russian aggression using its regular armed forces and through the mobilisation of its people into a territorial defence force.[31]

THE UKRAINE INVASION HAS BROUGHT to light some potential characteristics of future conventional conflict, and challenged some assumptions about how large-scale high-intensity combat will be fought. Three characteristics have emerged: (1) nowhere is safe from intelligence collection and conventional munitions strikes; (2) long-range precision weapons such as missiles, artillery and combat drones are ubiquitous; and (3) sustained conventional warfare creates unprecedented industrial demand for resupply.

The first characteristic is that nowhere is safe from intelligence collection or strikes by conventional munitions in a conflict zone. The contemporary conflict space is physically and electronically congested. Unmanned aircraft systems (UAS), electronic warfare assets, communication networks, radar, navigation systems and human intelligence networks compete for coverage of the battle space to identify key assets and information in order to gain an advantage over opposing forces. The proliferation of UAS and electronic sensors to all levels of war means that the ability to achieve surprise is increasingly difficult.

The challenge for the use of UAS has been the rapid learning curve for personnel required to become proficient in the employment of these systems to maximise their effectiveness.[32] Early adopters of UAS, such as Britain and the US, focused the procedures for their use at the strategic level, as early types of UAS were large, long-range and expensive.[33] As technology has reduced the size, extended the range and decreased the cost of these systems, adjustments to how UAS are used have not kept pace. Many of the processes guiding UAS use are linked to battle-space coordination to prevent collisions between UAS and friendly manned aircraft.[34] While the risk of accidental collisions remains, in a conflict zone the level of risk acceptance is increased beyond legislation governing air operations within civilian airspace. Battle-space coordination is becoming increasingly difficult as the number of objects moving throughout a conflict zone increases.

However, not only does use of military assets in the physical domain require coordination, so increasingly do operations in the electro-magnetic spectrum. The necessity for effective frequency management between the demands of radio networks, digital data transfer, radar surveillance, missile guidance, artillery fuse function and UAS control networks is important to prevent electromagnetic spectrum fratricide, as well as to minimise electronic signatures that can be targeted by long-range fire. The ability to detect targets anywhere in the operational area, through visual or electronic means, allows those targets to be engaged by appropriate weapon systems throughout the conflict space.

This targeting capacity leads to the second important characteristic of the Ukrainian conflict — the ubiquity of long-range precision weapons. The increased availability and employment of a variety of sensors and human intelligence networks, which can remain hidden in operational depth, ensures that key targets can be identified and indicators of intent, such as troop and logistics movement, can be observed and updated continually. The presence of intelligence networks directly linked to long-range weapon systems means large and static support areas are increasingly vulnerable to destruction by missiles and artillery munitions. Smaller, dispersed and highly mobile command-and-control nodes and logistics-supply assets are used to maintain effective military manoeuvres.

Training establishments and maintenance facilities deep in Ukraine territory were struck when identified. This led to Ukraine's greater use of smaller, deployable repair and resupply units and rapidly relocatable supplies dispersed over a greater area of the battle space. The Ukrainian Air Force also used dispersion to ensure continuity of operations, by using secondary and tertiary airfields and creating redundancy in its maintenance and supply elements responsible for servicing and re-arming aircraft. The vulnerability of static installations extends to the command-and-control nodes. The notoriously large electronic signatures of these installations make them particularly vulnerable to identification by electronic warfare systems.

The use of dispersed operations, besides raising the cost of targeting key military assets by forcing an opponent to expend more time and resources searching large areas of the battle space, also presents some challenges for the force employing this approach. As more assets are pushed down to tactical level to enhance intelligence collection and survivability, a greater burden is placed on individual leaders to manage their span of command effectively. Greater demands on the commander's attention from subordinates, higher headquarters and information collection systems assigned to support their activities have an impact on the timeliness of decision-making.

Aligned to this demand is the fluid nature of contemporary manoeuvre operations, in which commanders must judge where and when to concentrate to achieve an effect before redispersing to ensure survivability. Throughout these manoeuvres, speed is important both as a means of protection and for seizing opportunities as they are presented.

The Russian failure to rapidly reinforce its air assault forces that had penetrated Ukraine's defences demonstrates how a window of opportunity can close quickly, allowing a potential advantage to remain unrealised. Land and air force experiences in this regard were the same; the impact in the maritime environment was different due to the greater mobility of naval operations. The risk to naval assets increased only as vessels were required to operate closer to land when providing land strikes or facilitating amphibious operations.

The final characteristic of the conflict in Ukraine discussed here is the intense industrial demand of conventional warfare. To enhance the survivability of force elements and key weapon systems, dispersion and speed have been identified as best practice. To counter this, opposing forces have employed increased amounts of munitions to achieve their desired effects. Mykhaylo Zabrodskyi and others state that at the peak of fighting in Donbas, Russia expended the equivalent of Britain's entire ammunition stock in two days.[35] At Ukraine's rate of consumption, British stocks would last no more than a week. The true challenge with such a high-intensity consumption of ammunition is not in delivery but in production.

The limitations of a single-state military industrial complex to meet expenditure rates of equipment in conventional warfare were often downplayed with the idea that a state's allies could provide additional stocks.[36] For large alliances such as NATO, whose members field weapon systems and equipment of various calibres, and from a variety of manufacturers, the ability to draw on allied stocks becomes difficult.[37] The ability to increase the scale of their own military industrial complex quickly in response to conflict should be a key consideration for any state likely to engage in conventional warfare.

The employment of military capabilities in the Russian-Ukrainian conflict, despite the characteristics discussed above, aligns with the commonly understood concept of conventional warfare. The use of force from both parties in the conflict is focused on establishing military conditions to achieve a political solution. The primary actors are states driven by political interests. The conduct of combat is largely between the military forces of Ukraine and Russia and volunteer foreign fighters drawn to their causes. Targets within the conflict have for the most part been of military necessity, with the deliberateness of strikes on non-military targets open to debate. The Ukraine conflict thus far has demonstrated that conventional capabilities can be employed in concert with emerging technologies to achieve effects that may shape the next generation of military equipment and the constitution of military force elements.

The Russian-Ukrainian war conforms to conventional warfare paradigms because of the context in which it originated. The physical operating environment is a large continental land mass; the primary actors are states with adjacent land borders. These factors lead the warfare to be land-centric, which in turn also makes it people-centric: military objectives will be based on influencing people's behaviour. An example is the initial Russian drive to encircle and seize Kyiv. By taking control of this city, Russia could undermine the power of the Ukrainian government. The political significance of losing the capital city has always affected a state leadership's ability to control effective defence. In 2003 the loss of Baghdad rapidly brought an end to the conventional operations between the US and Iraq military forces.[38] Additionally, Russia's intent to focus on the people is clearly indicated in its strategic objectives. Securing Kyiv may have decapitated the Ukrainian leadership, but seizing critical heating, electrical and financial infrastructure would also have supported the Russian control of the populace.

Taking a conventional warfare approach meant that Russia was signalling its intent to a broader audience. It was demonstrating that it had returned as a major power with significant military capability. It likely wanted to demonstrate parity with the US on the world stage. In particular, Russia wanted to demonstrate that it was the pre-eminent power within its immediate region. Conventional military operations were the best way to send this message. An overt, operationally savvy invasion of a large opposing state would provide a good example of Russia's power. Only history will decide whether this approach by Russia was successful or not.

WHAT DOES THIS CONVENTIONAL WAR mean for New Zealand? A number of questions arise — all of which are difficult to answer. Thus far, New Zealand has offered training, intelligence and logistics support to Ukraine's defensive operations.[39] Should this conflict escalate to include the commitment of NATO combat forces actively participating in Ukraine, would the New Zealand Defence Force (NZDF) be asked, or able, to provide a more tangible contribution to multinational operations? Would such a request to a small military force like New Zealand's be feasible? Could the NZDF realistically be expected to engage in high-intensity combat operations within a conventional operational theatre like Ukraine?

We can consider the possible characteristics of a conventional war in which New Zealand could be involved. Conventional warfare in New Zealand's immediate strategic environment would be different from the Ukraine conflict. The most likely context of such a war would be conflict between the US and China due to tensions over the latter's claims in the

South China Sea and its expanding defence involvement in the Indo-Pacific region.[40] The dominant physical environment would likely be the maritime domain, with increased exploitation of the electromagnetic spectrum. The anti-access area denial (A2/AD) concept developed by China, Russia and Iran to negate the US ability to get its forces to any place of conflict would likely be used to shape US manoeuvres and defend any gains made.[41]

This type of conflict will mean a limited role for land forces and a greater reliance on naval and air assets. Land forces will be valuable in capturing key terrain that enhances a force's ability to block their opponent's manoeuvres, such as locations for forward-basing of aircraft and supplies or positioning in defence or anti-ship weapon systems.[42] As in Ukraine, engagements will be long range and mobility will enhance survivability. UAS and dominance of the electromagnetic spectrum will remain key and battle-space coordination to deconflict assets operating in multiple dimensions will be increasingly necessary. Effective intelligence surveillance and reconnaissance suites that are linked to highly responsive command-and-control and weapons-control systems will be important enablers of success.

This approach will move the warfare away from the people-centric focus seen in Ukraine to a platform-centric focus.[43] With this type of focus, military operations will be centred around the particular effect that the vessels within a naval task group, for example, have been designed to achieve. These task groups will be centred around a capital ship such as a battleship or aircraft carrier. Populated areas will be less important unless they dominate access to key parts of the operating environment.

Unlike in Ukraine, conventional naval warfare in the Pacific Ocean or South China Sea will not be fought with the easy access to social media, and any mass media involvement will likely be carefully managed. This means that the raw human stories that appeal to global audiences, such as have emerged from the Ukraine operational theatre, will be largely absent, and a US-China naval conflict will not generate the same emotional response from the international community. Human suffering will still occur but will be less obvious, as it will likely be confined to the loss of ships and aircraft crews killed in combat.

So where do these modern conflicts position the NZDF in being able to contribute to contemporary conventional warfare effectively? The war in Ukraine demonstrates that the fundamental nature of war has not changed despite the inclusion of new technologies such as drones, precision missile systems and advanced electronic sensors. These technologies, however, have impacted the character of this conflict by demonstrating that nowhere in the operational theatre is safe from intelligence collection and conventional munitions strikes, the ubiquity of long-range precision weapons — which is forcing more dispersed and mobile command and control, logistics and ground forces — and the intense industrial demands of conventional warfare.

While some important lessons may be gleaned from the Russia-Ukraine war for future conventional conflict, it should be remembered that this conflict's character will be unique to its particular context. Lessons observed in Ukraine may not be directly applicable to conventional warfare in a different region or environment. A conventional war in the Pacific region, for instance, is likely to have a greater maritime focus. Force projection will likely occur through amphibious manoeuvre, and A2/AD strategies will be employed to counter this. Long-range precision weapon systems are likely to dominate, and land forces are unlikely to play a significant role. Naval and air forces and their accompanying uncrewed systems and cyber assets will be the decisive military capabilities.

The challenge for preparing for multiple conventional warfare contexts places New Zealand defence planners in a quandary as to where to focus the country's limited financial and personnel resources.

New Zealand could make four potential choices in its future force planning:

1. Take the lessons from Ukraine as the best indicator of future conventional conflict and focus capability and force development plans around these lessons;
2. Analyse the scenarios for future conventional warfare in the Pacific region and use the data and conclusions from this analysis to inform NZDF future planning;
3. Identify commonalities between the Russia-Ukraine war and a Pacific conflict scenario and develop strategies and capabilities concentrated on operating effectively within these common characteristics; and

4. Focus on key issues within New Zealand's direct defence environment to guide future force development.

Each option brings its own unique implications. The characteristics of the Ukraine conflict will require military capabilities at the expensive end of the contribution spectrum. This option may only be feasible by focusing on a specialist military function or niche capability to lighten the burden of larger defence partners. The option of focusing on a conventional war in the Pacific region may also be a costly choice as it would require rebalancing the NZDF towards the maritime domain and accepting the need to purchase additional naval capabilities.[44]

Option 3 seeks to achieve an effective balance between conventional warfare as it is currently being conducted, and a hypothetical scenario of future war. This may be New Zealand's preferred option, as it has the certainty of being relevant within today's context as well as building in the flexibility to pivot towards a different operational environment. However, given New Zealand's economic and human resource limitations, an important factor in choosing this option will remain its feasibility.

The final option is to focus on the issues and challenges both present and emerging in New Zealand's immediate defence environment. In choosing option 4, New Zealand could address the defence interests and concerns of its citizens directly. However, Aotearoa may be seen as 'free riding' on the broader sense of security created by its larger defence partners. For small states such as New Zealand, who rely on the support of larger allies and the international community to defend against conventional military threat to their sovereignty or territory, the perspective of these partners may outweigh the interests of their own people.

Each choice will have its advantages and be open to criticism. Finding the balance that best serves New Zealand's interests and is achievable within its resource limitations, as well as meeting the expectations of defence partners by contributing effectively to international stability, is key for New Zealand defence planners in determining the country's place in future conventional warfare.

3.

RETAINING A NATIONAL SECURITY WORKFORCE

Army personnel shortages in a mobile neoliberal society

Nina Harding

The platoon is returning from Physical Training. Corporal Wilson says he hated that session and, as the soldiers often do when frustrated, he jokes that he is going to '717' — 717 is the numerical designation of the resignation forms. Private Stewart responds by taking a copy of the 717 forms out of his locker and handing them to Corporal Wilson. Corporal King, who has just arrived and missed the joke, immediately notices, and recognises the resignation forms his mate is holding. 'Joining the crew!' he says excitedly.
— Harding, Fieldnotes, Royal New Zealand Infantry Regiment

During the period 2021–23, 29.8 per cent of regular personnel left the New Zealand Defence Force (NZDF).[1] Consequently, the institution on which Aotearoa New Zealand currently relies to address a wide range of security threats is not fully staffed. The state deploys the NZDF to deal with not only combat and peacekeeping but also natural disasters, humanitarian assistance, search and rescue, transnational organised crime, patrolling the exclusive economic zone and more.[2] The NZDF supports national, regional and global security, as the international rules-based order is considered 'the foundation for New Zealand's security'.[3]

The NZDF's ability to achieve all these tasks may be limited by personnel shortages. But the defence force is not alone: attrition is a long-term trend in neoliberal nation-states in which all-volunteer militaries struggle to retain personnel. A standing army of career soldiers with experience and specialised training is incompatible with neoliberal societies in which people are taught to pursue mobility over stability in their careers.

This case study focuses on one of the NZDF's three services, the New Zealand Army, to illuminate the wider NZDF struggle with attrition. It examines one cohort of infantry soldiers to explore what motivates soldiers to join the army, and why those same motivations then lead them to leave the army.

I conducted this research with a cohort of soldiers who joined the army around a decade ago.[*] The research was designed to follow this cohort through the first four stages of their army careers: basic training, specialised infantry training, life in an infantry battalion in camp in Aotearoa New Zealand, and their first overseas deployment, the Regional Assistance Mission to the Solomon Islands. I was embedded with a platoon at each of these stages, 'hanging out' with the soldiers every day, hearing their hopes and frustrations.[4] At the beginning of basic training this cohort was 63.6 per cent Pākehā, 22.1 per cent Māori, 2.8 per cent Pasifika and 1.4 per cent Asian. Fifteen per cent of recruits at basic training were women, but few women went on to the infantry units. This case study discusses career motivations shared across these groups.

Although the research was designed to cover only the first 18 months of the cohort's careers, I also witnessed, unexpectedly, the last stages of some soldiers' careers. When the cohort finished training and entered the Royal New Zealand Infantry Regiment, they joined platoons of soldiers, many of whom were quitting or talking about quitting, as in the fieldnotes above. Eighteen months, then, was long enough to witness not only the beginning but also the end of some of the cohort's army careers. During the second year of their service, 5.7 per cent of them resigned; a further 8.6 per cent quit the year after.

---

[*]   I am approximating the time to protect the soldiers' anonymity. Pseudonyms are used for research participants.

NEW ZEALANDERS JOIN THE ARMY to learn new skills, develop new attitudes and habits and improve themselves, all of which makes them more employable. They leave the army when it no longer provides them with opportunities to develop themselves. Neoliberal reforms and the reduction of the welfare state in the 1980s made New Zealanders individually responsible for their own everyday economic security. Young people are taught that their primary responsibility as citizens is to continually acquire skills that will make them attractive in the job market, allowing them both to take care of themselves and to contribute to the prosperity of the nation. As people come to enjoy acting in the ways that bring social approval and reward, they experience upskilling as both a necessity and a desire.

This has meant that citizens may be less able or likely to contribute their labour towards national security by maintaining long-term army careers. An army salary, minus many of the benefits past soldiers received, isn't always enough for a family to live on. Further, the army can't always provide the personal development soldiers desire. Maintaining a peacetime army ready to respond to crisis often involves soldiers waiting around during long periods of inactivity. The increasing range of non-combat tasks the army is assigned may also not be what people attracted to the military life consider fulfilling. After initial training, if further opportunities for self-development are unforthcoming, soldiers feel both compelled to and responsible for leaving the army to seek those opportunities elsewhere.

Neoliberal reforms have therefore caused national insecurity in two cascading ways. They have made individual citizens economically insecure, which has made them less capable of working for the institution that addresses more extraordinary threats. The incompatibility of career armies and neoliberalism suggests a need to look beyond the military for some national security tasks. More broadly, army workforce shortages demonstrate the issue that the term 'human security' was coined to describe: national security is unachievable if citizens don't have everyday security in the form of food, shelter, income and fulfilling jobs.[5]

ATTRITION IN THE NEW ZEALAND ARMY rose from a projected 8.6 per cent to 10.6 per cent in 2021, rose again to 16 per cent in 2022, and remained at 16.7 per cent as of April 2023.[6] In 2021, attrition was driven by the pressures of serving at managed isolation and quarantine (MIQ) facilities during the Covid-19 pandemic.[7] However, even after MIQ closed, attrition continued to increase, because army salaries cannot compete with civilian salaries at this time of low unemployment.[8] In exit surveys, soldiers reported dissatisfaction with the opportunities for career development in the army.[9] Increased opportunity in the job market means such development can be found elsewhere.

What are the potential impacts of army workforce shortages for national security? The NZDF warns that shortages could limit its responses to the many security issues it may be asked to address. According to a *Capability and Readiness* update, which Chief of Defence Force Air Marshal Kevin Short provided to Cabinet ministers in 2022, 'workforce gaps are now placing limitations on how the NZDF can respond to domestic needs [. . .] and sustain operational activity for any length of time'.[10] The report repeatedly uses words like 'fragility' and 'hollowness' to characterise current capability. It states, with qualification, that the army can carry out key tasks: the army can 'provide full responses in support of domestic and civil defence tasks' but 'with some risk'.[11] Likewise, it can 'provide high readiness forces for regional humanitarian assistance and disaster relief responses' but 'with some limitations on scale and sustainability'.[12]

In February 2023, workforce shortages impacted the NZDF's response to Cyclone Gabrielle. The NZDF was involved in rescue, resupply and recovery, but couldn't always use what had been assessed as the best planes and ships for the job due to an inability to crew them, and had to deploy personnel for longer than is ideal.[13] Air Marshal Short concluded that 'the NZDF was currently operating at a lesser standard than he would like'.[14] Both the NZDF and Defence Minister Andrew Little expressed concern about the decisions that would need to be made if two events requiring a response were to occur simultaneously.[15] The army 'ring-fences' units during major deployments to maintain capability to respond elsewhere, but large-scale and long-term responses would be difficult.[16]

This isn't a short-term issue; it takes time to rebuild numbers. Military positions cannot be filled from other industries, as servicepeople go through initial military training and work up from the bottom of rank structures. Chief of Army Major General John Boswell stated it will take two to three years for the army to regain numbers. Short wrote, 'it takes 5–15 years of education, training and experience to develop staff [. . .] this puts the NZDF's ability to generate outputs for the next 10 years or more at considerable risk'.[17] Given that the role of the NZDF is to 'support New Zealand's security, resilience and wellbeing', when the army says their ability to 'generate outputs' is at risk for the next decade, they mean their ability to provide national security.[18]

Personnel shortages, particularly acute in Aotearoa New Zealand currently, are part of a broader trend: all-volunteer militaries in neoliberal nation-states have been struggling with recruitment and retention for the last few decades.[19] MIQ duties didn't provide the self-development soldiers are looking for, and low unemployment means they can find it elsewhere comparatively easily. However, it is the desire to develop themselves that drives the longer-term trend. My research, which took place during another period of high attrition, can speak to this trend.[20] Soldiers leave the army if they are unable to work towards economic security through self-development. National security relies on citizens being secure enough to contribute their labour towards the collective.

WHEN MY RESEARCH PARTICIPANTS ARRIVED at basic training, what excited them most about beginning their army career was that they were going to 'change' as people. 'We're going to change so much,' one recruit said in the first week. Another recruit, after talking on the phone, assured everyone else, 'we're going to change so much, even my girlfriend already noticed [that I had changed]'.

This focus on transformation is part of a trend in neoliberal nations, in which joining the military is conceptualised as a way of developing oneself rather than as a sacrifice of oneself for national security. Soldiers in conscripted militaries during the world wars were seen to be sacrificing themselves for 'a purpose transcending individual self-interest in favour of a presumed higher good'.[21] Soldiers faced possible death, and were paid less than civilians, but in return received high social status. As militaries moved from conscripted to all-volunteer forces in the last quarter of the twentieth century, soldierhood instead became an occupation undertaken to gain income, 'self-fulfilment' and 'a meaningful personal adventure'.[22] The military now followed the logic of the marketplace, paying soldiers for their skills and labour.[23] Militaries must compete with other workplaces for personnel, and have trouble doing so.[24]

The fact that soldiers join the army to develop, rather than sacrifice, themselves, can be seen in my research participants' responses to the punishments they received during training. These new soldiers embraced any activity explicitly linked to self-development. Although the cohort had to accept army control over their everyday lives, and learn to act and present themselves in a uniform manner, they didn't perceive this as a subsummation of the individual to the collective. Rather, developing the ability to follow orders and match colleagues was explicitly linked to learning new skills, and therefore to individual growth.

The army requires that any punishment must help recruits correct their initial fault. Therefore, staff almost always told recruits how what they were doing would help them develop skills. Recruits would, for example, accept any punishment they were told would assist them to practise a 'sense of urgency' that would allow them to conduct tasks quickly but effectively on a battlefield. One corporal gave recruits only 20 minutes to clean the barracks but repeatedly called them into the corridor to stand at attention, where they achieved nothing as their minutes ticked away. Because the corporal stated that this had taught them how quickly they could complete tasks, recruits saw it as a valuable learning experience.

However, the cohort resented any activity that provided no opportunity for self-development and seemed designed to humiliate the individual. They were angry when a corporal made them eat, sleep and shower simultaneously on command, complaining that this was not 'getting [any]thing done'. Although this punishment wasn't much different to others they had valued, the corporal didn't explicitly connect it to any new skill; he told me that he was just 'messing them around'.

This focus on themselves does not suggest that soldiers are unwilling to work for collective national security. Rather, they have been taught that the way to do this is to work on themselves first, and that economic prosperity represents security.

From the 1930s to the 1980s, the welfare state took collective responsibility for the economic and social security of citizens.[25] Soldiers sacrificed for the nation; if they made it home, the nation would look after them, their families and everyone they had sacrificed for 'from the cradle to the grave' (at least in theory, and particularly if you were Pākehā).[26] Beginning in 1984, New Zealand underwent a comprehensive neoliberal restructuring that minimised state intervention.[27] The state 'abandoned its full employment goal and commitment to adequate social welfare provision in favour of privileging the market in allocating employment and resources'.[28] Even social benefits given to soldiers, such as subsidised housing, have been eroded over time.

Citizenship used to be guaranteed by military service, but is now assessed through participation in the labour market.[29] In a 'new form of patriotism', a good citizen is someone who 'develop[s] the skills, knowledge and attitudes that will enable them to succeed in world markets', and which will enable New Zealand to develop an 'internationally competitive knowledge-based economy'.[30] A study of New Zealanders who grew up in this neoliberal context found that, across ethnicities and genders, they see themselves as individually responsible for striving to make themselves employable and for upskilling through-out their lives, as mobility characterises the competitive marketplace.[31]

However, upskilling is also considered desirable. Young people today find self-development enjoyable and expect to find pleasure, or at least fulfilment, at work.[32]

People in neoliberal societies initially join the military because the training, long perceived as transformative (it will 'break you down and rebuild you'), offers an opportunity for self-development.[33] In fact, some of my research participants had joined the army planning to stay only a few years; the army would provide them with skills that would then make them attractive in the wider job market. The cohort believed that it is easier to get accepted into the New Zealand Police if you are ex-army. One private planned to spend three years as an army driver to gain the vehicle qualifications needed to move on to Fire and Emergency New Zealand. Others saw deployment as a short-term financial starter; every Afghanistan veteran they heard about had come home with enough money for either a car or a house deposit. Some soldiers therefore left the army as soon as they had achieved what they came for.

AFTER COMPLETING INITIAL TRAINING, the soldiers I followed found themselves in comparatively inactive platoons with nothing new to learn. Soldiers were quitting because they 'weren't getting anything' out of the job. One of these platoons was stuck in camp in Aotearoa, tasked with maintaining readiness rather than with any advanced training or deployments. The other platoon was deployed to the Regional Assistance Mission to Solomon Islands (RAMSI). Neither platoon did much each day. The soldiers in camp mostly waited to be tasked, cleaned already clean kit and took quizzes on weapons specifications. The RAMSI soldiers were one of the last rotations sent to a conflict that had already been stabilised, and their only job was to stand by to respond to potential incidents that never occurred.[34]

Both platoons did go on some training exercises, but were as unhappy on these as they were when doing nothing. When asked about this seeming contradiction, they told me this was training they had already done, and therefore it was as bad as doing nothing. The soldiers in camp were drilling the same core infantry skills (patrolling, live-fire manoeuvres) in the same places. The soldiers on RAMSI were drilling the same skills in a new environment (the jungle), but did not feel it was sufficiently different to help them develop as soldiers.

The fact that the RAMSI soldiers were still technically contributing to New Zealand's responsibility towards regional security did not make them any less critical of their situation than the ones in camp. Rather, both sets expressed restlessness and a sense that they were undervalued because they were not given opportunities to upskill. They spoke of opportunities elsewhere, for example in the Australian mining industry. In a society in which economic security is not provided collectively but is supposedly awarded to those who work hard on themselves, the new social contract is that employers should provide employees with opportunities for self-development. When one soldier complained, 'If they haven't got anything for us to do, they should knock us off,' another responded, 'No, the thing is, they should have something for us to do.'

I arrived at the platoon in camp in time to see a soldier from the basic training platoon I had followed quit the army. Private Ellis had intended a long-term army career, yet asked for his resignation papers just a year and two weeks after he had joined. He still wanted to be a soldier and planned to join the Australian Army, and told me, 'I'm getting nothing out of sitting around here.'

The idea that ensuring national security may require forces to wait around, not doing much, ready just in case, did not inform the decisions of Ellis or his colleagues. They had grown up in a society in which anyone who was not seen to be working on themselves to enable their full participation in the labour market was criticised, cast as a drain on the rest of 'hard-working' society.[35] You cannot live in New Zealand today and avoid hearing references to people who need assistance, those on social welfare, as 'bottom-feeding' dole-bludgers.[36] Not working, or not improving, is seen as an abrogation of one's responsibility to the collective. Ellis was concerned about what the New Zealand public would think of soldiers if I publicised how little work his platoon did every day. He was worried that readers would think that soldiers are 'glorified dole-bludgers'. Feeling like a 'bludger' is incompatible with feeling secure in New Zealand.

PEOPLE RAISED IN NEOLIBERAL SOCIETIES associate good citizenship and security with continual self-development. It is not that they do not want to help fellow New Zealanders — recent NZDF research shows they do, and careers some of my participants left the army for (police, fire and emergency) are perceived as service roles.[37] Rather, due to their relationship with the nation-state in its neoliberal form, some activities feel like a contribution and others do not. Soldiers generally stay in the army if opportunities to upskill are provided, and leave if they are not.

Neoliberal nations are insecure in particular ways. The result of neoliberal reforms has been increased inequality and precarity.[38] Citizens face individual economic insecurity daily. This undermines collective national security in that some soldiers cannot afford to stay in the army if it isn't providing competitive salaries or opportunities to improve their skills and employability.[39] The long-term retention of career soldiers is incompatible with a neoliberal nation-state.

One potential partial solution to army workforce shortages is to increase salaries, and thus soldiers' economic security. The 2023 budget allocated $419 million to boost salaries NZDF-wide, which the government asserts will bring 85 per cent of salaries to competitive levels.[40] Personnel have also been given one-off 'retention payments'.[41] However, even soldiers who are not struggling economically are compelled to upskill, especially if previous efforts are perceived as the reason for their economic security. But upskilling has become more than an economic necessity. In teaching citizens that the way to create a good life in a precarious neoliberal nation is to work on self-improvement, upskilling has become a socially rewarding, enjoyable activity.

Aotearoa New Zealand faces a range of new security challenges. Some of these will allow soldiers to develop themselves; some will not, and may inspire soldiers to quit and make themselves no longer available to secure the nation. One recent domestic deployment, climate change-exacerbated Cyclone Gabrielle, seems to have been experienced as fulfilling.[42] Another, however — manning MIQ during the Covid-19 pandemic — was named as a reason for quitting in one-third of exit surveys in 2021.[43]

MIQ, at least in the first stages, was a major contribution to the security of New Zealanders, given that it is estimated to have saved thousands of lives before vaccinations became available.[44] Soldiers do not seem to have experienced it as fulfilling, however: it was difficult on their families, and therefore did not enable them to practise their individual responsibility towards their families' wellbeing.[45] As well, MIQ duties actually impeded career development in that many were unable to complete courses that promotion (and therefore pay rises) depend on.[46]

Chief of Army Major General John Boswell stated that 'the type of role being performed by soldiers is not why a lot of them joined the army'.[47] The army promised soldiers that, after MIQ, they would re-focus on 'training, travel' and 'the individual'.[48] This indicates that the army hierarchy is aware of, and sympathises with, the perception that MIQ did not provide self-development.

The army has no control over what security threats will arise and which of a broad range of potential tasks the government will assign it.[49] If a stable workforce of career soldiers is unlikely in present neoliberal society, the assumption that soldiers are the best people to address almost any non-traditional security threats that may arise in the future needs to be questioned. New Zealand academics have been questioning the assumption that the army and wider NZDF are the best, or only, already existing or potential agencies that could respond to non-combat threats for some time. This is for many reasons, including the problematic assumption that combat training equips flexible soldiers to deal with non-combat tasks, and the risk of militarising civilian spaces.[50]

The army's personnel shortage highlights another, practical, reason: over-reliance on a 'fragile' NZDF is just not necessarily secure. Some people — reserve soldiers who primarily work in civilian jobs — did in fact experience MIQ as an opportunity for self-development, and reported that MIQ allowed them to develop civilian skills like facilitation management and customer service.[51] People attracted to non-military careers as the site in which to improve themselves may well find addressing non-combat security threats fulfilling and be motivated to continue working towards national security.

If New Zealand is to achieve collective national security, we need first to ensure that individual New Zealanders are economically secure and fulfilled in their daily lives. Neoliberal economics has never yet provided this security.

4.

MARITIME TRADE SECURITY THREATS*

Protecting New Zealand's economic lifeline to the world

Stephen Hoadley

High on the list of factors enabling modern prosperity is trade. Adam Smith, David Ricardo and subsequent economic analysts have developed the principles of specialisation, mass production, economies of scale, comparative advantage and exchange that clarify the economically beneficial aspects of what we loosely call globalisation.[1] Since time immemorial, maritime commerce, the profitable cartage of goods by ships from producers to consumers, has been essential to human economic welfare. But so, too, has been predation of that commerce by criminals, pirates, freebooters and navies, and interruptions due to wars, accidents and natural disasters. Enhancing the security of maritime trade has always been imperative to governments committed to economic growth, especially those of island states such as New Zealand.

Admittedly, airborne commerce and e-commerce now rival maritime commerce, at least in people's minds, their glamourous innovations and increases of international market share often attracting more attention than the mundane and traditional activities of ports and ships.

---

* This chapter elaborates on my keynote presentation to the *Conference on Maritime Trade Operations*, convened on 31 March 2023 by Captain Phillip O'Connell, Assistant Chief of Navy (Reserves). I am grateful to officials from the Ministry of Transport, the Ministry for Primary Industries and the New Zealand Defence Force for advice, but take responsibility for the information presented, opinions expressed and conclusions drawn herein.

However, the United Nations Conference on Trade and Development (UNCTAD) and other agencies note that despite the entry of air and electronic commerce, it is still the case that 'around 80 per cent of global trade by volume and over 70 per cent of global trade by value are carried by sea and are handled by ports worldwide'.[2] Furthermore, the volume of maritime trade has grown more than 400 per cent in the past half-century, from 2605 million tons in 1970 to 11,076 million tons in 2019 (see Figure 1).

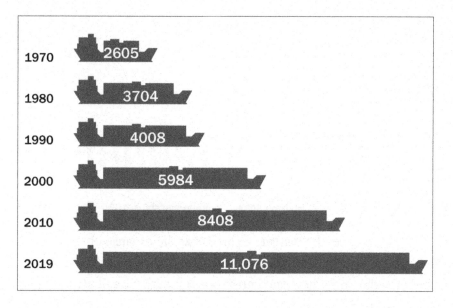

Figure 1: Total volume of international maritime trade in million tons loaded, 1970–2019[3]

In contrast to commercial fleets, the size of national navies, one of whose missions is to protect sea lines of communication, is declining on average as governments choose larger, faster and more sophisticated vessels at the expense of numbers. As a case in point, the US Navy has shrunk from over 900 ships in the 1960s to just over 200 ships in 2023.[4] In the same period, the number of commercial ships plying the oceans rose from 40,000 to over 100,000 (see Figure 2). Ports, too, have proliferated: there are now almost 1000 container ports plus a comparable number of liner, local and recreational ports.[5] While each ship and port represent an opportunity for the facilitation of trade, each is also an opportunity for exploitation of vulnerabilities by unscrupulous agents — corporate, criminal or sovereign.

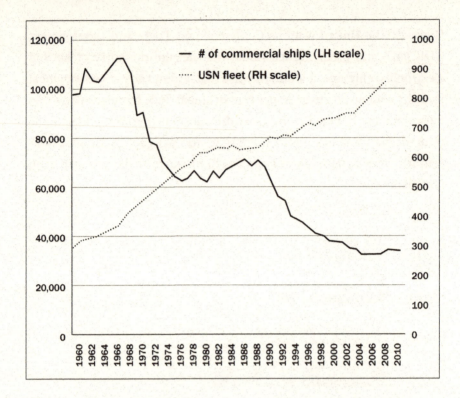

Figure 2: Changing ratio of US Navy ships to commercial ships, 1960–2010[6]

Furthermore, the merger of carriers at the expense of small local firms, such as have traditionally conducted trade in New Zealand, has made regulation by host governments more difficult and evasion and abuse easier.

Over the years, mergers and acquisitions have consolidated and transformed the container shipping sector. The result is that over the last 25 years, the top 20 carriers have almost doubled their market share from 48 per cent to 91 per cent; the four largest carriers now control more than half of the global container shipping capacity.

Carriers have also pursued vertical integration by investing in terminal operations and other logistics services. This integration has given carriers and their alliances stronger negotiating and bargaining positions vis-à-vis port authorities, as they now have two seats at the table — as both tenants of terminals and providers of shipping services.

Consolidation in the shipping market reduces competition and constrains supply. It can lead to market power abuse, higher shipping costs for businesses, and thus higher prices for consumers.[7]

THE RISE OF CHINA'S MARITIME predominance is another threat to an equitable and secure maritime trade regime. Whereas in the past the regulating of irresponsible ships operating under diverse 'flags of convenience' (where ships might change their flag for nefarious purposes) was the primary challenge to maritime order, the emerging challenge is how to monitor and manage the consequences of the growth of China's merchant fleet and the port facilities operated or managed, overtly or covertly, by China's state corporations around the world. As UNCTAD reports, China's merchant fleet is already the world's largest in total number of ships (although third in deadweight tonnes), as shown in Figure 3.[8]

Through its Belt and Road Initiative, China has positioned its state corporations in over 100 ports in 63 countries (see Figure 4).[9]

A majority of the world's countries, including New Zealand, record China as their largest single trade partner, and transport the bulk of their exports and imports by sea. This degree of trade concentration entails vulnerability. Apparently motivated by political irritations, China in recent years has curtailed imports from Canada, Japan, Lithuania, Mongolia, Norway, the Philippines, South Korea, Taiwan and Australia. China could easily reduce New Zealand's exports by sea of non-essential products.

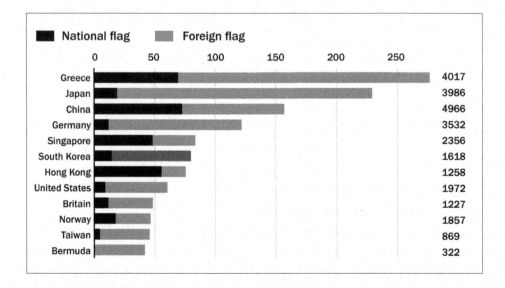

Figure 3: World merchant ship fleets as of 1 January 2015 in million deadweight tons[10]

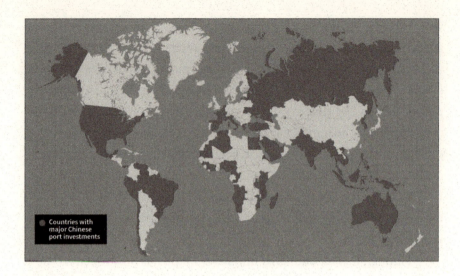

Figure 4: Countries hosting China's investments in seaports[11]

China's subsidised and semi-militarised maritime militia and fishing fleets, its satellite control vessels (which allow for the atmospheric tracking of spacecraft and ballistic missiles while at sea) and oceanic survey ships are active in all the world's oceans and support China's four research stations in the Antarctic; its navy has emerged as the largest in the world.

According to a recent report, China has begun inspecting commercial ships passing through the Taiwan Strait.[12] If true, this would constitute a violation of international law of the sea on the right of innocent passage through exclusive economic zones (EEZs). And China's aggressive deployments and live-fire exercises around Taiwan, and assertions of 12-mile territorial limits around its artificial islets in the South China Sea, are also disruptive of efficient high-seas navigation and constitute threats to safety. The consequences for New Zealand of normalisation of these actions would include supply chain interruption, less reliable service and higher costs; knock-on effects might include socioeconomic stress, eroded support for the government of the day and reduced trust in governing institutions generally.

Russia's illegal invasions of Ukraine in 2014 and 2022 have added to the maritime threat environment, directly in the Black Sea and indirectly throughout the maritime realm. Threats range from the physical and financial to the intangible undermining of the international rules-based order.

President Putin's military and political aggression have also precipitated several negative consequences for maritime trade. These include: rising risk to ships of crossfire and mines; elevated insurance rates and cost of fuel; declining volume and reliability of maritime commercial services in the eastern Mediterranean and beyond; disruption of supply chains worldwide because of sanctions, counter-sanctions and shipping shortfalls; the decline of grain, oils and fertiliser shipments from Ukraine and Russia with consequent price increases and hardship for consumers, especially those in the developing world; and depression of world economic growth rates due to rising energy, food and shipping costs and erosion of trust in international trade rules. Annual UNCTAD reports on maritime conditions examine and assess Ukraine war-related and other threats in detail.[13]

THE NEW ZEALAND MINISTRY OF TRANSPORT has adapted the generic overseas threat inventories noted above for local policy guidance. Its *Maritime Security Strategy 2020* listed 14 potential threats arising in the maritime space.[14] Slightly abridged and consolidated, the threats are as follows:

- Imports and exports by sea of prohibited goods;
- Arrival of undocumented persons by boat;
- Detection of plant or animal diseases aboard arriving vessels;
- Transmission of human communicable diseases from arriving vessels;
- Illegal, unregulated and unreported fishing (IUU) in EEZs or marine protected areas (MPAs);
- Exploitation of non-living resources and protected species;
- Interference in maritime infrastructure such as undersea cables, navigation beacons, communications installations, GPS satellites;
- Piracy, robbery and violence in EEZ waters or impacting on New Zealanders on the high seas;
- Crime in territorial waters;
- Security threats to ports or vessels in port;
- Marine pollution (including oil spill response);
- Maritime emergencies and accidents requiring maritime search and rescue;

- Threats to New Zealand's flagged ships, sovereignty and territorial integrity; and
- Challenges to the maritime rules-based order.

Given New Zealand's limited resources, each of these diverse maritime threats represents a multifaceted challenge. The traditional New Zealand response, used in dealing with global challenges of diplomacy, economics or defence, is to engage in international cooperation.

New Zealand is a beneficiary of the post-Second World War rules-based order. Many of the rules and institutions related to maritime security originated a century or more ago, such as the legal principles advanced by Hugo Grotius in the 1600s, and manifest today in modern and refined forms.[15] The UN Convention on the Law of the Sea (UNCLOS), adopted in 1982 and fully in force since 1994, is now the overarching legal framework. Its definitions, standards and rules are given focus and voice by International Maritime Organization conventions, dispute settlement mechanisms and numerous affiliated institutions.

Within the UNCLOS framework, specialised agreements and institutions, some established earlier than 1982, function to address specific maritime issues. In many cases, disasters and crises were the triggers leading to intergovernmental negotiations and agreements. For example, the Convention for the Safety of Life at Sea of 1914 (SOLAS) was adopted following the sinking of the *Titanic*, which highlighted the need for better passenger safety standards. The rising number of commercial vessels and their longer voyages led to increased collisions, which in turn stimulated the negotiation of the 1972 Convention on the International Regulations for Preventing Collisions at Sea (COLREGS).

The *Torrey Canyon* spillage disaster off the southwest coast of the UK in 1967 attracted widespread media and public condemnation and led to the conclusion of the London Convention on the Prevention of Marine Pollution (MARPOL). And the 9/11 terrorist attacks, although airborne, focused negotiators on the potential for similar attacks at sea and led to the adoption of the International Ship and Port Facility Security (ISPS) Code. It is likely, and appropriate, that future crises will trigger closer international cooperation and new protocols aimed at managing maritime security threats; New Zealand will participate in these initiatives.

WITHIN THIS ENVIRONMENT OF INTERNATIONAL law and institutions, in 2020 New Zealand's Ministry of Transport led an interagency consultation process that culminated in a comprehensive national approach to maritime security: the *Maritime Security Strategy 2020*.[16] This strategy features four pillars: understand; engage; prevent; and respond.[17]

Understand: The collection of maritime security intelligence and information.

- Information, research collaboration and intelligence-sharing with domestic and international partners;
- Persistent wide-area maritime surveillance collection activity backed up by data fusion and analytic capabilities;
- Contributions to situational awareness made by regular maritime patrol and compliance activities; and
- Coastal and shore-based surveillance, intelligence and community outreach.

Engage: The strengthening, protection and use of international rules that underpin maritime security and order.

- Leveraging New Zealand's diplomatic, military, economic, intelligence and law enforcement resources to benefit us internationally;
- Development of key bilateral relationships, in particular with Australia and Pacific Island countries;
- Support for the international rule of law and international institutions, for example the UN system, the Antarctic Treaty system and the International Maritime Organization;
- Adherence to and promotion of international law related to maritime security; and
- Support to regional organisations, programmes and groups, such as Pacific Islands Forum; Forum Fisheries Agency; South-West Pacific Heads of Maritime Forces; Australia's Pacific Maritime Security Program; Western and Central Pacific Fisheries Commission; South Pacific Regional Fisheries Management

Organisation; Pacific Transnational Crime Coordination Centre initiative; Pacific Quadrilateral arrangements.

Prevent: Dealing with root causes, enhancing regional maritime security, deterrence and target hardening (strengthening any perceived vulnerabilities in our maritime infrastructure).

- These efforts can range from supporting refugee assistance and processing systems to reducing the attractiveness of irregular immigration, through to the promotion of alternative forms of economic activity to divert people from harmful activities
- New Zealand maintains a visible and sustained maritime patrol; effort covering its EEZ and the high seas (with a particular focus on the South Pacific) by means of NZDF maritime surface and aerial patrol assets alongside the inshore surface patrol capabilities operated by New Zealand Customs and New Zealand Police;
- Physical security of ships visiting New Zealand and our international trading ports is managed through the provisions of the Maritime Security Act 2004, which implement the International Ship and Port Facility Security Code; and
- Enhancing the resilience of port and ship electronic systems.

Respond: Capabilities that provide New Zealand with the ability to respond in a targeted and timely manner.

- The ability to intercept non-compliant vessels at sea and, if necessary, board with multi-agency teams, disrupt with appropriate aerial and surface assets and take swift diplomatic and law enforcement action from the Antarctic through to the tropics; and
- The environmental challenges, various threats and scale of our domain means New Zealand maritime security response capabilities aim to be available, efficient, robust, appropriate and balanced. Compliance with international law and expectations is a priority.

The New Zealand Ministry of Transport is the lead agency for maritime trade security. Its permanent secretary, representing the minister of transport, chairs an interagency body of senior officials — the Maritime Security Oversight Committee (MSOC). Its role is to coordinate the implementing capabilities of the various agencies with maritime security roles and capabilities throughout government.

WITHIN THE GUIDELINES SET BY the Maritime Security Strategy, the Ministry of Transport and MSOC, the role of policy coordination for maritime safety and port security-related matters at the operational level is assigned to Maritime New Zealand.[18] At present its staff of about 300 play three key roles: regulation and compliance; provision of maritime safety infrastructure; and response to incidents. They liaise with and, as appropriate, facilitate coordination and execution of the policies and actions of other agencies of the New Zealand government and the activities of private and voluntary actors, including a number of partner agencies.[19]

Maritime New Zealand also serves as a focal point for awareness of and compliance with international maritime security agreements to which New Zealand is a party and participation in international institutions of which New Zealand is a member, and as such advises the Ministry of Foreign Affairs and Trade. Among its overseas partners are the International Maritime Organization, the US Coast Guard and the Australian Maritime Safety Authority. Among Maritime New Zealand's responsibilities is support of, and monitoring compliance with, 17 international agreements.[20]

Maritime New Zealand advises Cabinet and Parliament on legislation and policy, and administers, enforces or has responsibilities under various acts of Parliament, which incorporate international agreements into statute law.[21]

ONE OF MARITIME NEW ZEALAND'S more visible core activities is coordinating search-and-rescue operations through its Rescue Co-ordination Centre. This entails working closely with navy, air force, police and private vessel operators. In 2021–22, the centre oversaw operations that resulted in 248 persons rescued, 38 lives saved and 18 lives lost.[22]

The interdiction of illegal drug smuggling by ships' personnel or in cargo is conducted constantly and involves defence, customs, police and intelligence, and related agencies. In February 2023 a Royal New Zealand Navy ship, working with police and intelligence agencies, seized a half-billion dollars' worth of smuggled cocaine.[23]

Biosecurity operations under the lead of the Ministry for Primary Industries involve similar agencies, with the addition of the ministries of agriculture and health. In past decades, threats ranging from fruit flies to snakes and a number of plant and animal diseases have been identified, intercepted or suppressed.[24] The growing number of arriving ships and ship-borne containers has necessitated the training of some 12,000 inspectors.[25] The interception of recreational yachts approaching New Zealand's shores is conducted by the Royal New Zealand Navy, the New Zealand Police, New Zealand Customs Service, and health and biosecurity officials as appropriate.

The advent of Covid-19 in 2020 precipitated a serious threat to New Zealand's maritime trade supply chain.[26] As dockside cargo handlers in northern hemisphere ports fell ill, ship turnarounds slowed and the queues of ships waiting to be processed lengthened. As a result, some shipping firms delayed or cancelled less profitable port calls in the southern hemisphere, including in New Zealand. Instances of unscheduled diversions and offloading of containers threatened perishable product quality, and the cost of hiring containers, which were in short supply, skyrocketed.

All this slowed not only the importing of essential bulk goods such as fuel and general cargo in containers but also the exporting of products on which New Zealand's economic wellbeing depended. Rising costs eroded profitability and threatened smaller firms' solvency. Given the small scale of New Zealand's enterprises and the growing concentration and size of international shipping, container and port firms, this vulnerability is structural. Supply chain and export challenges are likely to arise again in future, and some could become crises if armed conflict between major powers breaks out. The challenges can be mitigated, but only partially, by the resilience of New Zealand's peak exporter firms such as Fonterra, and their willingness to work with the government to assist smaller firms.

During the Covid-19 crisis the Ministry of Transport, working with the Ministry for Primary Industries, consulted with leading producers — Fonterra, Zespri and peak associations for meat, forestry, horticulture and seafood, among others — and with the Shipowners' Association and Ports Association to facilitate the chartering of ships and containers to move products to ports in China, East Asia, North America and Europe.

The minister of transport convened a Supply Chain Ministers Forum and set up a senior officials' group, which included Maritime New Zealand, to advise on helping producers, importers and exporters to mitigate supply chain weaknesses. The government's role was to collect and disseminate maritime trade intelligence, conduct risk analysis, streamline official processes and coordinate private sector firms' export adaptation initiatives. This could be described as government playing a catalytic 'brokering' role to mobilise and focus existing private sector capacity and adaptability.

Encouraged by government agencies, exporters were able to charter break-bulk (non-containerised) ships and coastal vessels to move their products to ports and thus to markets. Large exporters made space for smaller exporters' niche products aboard the ships they had secured; and some high-value or time-urgent exports were diverted to air freight. This public–private cooperation obviously could not solve the maritime supply chain problems that had arisen beyond New Zealand's control, but it did succeed in averting a severe reduction of imports and exports and a potential maritime security crisis, and suggests that although we proved less secure than hoped, we are more secure than feared.

OTHER TENSIONS EXIST IN THIS domain, which are not exactly security threats but could potentially lead to protest regarding concerns around fossil fuel use, carbon production or animal rights. A current issue is the tension between commercial interests and environmentalists. Importing and exporting leaders want minimum regulation and lower compliance costs; at the same time environmentalists demand tighter controls on the entry of potentially environmentally harmful items. Bulk imports of materials that contribute to greenhouse gas emissions, such as coal and diesel fuel, have been decried by environmental activists. In another scenario, animal welfare campaigners have succeeded in inducing Parliament to legislate against exports of livestock by sea; this ban became effective on 30 April 2023.[27]

A potential challenge to New Zealand's maritime security is the low retention rates and specialised personnel shortages in the navy, which have several times restricted the deployment of ships.[28] Reduced time at sea impacts New Zealand's ability to carry out the 'understand, engage, prevent, respond' roles mandated by the *Maritime Security Strategy 2020*. Maritime surveillance, disaster relief, search and rescue and interdiction capabilities are jeopardised, and New Zealand's international status, particularly in the South Pacific, comes into question. No doubt navy leaders are arguing their case for budgetary resources. Whether recent bonuses and pay rises will raise the retention rate and resolve this situation, and whether the public will regard the issue of an under-resourced navy with the same urgency as rising food prices and mortgage interest rates, homelessness and youth crime, remains to be seen.[29]

Cabinet's clear designation of the Ministry of Transport as the lead agency in maritime trade security, endorsement of the *Maritime Security Strategy 2020*, establishment of the Maritime Security Oversight Committee, passage of appropriate legislation and support of Maritime New Zealand's operational roles have established a clear hierarchy of authority and assigned responsibilities to each specialised agency. As a result, the interagency rivalries sometimes apparent in larger countries such as the US have not appeared here.

THE MUTED NATURE OF POLITICAL debate surrounding maritime trade security, and the relative paucity of security breaches reported in the media, constitute indirect evidence that the New Zealand regime is operating with relative efficiency and effectiveness. A sceptic might argue, however, that New Zealand is already the world's safest country: the incidence of threats is low by international standards, and the nation's regime has never been severely tested.

I would reply that alarmists would argue the opposite: that New Zealand is the most vulnerable of countries because its products and markets are expendable. Covid-19, the Ukraine war, the China challenge, extreme weather and natural disasters here and abroad have not drastically lowered the average Kiwi standard of living (immediate victims of floods, diseases, inflation and interest rate rises aside). New Zealand's political and administrative leaders, and import and export sector business elites, are well aware of maritime threats and moderately well prepared to address them, when and if they emerge.

In the meantime, although desirable, it may not be prudent to overinvest in preparations for hypothetical crises at the expense of responding to visible and imminent demands on government funding and institutions. The routine calls by academic experts for theoretically ideal coordination and efficiency, better prioritisation of resources and more comprehensive planning is a counsel of perfection that does not align with the pluralistic and bureaucratic nature of New Zealand's democratic decision-making system.

Drafting a comprehensive strategy and creating institutions to anticipate every possible maritime threat is a Sisyphean task, and a costly one, and would drain resources from the necessary tasks of daily governance. In a situation of skilled personnel shortage, timely response for damage control is the highest priority. Long-horizon maritime threat contingency planning for crisis management is important, but much is already being done by larger partner governments, the results of which can be adopted and adapted by New Zealand and applied when needed.

It is said that no strategy survives the initial contact with the enemy. But history has demonstrated that a capable and resilient army led by a responsible and resolute government can adapt and prevail despite initial setbacks. The same applies to New Zealand's current maritime security strategy and institutions. They have adapted in the recent past, and the burden of proof lies on those who assert that they cannot do so in the future.

5.

SUPPLY CHAIN DISRUPTIONS AND DEEP UNCERTAINTY

Implications for New Zealand in a post-Covid environment

Germana Nicklin

Growing supply chain disruptions are an effect of increasing global uncertainties, such as tensions between the great powers, climate change and resource insecurity. Being well prepared for such disruptions is an important part of national resilience. The Covid-19 pandemic showed that supply chain disruptions can reach deep into society, affecting the necessities of life — food, the goods needed to run a business, the provision of healthcare. Previously taken for granted, supply chains became something that people cared about during the pandemic.

How did the supply chain disruptions during the pandemic affect New Zealand government officials, and what are the implications for future societal preparedness? Drawing upon research undertaken to scope the vulnerabilities the New Zealand government faces from supply chain disruptions, using Covid-19 as a case study, and including interviews with 20 government officials from eight New Zealand government agencies,[1] this chapter outlines how goods move in supply chains. It examines implications for future resilience from supply chain uncertainties and the need to address three key absences: (1) the absence of knowledge about supply chain systems; (2) the absence of relationships; and (3) the absence of testing long-held assumptions about how society works.

SUPPLY CHAINS ARE PART OF a global trade regime that is not designed to go wrong. Rather, the regime is based on the need for goods and the vehicles that carry them to circulate smoothly around the globe in an orderly and predictable fashion.[2] This circulation includes the frequent pausing of goods at places such as ports, airports, fuelling stations and warehouses on their way from one place to another. These pause points maintain orderliness as goods are loaded, unloaded and moved from one mode of transport to another. Government legislation and policies play a part in maintaining this order.

Before the pandemic, supply chains operated as if there were no hold-ups in the circulation of goods, even when there were.[3] Occasional malfunctions occurred at pause points, with flow-on effects. For example, the *Ever Given* tanker that blocked the Suez Canal for six days in 2021 resulted in a backlog of ships waiting to get through the canal. The backlog rippled out to transport operators, manufacturers, distributors and consumers, with severe economic consequences.[4] Until Covid-19, however, such malfunctions were fairly short-lived. The full effects of Covid-19's much more sustained disruption were increasingly cumulative and impacted all areas of society.

In government, too few agencies understood the interconnections between supply chains, government and society and therefore the likely effects across the country. This lack of understanding added to the workload of border agencies in particular, diverting them from more pressing work. Importantly, this highlighted that a sound understanding of supply chains is essential in preparing for sustained disruptions and their associated uncertainties.

There is widespread agreement that the uncertainties and unpredictability of the supply chain disruptions experienced during Covid-19 are likely to become more frequent. Possible causes include global pandemics, natural disasters, global economic recession, trade conflicts, terrorism and piracy, the destruction of information systems and transport infrastructure, and disruption to energy supplies (the last two can also be a result of other disruptions).[5]

These examples highlight three key points. The first is that the world is experiencing some of these disruptions right now. The second is that the interconnected nature of global trade and supply chain systems dictates that when there is a disruption in one country, if that country is a major global supplier, supply chains everywhere will be affected. Third, the confluence of two or more disruptions will have a multiplier effect.[6]

Climate change is intensifying weather events such as cyclones, floods and droughts.[7] It is therefore likely that a financial crash coupled with climate change events in a major supplier country, such as China or the US, will have significant effects on New Zealand's supply chains and the supply of some goods. When disruptions converge, they result in unpredictability and uncertainty. Unpredictability and uncertainty affected officials' ability to plan and provide advice. In their interviews, officials articulated some of these unknowns:

> No one knew when things were going to change [. . .] And I think in hindsight, probably no one thought it would go on for as long as it has either, because we haven't been exposed to this in the modern climate before. (Interviewee 1)

And the effects on officials:

> There'd be some problem, and there was literally no precedent for what they were having to grapple with but they were being charged with coming up with some options basically overnight and being able to present them to ministers and potentially have them put in place the next day. (Interviewee 19)

These are descriptions of 'deep uncertainty', in which the nature of a disruption is unknown, how to address it is unknown and all criteria normally used to analyse data are uncertain.[8] Interviewees referred to all these elements — a lack of data to analyse problems; policies that changed frequently, sometimes daily; and not knowing how long uncertainties would continue.

An implication of deep uncertainty is that situations can only be responded to, not controlled. But the effects of responses in these situations are also uncertain. Populations want their government to take control in times of uncertainty, as with the New Zealand government's decision to close the border and the population lockdown in March 2020. Officials noted the tension between these sorts of control measures and successive New Zealand governments' preferred position of stewardship or kaitiakitanga:

> The point is that in times of crisis, governments need to take control, even if the underlying philosophy is stewardship. However, this also raises the question, 'What is stewardship in times of crisis? Is it different from BAU [business as usual]?' (Interviewee 12)

Part of this stewardship role is controlling collective behaviour, for which collective trust in government information is essential.[9] However, exerting this control can be problematic. The continuous restrictions in New Zealand from 2020 to 2022 arguably resulted in the loss of this control and thus of social licence. The three-week-long protest on Parliament's lawns in February–March 2022 was triggered by the government's 90 per cent vaccine mandate, but it incorporated a build-up of frustrations experienced over the previous two years.[10]

Underpinning these ideas of control, stewardship and social licence are fundamental assumptions about how a particular society works. Many such assumptions are grounded in government policies that have remained stable over time. For example, the Fourth Labour Government's reforms of the 1980s were based on neoliberal values of efficiency and effectiveness. These values, actualised in part as 'hands-off' government in market regulation, continue to the present day.[11] Decades of policy, based on these values, have led to their internalisation among many government officials. When Covid-19 hit, officials assumed that private sector supply chain resilience was much stronger than it was.

But two values-based assumptions surprised officials. The first was that supply chain processes within the free market would continue to operate as normal, as illustrated in the following two quotes:

> Through the end of 2020/beginning of 2021, people started talking about supply chain issues [. . .] — supply chain vulnerabilities — and just how sensitive those systems are and

> perhaps not as resilient as we thought. I'd have assumptions
> that people would just be able to work around it. You'll go to
> a different supplier. Not really. In that sort of environment of
> specialisation and 'just-in-time', that combination starts to
> create quite a fragile system. (Interviewee 2)

And:

> There has been an assumption that if you have free trade
> between you, that should create some resilience in your supply
> line. But I think that we're all acknowledging that that's probably
> not enough by itself. (Interviewee 20)

These quotes reveal the mistake in these assumptions — a fragile supply chain system in a free-market environment is not a resilient system. Interviewee 20 then described their realisation that their three working assumptions — 'markets would become more open over time, the rules-based system would be preserved and expanded [. . .] and the social licence for trade would be sustained' — no longer held. This person was forced to revise their working assumptions.

Indeed, the dynamics of international trade had changed dramatically in the early stages of the pandemic. Robert Handfield and colleagues argued that during a crisis, countries become very selfish.[12] New Zealand's biggest trading partners, China and the US, turned inwards, disregarding global trade rules and looking after themselves only. As one senior official said, it was the small countries that banded together and helped one another. Understanding the flow-on effects of this change, and the implications for New Zealand, took time, as officials and industry actors reoriented their thinking:

> Our sense of resilience was always through open markets.
> But the challenge when [. . .] vessels were not able to move or
> airlinks dropped away dramatically, a sense of what that meant
> for New Zealand took some time to come. (Interviewee 19)

Although New Zealand's Trade Recovery Strategy is already addressing these changed understandings, there is a lesson here.[13] Deeply embedded assumptions hold our systems steady and enable goods to flow. But long-held assumptions can become so ingrained that they are perceived as facts and, as such, are beyond question. This non-questioning is a vulnerability.

The second deep assumption — that the way goods move through borders is an operational matter — exposed gaps in knowledge that had real effects. For example, Ministry of Health officials did not understand how imports are regulated, resulting in delays to increasing the range of government-approved Covid-19 rapid antigen tests (RATs) being imported. One ripple effect was the need for New Zealand Customs Service staff to seize and process huge volumes of unregulated RATs at the border, which diverted resources from providing important industry support and intercepting criminal offending. The pandemic showed that many agencies have an interest in how goods move, not just border agencies.

Once such assumptions are made visible they can be used to gain foresight into future resilience. This surfacing is important because it raises the important question, 'What do our assumptions mean for future resilience?' I propose two answers. First, the interconnections across society that keep supply chains flowing smoothly need to be widely understood. For example, officials talked about consumers not understanding that increased online purchasing during lockdowns would create bottlenecks, delays in supply chains and price increases. Such ripple effects are not always obvious to consumers.

Officials also gave examples of industry actors not understanding the ripple effect. One story involved foresters. During the lockdown they wanted to keep cutting and processing logs to take advantage of good prices. It was only after the lockdowns ended that the foresters realised that if they had continued to send logs to the ports, those logs would have been sitting there potentially for weeks, rotting and clogging up the wharves. The story highlighted the gap in knowledge and understanding between industry and logistics actors.

Second, such examples illustrate a need for more connectivity between different groups, within government, between government and the private sector and with local communities. Some researchers argue that a functioning society requires cooperation that is born out of a relational paradigm.[14] Supply chain systems are complex and need the glue provided by human relationships to keep them working smoothly. When things go wrong, institutional relationships, and the personal connections that arise from them, become particularly important.

Interviewees from multiple agencies stressed the need to develop the 'right' relationships with supply chain actors, which they could then draw on in times of disruption. These officials identified both the lack of knowledge available to them when key relationships were missing, and the positive effects on the government response when relationships did exist. Interviewee 17's statement, 'you walk into an emergency response with the relationships you've got, not the ones you want', emphasises the need to make sure relationships that are likely to be important to respond to a disruption are built *before* disaster occurs.

Covid-19 illustrated how relationships for government officials were strong in some ways but needed work in others. Interviewees described a plethora of working groups that were set up within and between agencies during Covid-19, coordinated by the Department of the Prime Minister and Cabinet. These groups were often interconnected. For example, the Ministry of Business, Innovation and Employment was the Safe Goods lead agency. Its Safe Goods group included New Zealand Customs Service, as the Border lead agency, and the Ministry of Transport, as the Supply Chain lead agency. All were represented in the Ministry of Health's National Crisis Management Centre, as was the Ministry for Primary Industries. Each agency in turn had their own Covid-19 group.

Some officials assumed that, within government, relationships between agencies related to supply chain matters were more widespread than they actually were. For example: 'we kind of made an assumption that there was a lot more coordination going on that we weren't privy to [. . .] That wasn't as true as I would have liked.' (Interviewee 12)

Critically, these governmental groups did not seem to include industry:

> I know the healthcare sector is quite connected. Border certainly
> is. Domestic production is. Logistics didn't seem to be. That
> seemed to be a novel thing, that we'd get industry and agencies
> that play a part in logistics, regulatory stewardship functions —
> people didn't know each other. (Interviewee 12)

Nevertheless, particular agencies frequently met with industry groups; these groups tended to represent exporters, who are generally larger companies. Officials also met with a wide range of other actors, such as freight owners, transport and logistics operators, large retailers and distributors, to find out how the Covid-19 environment was affecting their operations. The logistics operators and freight forwarders tended to be proxies for small and medium enterprises (SMEs). Officials noted that SMEs are less networked, have less 'fat' in their systems and less capability, making it harder for them to adapt in times of disruption. As such, SMEs were much more vulnerable than larger enterprises during Covid-19, which suggests a need for government to be more deeply connected with them.

International relationships are also important for adapting to major supply chain disruptions. First, they can provide advance signals of changes in the international trade/supply chain environment. Second, they enable the government to work through specific supply chain issues quickly. One example was the trade relationship New Zealand has with Singapore, which enabled the two countries to negotiate a mutually beneficial deal to keep critical goods, such as personal protective equipment, moving during the pandemic.[15]

One interviewee noted that local government was generally absent from the government's consideration of supply chain and freight disruptions, yet local government is responsible for local roading and other infrastructure and has strong community relationships. Research on the Canterbury earthquakes has shown that societal support systems and strong local knowledge contribute to resilience.[16]

Research on Māori business models has identified that social values and community connections form part of their resilience.[17] One interviewee described how connections with other iwi across New Zealand enables one Māori honey business to produce honey all year round; importantly, the business also trains and supports other iwi and whānau to produce their own honey. This story illustrates the possibilities from connections built on understanding — of local conditions for honey production, of the value of reciprocal relationships and of the way to create a long-term business. The story came to light during the pandemic, from a government agency engaging with Māori businesses to help them with their exports.

The challenge is that government efforts to prepare for future disruptions may be seen as 'soft' and discretionary and not be prioritised in strategies, plans and budgets. However, addressing relationships and understanding will have observable effects. Creating relationships where none existed before will mitigate the effects of supply chain disruptions through actions such as co-creating new ways to navigate blockages; understanding how goods are moved will change assumptions and expectations and thus behaviours. Two specific actions that could be built into government plans are to revisit the breadth and depth of institutional and local relationships to build resilience in supply chain and freight systems; and to interrogate how core societal assumptions could affect supply chains in times of disruption. Importantly, though, all sectors of society need to play a part.

IT WOULD SEEM APPROPRIATE FOR government to initiate the mapping of potential and existing institutional and local relationships between participants in supply chain systems across New Zealand communities, including the private sector, local and central government, and even internationally, to see what and where relationships exist or are missing. Local and central governments also have a key role in generating interest and mobilising people to become involved. This sort of work lends itself to co-design and co-discovery exercises involving multidisciplinary and diverse groups.

Multiple worldviews will be needed to make sense of complex supply chain threads and interconnections and to create new insights into problems and solutions.[18] Climate change projects such as The Deep South Te Kōmata o te Tonga National Science Challenge research programme have been working this way for some time.[19] Such a big and complex task could be simplified by examining security and resilience on a sector by sector basis, as suggested by the Productivity Commission.[20] Food security has already been identified; the health system has made a start because of the pandemic; other sectors include transport, education, agriculture, manufacturing, water, energy and defence.

The cross-societal relationship work could lead to uncovering core societal assumptions and their inherent vulnerabilities. Many interviewees commented on their surprise at the border closing; some were surprised by the importance of supply chains that had been invisible to them prior to the pandemic; others were surprised that supply chain systems were not as flexible or responsive as they thought, or were astonished by the speed with which some companies could pivot their operations. Such assumptions framed their policy and operational responses, with varied results.

In times of deep uncertainty, if the effects of supply chain disruptions cannot be controlled, then at least having a clear understanding of the effects of those core and apparently unquestionable societal assumptions will help with responses. To deeply understand and question the unquestionable will require input from diverse experiences and people with assorted worldviews from across society.

THE EFFECTS OF ABSENCES ON the resilience of supply chain systems — absence of knowledge about how goods are moved; absence of relationships needed to respond to disruptions; and absence of testing of long-held assumptions about how society works — are perhaps underrated. Under-appreciating the importance of relationships and of underpinning assumptions about how society works is a concern for all New Zealanders. Cross-societal work on relationships and core societal assumptions relating to the movement of goods will go a long way to addressing these absences and helping New Zealand prepare for future disruptions. Much of this work is likely to be exploratory and led by government. It will take time, effort and money, and will require sustained commitment not only from future governments, but also from industry and communities. The government and New Zealand communities must work together on removing these absences.

Part 2

INTELLIGENCE AND DOMESTIC SECURITY

While automated detection has a role, it is unlikely to replace human labour.

6.

OUT OF SIGHT AND OUT OF MIND

The absolute importance of submarine cables to New Zealand

Phil Holdstock & John Moremon

New Zealanders depend on a critical communications infrastructure that few ever think about. Most of us are familiar with the internet and are accustomed to such terms as cyberspace, the cloud, 3G, 4G and 5G, but many of us may think our ability to complete everyday online tasks such as banking, emailing, social media, news and streaming is the result of something that happens 'up there' thanks to satellites and Wi-Fi. The truth is that our internet experience is shaped by a more mundane yet incredibly sophisticated technology: a worldwide network of copper and fibre-optic cables buried underground on land and laid across ocean floors. This cable network carries a staggering 95–99 per cent of global electronic communications — and includes more than 1 million kilometres of undersea submarine cables.[1]

The lack of public awareness of this infrastructure is not unique to New Zealand. Even though submarine cables are laid across almost every ocean and sea, connecting virtually every continental and island state, scholars have noted that it 'remains surprising how little is known in public or among policymakers about how the network operates, how it is regulated, who controls it, and how it is protected from vulnerabilities'.[2]

This lack of awareness stems from a 'triple invisibility'. First, as a society, we tend to take for granted most forms of infrastructure, such as roads, buildings, sewers and cables, until something goes wrong. Second, cables are out of sight, with perhaps the only visual clue to their existence in our lives being the easy-to-ignore flashing lights on the ONT (Optical Network Terminal, aka modem) inside our home or business. And third, not only is most of the cable network under the surface, but most of it is in the darkest depths of the ocean.[3] Despite their lack of visibility, however, submarine cables are vital to our national prosperity and security. In essence, submarine cables provide the physical bedrock of cyberspace and the cloud and thus play a tremendous part in our social connectedness and contributions to global governance and the global economy.[4]

New Zealand's geographic location as an island nation in the south of the South Pacific means that submarine cables are critically important. However, although New Zealand has legislation to protect submarine cables in its territorial waters from accidental or deliberate damage, most are foreign-owned, outside territorial waters, and facing an array of potential military, terrorist and natural threats. As Rishi Sunak noted before he became British prime minister, submarine cables can be summed up with two words: 'indispensable, insecure'.[5] The importance of submarine cable networks is such that they must be factored into public dialogue and decision-making around national and international security.

THE USE OF CABLES FOR governmental, commercial and social communication goes as far back as the 1840s. Following the invention of electromagnetic telegraphy, vast networks of above-ground copper lines were constructed on continents and large islands, and telegraph operators used Morse code to send and receive messages. Postal mail services were important, but the telegraph enabled faster delivery of messages and faster responses.[6] From the outset, cables tended to be laid and owned by companies rather than governments, thus avoiding the political friction that could come from having telegraph cables linking different countries. To this day, commercial entities are responsible for most cable development. However, despite their private appearance and legal status, 'international telecommunications companies have almost always been hybrid creatures: private in appearance and by law, but intimately tied to their home governments'.[7]

The earliest cable networks were on land, but people soon realised that sending telegraph messages across the seas would also be advantageous and profitable. The first undersea cable was laid across the English Channel in 1850–51, and during 1854–58 a submarine cable was laid across the Atlantic Ocean, connecting Europe and North America. This transatlantic cable failed after three weeks. However, even in that short time it proved its worth, allowing for investment to produce a cable able to withstand oceanic conditions. Further submarine cables were laid across important passages, including the Mediterranean and the Red Sea, and in 1865–66 another was laid across the Atlantic.[8]

The submarine cable networks offered tremendous commercial and social benefits. However, they were also strategically important, being more secure than overland lines and less troublesome diplomatically, as cables could be laid across oceans and seas without negotiating with foreign governments. From the 1870s, Britain supported laying an extensive submarine cable network, the All-Red Line, to service the British Empire. With security front of mind, the route of the All-Red Line was planned to avoid foreign soil as much as possible, only coming ashore on islands or continental coastlines of the British Empire or close allies. Royal Navy warships would patrol sea lanes over the cables, and defences were constructed at relay stations where the cables come ashore.[9] The 1884 Convention for the Protection of Submarine Telegraph Cables meanwhile compelled signatory states (even to this day) to enact laws making it an offence to wilfully or negligently break or damage a submarine cable, or to interfere with the activities of cable-laying and cable-repair ships.[10]

New Zealand's first submarine cable was laid in 1866 between Lyall Bay in the North Island and Whites Bay in the South Island to connect the domestic telegraph network. In 1876 the first trans-Tasman cable, between Botany Bay near Sydney and Cable Bay near Nelson in the South Island, was completed, with another then laid from Cable Bay to Whanganui to connect with the North Island. The trans-Tasman cable was a technological marvel, in places 5 kilometres deep and strung across undersea mountains, canyons and plains, despite the fact that deep ocean surveying was not possible at that time.

In 1902 a New Zealand branch of the British-American Pacific cable (part of the All-Red Line) was laid between Doubtless Bay in Northland

and Norfolk Island, from where lines ran west to Brisbane, north to Hawai'i and on to Vancouver, Canada.[11] These cables gave New Zealand direct connections to Australia and indirect connections to Asia, North America and Europe. The communications infrastructure was strategically, commercially and socially significant, allowing messages to be sent between governments, militaries, businesses and families around the world in peacetime and in wartime.

IN THE MID-TWENTIETH CENTURY, SUBMARINE telegraph cables experienced a decline in use due to the introduction of new technologies, including wireless (radio) transmission from the 1930s. In the 1950s new submarine coaxial telephone cables were laid, but they proved technologically challenging and expensive and offered limited bandwidth. As a result, by the 1970s most transoceanic communications traffic was carried by satellites.[12]

New Zealand became part of the 'space age' in 1965 when the first satellite call was made between Britain and New Zealand, and in 1971 the opening of Warkworth Satellite Earth Station, north of Auckland, enabled the use of satellites for television broadcasts.[13]

A more far-reaching development occurred in 1986 when the University of Waikato connected to the world wide web via a dial-up telephone connection. As internet technology and accessibility developed, in 1989 New Zealand became the first country in the Asia-Pacific region to connect to the United States' internet backbone; 1193 New Zealand customers were connected in the first two years. This grew to 15,000 in the following two years — globally the fastest growth rate in internet accessibility.[14]

The renewed focus on submarine cables came about because the satellite network was inadequate for the increased data traffic generated by the internet. High-bandwidth fibre-optic cables provided the solution. The growth of the internet and the laying of fibre-optic submarine cables have gone hand-in-hand since the 1990s: 'In essence, the two technologies complemented each other perfectly: cables carried large volumes of voice and data traffic with speed and security; the internet made that data and information accessible and useable for a multitude of purposes.'[15]

In fact, there has never been another period when submarine cables have been more significant to humanity. Global connectivity depends on some 450 submarine cable networks worldwide with a total undersea cable length of over 1 million kilometres. Low-orbit satellites have started to take some of the load from the local fibre-optic networks; indeed, New Zealand mobile providers have begun to utilise the Starlink satellite network. However, even with the move to using satellites, the submarine cables remain crucial, linking the satellite ground stations to data storage and providing the critical commercial links between countries. Christian Bueger and Tobias Liebetrau argue that submarine cable networks should not be seen merely as data transmission conduits but rather as 'an economic trade route carrying the most important commodity of the information age: data'.[16]

The 1982 United Nations Convention on the Law of the Sea (UNCLOS) allows governments and companies to maintain existing submarine cable networks and lay new networks in non-territorial waters without requiring environmental impact studies. Studies by the United Nations Environment Programme, the World Conservation Monitoring Centre, the International Cable Protection Committee (a non-profit member organisation that promotes the security of cable networks) and research teams from other organisations have, in any case, found that modern submarine cables have a neutral to minor impact on the marine environment.[17]

In recent years there has been significant investment from an array of communications companies and content giants, all free to pursue the growth of submarine cable networks. Collectively, Google, Meta, Amazon and Microsoft make up four-fifths of recent investment in submarine cables, although competition from Chinese companies is increasing rapidly, particularly in the Indo-Pacific region.[18]

THE SUBMARINE CABLE INFRASTRUCTURE THAT serves New Zealand has continued to grow exponentially. The Southern Cross fibre-optic cable connecting Hawai'i to Takapuna was completed in 2000 and rapidly reduced the country's reliance on satellite communications.[19] Domestically, in the late 1990s and early 2000s, the Aqua Link network was laid along the coastlines of the northeastern South Island and western North Island to link main centres. In the last decade a second loop link of the Southern Cross Cable was laid from Whenuapai to

Hawai'i; another connection to Hawai'i is provided by the Hawaiki Cable spur connected to Mangawhai Heads. In addition, the Tasman Global Access Cable connects Raglan and Sydney.[20] The latest submarine cable connected to New Zealand is a spur of the Southern Cross Next cable, which in July 2022 linked Takapuna and Los Angeles (with connections to Australia, Fiji and Kiribati); this cable alone doubled New Zealand's data transmission capacity.[21]

The New Zealand activity is essential but pales in comparison to the global race to develop submarine cable networks, especially across the Atlantic, Indian and Pacific oceans. On top of American commercial interest in developing new networks and hubs, China intends to lay networks across the Indian and Pacific oceans as a digital extension ('a digital Silk Road') of China's Belt and Road Initiative.[22]

The developing networks influence New Zealand's commerce, security and society both directly and indirectly: without access to the internet provided by submarine cable networks, it would be impossible for the country to transmit and receive vast amounts of data generated in real time. To give one indication of the importance of the digital link, New Zealand's banks belong to the Society for Worldwide Interbank Financial Telecommunication (SWIFT), which links 8300 banking members in 195 economies; every day, SWIFT is responsible for US$10 trillion in financial transfers and over 15 million financial messages: most of this is transmitted using cable networks.[23] While New Zealand's share of SWIFT communications is modest, the ability to link with such networks is of fundamental importance.

The significance of the submarine cable infrastructure to the country cannot be underestimated. Yet, this critical infrastructure is still often overlooked in broader public discussions of New Zealand's security interests.

AS NOTED AT THE OUTSET, submarine cables are 'out of sight and out of mind' for most New Zealanders. At governmental and intergovernmental levels there is awareness of the submarine cable network and the array of security threats, as demonstrated in policies and agreements at these levels. For example, in 2018, as part of the Pacific Islands Forum, New Zealand signed the Boe Declaration on regional security. While most attention has been given to the declaration's affirmation that climate change is the primary threat to the livelihoods in the Pacific, it also acknowledges the vulnerability of member states to threats to their security, with an intention to 'maximise the protection and opportunities for Pacific infrastructure and peoples in the digital age'.[24] It is impossible to achieve regional security in the digital age without considering the submarine cable network.

New Zealand has appropriate legislation that specifically covers the security of submarine cables in its territorial waters with the Submarine Cables and Pipelines Protection Act 1996, as required under the 1884 Convention for the Protection of Submarine Telegraph Cables, of which New Zealand is a signatory. This is concerned principally with the types of physical threats from shipping activities that existed when the convention was drafted in the early 1880s.[25] Under this Act, New Zealand has 10 declared Cable Protection Areas (in areas of Great Barrier Island, Hauraki Gulf, Kawau Island, Whangaparāoa Peninsula, Muriwai Beach, Taharoa, Cook Strait, Oaonui, Hawke's Bay and in Taranaki around the Maui A and B gas pipelines) where anchoring and most types of fishing are banned.[26] But the Act does not address modern challenges such as the physical distance required between the now greater number of submarine cables in congested sea spaces, co-location with other activities such as undersea mining and fisheries, cybersecurity threats or natural threats.[27]

SUBMARINE CABLES FACE AN ARRAY of threats attributable to three leading causes: negligence, intentional damage or destruction, and natural events. While there is no cable damage reporting requirement, worldwide some 150–200 faults affecting submarine cables occur annually, of which fewer than 10 per cent result from natural hazards. Some 65–75 per cent of damage events occur mainly as a result of fishing and shipping activities, in areas where water depth is 200 metres or less. In much deeper waters, natural hazards become the primary cause of damage: approximately 31 per cent of faults in deep water are traceable to natural events, 14 per cent to fish bites on cables, and 28 per cent to unknown causes.[28]

The military use of submarine cables was not considered initially, despite the military achievements during the Crimean War of 1853–56. The British Colonial Office's Colonial Defence Committee recognised the cable vulnerabilities in the nineteenth century, and the 1884 Convention for the Protection of Submarine Telegraph Cables sought to deal with the most obvious form of physical threat: accidental physical damage. As noted, New Zealand's Submarine Cables and Pipelines Protection Act 1996 seeks to provide the grounds for prosecution in the event of such damage in territorial waters. However, there is a more sinister possibility of deliberate human interference that may be harder to counter.

The vulnerability of submarine cables to foreign interference was realised during the early twentieth century. The first significant deliberate attack on a submarine cable occurred within hours of the start of the First World War when British forces cut all but one of Germany's transatlantic cables; they left one intact to allow codebreakers to intercept and read messages.[29] Similar action was taken early in the Second World War. Then in 1971, at the height of the Cold War (1947–91), the United States began tapping into Soviet-owned submarine cables for intelligence gathering. These episodes established a practice of sabotage and espionage that continues today in various forms. In recent years there has been a small number of reported physical attacks on, and interference with, submarine cables, ranging from criminal theft of cable components to state-sponsored sabotage and cyberattacks by different groups.[30]

In 2014, documents leaked by Edward Snowden highlighted that the US National Security Agency had implemented a metadata collection programme, codenamed Speargun, in which New Zealand's Government Communications Security Bureau (GCSB) played a supporting role. According to the leaked documents, Five Eyes partners regularly use surveillance probes to tap into fibre-optic cables to gather information deemed to be of importance for international and national security.[31]

Given the rising superpower tensions in the Asia-Pacific region, the prevalence of transnational crime and the potential for terrorism, the vulnerability of submarine cables is a genuine concern. Military, terrorist or criminal physical attacks have the capacity to damage or cripple submarine cable networks.

Cyberattacks pose another serious threat, with the possibility of states, criminal groups or hostile groups hacking into network management systems to seize control of transmissions, skim personal and financial information transmitted over the cables, or mount ransom attacks. The US Department of Homeland Security thwarted at least one serious cyberattack on a submarine cable network in April 2022, although it could not confirm the attacker or the motivation.[32] Countries like New Zealand, which rely heavily on foreign-owned submarine communication infrastructure for economic and national security, may be impacted directly or indirectly by any of these forms of attack on the cable infrastructure. The GCSB is likely to play a further role in securing submarine cables serving New Zealand.

The vulnerability of submarine cables was brought to the attention of politicians in 2017 when Rishi Sunak, then a British member of parliament and now British prime minister, released a discussion paper, *Undersea Cables*, arguing that submarine cables are vitally important for international communications but are 'inherently vulnerable', and explaining that 'their location is generally publicly available, they tend to be highly concentrated geographically both at sea and on land, and it requires limited technical expertise and resources to damage them'.[33]

Sunak also warned of potential Russian aggression, and discussed how Russia's hybrid warfare model extends to utilising sabotage to destabilise an adversary's communications. Indeed, this occurred as part of Russia's invasion and annexation of Crimea in 2014: Russia cut the submarine cable that linked mainland Ukraine and the Crimean Peninsula, which enabled it to control the flow of information (and disinformation) concerning the invasion. Furthermore, Russia, and possibly other countries too, has invested in deep-sea submersibles and intelligence-gathering ships that can attack undersea infrastructure, including pipelines and submarine cables. Unfortunately, existing laws of armed conflict and laws of the sea do not provide robust protection for submarine cables.[34]

Rising tensions in the Asia-Pacific also open the possibility of hybrid warfare in this region, including potentially state-sanctioned attacks on South Pacific communications networks, which would threaten the interests of New Zealand and other South Pacific nations. The undersea infrastructure is mainly foreign-owned, particularly American-owned, and most cables terminate at four chokepoint locations: Sydney, Hawai'i, Guam and Los Angeles.[35]

While much of the cable network rests at depths where direct physical interference is not likely or possible, shallower waters and any locations where cables come ashore are points of physical vulnerability. Potential threats include disguised ships loitering in shallow waters and using submersibles to cut cables, or the worst-case scenario of missile or air strikes on key communication hubs.[36] As China gains influence across the Asia-Pacific region, it gains greater access to critical infrastructure in the area, including points where cables are accessible on land.

The United States (and no doubt its Five Eyes partners) monitors the situation, including reviewing ownership of critical infrastructure, intending to mitigate threats.[37] Future state or non-state sabotage, espionage, military attack or cyberattack against cable networks could potentially leave New Zealand with only an indirect submarine cable route via Sydney, either temporarily or for some duration. If the Sydney connections were also compromised, it would severely disrupt New Zealand's communications capability.[38] While a direct military attack on cable locations seems unthinkable, as it would mean a war had broken out, we should be aware of the inherent vulnerabilities built into the submarine cable networks.

There is, in addition, an ever-present natural threat to submarine cables — the potential for damage from natural events particularly evident within the Pacific's Ring of Fire, where triggering events include volcanic eruptions, earthquakes, tropical and sub-tropical cyclones and typhoons. These events can cause strong turbidity currents that result in underwater landslides. The impact of such events was illustrated in December 2006 when a magnitude 7.0 earthquake occurred off southern Taiwan, triggering a series of underwater landslides that produced dense sediment-laden turbidity currents that fell rapidly to the ocean floor, breaking nine fibre-optic submarine cables. The event seriously impacted Southeast Asia's regional and global communications, including telephone, internet and other data-transfer services.[39]

Recently, the January 2022 eruption of the Hunga-Tonga-Hunga-Ha'apai underwater volcano off Tonga showed clearly the vulnerability of the cables in our region. The eruption shredded 80 kilometres of submarine cables, making the repair mission far more complex than a simple cut from an anchor or fishing equipment, as might occur in shallower waters. The reinstatement of the undersea cable took five weeks, including two weeks to get a repair vessel to the location.[40]

Recent natural disasters have shown in stark detail the vulnerability of New Zealand's communications infrastructure. Cyclone Gabrielle in 2023 caused widespread damage across the North Island, damaging power-lines, fibre cable networks and mobile phone networks on land, isolating towns and rural communities and hindering emergency services. The loss of electronic payment systems and internet access caused disruptions to local commerce and economies and highlighted what can happen when communication infrastructure is impacted or compromised.[41] Significantly, the cyclone struck at a point where three submarine cable landing sites are located, and while on this occasion damage to submarine cable infrastructure was avoided, the event should serve as a reminder of the potential for damage from serious storms and flooding.

In the past when the locations of cable landing stations were chosen, no thought was given to accelerated climate change and its effects on coastal environments. Cable hubs in many countries tend to be located on low coastal ground, and many land-based cables are in low-lying coastal zones. Possible future responses to the climate change threat may include enhanced monitoring of storm-surge predictions, relocating cable stations if necessary, and developing back-up systems to ensure that networks can continue to operate if a cable network is damaged.[42]

New Zealand can, in fact, start to mitigate the impact of infrastructure loss by planning to relocate cable infrastructure and potentially add government-owned low-level communication satellites to provide additional redundancy pathways. Using satellites for redundancy for New Zealand has become a viable option because the launching facilities at Māhia Peninsula are significantly cheaper to use than traditional launching sites.[43] Ulrich Speidel suggests also increasing the resilience of New Zealand's communications infrastructure by having a back-up microwave capability between mobile phone towers, with satellite use ensuring sustained connections in times of emergency. However, while the emerging low-level satellite networks can play a part in national and regional responses to local disasters, they do not have the capability to make the submarine cable networks redundant.[44]

IN THE MODERN AGE, CLOUD computing is synonymous with global connectivity. While submarine cables may appear archaic, they are essential to modern life and serve as the backbone of the internet. These cables link countries to create, in effect, a submarine web; however, like a giant spider web, the infrastructure is vulnerable to threats, including natural disasters, accidental damage and deliberate interference.

The South Pacific region presents unique challenges for laying and maintaining submarine cables due to its location within the Ring of Fire and its transformational boundary, which makes the region prone to seismic and volcanic events. Climate change threatens further significant risks, as rising sea levels can affect landing stations and onshore cables connected to the submarine cables. Great power competition, rising geostrategic tensions, transnational crime and the ever-present potential for terrorism mean that the submarine cables are also susceptible to human interference.

These vulnerabilities are significant because of the critical nature of the infrastructure, particularly for New Zealand, which relies heavily on submarine cables for global communications and connectivity. Protecting these cables must be considered a national security issue, and steps must be taken to ensure resilience in the face of the array of potential threats. However, this will require sustained government action.

It would be timely for the New Zealand government and private sector entities to publicly assess the threats to submarine cable networks, ahead of investing in back-up systems and developing protocols for expeditious and effective responses in the event of serious damage to a network or networks. This may include consideration of active steps that can be taken to improve national and regional responses, such as maintaining regional stocks of spares for the repair of damaged cables, and providing input into the strengthening of national and international legal frameworks required to enhance the protection of submarine cables against such threats as hybrid warfare, cyber warfare and criminal activity.

The inherent vulnerability and criticality of submarine cables for global and national communications make it imperative to take these steps both for New Zealand and its Pacific partners. By understanding and acknowledging the vulnerabilities in the infrastructure and implementing appropriate measures, we can mitigate the risks and ensure that the submarine cables remain a reliable and secure resource for as long as they are needed. It is critical that we act to protect the submarine cables against the array of threats to ensure that in the event of a failure, an incredible technological innovation does not become our undoing.

7.

OUTLAW MOTORCYCLE GANGS AND THE ILLEGAL DRUG TRADE

▮ What national security risks do they pose?

Chris Wilkins, Marta Rychert, Jose Romeo, Thomas Graydon-Guy & Robin van der Sanden

Aotearoa New Zealand is considered to have one of the highest rates of gang activity in the world, and has experienced a dramatic rise in gang membership over the past decade according to law enforcement intelligence estimates.[1] Since the early 2000s, law enforcement has reported that gangs in Aotearoa have developed more sophisticated and internationally networked criminal enterprises focused on profit, including cooperating with each other to import and manufacture methamphetamine.[2] The growth in gang numbers and the establishment of New Zealand-based chapters of global gangs have also been linked to a surge in the incidence and intensity of gang violence, with unprecedented levels of drive-by shootings and murders.[3]

There remain, however, significant gaps in our understanding of the extent of gang involvement in illegal drug markets and the implications for violence and community security in Aotearoa New Zealand. The current assessment of the situation is overwhelmingly based on New Zealand Police, Customs and Corrections statistics and intelligence assessments.[4] Although these sources provide valuable analysis based on street-level observation of gang activity, wire taps of gang communication, first-hand accounts by undercover officers, and the aggregated agency data on gang involvement with the criminal justice system, they also have some important limitations.

First, much of the enforcement intelligence on gang activity is restricted from public release and consequently not available for external analysis.[5] This has the practical purpose of not revealing sources and knowledge to the criminal fraternity, but it also limits the level of independent critical analysis of information and conclusions. All information sources have limitations, and one powerful means to minimise these limitations is to triangulate from multiple independent information sources and draw on multidisciplinary perspectives.

Second, as for crime in general, much gang crime is under-reported and clandestine in nature.[6] Under-reporting is likely to be particularly pronounced with respect to gang activity since gangs are known to retaliate violently against those who cooperate with the authorities; some notable New Zealand examples have likely had a lasting chilling impact.[7] In addition, victims of gang threats and violence may themselves be involved in illegal activity, such as drug use, sales and manufacture, and may hold drug debt, and consequently risk incriminating themselves if they report incidents of gang violence related to drug markets.

Third, enforcement agencies tend naturally to focus on a narrow set of statistical indicators directly related to criminal offending (such as arrests, seizures and imprisonment) rather than drawing on wider sociological and economic market theory and analysis.[8]

Fourth, the reliance on criminal justice statistics tends to favour a national focus, as government statistics are most commonly published at the national level. This can obscure important regional differences in levels of gang activity and community impact.[9]

Consequently, much remains to be explored about the national security risk posed by gangs and the extent of their involvement in the illegal drugs trade in Aotearoa New Zealand. We provide here an overview of current understanding of recent gang trends and the influence they have on illegal drug markets in Aotearoa New Zealand, and draw on findings from the latest New Zealand Drugs Trends Survey (NZDTS). The final section of the chapter draws some tentative conclusions and identifies a future research agenda for understanding gangs and drug markets in Aotearoa New Zealand.

THE GOVERNMENT'S MULTI-AGENCY GANG HARM Insights Centre (GHIC) maintains a register of gang members in Aotearoa New Zealand, known as the National Gang List (NGL). The NGL is validated by police districts and national intelligence staff and is based on evidence from operations and search warrants, including observation of and intelligence on patch wearing and gang tattoos.[10] New Zealand Police consider the NGL the best source of information on the number of gang members, although it is acknowledged that counting (generally secretive) gang members is challenging and inexact; as well, those who drift away from the gang scene are unlikely to be removed from the list.[11]

In January 2019 the GHIC reviewed the methodology of the NGL to improve the national consistency of the recording and validation of gang numbers. According to the NGL, the number of patched and prospect gang members increased from 4361 in February 2016 to 6361 in February 2019, and 7722 in April 2022.[12] Most recently, a 'new record' number of 8357 gang members was reportedly reached in October 2022.[13] Overall, this amounts to a 91 per cent increase in gang members over six years (and a 21 per cent increase from the implementation of the enhanced NGL in February 2019).

There is regional variation in gang numbers. The NGL suggests 19 per cent of gang members are based in the Bay of Plenty, 17 per cent in Gisborne/Hawke's Bay, 13 per cent in wider Auckland, 12 per cent in Wellington, 8 per cent in Canterbury and 8 per cent in Waikato.[14] The largest regional increases in numbers since 2016 were recorded in Tasman (+232 per cent), Canterbury (+124 per cent), Waitematā (+123 per cent), Waikato (+102 per cent), Southland/West Coast (+102 per cent) and Wellington (+94 per cent).[15]

NEW ZEALAND LAW ENFORCEMENT HAS long associated gangs with the illegal drugs trade, specifically the emergence and expansion of the methamphetamine trade since the early 2000s, but also previously the cultivation and sale of cannabis from the 1980s onwards.[16] The amount of methamphetamine seized has increased substantially in recent years, from 212.5 kilograms in 2018 to 1183.1 kilograms in 2019.[17] The large increase in seizures likely reflects the industrial-scale increase in the illicit production of methamphetamine in some Asian regions where government control is weak or compromised, which has resulted in a surge in methamphetamine supply throughout the East and Southeast Asia and Oceania regions over the past decade or so.[18] It has been estimated that gangs in Aotearoa New Zealand make approximately NZ$500 million in profit from the methamphetamine trade every year.[19] The illegal market for cannabis has been estimated to be over NZ$1 billion per year, but it is not clear what proportion of this market is controlled by gangs.[20]

Police intelligence and local sources have reported that North Island gangs with a 'business focus' on the drugs trade have been moving into smaller towns and rural areas in recent years, notably in the South Island, to expand their methamphetamine sales and markets.[21] It has been claimed this is because the methamphetamine trade is particularly lucrative in rural areas.[22]

Our previous modelling found the price of a gram of methamphetamine was $26 higher in small towns and rural locations (+5 per cent higher) compared with in the cities; availability was also greater in small towns and rural locations than in cities.[23] The higher price may reflect the 'thin' nature of methamphetamine markets in small towns (where there is a small number of sellers), the vulnerability of these local sellers to detection, and the limited alternative sources for buyers. A number of factors may contribute to the higher availability of methamphetamine in small towns and rural areas, including proximity to methamphetamine laboratories located in rural areas to avoid detection, regional economic decline, a lack of entertainment options, limited police presence, and geographical distance from drug treatment and other health services.[24]

Our previous analysis also found that respondents reported a gram of methamphetamine was $29 cheaper (−5 per cent) and availability greater when they purchased from a gang member. The reduced price may reflect gangs' access to lower-cost methamphetamine as a result of the scale of their own production and/or importation of cheaper methamphetamine and precursor chemicals via relationships with international drug-trafficking groups.[25]

Gang-affiliated drug dealers may also face lower risks of victimisation and retaliation than independent drug dealers, as they can call on the collective protection of their fellow gang members. They may also be able to lower their risk of arrest by intimidating local communities and perhaps even local police officers, who do not have timely access to back-up.[26] Gangs may also have a particular advantage when opening new drug markets as they can coordinate the entry of large numbers of drug dealers to a nascent market and thereby swamp the existing local drug enforcement activity.[27]

THE PROPORTION OF NATIONAL FIREARMS offences that are committed by gang members has increased from 6.6 per cent in 2010 to 12.6 per cent in 2019.[28] The recent increase in the incidence and intensity of gang violence has often been attributed to the creation of New Zealand-based chapters of international outlaw motorcycle gangs by Australian deportees (so called '501s'), such as the Comancheros, Mongols and Rebels. It has been suggested that these newcomers upset established gang divisions of territory and illegal enterprise and the diplomatic channels previously utilised to resolve gang disputes peacefully.[29] It is also contended that these 'new' gangs use more brutal forms of violence and criminal business practices than existing groups, and have brought with them international networks for larger-scale drug trafficking, for example new supply source countries, such as Mexico.[30]

Police intelligence reports caution that not all of these developments can be attributed to the arrival of new Australian actors. For example, the number of gang-related firearms offences increased from early 2013, two years before the 501s began arriving in New Zealand.[31] As well, some domestic gangs had been developing a new 'business focus' to exploit the lucrative methamphetamine trade since the early 2000s.[32] This evolution of the gang subculture has brought about competitive rivalry between modernised gangs focused on the drugs trade and more traditional turf-based gangs.[33]

AS NOTED EARLIER, THERE ARE important gaps in data regarding gang involvement in illegal drug markets in Aotearoa New Zealand. The New Zealand Drugs Trends Survey (NZDTS) is the only survey that examines the structure of illegal drug markets and the role of gang sellers in New Zealand. The NZDTS is an anonymous online convenience survey designed to provide an annual snapshot of frequent drug use and illegal drug market indicators, such as availability and price, in Aotearoa New Zealand. Respondents are asked a range of questions about their use and purchase of drugs, including whether they have purchased different drug types from gang members and gang associates, and their perceptions of gang influence and community safety in their region. Respondents are not required to provide their name or any contact details, and no incentive payment for participation is offered. The anonymity of the online survey encourages respondents to be honest about gang involvement in drug markets without fear of retaliation.

The NZDTS was conducted on three previous occasions: 2017/2018, 2018/2019 and 2020/2021. The questionnaire is reviewed annually, and core questions are derived from established drug use and drug market studies conducted in New Zealand and Australia (such as New Zealand Arrestee Drug Use Monitoring; Illicit Drugs Monitoring System[34] and Drug Use Monitoring in Australia) and draw on the international academic literature. Recruitment for the NZDTS is via a widely targeted Facebook promotion campaign among people aged 16 years or older and living in New Zealand who have expressed interest in a range of entertainment options associated with alcohol, tobacco and other substance use.[35] The 2022/2023 NZDTS was conducted from August 2022 to February 2023. Surveys were audited for quality and extent of completion, leaving a total of 13,026 completed surveys.[36]

It is important to be clear that the NZDTS is not designed to be a representative survey of all frequent drug users; instead, it seeks to obtain a snapshot of drug market trends from people who have recently participated in those markets.[37] While the NZDTS has a large sample size, it may be less effective at reaching certain groups, such as those who do not use Facebook and the internet; and those with a particular interest in drug issues may be more likely to engage with the survey (although we employ quality controls to address the risk of multiple surveys from the same person).

New Zealand has a high level of digital engagement by international standards.[38] For example, 2.3 million New Zealanders (from a total population of 5.1 million) log on to Facebook every day.[39] There is evidence that self-administered online surveys provide greater perceived anonymity for sensitive topics.[40] The NZDTS sample was broadly consistent with the regional population distribution and the demographic profile of the wider New Zealand population: 19 per cent of respondents were Māori and 73 per cent Pākehā European, which aligned with the 2018 census returns, of which 16.5 per cent were Māori and 70.2 per cent European.[41] Sixty-five percent of the NZDTS sample were employed, 24 per cent were students and 11 per cent were unemployed or on a sickness benefit, compared with the wider New Zealand population with 66 per cent employed, 15 per cent students and 10 per cent receiving some kind of government benefit.[42]

Those respondents who reported purchasing a drug type in the previous six months were asked what types of sellers they had purchased from and provided with the following options: 'gang member or gang associate', 'drug dealer', 'social acquaintance', 'friend/partner/family'. The drug type most commonly purchased from a gang member was methamphetamine (31 per cent), followed by cannabis (17 per cent), ecstasy (MDMA) (6 per cent) and LSD (2 per cent). The regions with the highest proportion of methamphetamine purchasing from a gang member were Northland (41 per cent), Canterbury (40 per cent), Tasman/Nelson/Marlborough (38 per cent), Wellington (36 per cent) and Southland (36 per cent) (see Figure 1).

The New Zealand Police Association president has previously identified the Tasman and Southern districts as regions that have experienced the largest growth in gang activity.[43] As quoted above, the NGL has also recorded large increases in gang numbers in the Tasman (+232 per cent), Canterbury (+124 per cent) and Southland/West Coast (+102 per cent) districts. This rise in gang-related methamphetamine sales in the South Island is consistent with the previous accounts of 'business focused' North Island gangs moving into these South Island regions as part of a strategy to expand their methamphetamine markets.

The regions with the highest proportion of cannabis purchasing from a gang member were Manawatū-Whanganui (29 per cent), Gisborne/Hawke's Bay (25 per cent) and Bay of Plenty (22 per cent) (see Figure 2). Some regions reported relatively low levels of purchasing cannabis from a gang member, including Auckland (11 per cent) and Otago (13 per cent). For Auckland, this may represent the greater involvement of mid-level cannabis dealers within a large urban population who insulate retail buyers from gang-associated cannabis cultivators and wholesalers based in rural regions. Given the broader base of cannabis users, sale of this drug often happens within personal networks rather than from a clearly defined 'drug dealer'. Some regions, such as Tasman and Marlborough,

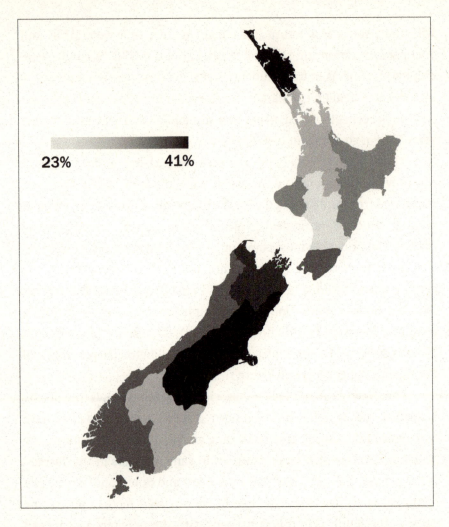

Figure 1: Proportion of respondents who had purchased methamphetamine from a gang member or gang associate by region, 2022/2023

have a long cultural history of small-scale cannabis cultivation, and this social supply network may have inhibited the greater involvement of gangs in cannabis cultivation and sale in these regions.

All NZDTS respondents were asked, 'What influence do you think gangs have in your community? (e.g. people fear or admire them, or authorities fail to act against them)', and were provided with a scale of 1 = no influence to 7 = very influential. Gang influence may involve a range of observed behaviours beyond drug manufacture and selling, and perceptions of gang influence will be subjective based on an array of first- and second-hand experience and knowledge. In places where gangs are highly active, they often partake in ritualistic public displays of power,

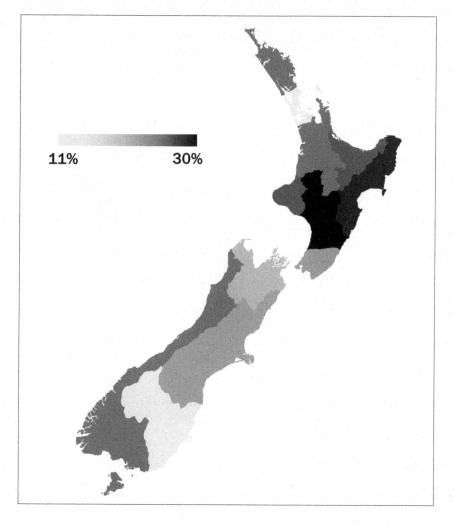

Figure 2: Proportion of respondents who had purchased cannabis from a gang member or gang associate by region, 2022/2023

including wearing patches and gang regalia in public, participating in motorcycle rallies and funeral processions, flaunting road rules, occupying public spaces and establishing visible headquarters. The reported perceptions of gang influence are also based on a large sample size and so represent collective assessment (a total of 8982 answered this question).

Figure 3 presents the proportion of respondents who rated the influence of gangs as 6 or higher on the 7-point scale. The two regions with the highest proportion describing gang influence as very high (6+) were Gisborne/Hawke's Bay (33 per cent) and Northland (25 per cent), followed by Bay of Plenty (19 per cent) and Waikato (18 per cent). There

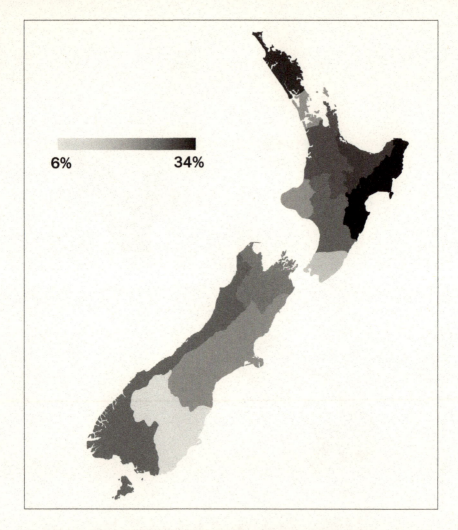

Figure 3: Proportion of respondents who rated the influence of gangs in their community as 6+ on a 7-point scale (1 = no influence to 7 = very influential), 2022/2023

is some overlap with the previous reports of the prevalence of buying drugs from gangs, notably the higher proportions reported buying methamphetamine from gangs in Northland, and the higher proportions reported buying cannabis from gangs in Gisborne/Hawke's Bay, Bay of Plenty, Waikato and Manawatū-Whanganui. High gang influence in specific regions will also represent long-standing cultural and socio-economic drivers of gang activity, such as experiences of racism, social and economic dislocation, and distrust of the authorities, often within Māori communities.[44]

All NZDTS respondents were asked, 'How safe do you feel to walk around your neighbourhood after 11pm?' and were provided with a scale

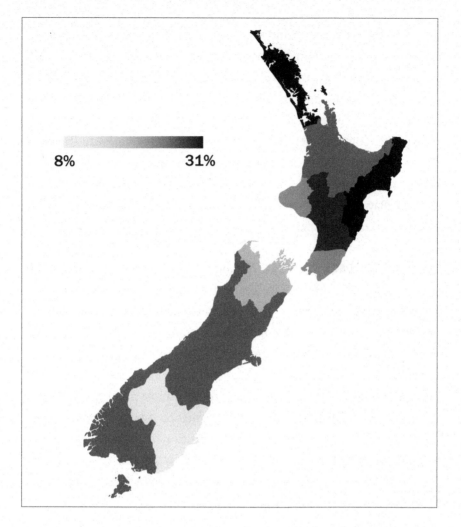

Figure 4: Proportion of respondents who rated the safety of their community after 11pm as 2 or less on a 7-point scale (1 = very unsafe to 7 = very safe), 2022/2023

of 1 = very unsafe to 7 = very safe. Perceptions of community safety are subjective based on an array of first- and second-hand experience and knowledge, and gang activity may only comprise a small component of any overall assessment of community safety. Nevertheless, typical public displays of gang activity, such as the wearing of gang patches and regalia, motorcycle rallies, flaunting traffic rules and occupying public spaces intimidate members of the public and influence perceptions of community safety. Previous studies have shown that gang members are more prevalent in neighbourhoods that are perceived as unsafe.[45] High gang membership can be viewed as both a cause of low neighbourhood safety and a driver for people to join gangs for protection.

The assessment of community safety from the NZDTS is based on a large sample size representing collective knowledge (a total of 9125 answered the question). Figure 4 presents the proportion of respondents who rated the safety of their neighbourhood at night as 2 or lower based on the above 7-point scale. The regions with the highest proportion rating their communities as unsafe (2 or less) were Gisborne/Hawke's Bay (30 per cent) and Northland (29 per cent), followed by Manawatū-Whanganui (25 per cent). As detailed in the previous section, Gisborne/Hawke's Bay and Northland also reported the highest levels of gang influence in the country.

THERE IS EVIDENCE THAT THE number of gang members has increased significantly in Aotearoa New Zealand in recent years, and that some gang members are adopting 'business-focused' modes of operation to exploit the lucrative methamphetamine trade, including drawing on international drug-trafficking networks, cooperating with members from other gangs, modernising the gang subculture and seeking to expand local drug markets. Gangs were reported to be most directly involved in retail sales of methamphetamine and cannabis. It is possible that they are involved in the importation and distribution of other drug types, for example MDMA, LSD and cocaine, but as they are not closely aligned with the social milieu of these consumer groups (dance party culture for MDMA and LSD or affluent urban elites for cocaine) their involvement in these markets may not be readily recognised.

Statistical modelling has shown that gang selling has increased the availability and lowered the price of methamphetamine, particularly in small towns and rural areas. Gang information gathering and utilisation of intimidation and violence may be especially effective in small isolated rural communities, particularly those with long-standing distrust of the authorities, such as Māori and Pasifika communities.[46] Rural communities often also have a limited number of police officers covering a large rural territory, far from the possibility of reinforcement.[47]

The fact that gangs offered lower prices for methamphetamine suggests they may not have monopoly control of these local markets, but rather are price competitors and offer lower prices to attract more customers, perhaps as part of a market growth strategy. It may be the case that gang sellers in these contexts are able to reduce prices because they face a lower risk of arrest, since people are nervous about reporting gang drug-selling activity, and a lower risk of victimisation by rival drug dealers due to their collective security and capacity to retaliate violently. The extent to which gangs utilise the profits and influence from the methamphetamine trade to gain information on local police operations and a competitive advantage over rivals is not publicly known.

There appears to be some regional association between the extent of purchasing of methamphetamine and cannabis from gangs, levels of gang influence and perceptions of public safety. Further statistical modelling of these associations with controls for a range of confounders, such as lower socioeconomic status, is required to confirm the strength of any relationship.

8.

BIOSECURITY INTELLIGENCE IN AOTEAROA

Adapting to changing national and international conditions

Madeline Marshall

As a result of its lack of land borders and relative isolation, Aotearoa New Zealand has many rare and unique plant and animal species.[1] Endemism (defined as geographic isolation of a species to a distinct area) is associated with high extinction rates in our modern global society due to the introduction of exotic species to new environments via human activity. Introduced species often cause significant environmental harm. They may outcompete native species for resources such as food, water and habitat; they may prey on native species, reducing their populations, potentially to extinction; and they may introduce pathogens to which native species have not developed immunity or resistance. Environmental damage from introduced species can lead to economic impacts such as reduced crop yields, outbreaks of agricultural diseases, reduced revenue from ecotourism due to changes in native landscapes, and costs associated with managing introduced species' populations and impacts.[2]

Preventing and managing the introduction of exotic species (such as insects, animals, ecological pathogens and weeds) is an essential component of national security as it protects a country's natural resources, economy and citizens from potentially harmful effects. In Aotearoa this process is known as biosecurity, defined by the government as the protection of the economy, environment and people's health from the risks posed by unwanted exotic pests and diseases entering the country, and the control of endemic pests and diseases within the country.[3]

Biosecurity practices and principles in New Zealand are governed by the Biosecurity Act of 1993. This foundational piece of legislation established the governmental responsibilities for comprehensive prevention and management of harmful species introduction to Aotearoa. The Act was the first of its kind globally and has influenced and spurred biosecurity legislation around the world.[4] The Ministry for Primary Industries Manatū Ahu Matua (MPI) is the lead agency for administering the Biosecurity Act in New Zealand. Implementation is carried out via pre-border, border and post-border activities.

Biosecurity management at the border involves the screening of imported goods, travellers and transportation vessels that could potentially introduce harmful, unwanted organisms. Post-border management involves detecting and responding to newly identified introductions of unwanted species, and managing the long-term impact of unwanted species that have established self-sustaining, spreading and/or environmentally damaging populations within the country.[5] While these border and post-border components are critical, this chapter is largely concerned with pre-border biosecurity practices.

Pre-border operational activity is focused on prevention. Preventative biosecurity aims to protect environments from the potential lasting effects of harmful species and is more cost effective than the post-border management of a harmful introduced species. Pre-border biosecurity operations are multifaceted; emphasis is placed on evaluation of risk factors and implementation of import health standards (IHS). IHS outline compliance requirements for importation with the aim of excluding unwanted organisms at the point of origin. Risk evaluations determine which offshore organisms could negatively impact New Zealand's ecosystems, how these organisms are most likely to enter the country, and what preventative strategies can be employed. Border inspections of imported goods via activities such as random sampling of produce imports, X-ray scanning and visual inspections augment these pre-border biosecurity measures.

The functionality of New Zealand's biosecurity system is dependent on continual review and adaptability to changing national and international conditions. This adaptability is necessary because the conditions that influence biosecurity are not static: among other possibilities, organisms evolve and spread to new environments; political changes influence resource allocation to pest and disease treatment in other countries; climate change alters the habitat and fitness of organisms; and political shifts and conflicts alter shipment routes and primary production.[6]

Adaptability is structured into MPI's biosecurity management by continual re-evaluation of risk profiles based on the global spread of unwanted organisms, regular re-review of IHS based on changes to trade partnerships and global environmental conditions, and monitoring of global changes (social, political, natural, etc.) that alter the international biosecurity threat environment. This last function is conducted by the Biosecurity Intelligence team (BSI), which was created under MPI's Biosecurity New Zealand business unit in 2018.

BSI contributes to biosecurity operations through the monitoring of offshore indicators of biosecurity threats. Intelligence gathering related to biological, environmental and social/human events allows for a holistic assessment of the changes that could influence opportunities for exotic species to enter New Zealand, and is used to reduce uncertainty surrounding exotic species and further protect Aotearoa New Zealand from their introduction and establishment.

BSI CONTRIBUTES TO AOTEAROA NEW ZEALAND'S wider biosecurity system via the fusion of two disciplines: biosecurity and intelligence. Intelligence is defined here as the collection and analysis of information to produce insights that inform decision-making. These insights in turn influence the observed domain or environment — in this case, biosecurity in Aotearoa. Intelligence collection can be a challenging and complex process that often involves dealing with incomplete or contradictory information from sources that may not always be reliable. Critical thinking, information evaluation and bias recognition are essential skills in this process. In BSI, intelligence collection occurs during horizon-scanning, a structured process of looking across a wide variety of sources for early signs of disruptive change. Figure 1 illustrates

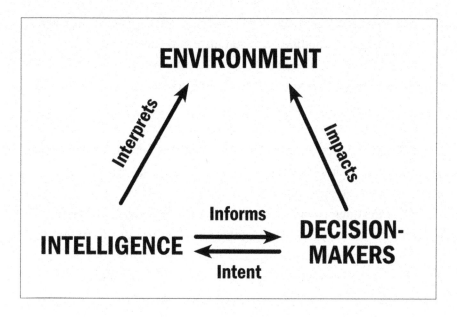

Figure 1: The 4i model of intelligence-led operations, detailing the interconnection between intelligence and decision-makers and how these connections influence changes within the observed environment

where and how intelligence sits and functions within an organisation. In BSI, the decision on what to collect is informed by drivers and indicators. Drivers are high-level themes or trends that influence the direction and magnitude of changes in the threat environment. Indicators are specific, observable events or conditions that, should they occur, provide an early warning of changes to threat, particularly if changes to several indicators occur simultaneously.[7]

This driver- and indicator-led approach is predicated on the idea that a significant event, regardless of its nature, is the result of smaller, interconnecting factors that collectively influence an outcome. When analysed alongside other related data, indicators can help to identify patterns and trends that may suggest a developing threat. BSI analysts monitor specific indicators and report on developments. Their role is to understand the potential consequences of particular changes and to provide timely and accurate threat assessments to decision-makers (such as evidence of biosecurity non-compliance in trade between two countries that do not include New Zealand). In BSI's system, each high-level driver is broken into several specific indicators.

Indicators can also be used to inform policies by providing a baseline of situational awareness. Intelligence assessments are not always about increasing threat: situations can stabilise, and threats can decrease or fluctuate in severity.[8] Regular updates against a set of indicators can be useful for informing business-as-usual practices.

The use of indicators as part of a warning system was developed for military use to identify early signals of military action during the Cold War. The practice has since been modified for use in many other disciplines. Indicators in the military sense are designed to help analysts evaluate the strategic significance of another country's preparations and activities. But how can military intelligence strategies apply to species and diseases that do not plan in the way that humans do? Applying traditional intelligence methodologies to biosecurity requires a rethinking of the threat equation, commonly expressed as: threat = capability + intent + opportunity.[9]

In biosecurity contexts, the basic intent of an organism to sustain itself and reproduce can be taken as fixed, even though its behaviour in an environment is not fixed. The biological capability of a pest or disease to survive and thrive in an environment is also relatively stable compared with the parameters of that environment, as it is much less dynamic than human capabilities. The capability of a biosecurity threat organism to survive and reproduce in Aotearoa is assessed using scientific methods by MPI's Emerging Risks System.

Therefore, the core of biosecurity intelligence threat assessment sits in the 'opportunity' space where the fundamental questions are: how can unwanted organisms reach New Zealand, and are the opportunities for arrival increasing or decreasing? Methodologies for generating and selecting indicators vary because the type of indicator needed depends on the context. Biosecurity threats require indicators that point to opportunity for non-human environmental organisms (such as viruses, insects, fungal spores) to reach New Zealand. There is no 'correct' way to approach indicator selection, but some common strategies include employing experts in the field who can identify indicators; historical assessments of previous events; creating hypothetical scenarios and then identifying the indicators that would signal the progress towards these scenarios; and think-tank style brainstorming.[10]

ADAPTING INTELLIGENCE METHODOLOGY FOR USE in a biosecurity system began with an understanding of the core objective of the BSI team: to forecast how changes to the global biosecurity threat environment could impact Aotearoa. The operational activity of BSI had to include an understanding of what global biosecurity threats exist, how they can be monitored, and how the status of these global biosecurity threats can be reported in a manner that increases the efficacy of the greater biosecurity system.

BSI uses a combination of scenario generation, expert judgement, structured analytic techniques (SATs) and historical analysis in order to develop a comprehensive set of drivers and indicators that are monitored pre-border, are relevant to the biosecurity threat environment in New Zealand and are adaptable to changing circumstances. This required multiple stages of development that resulted in the identification of the indicators. The key stages of this process are: (1) tasking; (2) environment scan (background research); (3) identifying indicators; (4) monitoring indicators; (5) collation; (6) analysis and assessment; and (7) reporting.

Each step is further outlined in the following sections and is accompanied by a hypothetical example involving a global pest of agricultural significance that is not present in Aotearoa New Zealand.

1. TASKING

The initial step in intelligence collection involves identifying the situations or issues where assessment is needed: what are the intelligence requirements (IR)? What are the issues that need intelligence assessment? For BSI, IRs relate to events or conditions that could alter the existing biosecurity threat environment, as identified by expert judgement and historical analysis of biosecurity events both within the country and abroad. IRs can be high level or very specific. High-level IRs usually relate to drivers, while specific IRs can help to generate indicators.

Example: Populations of the brown marmorated stinkbug (BMSB) are increasing in country X. A specific intelligence requirement here is: how do developments in country X in relation to BMSB affect the biosecurity threat to Aotearoa New Zealand? A high-level intelligence requirement might be: How are known biosecurity threats to Aotearoa changing over time?

2. ENVIRONMENT SCAN

Environmental scanning involves collecting information based on the known variables associated with the event. Establishing background knowledge is critical to effective intelligence assessment: although assessment is future-focused, a context which is inherently unknowable, a good grasp of the background ensures that decisions about the future are grounded in reality.

Example: Analysts will search open sources (media, academic publications, datasets, trade journals, etc.) in order to:

- better understand the presence of BMSB in country X;
- quantify reported population changes;
- identify factors that may affect BMSB spread (supply chains, political corruption, consumer preferences, climate change, etc.);
- learn how country X manages BMSB; and
- determine connections between country X and Aotearoa New Zealand, particularly import and traveller pathways.

3. IDENTIFYING INDICATORS

Once background knowledge is collated, SATs such as scenario development and back-casting are then used to derive indicators. Multiple alternative scenarios are developed, each representing a plausible future outcome related to the original event. These scenarios cover a wide range of possible outcomes, which analysts will rank from most to least likely. Back-casting (the act of working backwards from the chosen hypothetical scenario) can then be used to hypothesise the chain of events that would lead to each future outcome.

The steps in the chain of events can become indicators for monitoring changes relevant to the initial event. As well as being specific and observable, these indicators should be sensitive to changes in the scenario. Indicators can be grouped under high-level drivers, such as political, economic, social or ecological factors. The chosen indicators are then assessed for their ability to measure a potential change in the biosecurity threat environment.

Examples of developed scenarios: Through discussion and the use of SATs, the following two scenarios are deemed the most likely outcomes of the original event:

- Scenario 1: BMSB populations rise in high-volume trading partner countries, leading to a higher number of BMSB-infested goods and cargo arriving at New Zealand's ports and airports.
- Scenario 2: Increased international travel and trade post-Covid-19 increases the likelihood of BMSB-infested items arriving at the border via passenger and cargo pathways.

Examples of identified indicators: Back-casting or further brainstorming is used to identify indicators that would lead to these scenarios:

- Changing population dynamics: Track BMSB prevalence near production/shipping hubs that export to Aotearoa;
- Changes in imports: Changes to the types of goods received from countries with BMSB could alter opportunities for pest arrival;
- Changes in host range: BMSB has a wide range of host plants — changes in its host range could suggest a shift in its population levels or behaviour; and
- Detection in new regions: More BMSB infestations in trading partner countries could indicate biosecurity gaps or import standard non-compliance.

4. MONITORING INDICATORS

In BSI, specific indicators are assigned to each analyst, who then identifies sources of information for their respective indicators. These sources may include publicly available information, such as news articles, social media and online forums, as well as closed sources, such as in-house datasets, industry contacts or government intelligence reports. The intelligence analyst must assess all information collected to ensure that it is accurate, relevant and trustworthy.[11] This may involve verifying the source of the information or comparing it with other sources to check for consistency.

Intelligence collection against indicators is not a one-time event but an ongoing process that is ideally part of a daily or weekly routine. As new information becomes available, an analyst must update their collection to ensure it remains current and relevant.

Indicator monitoring often results in the collection of individual pieces of information that are, in themselves, quite weak and therefore do not independently reach an assessment threshold. Collectively, however, these can signal general shifts in the biosecurity threat environment. Analysts are tasked with recognising these patterns and trends, as a collective situational change is often greater than the sum of its parts.

Example: Analysts review intelligence sources for changes to BMSB populations. These include:

- data published by monitoring teams in countries with BMSB;
- reports of BMSB interceptions from border inspection departments in other countries; and
- field reports on BMSB feeding damage and relative populations in different regions.

5. COLLATION

Effective collation of data requires a robust information management system that can efficiently process and analyse large volumes of data from diverse sources.[12] The collation stage is critical in the intelligence cycle as it lays the foundation for the subsequent stages of analysis, assessment and reporting. One of the key benefits of effective intelligence collation is the ability to summarise the collected data in a manner that makes it searchable under specific contexts. This is often accomplished by categorising the data based on relevant parameters such as geographic location, relationship to an event, or other relevant factors. By doing so, intelligence analysts can quickly identify interrelated information that would otherwise be challenging to uncover.

Example: An article regarding discovery of BMSB in a previously unaffected area is published. This article is collated and summarised using searchable terms such as location name, host plant species, the organisation responsible for the discovery or management, and the mitigation strategies employed. Using searchable terminology allows the article to be easily referenced and accessed when searching for specific BMSB-related information.

6. ANALYSIS AND ASSESSMENT

Analysis involves identifying patterns and trends from multiple pieces of intelligence to generate insights wherein the level of agreement between multiple items of collected intelligence is used to make an intelligence assessment.[13] If the majority of intelligence items suggest a particular outcome or trend, this is taken as strong evidence in support of that assessment. Conversely, if intelligence pieces do not align easily, this may indicate that further investigation is needed or that the situation has a high level of complexity or uncertainty.

Quantitative methods, such as statistical analysis or data modelling, may be used in indicator analysis when relevant data are available. For example, if the indicators are numerical in nature (GDP, unemployment rates, population size, etc.), statistical methods can be used to analyse these data and identify patterns or correlations. However, intelligence collected by BSI is often more qualitative in nature and relies on judgement and interpretation, as many indicators are subjective or difficult to quantify (such as changes in consumer preferences, geopolitical tensions, species introductions to new areas, changes to international trade policy, etc.).

Once an assessment has been developed, it must be communicated effectively to the appropriate audience.

Example: The frequency of articles reporting new BMSB discoveries has increased. To understand why, an analyst examines the articles for patterns related to elements such as the crops or items BMSB were found on, the origin of the introduced BMSB, and the location of discovery. Analyses can identify commonalities that may indicate changes in BMSB behaviour or identify vulnerable areas and industries.

7. REPORTING

The decision to report intelligence is influenced by several factors, including the nature of the information, the intended audience and the urgency of the situation. Depending on these factors, the output of intelligence reporting can vary significantly in terms of complexity, content and regularity.[14] Biosecurity threats can emerge rapidly and require a swift response to contain these threats, and operations sometimes require quick decision-making under conditions of significant uncertainty. Intelligence reporting must be timely and actionable and provide decision-makers with the information they need to act quickly and effectively. Examples of the type of reports that stem from intelligence collection include the following:

- Routine updates providing ongoing situational awareness, compiled on a predetermined schedule (weekly, fortnightly, monthly, etc.).

- **Example:** Updates would include essential data on the spread of BMSB including new infestations, population densities, geographic distribution, affected crops and control measures. These routine updates could then be used to inform BMSB-related decision-making with the latest available data.
- Strategic assessments that provide insights to decision-makers by compiling an in-depth assessment of complex issues, and challenges that provide complexity beyond the scope of standard situational awareness.
  - **Example:** A strategic assessment may require analysis of the economic impact BMSB would have on agriculture, potential threats to food security, effectiveness of control measures, and/or behavioural patterns. Assessments could be used to inform the development of proactive policies and interventions to mitigate the threat BMSB poses to Aotearoa New Zealand.
- Bespoke items commissioned by and tailored to meet the needs of a particular stakeholder.
  - **Example:** A researcher may enquire about the efficacy of a particular BMSB control treatment. The resulting bespoke item can inform on the control treatment's suitability for use in Aotearoa New Zealand.

Intelligence reporting in biosecurity covers all aspects of the greater biosecurity system, including identifying potential threats, tracking pests and diseases, assessing vulnerabilities and more. Decision-makers can use intelligence to prioritise resources and implement targeted prevention measures, as well as enabling early warning and proactive measures to prevent the introduction of exotic species. Timely and actionable intelligence allows informed decision-making and the development of effective response strategies, increasing the likelihood of successfully mitigating biosecurity threats.

BIOSECURITY REMAINS A CRITICAL COMPONENT of national security as it functions to protect the economic and environmental security of Aotearoa New Zealand. The integration of an intelligence component for pre-border biosecurity contributes to the effectiveness of New Zealand's biosecurity system by providing situational awareness of emerging global biosecurity threats and reducing uncertainty surrounding these threats for decision-makers. By monitoring global trends, the BSI team assesses how international developments may impact biosecurity in Aotearoa.

The indicators developed for BSI's pre-border intelligence assessment are adaptable and involve multiple methods and inputs to ensure their accuracy and relevance, while also providing early warning of threats, allowing decision-makers to take action to mitigate these threats in a time-effective manner. Analysis of international developments provides the opportunity to identify emerging threats, anticipate potential pathways of introduction, and evaluate the effectiveness of existing biosecurity measures. The fusion of biosecurity and intelligence disciplines creates a unique and effective method for providing situational awareness and informing decision-making in an ever-changing global biosecurity threat environment.

9.

DOES AI DREAM OF PROTECTING SHEEP?

The role of artificial intelligence in national biosecurity

Jodie Chapell & Deidre Ann McDonald[1]

Artificial intelligence (AI) is an important tool for identifying and mitigating biosecurity threats to Aotearoa New Zealand. While AI's value may be clearly understood, there are some limitations inherent in this technology that require careful consideration. Those limitations can create problems for intelligence gathering, which means that the outcomes can potentially become less rather than more secure. Critically, developing an understanding of the benefits and drawbacks of AI for biosecurity can highlight certain intelligence problems that might be avoided, along with some avenues for best practice around the use of such technologies.

Focusing on AI that creates data about valued life, this chapter discusses the problems of uncertainty, inaccuracy and lack of inclusivity in the use of big data for pre-border biosecurity intelligence (that is, for understanding and locating future threats from offshore). An underlying premise here is that AI cannot replicate the human and geographical diversity required for situated biosecurity knowledge gathering and/ or sharing. Those who gather intelligence for biosecurity (and for other national concerns) have reason to reflect on those vulnerabilities inherent in AI. However, AI has an important role to play in preventing and/or mitigating biosecurity threats, and there are opportunities for government agencies to minimise potential harms from using AI so that its benefits may be more transparently realised.

The discussion about using AI for biosecurity can be framed around four categories, each dealing with a different type of knowledge that is required for building an intelligence picture. They are:

- You need to know which lives matter, and which do not.
- You need to know what else matters — where are the data gaps or blind spots?
- You need to know what data or knowledge can be ignored — what is irrelevant to the task?
- You need to know what knowledge gaps must be filled before you can understand and analyse what is there.

BIOSECURITY DESCRIBES A GROUP OF practices enacted by humans to secure valued forms of life from harm.[2] These practices foreground the never-ending work of securing biological life.[3] Biosecurity is concerned with the control of mobilities and spatial boundaries. The practices of biosecurity control and shape human and non-human populations, affect civil liberties and intersect with wider agendas. Governing bodies act to control or eradicate some forms of life for the purpose of protecting others.[4] A recent New Zealand example is the *Mycoplasma bovis* eradication programme, whereby some cattle were culled to eradicate the bacteria from the national herd. Another is the Covid-19 response, during which humans were confined and quarantined in a bid to eliminate the virus from these shores.

The Ministry for Primary Industries (MPI) is the lead agency for implementing biosecurity in Aotearoa New Zealand. MPI is concerned with trying to exclude or manage viruses, bacteria, fungal diseases, insects and other pests that can cause harm to the country's primary industries, indigenous biodiversity and human health.[5] Biosecurity is a key part of the bioeconomy, and its practices support the country's accumulation of wealth; but biosecurity is also part of the shadow 'necroeconomy', which requires some animal lives to be disposed of for the greater good.[6] For example, while most animals will recover from foot-and-mouth disease (FMD),[7] the disease impacts animal product exports, which means that animals are culled for the purpose of eradicating the virus.

Biosecurity surveillance, which is the act of gathering and analysing biosecurity information to obtain data about pests and diseases, plays an essential role in securing this country's economic and environmental security.[8] Standardised protocols and systems depend on technologies and are used to identify threats and emergencies, and the ability to predict these is critical for biosecurity.[9] Getting it right matters. During an FMD outbreak in the UK, one example of computer modelling misread the localised situation, resulting in the slaughter of over 10 million animals, many of which were healthy, and the loss of valuable and genetically diverse heritage breeds.[10]

WHAT EXACTLY IS AI? AI can be defined as 'a machine-based system that can, for a given set of human-defined objectives, make predictions, recommendations, or decisions influencing real or virtual environments'.[11] AI uses these 'predictive algorithms, models and systems' to define threats in the 'pre-border' biosecurity space.[12] Big data predictive analytics,[13] machine learning and natural language processing technologies in particular can make synthetic and other data, decisions about data, and large data sets for future biosecurity predictions.[14]

As mentioned, AI already benefits biosecurity professionals in Aotearoa New Zealand. Amazon and Google deep learning environments enable practitioners to use image-based data to protect Māui dolphins, detect biofouling and oversee fishing activity.[15] Other localised applications include diagnostic identification of pests at the border, wildlife monitoring, monitoring lameness in livestock, counting fish, inspecting bees and predicting rainfall.[16] Scientists have used AI to check for tree pests, make predictive models of pig disease, and identify marine species by sound.[17]

Since 2016, AI applications in animal health have increased markedly with a focus on pigs, cows and chickens, though many studies are at an experimental stage.[18] While AI is already being used to enhance biosecurity, its application comes with important drawbacks.

AI technologies promise to simplify the management of biological risks and to allow humans to be more prepared for and even pre-empt biosecurity incursions.[19] AI proponents claim to help agencies prioritise their resources by modelling the future spread of pests and diseases (e.g. for preparedness or response).[20] Promissory claims include reducing 'cost, time and bias in biosecurity data collection'.[21] But AI technologies are expensive, and validation of their effectiveness remains incomplete. Can biosecurity really afford to rely on these less supervised forms of data collection, rather than on human judgement and community perspectives? Will doing so better secure our valued lives? Four knowledge sections below attempt to address these questions by discussing how emerging threats are identified and the values that tell analysts which lives matter.

WHAT ARE THE HUMAN VALUES that determine what biosecurity will protect? Internationally, economic concerns largely determine if organisms become regulated or quarantine plant pests, and these set the majority of animal and aquatic diseases listed by the World Organisation for Animal Health.[22] Aside from monetary value, the lives that matter most in biosecurity are epitomised by biological ideas about where species belong (e.g. endemicity or invasive alien species) and cost concerns. Legislation reifies values by classifying organisms as unwanted, notifiable and prohibited, and determines when organisms are considered 'new' to Aotearoa New Zealand.[23]

These underlying values transform into biosecurity resourcing and decision-making. For example, bacteria that transfer from fleas to humans (such as the bubonic plague) would be a biosecurity priority, not for their impact on fleas but for their impact on human health. The same can be said for FMD, where the economy is the primary object being protected, and avian influenza, where protecting human health and the economy are the main objectives. Biosecurity is essentially about what matters to (some) humans, despite the subject being non-human life forms such as bacteria, viruses, animals and insects.

In Aotearoa New Zealand, biosecurity exists to protect environmental, cultural, social and economic values, along with human health.[24] Classification systems cannot list all the overseas life that matters for local biosecurity.[25] There can be no single source of truth for which biological lives matter for biosecurity. Consequently, discord and dissent are inherent in biosecurity decision-making, though scientific experts mobilise appeals based on ostensibly universal scientific truths by listing 'alien' or 'invasive' species. Yet, these categorisations themselves are the product of cultural histories, intense debate and human value judgements.[26]

AI promises to simplify these messy realities by impartially collecting data for enhancing biosecurity decision-making. The questions that this chapter raises are whether that data is reliable, whether it is meaningful, and whether it is 'enough' for biosecurity decision-making. Analysts need to know which lives do and do not matter, and these answers are influenced by time and space. We argue biosecurity intelligence requires situational awareness and knowledge of what else matters, and that 'what else' includes more than scientific knowledge or a remote collection of digital data.

IMAGINING A BIOSECURITY THREAT MEANS placing humans, non-humans, ideas and mobile objects together in specific arrangements, according to known associations that might cause concern. Together, the elements that create an emerging threat are not fixed as an immovable whole, however. Some elements of the threat situation could be removed without causing a change in assessment, while others are fundamental either singularly or because they act in combination with others.

We refer to these situations as assemblages — complex networks with social, biological, economic and technical components.[27] A biosecurity assemblage might be a situation involving tourists stepping in the faeces of sick swans before boarding a plane, then feeding wild ducks back home while wearing the same shoes. The consequential disease outbreak is then investigated by epidemiologists who trace its origins (and future spread). The humans, ducks, planes, time zones and disease are all part of an assemblage that we argue can only be understood through investigating all its parts. Assemblages can become emerging threats of potential harm to valued life, but only if temporal, spatial, conceptual and social criteria are met.

Knowing if a chain of events produced or became a threat is only possible with hindsight, and in this sense biosecurity knowledge is constructed post-event and can only ever be partial.[28] The influence of time on the data collected matters if border breaches are the only means by which the existence of emerging threats is validated by biophysical reality.

Projections from past data by themselves cannot satisfy analysts as to exactly why a current breach has occurred or how to predict a future outbreak. For example, knowing that a livestock truck inadvertently spread disease to 17 farms last year, and how that occurred, cannot tell us where the next truck will spread disease. Similarly, knowing how one virus emerged in a given place and at a certain time cannot tell us why another might emerge, even if the viruses are genetically similar. The assemblage elements will have changed and/or been reordered, impacting the threat assessment. This means that future threat assessments using AI can only ever be made using past (and partial) knowledge.

When surveilling objects expected to reliably contain data about valuable life, analysts will know in advance what types of trends they are watching for. Often, intuitive judgements and/or past experiences will pre-determine the assemblages that *should* matter. In order to interpret data to know which future assemblages matter, analysts must rely upon collective, situational knowledge and human imagination (for future application). For example, sentinel plants (those that alert us to the existence of diseases by succumbing more easily than others) can be identified through surveillance, using data about previous outbreaks, applying common sense or using mapping. These human qualities are the domain of biosecurity practitioners, scientists, and those who live and work with the natural world. There are nuances inherent in the way that data are collected, and how information is ranked and made sense of.

These important aspects of biosecurity intelligence gathering sit outside of the realm of AI, because AI has already been generated by humans at a point in time, so there has already been a narrowing and prioritising of assemblage elements within that data set. In short, AI cannot be relied on to tell us the whole story, and more than that, we need to understand which parts of the story AI can reliably tell us about. Yet, there is a seductive quality to an apparently 'universal' knowledge that simplifies the world and enables one place to be compared with the next.

Intelligence seeks to understand biosecurity threats, but it also looks to persuade and influence action with respect to them. Negotiating a biosecurity threat into existence means it must appear to be at least credible, likely or consequential. Any action recommended must be possible as well as deemed necessary.

Another of the seductive qualities of AI is that it presents threat data in ways that appear efficient, objective and valuable. Through qualitative summaries of that data, analysts will describe and validate assemblages, making necessary claims about 'the *so what* for biosecurity'. Any aspects of the data that are unconvincing, however, will become invisible through that process and this can lead to fundamental and enduring biases in the datasets being used for the future.

As alluded to above, articulating assemblages blends rhetoric, personal values, biologically derived ideas about organisms and their capabilities, institutional experiences and understandings of risk and uncertainty. Under conditions of high uncertainty, reductive and urgent processes can strip data from rich contexts to splice it together with different data. Iterative practices will then determine the biosecurity assemblages worth assessing. Biosecurity practices will exclude non-dominant forms of knowledge or versions of reality, and assemblages that challenge normative beliefs (e.g. about an organism's biological capability, pathways or risk) can seem unnecessary or inefficient.[29]

Cost savings from discontinuing existing data processes in favour of AI also mean accepting novel analytical compromises on what data (or what about it) counts. Some data might need significant interpretation, be highly contextual, impossibly mutable or resist categorisation. 'Keeping it complex'[30] challenges presentism and presumption in biosecurity, and acknowledges that 'nothing is, by itself, either reducible or irreducible to anything else'.[31] The ability to debate what matters is not only essential for critical thinking, but dissenting interpretations make space for preconceptions and biases to be revealed.[32]

CREATING UNIVERSAL DATA REQUIRES 'the exclusion of nature, and of culture', even though all data are created by humans assembling knowledge to confer meaning, and all datasets require interpretation to be made useful.[33] By the time experiences and knowledge have become a dataset, certain practices of curation, extrication and cleansing have already taken place. For example, laboratory research might inform us that brown marmorated stink bugs stop reproducing at 10°Celsius. What that research data will not reveal, however, is that the meaning and scope of those results has been debated by experts, or whether they disagreed among themselves. Perhaps those bugs were captured from local wild populations, fed on local foods and are always measured with specific technologies and methods. Applied in other places, by different experts, to different bugs, a different research outcome may arise.

Each dataset requires location and interpretation. Yet diverse perspectives that pose challenges for dominant modes of knowledge production are often under-researched and under-valued. Agencies seeking data-driven technologies to narrow (quantitative, 'big') data can inadvertently create persistent and pressing gaps that will at some point require redress.[34]

AI-LED BIOSECURITY TOOLS INCLUDE INFORMATION management systems and open-source intelligence platforms. These 'sets of material and processual work arrangements'[35] administratively govern the production of future biosecurity knowledge. As discussed above, however, these tools are not repositories; they drop off particulars rather than preserving whole data.[36] In addition, the searchability of the data that is held is often inflexible to user requirements.[37] Hence difficulties occur, especially when preserving qualitative, social scientific or indigenous knowledge. Users interpret classifications, and meanings change, compromising later interpretation of trends.

Algorithms make associations visible and valorise inferences by obfuscating neglected ('untagged') connections in data. But what if the associations only appear because of the data that are excluded? Data that are missing skew the data that are made present through their absence.[38] Patterns that show one variable (e.g. handwashing) linked to another (the training provided) may collapse and create false inferences if some data (the location of hand basins) are not included. Inputs do not equate to outputs and, at the end of the process, it may be impossible to identify the important and missing data, let alone see methodological gaps, because these are made irrelevant.

Databases particularise (separate fragments of knowledge from context), validate (abstract knowledge via scientific appraisals) and generalise (catalogue, store and circulate) assemblage elements. Matters of cultural significance, for example, including local and indigenous knowledges, are stripped by AI from the very practices that imbue the knowledge with meaning and power.[39] These issues arise, in part, because big data can never substitute for valid *or* representative data (because subsets cannot be used to generalise for populations).[40]

Extraction renders context-specific data, like culturally specific referents, meaningless, and the ensuing analysis will therefore be incomplete and potentially incorrect. In the extraction and interpretation process, the doctrinal values of those involved dominate and frame the data sets, connections and assemblages produced, along with inherent and often non-obvious biases.[41]

Moreover, the databases themselves are based on the dominant languages and values of those doing the processing.[42] Few languages (including indigenous languages) are included.[43] AI professionals create power in discourse by rendering familiar concepts technical, then blending them back into the everyday.[44] As biosecurity intelligence adapts and borrows terms (and therefore power) from other contexts (such as the terms 'vector' or 'vulnerability'), research should make these knowledge practices and claims to power overt.

Unlike empirical or experimental methodologies, machine learning data is 'more akin to the translation or interpretation of signs rather than [. . .] understanding chains of causation'.[45] Statistical models used to predict future border 'slippage', for example, do so by detaching data from previous biological interceptions.[46] Machines can then be trained on 'synthetic' data to produce analytics informing decisions that affect valued lives, but that may have no basis in the world.[47] Just as binary classifications (presence versus absence) cannot tell us if pests, pathogens and invasive species have arrived unseen, nor can predictions — which are 'past anticipation[s] of the future'[48] — tell us when they might arrive.

Algorithmic bias occurs in the modelling of statistical estimations, in training *and* in interpretation.[49] Interpretation biases are likely where outputs and information requirements differ, where algorithms are used in contexts that diverge from the intended use, or if users do not have enough information about the data to make correct assumptions.[50] Characterised by inherent uncertainty, AI surveillance presents a design problem. Machine learning works best when problems are clearly defined and understood, contexts are stable, samples are statistically identical, and training and end use are identical.[51] This is not the biosecurity landscape.

While AI technologies do provide greater opportunities for surveillance and for producing data about valued life, they also create new and unchartered vulnerabilities — and these vulnerabilities are not confined to biosecurity. For example, AI has not only enabled widespread use of facial recognition, but the technology has also enabled its avoidance. Attempts to exclude identifying data from big data predictive analytics can make human behaviour unpredictable and result in marginalisation, mistrust and voicelessness.[52] AI-led access to data creates potential concerns over both transparency and misuse as well as unsolicited access or attacks on stored and compiled data.[53]

AS BIOSECURITY BECOMES INCREASINGLY INFORMED by scenario-based predictions, social scientists have an important role highlighting the communication, framing and production of this discourse and its relevant assumptions.[54] Research might address, for example, whether machine learning predictions of biosecurity threats (based neither on observation nor understandings of causation) are even appropriate. AI's inherent unpredictability is problematic,[55] and its use threatens to significantly reduce awareness of the multiplicity and contingencies that impact on pest and disease movements and behaviours, both within and because of assemblages.[56] Big data predictive analytics have already led to delays (errors) in biosecurity responses where Eurocentric assumptions about cell-phone ownership have produced inaccurate correlations and reliance on mere 'common sense' observations.[57] The geographic and temporal distance at which biosecurity intelligence predictions are made means that these assumptions are expected.

Big data predictive analytics and AI tools not only make promises but also confer dependencies. At the global scale, these have worried UK and US government regulators.[58] Individual advisees with diverse expertise also give trust to advisors (e.g. system designers). This trust differs from personal trust between experts that offers greater opportunities for convergence of disparate and locally specific knowledge. As Peter Drahos explains:

> Technocratic trust is an impersonal form of trust in which the trust-giver comes to have an expectation about the performance of the system. The system designer has an interest in ensuring the reliability of the system since otherwise there is no possibility of an expectation about its reliability. Beyond that the system designer may not necessarily have the interests of the trust-giver in mind.[59]

Reliance on AI must also be balanced against the need to guard against inaccuracy, inequities and data loss from classificatory confusion. It is possible that algorithms used by government agencies will include prejudice and discrimination, and produce intrinsic (e.g. racist) and extrinsic (e.g. dirty data) biases.[60] AI efficiencies in knowledge production also need balancing against subsequent reallocation of agency and expertise, especially when AI applications and other analytic outputs are alienated from their original sources. Notable concerns are the biases that come with AI professionals, who are predominately white, technically educated males.[61]

Elsewhere, the 'misleading and undeserved imprimatur of impartiality'[62] in AI applications have produced 'self-fulfilling prophecies'[63] through runaway feedback loops (remembering the important shaping role of missing data as discussed above). For example, feedback about the accuracy or amount of data has created surveillance 'hotspots', which attract excessive policing and the use of powers that have caused disproportionate arrests of already marginalised groups.[64] AI embeds existing inequalities deep into software code, and makes the rules, decisions and framing of data opaque and difficult to examine.[65]

Used as a tool to increase the richness, diversity and quality of knowledge that shapes biosecurity practices through 'strong, balanced and reciprocal relationships', AI could aid decision-makers and kaitiaki or guardians of the land and species.[66] Poorly researched or non-transparent use of AI risks creating a lack of trust and alienating New Zealanders in the process. Social scientific, community and indigenous knowledges are rarely integrated with other scientific evidence.[67] Social science has highlighted the valuable and localised biosecurity knowledge existing 'out there' — on farms, in orchards and in forests[68] — and the relevance of non-human agency (or the way pests and diseases behave).[69] We suggest here that investment in AI technologies also requires research identifying how localised and expert knowledge is actually used to meet real-time and contextually driven challenges.[70]

Furthermore, engagement is required to understand the meaning of data, to create meaningful human relationships and build trust and agency in which knowledge ownership can be negotiated. As the 'Ko Tātou This is Us'[71] biosecurity campaign illustrates, it takes all New Zealanders to protect what we value, but this necessitates knowledge-sharing and participating in knowledge creation. There are many potential benefits of surveillance and these increase through engagement and by carrying out localised research that addresses issues of data equity, among others. Beyond biosecurity, agencies should use AI's inherent failings to identify situations where 'post-hoc interpretability' from social scientists will add essential value.[72]

PUTTING HUMANS BACK INTO BIOSECURITY intelligence and knowledge creation reveals issues of uncertainty, opacity, assumptions and biases. Yet these problems provide agencies with opportunities to use AI alongside more inclusive and diverse data and to negotiate a stronger social licence to operate. Identifying those responsible for processes within the invisible world of algorithms is near impossible across interoperable systems, agencies and national borders.[73] If agencies place trust in AI applications, interdisciplinary research should sit alongside and assess the validity and reliability of those applications. In addition, transparency is essential for decisions that affect the livelihoods, movements and freedom of New Zealanders from unwarranted surveillance.[74] Without transparency, knowledge gaps, biases or assumptions may result in severe, long-lasting consequences for stakeholders and communities, an inability to trust data and/or erosion of the social contract itself.[75]

Despite concerns about the opacity of AI's underlying systems and the lack of a national strategy for AI, agency interest in generative AI appears to be increasing.[76] Dreaming of AI's future ability to, say, solve climate change or improve environmental governance, distracts us from its profound concentration of information and power that furthers socioeconomic inequalities.[77] In addition, agencies that invest in AI, for example to counter mis/disinformation, play a 'cat-and-mouse game' as technologies on either side advance, making successes ephemeral.[78]

Investment in social science-led research could explore the different and differing knowledges inherent in biosecurity (and in other national security practices) with a view to assessing the risks, challenges and opportunities arising from the use of AI. One conclusion might be, for example, that biosecurity surveillance responsibilities should be the domain of those who benefit from biosecurity's practices.[79] Another could be that while automated detection has a role, it is unlikely to replace human labour and that at every stage of the process, data needs to be scrutinised for bias, partiality and inaccuracy as well as assessed by humans trained to interpret it. While AI platforms 'dream of electric shepherds',[80] we argue it is human shepherds who best protect their sheep.

Part 3

GOVERNANCE AND EXTREMISM

Expectations need to be managed. The detection of genuine threats will remain a highly demanding challenge.

10.

ACCOUNTABILITY AND OVERSIGHT

Democratic control over New Zealand's secret intelligence activities

Damien Rogers

hanges are needed in the way the New Zealand government manages its secret intelligence activities because ministerial responsibilities, which form an essential part of New Zealand's system of government and are the cornerstone of its public accountability arrangements, are limited. There are residual blind spots in oversight measures of the Intelligence and Security Committee, the periodic statutory reviews of the intelligence and security agencies, and the inspector-general of intelligence and security.

Weaknesses in mechanisms for democratic control over these arrangements and measures ensure that those individuals with the greatest responsibilities for New Zealand's secret intelligence activities — that is, the prime minister and other relevant ministers — will seldom, if ever, be held to account by the public for any violence, whether committed at home or abroad, that these activities might enable. These shortcomings ought to concern all New Zealanders because secret intelligence is collected in their name, is gathered using public funds, and is provided to agencies that are authorised to use lethal force.

Designing and enacting credible democratic controls over public accountability arrangements and oversight measures will be a crucial task for those planning to transform New Zealand's security infrastructure.

Democratic controls could be strengthened by treating the right to privacy as though it were a core human right, as this would oblige those who hold integrity assurance mandates to take a more concerted interest in intelligence matters. Yet the prospects for strengthening democratic control over public accountability arrangements and oversight measures for New Zealand's secret intelligence activities remain dim, because those with interests vested in the current approach will resist becoming objects of the integrity assurers' gaze. Interested members of the public ought to take this opportunity to think more deeply about how they might voice their views to influence how the government reforms the way it manages its secret intelligence activities.

MINISTERIAL RESPONSIBILITY IS A CORNERSTONE of New Zealand's Westminster-styled system of Cabinet government. The *Cabinet Manual* states that:

> Ministers decide both the direction of and the priorities for their departments [. . .] Ministers are responsible for determining and promoting policy, defending policy decisions, and answering in the House [of Representatives] on both policy and operational matters [. . .] Ministers are concerned not only with the short-term performance of their departments, but also with the capability of their departments to continue to deliver government objectives in the longer term.[1]

Ministerial responsibility for New Zealand intelligence and security agencies has discernible limits, however. Even though the Government Communications Security Bureau (GCSB) and the New Zealand Security Intelligence Service (NZSIS) generate separate ministerial portfolios, these two portfolios have been allocated to the same minister, and this removes any contestability of advice on secret intelligence matters within Cabinet.[2] Also, much of New Zealand's intelligence activities, including commercial services performed by former state intelligence professionals, occur beyond the minister's purview.[3] Significantly, the scope of this responsibility does not extend to intelligence activities conducted by all government departments that collect, analyse and assess intelligence for their own organisational purposes.[4]

Ministerial responsibility is the highest form of public accountability in New Zealand's system of Cabinet government. Parliament holds ministers to account for their department's proper and efficient conduct, even if a department errs and the minister has no knowledge of the error.[5] While the minister responsible for the GCSB and the NZSIS is accountable to the House of Representatives, specific oral questions on secret intelligence matters are relatively rare in the daily cut-and-thrust of parliamentary politics.

This spectacle of public accountability hinges on the quality of questions posed by members of the opposition and on the credibility of answers provided by the minister. This is a salient point because, unlike other parliamentarians with professional backgrounds to draw on to inform their parliamentary work, few parliamentarians have backgrounds as intelligence professionals and, given the low political rewards associated with a ministerial portfolio on secret intelligence, there is little incentive for them to develop subject-matter expertise in this area when they can merely master policy briefs provided by public servants.[6]

In discharging their ministerial duties, the minister(s) responsible for intelligence and security agencies remains bound by the collective responsibility of Cabinet while the prime minister, who chairs Cabinet, plays a determining role in promoting and demoting ministers. Like all ministers, those responsible for New Zealand's intelligence and security agencies serve at the prime minister's discretion. Ultimately responsible for protecting citizens and permanent residents from the harms caused by political violence and ensuring the integrity of New Zealand's democratic institutions, the prime minister also holds a ministerial portfolio for national security and intelligence that gives them 'strategic, policy and legislative overview responsibilities for the GCSB and the NZSIS. This is a stewardship role, one that allows [the prime minister] to drive their work as part of the national security system.'[7] Equipped with the power to set the legislative and executive agendas, the prime minister sits at the apex of the public accountability arrangements.

The public accountability arrangements for secret intelligence activities have evolved since their invention. Previous arrangements focused on the prime minister, who traditionally served as minister-in-charge of the GCSB and the NZSIS. In 2014 Prime Minister John Key created separate ministerial portfolios for both agencies, handing these ministerial responsibilities to a senior member of his Cabinet. This change was then included in the Intelligence and Security Act 2017, which ensured the prime minister was no longer involved in authorising intelligence warrants. The previous arrangement permitted the prime minister to hold themself to account for the conduct of the intelligence and security agencies. Now, the minister responsible for the GCSB and the NZSIS is held accountable for the proper and efficient performance of agency functions by the House of Representatives through the Intelligence and Security Committee, which the prime minister also chairs.[8]

While these arrangements continue to evolve, recent transformations do not appear to remedy the above-mentioned limitations by, for example, extending ministerial responsibility to cover all secret intelligence activities or by enhancing parliamentarians' understanding of intelligence matters to ensure more rigorous parliamentary scrutiny. Although *Ko tō tātou kāinga tēnei: Report of the Royal Commission of Inquiry into the terrorist attack on Christchurch masjidain on 15 March 2019* recommended a new minister be responsible for leading New Zealand's counterterrorism effort across multiple agencies, this would likely further obfuscate the much-needed bright line of ministerial responsibility for secret intelligence activities. It would also problematise public accountability for ministerial responsibility, as blame for poor performance can be shifted to more junior ministerial colleagues with cognate responsibilities, or even to the intelligence professionals who perform counterterrorism practices.[9]

THREE INQUISITORIAL OVERSIGHT MEASURES BUTTRESS those public accountability arrangements, but each has blind spots. First, the Intelligence and Security Committee scrutinises the policies, administration and expenditure of the security and intelligence agencies by questioning the directors-general of the GCSB and the NZSIS on matters contained in their annual reports.[10] However, the committee's inquisitorial gaze does not cover secret transnational intelligence activities, including any connections with the deadly use of force by New Zealand's foreign security partners.[11]

The minister responsible for the GCSB and the NZSIS is caught in a conflict of interest because they are a standing member of the committee, rather than called before it to answer questions on the GCSB and the NZSIS. When that minister is involved in authorising intelligence warrants, they become deeply entangled in the agencies' routine operations, and this could jeopardise the committee's willingness to hold the agency to account. Chairing this committee as the minister responsible for national security and intelligence, the prime minister is also conflicted. The inquisitorial oversight performed by this committee is compromised because it is holding itself to account and the executive power over intelligence matters wielded by the prime minister is largely unfettered.

Second, legislation now requires independent periodic reviews of the intelligence and security agencies, the legislation governing them and their oversight legislation, in order to assure parliamentarians that the legislative frameworks enabling and constraining New Zealand's secret intelligence activities are fit for purpose.[12]

To date, two such reviews have been completed. The inaugural reviewers' recommendations to strengthen the public accountability arrangements merely suggested that 'the Agencies should continue to consult with the leader of the opposition about matters relating to security and the GCSB's intelligence gathering and assistance functions. The Agencies should also, as they see fit, consult with the leader of any other political party in Parliament as defined in the Standing Orders of the House of Representatives about such matters.'[13]

The final report did not consider the roles played by relevant ministers and members of the Intelligence and Security Committee, thereby exempting those with executive power from scrutiny. In contrast, the second review recommends the membership of the Intelligence and Security Committee should exclude members of the executive, but be supported by a new, small, permanent secretariat of staff, and be empowered to scrutinise the intelligence work undertaken by an array of other government departments and agencies.[14]

Third, the inspector-general of intelligence and security provides ministers with assurance that intelligence professionals working at the GCSB and the NZSIS act lawfully and with propriety. Yet the inspector-general's inquisitorial gaze has significant blind spots. Although the inspector-general is empowered to compel any person to answer questions, produce documents or give sworn evidence, they are not empowered to examine the use of all products and services provided by the NZSIS and the GCSB to all of its customers within the wider intelligence community, or to examine the use of all products, services and capabilities shared by the NZSIS and/or the GCSB with its cooperating agencies.[15]

The inspector-general is not empowered to examine all information that flows between New Zealand's intelligence and security agencies and their international partners, as well as the activities of New Zealand intelligence professionals working at foreign intelligence organisations and foreign liaison officers working at the GCSB or the NZSIS. The inspector-general does not have the power to inquire into the use of New Zealand intelligence, equipment or techniques by its foreign partners.

While the inspector-general may peer beneath the veil of secrecy that shrouds intelligence activities, they cannot convey those secrets to the public and, in so doing, help to enact limits on public knowledge. Moreover, while the inspector-general has released several substantive reports on New Zealand's secret intelligence activities, one report investigated the release of incomplete, inaccurate and misleading information from the NZSIS to the prime minister's parliamentary office. This cast light on how senior staff within the prime minister's office used intelligence-related information to unfairly criticise the leader of the opposition, but stopped at the prime minister's door.[16] The inspector-general's inquisitorial gaze does not extend to ministers who are responsible for the intelligence and security agencies.

These oversight measures evolved since they were established in 1996. While the Intelligence and Security Committee has always been chaired by the prime minister and included members of the opposition, its membership was merely broadened from five to seven parliamentarians in 2017. The scope of the inspector-general's powers was recalibrated to match the intelligence and security agencies' new functions under the Intelligence and Security Act 2017.

The prohibition on inquiring into any matter that is operationally sensitive, including matters relating to intelligence collection, methods and sources, was removed in 2013 following revelations that the GCSB had undertaken unlawful surveillance of internet entrepreneur and New Zealand permanent resident Kim Dotcom. According to Cheryl Gwyn, '[p]reviously the Inspector-General had been a retired judge, working part-time, with no investigatory capacity. Under the 2013 amendments, it became a fulltime role and the powers and resources of the office now more closely match the mandate.'[17]

These inquisitorial oversight measures continue to evolve, but not in ways that will remedy those blind spots. Even though *Ko tō tātou kāinga tēnei* recommended the Intelligence and Security Committee be strengthened 'so that it can provide better and informed cross-parliamentary oversight of the national security system (including the counterterrorism effort) and priority setting, and members can access sensitive information for such oversight', it did not recommend broadening the scope of the inspector-general's powers to include ministerial involvement in secret intelligence activities.[18]

Although a separate inquiry into allegations of war crimes committed by members of the New Zealand Special Air Service recommended an independent inspector-general of defence be established to facilitate independent oversight of the New Zealand Defence Force and enhance its democratic accountability,[19] the decision to keep separate the inspectors-general — who will perform common functions but with different objects of inquiry — will do little to enhance oversight of the connection between New Zealand's intelligence activities and the use of armed force.

STRENGTHENING THE DEMOCRATIC CONTROL OVER these public accountability arrangements and oversight measures is important, given the lingering public unease over the connection between New Zealand's secret intelligence activities and the use of deadly force.[20] The significance of this unease is reflected in the commission of various official inquiries, the purposes of which include restoring public confidence and trust. The armed raids conducted by the New Zealand Police in Te Urewera mountain ranges during October 2007 generated sufficient unease that the Independent Police Complaints Authority undertook a review.[21]

Public unease also manifested in concerns expressed by minority communities that were captured in *Ko tō tātou kāinga tēnei.* They complained that intelligence professionals regularly treated them as a suspect community and were engaged for the sole purpose of cultivating informants as sources of information on their co-religionists, even though they held well-founded fears of becoming the subject of hate crime.[22]

Unease is discernible, too, in the formal inquiries conducted by the inspector-general of intelligence and security examining the role played by intelligence professionals, not only in connection to the New Zealand Special Air Service accused of killing civilians in Afghanistan, and to the US Central Intelligence Agency's use of torture, extraordinary rendition and targeted killings, but also in the killing of Ahamed Aathil Mohamed Samsudeen as he attacked shoppers with a knife in an Auckland supermarket in 2021.[23]

There have been other observable efforts to make information on secret intelligence activities available to the public. Widening the window of transparency on unclassified aspects of New Zealand intelligence activities, the prime minister and the minister(s) responsible for the GCSB and the NZSIS have made occasional speeches on those activities within and beyond Parliament.[24] The directors-general of the intelligence and security agencies have followed suit in their unclassified annual reports and public statements. Oversight bodies now release longer reports, and more frequently.

Yet these public displays of limited transparency do little to lift the veil of official secrecy that shrouds intelligence activities. Nor do they necessarily result in a better-informed public, because most New Zealanders do not fully understand that information or are not able to act collectively on it. Although a poorly informed public makes the art of governing easier, a docile and passive population undercuts the constitutional safeguards that buttress the public accountability arrangements over secret intelligence activities. An enfranchised public can form an electorate that can reward or punish the ministerial record of parliamentarians at the ballot box.

Given that most New Zealanders remain poorly informed about secret intelligence matters, the public's ability to exert democratic control over these public accountability arrangements and oversight measures is weak.

Members of the public rarely obtain access to Cabinet members, including the minister(s) responsible for the intelligence and security agencies. Notwithstanding opening statements made by the directors-general of the intelligence and security agencies, meetings of the Intelligence and Security Committee are closed to the public and, when the committee receives information from members of the public, the meeting minutes do not indicate if this information is discussed; nor is there anything to indicate that independent subject-matter experts have ever been invited to address the committee.

When Cheryl Gwyn was inspector-general of intelligence and security in 2014, she sought out the views of civil society by creating a public advisory committee; this important initiative appears now to be in abeyance. Although the first periodic statutory review, undertaken by Sir Michael Cullen and Dame Patsy Reddy, did not set up a formal engagement with academic experts, the most recent review undertaken by Sir Terrence Arnold and Matanuku Mahuika did so.

Ko tō tātou kāinga tēnei recommended ways to help build the public's capability to understand intelligence matters *and* create meaningful two-way consultation pathways between the intelligence professionals and civil society representatives. It recommended, for instance, involving communities, civil society, local government and the private sector with ongoing work on strategic intelligence issues, as well as the co-creation of a whole-of-society strategy to counter violent extremism and terrorism.[25]

The report also recommended an advisory group comprising a membership drawn from the community, civil society and the private sector be established to provide advice to the government on countering terrorism. It recommended, too, that the government establish a programme to fund independent New Zealand-specific research on the causes of, and measures to prevent, violent extremism and terrorism, and host an annual hui (meeting) as a means of building relationships and sharing understanding of countering violent extremism and terrorism among central and local government agencies, communities, civil society, the private sector and researchers.[26]

Efforts to implement these recommendations have not enhanced the democratic control over the above-mentioned public accountability arrangements and oversight measures, however. They do raise uncomfortable questions around the extent to which representatives of civil society may have been co-opted through their formal membership to advisory groups, bringing these potentially dissident voices within the establishment where they can be more easily muted.[27]

New Zealand has several independent Crown entities with so-called integrity mandates — namely, the chief human rights commissioner, privacy commissioner, race relations commissioner, chief ombudsman, chief censor and the auditor-general — each of which has a potential role to play in assuring New Zealanders that the public accountability arrangements and oversight measures concerning secret intelligence activities are fit for purpose. Yet on the rare occasions that these entities have taken an interest in secret intelligence matters, they have focused on the activities undertaken by the intelligence and security agencies, rather than the public accountability arrangements and oversight measures. This might be, in part, because these integrity officers report to a minister, rather than to the House of Representatives as officers of Parliament would. The lack of sustained, systemic and coordinated scrutiny by these integrity assurance officers curtails the democratic controls over New Zealand's secret intelligence activities.

This can be remedied, however. The latest research into intelligence oversight emerging from Europe lights a promising pathway forward in this respect.[28] This research builds upon an international consensus that the right to privacy applies to all individuals and groups regardless of their citizenship status or nationality.[29] It also reflects states' increasing recognition that the sanctity of this right must be protected by law, especially when states arbitrarily or unlawfully interfere with it through their widespread and systemic digital surveillance of domestic and foreign populations. And it supports the international consensus that when states justify their derogation from their responsibilities on national security grounds, the evidence supporting these justifications warrants close and expert scrutiny by independent judicial means, rather than by 'quasi-independent bodies established by executives already convinced of the value of intrusive surveillance by their intelligence agencies'.[30]

Parliament and the executive could consider establishing a monitoring mechanism against infringements of privacy in the form of digital surveillance, which might mirror one developed against state use of torture under the auspices of the Optional Protocol to the Convention against Torture that requires states to create a National Preventative Mechanism.

Serious consideration could also be given to amending the functions of the intelligence and security agencies so that privacy rights are respected as though they ranked among core human rights, and the protection of these rights become a function of those agencies.

New Zealand's integrity assurance officers could then collaborate to routinely scrutinise the quality of oversight provided by the Intelligence and Security Committee, the periodic statutory reviews, and the inspector-general of intelligence and security.

In so doing, the gaze of these integrity assurance officers would, in effect, watch the watchers who, in turn, watch the intelligence professionals, but from outside the configurations of power that radiate from the prime minister, through Cabinet, to the government's intelligence professionals. From this Archimedean point, that gaze becomes more than a proxy for civil society, but can serve as a vehicle for information, analysis and reporting, informing interested members of the public and, potentially, inspiring their greater participation in our democratic institutions and traditions.

IN SPITE OF THE WIDENING window of transparency on unclassified aspects of secret intelligence activities taking place within and beyond Aotearoa New Zealand, public accountability arrangements are quite limited, oversight measures have residual blind spots, and the mechanisms of democratic control over these arrangements and measures remain weak. This is because ministerial responsibility is limited to the secret intelligence activities undertaken by the GCSB and the NZSIS, and is not effectively checked by an informed opposition, news reporters, community leaders, academics or members of the wider public that, together, might constitute a vibrant or robust civil society.

This weakness is also because the inquisitorial gaze that lies at the heart of the oversight measures genuflects to its authorising configurations of power and does not take a wide view that encompasses the transnational dimension of New Zealand's strategic and operational intelligence activities.[31] It would be a mistake to suppose that parliamentarians were a proxy for civil society. Yet democratic control over oversight measures cannot be enhanced by civil society representatives who are co-opted within the official establishment or by integrity assurance officers without a sustained and coordinated focus on those measures.

These shortcomings mean that directors-general of the GCSB and the NZSIS cannot meet their lawful duty to perform their functions 'in a manner that facilitates effective democratic oversight'.[32] Moreover, these shortcomings grant the gift of impunity to the prime minister and the relevant minister(s) who are most responsible for New Zealand's secret intelligence activities, but are never held accountable by the public for any violence committed at home and abroad, or by New Zealand's foreign security partners, that these intelligence activities might enable.

An array of actions could foster increased levels of public awareness and understanding of secret intelligence activities. The directors-general of the NZSIS and the GCSB could more often respond positively to interview requests from researchers and reporters, better resource their processes for declassifying documents, proactively release assessments on issues and trends impacting on New Zealand's security, and fund independent research on security issues that introduces contestability to the intelligence advice given to ministers.[33]

The government could establish a parliamentary commissioner for security who could become an independent source of authoritative information, analysis and advice on New Zealand's security challenges.[34] Given the strong connection between secret intelligence and the use of armed force at home and abroad, the inspector-general of intelligence and security could incorporate the soon-to-be established inspector-general of defence so that their collective inquisitorial gaze covers all government agencies involved in defence, intelligence and security activities.[35]

Of course, each of these remediations will likely be resisted by those who, possessing vested interests in the institutional status-quo, would become subject to an invigorated democratic control. However, treating the right to privacy as a core human right would oblige those who hold integrity assurance mandates to take a more concerted interest in secret intelligence matters. Positioned outside the configurations of power that sustain the status quo, the gaze of these integrity assurance officers would function as a proxy for civil society while furnishing information, analysis and reporting that can inform interested members of the public and, potentially, inspire their greater participation in our democratic institutions and traditions. This is where the promise of greater democratic control over New Zealand secret intelligence activities could be realised.

11.

LEADING NEW ZEALAND'S SECURITY SYSTEM

| Ministerial responsibility for national security and intelligence

Wil Hoverd

Most New Zealanders will be surprised to learn that we have a minister for national security and intelligence. The role has been held by four prime ministers since the portfolio was established in 2014: Sir John Key, Bill English, Dame Jacinda Ardern and, most recently, Chris Hipkins.

In government, much of the everyday work in the realm of intelligence and security is classified, which makes it impossible to gauge the volume of national security work undertaken by the minister for national security and intelligence. Only two speeches have been made in this ministerial capacity in the last 10 years. Examination of these and the briefings to this incoming minister (known as BIMs) can help us to understand the minister's function, viewpoints and visions of national security, and to examine how these leaders communicate 'threat' to New Zealanders.

The role of minister for national security and intelligence has expanded over the last 10 years in response to the changing security environment. The definition of national security has also evolved, from an 'all hazards, all risks' approach to a focus on 'malicious threats', and the minister has the emotive role of telling the people of Aotearoa when to feel secure or threatened.

New Zealanders do not often discuss national security. Nor has this ministerial role received or invited scrutiny. If we are to be an informed public who can talk more confidently about national security, then we should know more about these roles and functions of government and how ministers discuss and frame our national security.

ON 6 OCTOBER 2014 PRIME MINISTER Sir John Key established and took on the ministerial portfolio for national security and intelligence. In a media release the National Party leader stated that he would be 'responsible for leading the national security system — including policy settings and the legislative framework'.[1]

Key also announced the creation of a second ministerial portfolio, that of minister for the Government Communications Security Bureau (GCSB) and the New Zealand Security Intelligence Service (NZSIS). This was initially held by minister Chris Finlayson and then, under the 2017 and 2020 Labour governments, by the Hon Andrew Little.

The 2014 creation of these roles appeared to have two purposes. The first was to separate responsibility for the NZSIS and GCSB from the prime minister, effectively distancing the nation's leader from the everyday business of these agencies. Questions had arisen regarding the intelligence agencies' relationship with Prime Minister John Key when it came to state action made against Kim Dotcom.[2] Certainly, there were concerns about the legality of some of the intelligence agencies' actions. The 2012 Kitteridge Report found cultural changes were necessary at the GCSB, and the Cullen Reddy report into the Intelligence Security Act was about to be initiated.[3]

The second purpose was to devolve the ministerial functions associated with the intelligence agencies to another member of Parliament to lighten the prime minister's workload. The responsibilities of the minister for national security and intelligence include:

- leadership of the national security system;
- responsibility for the overall policy settings and legislative framework of the sector;
- chair of the National Security Committee of Cabinet;
- chair of the Intelligence and Security Committee (as prime minister);

- final approval to the sector's four-year plan in the Budget process; and
- recommending (as prime minister) the appointment of the director of security, director of GCSB, inspector-general and deputy inspector-general of intelligence and security, and commissioner of security warrants.

The revised role situated the prime minister as leader of the national security crisis response system, chair of two committees, and responsible for the overall legislative, budgetary and policy dimensions of the sector. Key had quietly ushered in a powerful revised ministerial role for the prime minister that has received surprisingly little scrutiny, especially after 2019 when it underpinned Dame Jacinda Ardern's responses to the Christchurch terror attack and the Covid-19 pandemic.

The next publicly available document about the ministerial role is the 2017 briefing for the incoming minister of national security and intelligence (BIM 2017), Dame Jacinda Ardern. BIM 2017 states, 'as prime minister you have overall leadership of the government's response to any crisis'.[4] It explains that the minister has two roles when it comes to national security: to provide governance in terms of the security institutions of government; and to activate the national security system contained within the Department of Prime Minister and Cabinet (DPMC) in response to crises.[5] Utilising a risk and resilience model, the BIM 2017 defines the crisis response system as:

> an 'all hazards, all risks' approach to national security. This means we have developed an adaptable and responsive national security system that can govern a wide variety of hazards — from earthquakes and floods to bio-security events to terrorism and instability in the South Pacific, and everything in between.[6]

In my 2017 book *New Zealand National Security* I noted the definition's strength and weakness was its broad scope, which enabled scrutiny of a variety of non-traditional threats as matters of national security.[7] The strength of an 'all hazards, all risks' definition was that it was able to extend to any contingency, but it was simultaneously ambiguous: anything could be named a national security concern. Non-traditional events included incidents such as the sinking of the TS *Rena*, the Kaikōura earthquakes and Operation Concord (the 2014 infant formula 1080 poisoning threats).

The sources of these threats were not states and were not always human in origin: those that were of human origin could equally be the result of accident or error (such as the TS *Rena*'s sinking) or malicious activity. Much of the BIM 2017 is devoted to explaining to the prime minister how the ministerial role and responsibilities operate within a crisis, how the national security system operates across government in terms of crisis response, and how to monitor threat assessments as they may emerge from the assessments of the intelligence agencies and other government agencies. BIM 2017 also notes that Civil Defence mechanisms are included as part of the DPMC and the national security system as part of the 2014 portfolio changes.[8] It describes the prevalence of threats and risks covered by the workstreams of the national security system between 2016 and 2017:

> there were 51 watch groups and 25 ODESC [Officials Committee for Domestic and External Security Coordination] meetings, on a number of different topics, including the Kaikōura earthquake, myrtle rust, cyber threats, counterterrorism, major events security, severe weather, aviation security and the contamination of Havelock North's water supply.[9]

The ODESC comprises the chief executives of the security agencies, who meet as necessary to coordinate a whole-of-government response to particular threats. The ODESC is informed by watch groups (multi-agency teams devoted to one particular risk/threat)[10] and its task is to advise and brief the prime minister and Cabinet when activated.

Not every activation will be deemed a crisis, and as a consequence the minister is not necessarily involved at that working level but rather is kept informed through briefings and, when expedient, offers public leadership to any crisis response. Interestingly, the ambit of potential risks, threats, assessment and management from the system in 2017 is wide ranging, from natural disasters to biosecurity, cyberthreats and counterterrorism. In BIM 2017, most of the briefing describes threat assessments and crisis response rather than sector governance. Two paragraphs are devoted to the need for the prime minister to engage in conversation with the public about national security and note that such discussions have hitherto been absent.[11]

BIM 2020 WAS SET IN the context of the ODESC responses to the Christchurch terror attack, the Whakaari White Island eruption and the Covid-19 pandemic, which had been led by Prime Minister Dame Jacinda Ardern.[12] BIM 2020 reiterates the government's commitment to the 'all hazards, all risks'[13] approach to national security, and details the ministerial responsibilities now legislated under the Intelligence and Security Act 2017 (ISA 2017). These are revised versions of the ministerial responsibilities, noted by Sir John Key (above) in terms of the function of the ministerial role and now formalised under the legislation.

In BIM 2020, significant governance workstreams are detailed, primarily in response to the recommendations of the Royal Commission of Inquiry into the terror attacks on the Christchurch mosques (RCOI).[14] Specific attention is paid to the nation's cyber defence and counterterrorism functions.[15] Other workstreams are devoted to the Operation Burnham Inquiry (exploring an inspector-general of defence oversight mechanism) and the ongoing national security system response to the Covid-19 pandemic.[16] No mention is made in BIM 2020 of the need for public conversations about national security, but this need was partially implicit in Recommendation 15 of the RCOI, which argued for the initiation of public conversations about counterterrorism with a focus on prevention and social cohesion.[17]

In January 2023 the sudden resignation of Dame Jacinda Ardern necessitated the production of BIM 2023a to brief the incoming minister, the Rt Hon Chris Hipkins.[18] BIM 2023a is focused on the first 100 days in office. It details a wide range of governance work already under way (including the ISA 2017 review and a draft National Security Strategy).[19] Crucially, BIM 2023a radically revises how national security is defined. It notes: 'New Zealand's new definition of national security is based on actively protecting New Zealand from malicious threats to national security interests from those that would do us harm.'[20] These threats are specified as follows:

- Strategic competition and the rules-based international system;
- Economic security;
- Disinformation;
- Foreign interference;
- Cybersecurity;
- Emerging, critical and sensitive technologies;
- Terrorism and violent extremism;
- Space security;
- Pacific resilience and security;
- Maritime security;
- Transnational organised crime; and
- Border security.[21]

The new definition was ratified by Cabinet the previous year, in 2022.[22] The definition focuses on malicious threat, and the list narrows the focus of national security to challenges that tend to emanate from states and human actors. One could argue that this more traditional state-centric definition prioritises the defence, law enforcement and intelligence apparatus of state rather than the broader 'all hazards, all risks' definition. Quite how an event like the TS *Rena* sinking or an environmental disaster would now be responded to by the system is not clear.

BIM 2023a specifically notes a changing security environment characterised by geopolitical tension, pressure on the international rules-based system, counterterrorism and cyber threats.[23] While cybersecurity and terrorism were consistent threats throughout 2014–23, the geopolitical tension and threats to the rules-based order are new and indicate that human actors and nation states are potential threat vectors. New priorities for the minister include improving the resilience of the nation's critical infrastructure, and providing sector leadership in terms of the challenges to Aotearoa of 'foreign interference'.[24]

The discussion around foreign interference is new and is focused upon ensuring that supply chains, resilience, procurement processes and the Crimes Act 1961 are secured against external interference across our economic and democratic institutions. A resulting priority is to revise legislation to develop the ability to prosecute any actor who might engage in foreign interference.

BIM 2023a's emphasis on foreign interference in combination with its definitional shift toward 'malicious' is chilling. It suggests foreign actors are already intentionally interfering with critical infrastructure in ways that cause harm or create vulnerabilities. It also hints that these individuals have avoided prosecution because of the outdated Crimes Act 1961. Also noted is the ongoing governance work in response to the RCOI recommendations, the Intelligence and Security Act 2017 review, and the development of an overarching national security strategy for Aotearoa.[25]

ON 4 AUGUST 2023, NEW ZEALAND'S National Security Strategy 2023–2028, *Secure Together Tō Tātou Korowai Manaaki*, was released at Parliament by Rebecca Kitteridge, acting chief executive of the DPMC.[26] The strategy avoids presenting a definition of national security and instead states that 'National security is about protecting New Zealanders from threats that would do us harm.'[27] The word malicious is absent from the document, but there is clear language that New Zealand exists in an 'increasingly disrupted and contested world'. In the foreword, Prime Minister Chris Hipkins argues that 'National Security is fundamental to our country and our people'.[28] However, despite this claim, and that the document is a key government response to the Royal Commission of Inquiry's recommendations and that it coordinates the DPMC's national security core focuses, the minister was not present at its release.

Given the significant infrastructure supporting the minister of national security, it is surprising that only two public governance speeches have been made by the minister in the last 10 years.[29] These two speeches usefully occurred in 2014 and 2022, and therefore provide an insight into the common themes associated with the ministerial role, as well as allowing us to explore any changes over time.

On 6 November 2014 Sir John Key made the inaugural speech as minister for national security to the New Zealand Institute of International Affairs in Wellington. The occasion of the speech was to outline the threat posed by the Islamic State of Iraq and the Levant (ISIL):

> Given the nature of national security, I don't give many speeches about it. But I want to talk to you today — and to New Zealanders — about how our risk and threat profile is changing, the challenges we face, and how the government is responding

to them. Much of that is due to the rapid rise of the Islamic State of Iraq and the Levant, or ISIL.[30]

Key commenced, somewhat paradoxically, by stating that national security is not something that is everyday business for the minister or for the public; he felt the need to discuss it on this occasion because of the threat of ISIL. This suggests that we only discuss national security when threatened rather than as part of the regular structure of our democracy. Key went on to explain that the threat environment had changed in relation to ISIL, both in terms of that group's expansion in Iraq and Syria and its campaign of global terrorism. He spoke in the role of crisis leadership of the national security system, presumably informed by defence and counterterrorism assessments of the ISIL threat that required action, additional governance and funding.

Key described the threat posed by ISIL, saying it could motivate jihadist violence both within its borders and abroad in nations such as New Zealand.[31] He continued:

> ISIL exposes us to a type of threat that we lack both the legislative tools and resources to combat. We need to have both a short-term strategy, designed to deal with the immediate threat to our national security, and a longer-term strategy, designed to deal with the root causes of extremism. Today I intend to outline, as clinically and clearly as I can, the nature of the immediate threat to national security.[32]

Key outlined the legislative and governance changes required to secure Aotearoa domestically and pointed to resource constraints. The minister's function is then to supply the executive authority to make changes in legislation and funding, and to redirect the apparatus and priorities of the security sector.

> I want to assure New Zealanders that our agencies are doing everything they can to monitor the potential threat posed by radicalised individuals. But as prime minister, and minister for national security and intelligence, I would not be doing my job if I didn't ask whether there was more we could do to address this

risk. My government will ensure the agencies have the resources and tools they need to do this work.[33]

Key was also performing an assurance function for the public. He set out a range of response measures to mitigate the ISIL threat: domestic surveillance powers for potential foreign fighters, legislative review of the Search and Surveillance Act and international deployment of the NZDF.[34] His speech ended with reassurance:

> New Zealanders can be sure we are taking careful and responsible steps to protect their safety and security and we will continue to do so. Our national security is something that affects all New Zealanders and all of them have a stake in it.[35]

National security speeches have an emotive dimension. They attempt to create a shared understanding that there are risks and threats that make Aotearoa feel insecure. Their task is to name an insecurity, then to explain and justify the necessary government deployment of its instruments of state power to address that insecurity. The naming of the insecurity tells the public what they should be concerned about and functions to generate support for additional security measures that will make us feel more secure. This emotive role is perhaps one reason why the minister speaks so rarely.

Some nine years later, on 1 November 2022, Dame Jacinda Ardern gave the second ministerial national security speech to He Whenua Taurikura: New Zealand's Hui on Countering Terrorism and Violent Extremism. Earlier that day the DPMC had released its first National Security Long-term Insights Briefing in which it had surveyed the security threats that were of concern to New Zealanders.[36] Ardern spoke primarily to the briefing and to counterterrorism. Early in her speech she stated:

> I want to use this opportunity to speak openly about the national security threats facing New Zealand. And what we all must do about them. We do that with a lens on the global situation. But I also want to be very specific about what New Zealanders have told us, about what worries them, their views on our ability to act, and what more they need to play their

part too. Put simply, New Zealanders need to know more about the current and emerging threats to our national security — because ultimately, we all have a role to play in preventing the worst, and being open about our risks is part of that.[37]

Fulfilling the communication and emotive element part of the ministerial role, Ardern outlined what national security threats we should be worried about, and what New Zealanders are concerned about in terms of risks and threats that need to be prevented. There is a semantic shift in this speech: unlike Key, who detailed the government responses in terms of 'us' (the government) and 'them' (the public), Ardern emphasised a combined public and government response through the use of 'we all'. She then detailed the threats the public had identified as concerning in the 'National Security Long-term Insights Briefing' and explained the responses already in place to mitigate those threats.

Again, there is a semantic shift here: from naming a threat and providing a rationale for additional response to noting the named threats that already have government mitigations under way. Her discussion of threats and their mitigation ranged from natural disasters to mis- and disinformation, climate change, pandemics, cybersecurity and transnational crime.[38]

In terms of counterterrorism, Ardern outlined three government responses that engaged the public: the Christchurch Call, the Strategic Framework for Preventing and Countering Violent Extremism, and He Whenua Taurikura — the new National Centre of Research Excellence for Preventing and Countering Violent Extremism.[39] In all examples, Ardern named the threat then detailed the government and community engagement that had been initiated to mitigate that threat. She concluded with comments on the need for national security conversations:

Talking about national security can be tricky, but it's something we need to do more. I'm committed to a public conversation on national security, and to advancing this conversation over the next months, as we continue to make progress on implementing the Royal Commission's recommendations. This includes developing our first National Security Strategy, which will embed this work for years to come.

This conversation on our collective national security requires trust in others, without seeing all the evidence. It requires courage to face serious issues, rather than living in fear. It requires openness and compassion, instead of suspicion and self-interest. I believe we can, and must, do this, together.[40]

Ardern returned to the consistent theme that conversations about national security and the government need to occur more regularly. She suggested that the upcoming National Security Strategy could be one place to have those conversations. She then discussed the nature of the required conversations: they would require cooperation between the government and the public and trust in others (particularly government), especially when aspects of the conversation would be classified. Here she pointed to a thorny issue: that the minister needs to create and sustain trust from the public and make them feel secure without sharing access to the security sector's classified assessments.

When we investigate this speech a little more closely, we see that Ardern primarily spoke to the mitigation responses only in relation to the threats New Zealanders had identified as concerns in the Insights Briefing. Unlike Key in 2014, she did not talk to the threats identified in BIM 2023, such as foreign interference. She discussed 'perceived threats' rather than those specified by the national security system. Absent also was the new definition of national security, which had already been agreed upon by Cabinet. It is possible that the Long-Term Insights Briefing initiated a national conversation in which the minister felt safe to talk about the public's perceived threats — a conversation that is quite different to the internal governance and national security system where malicious threats are monitored and acted upon through the agencies, watch groups and ODESC functions.

THE BIMS AND THE TWO speeches provide us with insight into the function, challenges and threats associated with this underdiscussed ministerial role. Together, the BIMs show a ministerial portfolio that commenced in 2014 as a separation of responsibility for the everyday business of the intelligence agencies to an executive role focused on national leadership in terms of crisis response through the national security system and overall sector governance. The ministerial role was legislated into the ISA 2017. Over those 10 years, the role's governance responsibilities had expanded, primarily from the counterterrorism and national security governance workstreams that emerged from the Christchurch terror attack.

The 10-year BIM review also demonstrates a changing security environment. The role was established in response to governance concerns around the intelligence agencies, and the minister's function was to lead a national security system that responded to 'all hazards, all risks'. However, it quickly initiated sector change in response to the threat of ISIL. Under Dame Jacinda Ardern, the ministerial role further evolved between 2017 and 2020. During this time a significant amount of national security system crisis response leadership was required, which resulted in increased policy governance and legislative work.

What is not clear is whether the role has naturally evolved to be fuller than was originally intended by Sir John Key, or whether 2017–22 was simply a busy period as a result of a series of particularly catastrophic security events. Certainly, BIM 2023a made the incoming minister aware of pressing security governance projects and a range of threats for the system to focus on mitigating, thus suggesting that the expanded ministerial role and DPMC functions may now be simply business as usual.

When security environments change, naturally the governance and national security system react and have to follow. The definitional shift from 'all hazards, all risks' to the term 'malicious', and then 'protection from threats that would do us harm', suggests a change in system and governance in response to an evolving security environment.

The ministerial role is held by the prime minister, and this needs further exploration. Through the role, the prime minister is able to make decisions informed by the intelligence assessment functions of DPMC, and this enables them, when necessary, to represent the security power of the state internationally and domestically.

The extent to which the prime minister's personality and/or agenda shape the language and prioritisation of work associated with the ministerial role is not clear, however. Ardern was visibly vested in the portfolio after the Christchurch terror attacks; state initiatives such as the Christchurch Call were successful as a result of her leadership. Of course, the prime minister and the minister for national security and intelligence are one and the same, which means the minister can speak authoritatively for government, but there will almost certainly be confusion by the public, who may have no idea that the prime minister holds this additional ministerial role. The ministerial role of crisis response leadership is politically and electorally useful for a prime minister. It empowers them to act on their responsibility for the nation's security and to be seen to be doing so by the public. The minister can communicate with the public about threats or insecurities but also has the emotive and state power to mitigate those threats to reinstate a feeling of security.

In combination, these explicit and implicit ministerial functions support the prime minister's leadership role when it comes to the security of Aotearoa.

The DPMC BIMs and the ministerial speeches note that New Zealanders do not talk much about security. The *2023 National Security Strategy* explicitly prioritises a public conversation on national security and, surprisingly, commits the minister to an annual speech.[41] New Zealanders do need to discuss security more, as does the minister. There have been just two national security speeches in 10 years, and both have mentioned this theme.

Clearly, despite a commitment to a broader conversation about national security, it is still to emerge. The lack of public discussion about the ministerial role and the lack of awareness that the role exists and is held by the prime minister point to another gap in the national security conversation. Given the central importance of this ministerial role in a national security environment characterised by malicious and harmful threats, we must hope that these conversations will occur in the near future.

12.

AS SAFE NOW AS WE WERE THEN

Countering terrorism in New Zealand 1968–2030

John Battersby

There has been a recent tendency to assume that New Zealand's terrorism story began in 2019, and that terrorism here should be considered through the lens of that event alone. However, the nature of terrorism in New Zealand needs to be considered over the past 50 years — a difficult assignment when most people have little memory of it, and no legislation here defined 'a terrorist act' as a crime until 2002.

The risks exposed over the last 50 years reveal a prevalence towards individual perpetrators (who are difficult if not impossible to detect), as well as a complacency towards preventative measures and an inability to consider overseas developments as having the real potential of occurring here. We must also consider that our police and intelligence agencies do not have a crystal ball to reveal every risk we face. These organisations will only ever have finite resources that will be prioritised into the areas they suspect most likely to harbour those who may harm us. As human institutions, they will have points of failure and their human judgement will at times be faulty.

Understanding the risk of actual terrorism and how to manage it is not a simple exercise — nor one that can result in a guarantee that any emerging attacker will be detected before it is too late. The first step towards better preparedness in the future is to understand the trends that are observable over the past 50 years, and the limitations there have been in mitigating them. There have been key occasions in our recent history, however, where opportunities to improve such mitigations have been missed. The challenge, now, is to grasp such occasions in the future.

PRIOR TO 2019, THE RISK of terrorism in New Zealand was considered insignificant. The bombings of the early 1970s, the anti-Vietnam War protest era, have been long forgotten.[1] The 'Ananda Marga four' (arrested in 1975 attempting to steal explosives from a quarry in Wellington in order to bomb the Indian High Commission) never entered the collective consciousness of New Zealanders as a terrorist plot.[2] Although more recent academic work has attempted to rejuvenate discussion about these events in the context of terrorism, they are generally assumed to be too far in the past to be relevant to current security assessments.[3] Memories of bombs, bomb threats, death threats and arsons during the 1981 Springbok Tour have also been conveniently forgotten.[4]

In 2018 the story of Chris Lewis, the individual who — acting alone — fired a shot at Queen Elizabeth II in Dunedin in October 1981, was recalled in a *Stuff* media series. Lewis's shot missed, his rifle was underpowered and crowd noise meant it was too muffled to be heard.[5] Had he been successful, the assassination of Queen Elizabeth II in New Zealand would have had far-reaching consequences, and the incident should have served as a clear 'red flag' that New Zealand was not immune from acts of this type. But as a 'terrorist' act it failed completely and was not discovered until well after the Queen had gone. New Zealand Police had no interest in publicising the fact they had not detected the plot, and the *Stuff* series did not encourage any greater discussion on terrorism than previously. The bombing of the New Zealand Police Computer Centre in 1982 was considered the act of a lone anarchist.[6] The 1984 Trades Hall bombing continued to be reported on from time to time in the media, but more as an unresolved cold case with the allure of a mystery than as a potential act of terrorism.[7]

The 1985 *Rainbow Warrior* bombing did see the frequent use of the term 'terrorism' in New Zealand, but mainly to express disgust at the French action.[8] Call them what we would, the two agents (Alain Mafart and Dominique Prieur) could not be charged with a terrorist act because there was no legislation that defined 'terrorism' as a crime in New Zealand.[9]

Historian Michael King, writing shortly after the event, observed that the two suspects were not informed that they did not have to accompany police when they were encountered in the days after the bombing, or that they did not need to answer any questions. There was insufficient evidence to arrest Mafart and Prieur at that point. Had New Zealand Police properly informed the agents of their 'rights', the pair would have been able to leave New Zealand before an arrest was possible.[10] In the space of just a few years, therefore, not only had events occurred that should have alerted New Zealand's political leaders to our vulnerability to terrorist acts, but legislative gaps in terms of policing such acts had been exposed.

In 1987, New Zealand passed its solitary twentieth-century piece of terrorism legislation, but the International Terrorism (Emergency Powers) Act still did not make 'a terrorist act' a crime.[11] Nor did the legislation improve the powers of police to investigate such an act.

The New Zealand Security Intelligence Service (NZSIS) and the New Zealand Police suspected a right-wing mass killing plot at the turn of the millennium, but either their subsequent action stopped the attack, or upon investigation it was discovered to be without foundation.[12] Regardless, the attack did not occur. Until details of the suspected attack were revealed in 2019, New Zealanders were completely unaware that there could have been any such plot, and so the twentieth century closed quietly with terrorism not considered a concern. There is a prevailing assumption that New Zealand's security agencies had historically ignored right-wing extremists. Clearly, they had not.[13]

In the meantime, gelignite — the essential ingredient in most bombings that had occurred in New Zealand — disappeared from the domestic market, replaced with less well-known commercial explosives. Bombings in New Zealand became almost non-existent from the 1990s. By this time, however, military-style semi-automatic (MSSA) weapons had become available here, and the first mass killing by a gunman using these weapons occurred on 13 November 1990 at Aramoana.[14]

Five years later a mass killing at Port Arthur in Tasmania made world headlines and prompted a New Zealand inquiry into firearms regulations here. The resulting Thorp Report in 1997 recommended banning semi-automatic weapons in New Zealand and re-establishing a firearms register.[15] Was it too much to expect our political leaders to notice that the reduced availability of explosives had resulted in fewer instances of their illegal use; and that the growing public availability of combat-style weapons could facilitate events similar to the Aramoana and Port Arthur tragedies in the future? Perhaps it was the fact that these two events were criminal mass-killings, and therefore deemed immaterial to any assessment of terrorism risk. At any rate, the Thorp Report was shelved and its recommendations were not implemented.

THE END OF THE COLD WAR caused the notion of terrorism to recede even further in the minds of New Zealanders. Geographically isolated, New Zealand could be forgiven for missing the deeper significance of formative events such as the Soviet withdrawal from Afghanistan, the US-led liberation of Kuwait, the ethnic cleansing in the former Balkans and the impact all of this was having on a little-known wealthy Saudi militant, Osama bin Laden. Attention seldom strayed overseas, but when it did, it dwelled on New Zealand being a good international citizen amid this international chaos. New Zealand sent a record number of overseas peacekeeping operations around the globe in the 1990s.

As shocked as everyone else was by the events of 11 September 2001, New Zealand kept in time with the international community as it started to construct an international 'counterterrorism' response. The UN Security Council produced a series of resolutions focused on member nations taking actions intended to suppress international terrorism. New Zealand was compelled to legislate more forcefully with the Terrorism Suppression Act (TSA) in 2002. As a result, a 'terrorist act' was now a crime. Coincidentally, threats were made in New Zealand in the early 2000s, during the America's Cup regatta and Tiger Woods' visit, to contaminate public utilities if political demands were not met. It is unclear if those who made the threats were ever identified, but at any rate no act of terrorism occurred.[16] New Zealand remained largely an unaffected spectator as, globally, developments in terrorism gathered pace in the first years of the twenty-first century.

THE TSA WAS APPARENTLY TAUTOLOGICALLY flawed — its wording was too complex to be used.[17] But this went unnoticed in 2007 as New Zealand Police began an operation in which successive surveillance warrants were issued by the High Court to monitor activists (from a range of groups) who were suspected of militant training and allegedly fostering violent intent. The TSA was cited several times in these warrants, and again finally in a search warrant issued for multiple addresses in four provinces across the North Island.[18]

When it came to laying charges under the TSA, however, the solicitor-general decided the wording of the Act made it unworkable, and in November 2007 announced that no terrorism charges could be laid as a result.[19] Two questions have lurked here ever since: Why was an Act so patently unworkable able to exist unchallenged for five years? And, in the several months preceding October 2007, in which the TSA had been deliberately placed before the judiciary as part of a police investigation, why was this flaw not discovered?

The *Dominion Post* initially published parts of the police affidavit, which (contrary to popular belief) were not leaked by the police.[20] Cashing in on sensationalism and arguing that public interest demanded it, the *Dominion Post* published parts of the document it knew it shouldn't.[21] Prosecuted for doing so, the dominant media narrative then became that police had misstepped over the whole affair. The police successfully prosecuted four people for firearms offences, but then apologised for aspects of the police action that were deemed excessive.

The TSA was referred to the Law Commission for review by the Helen Clark Labour Government. The subsequent John Key National Government cancelled the review and the TSA remained untouched. Was the Act not flawed after all?[22] Police had uncovered expressed intentions of violence, race war and assassination. They had seized a number of firearms, several of which were MSSAs, as well as ammunition. They had uncovered evidence of improvised explosives, suspected the importing of rocket launchers and photographed what appeared to be tactical training by the activists involved.

But the issue of the TSA's wording allowed for the fundamental problem to be ignored; what did, and what did not, qualify as terrorism in New Zealand? What steps needed to be taken to counter it if terrorism occurred? If the October 2007 suspects had been a group of right-wing extremists, would there have been any doubt about what terrorism was or what should be done about it? Had New Zealand faced up to these questions at this time, and tightened regulations for MSSAs, it's just possible Brenton Tarrant would have come here 10 years later and left again, finding he was unable to carry out his plan.

IN THE MEANTIME, CONCERNING DEVELOPMENTS occurred overseas. Mass killings using improvised devices containing homemade explosives and MSSAs became common. Even everyday items such as motor vehicles and kitchen knives were weaponised. A new word emerged — 'radicalisation' — referring to a state of mind adopted by individuals who had progressed through stages towards a violent ideological nirvana.[23] This process could not be defined. Despite a proliferation of models, there is still no consistency in understanding how anyone is radicalised. This radicalisation came amid the rapid advance of communication technologies and their utility for distributing content that was graphically violent, uncompromisingly extremist, which justified and incited violence and was able to provoke impulsive, or even planned, isolated individual actions with devastating consequences.

New Zealand saw all of this develop as if watching a TV series; it was compelling viewing, but it wasn't happening here. We stayed in step with UN expectations through minor legislative amendments concerning terrorist financing and foreign fighters. But no measures were taken here to prepare for the possible occurrence of the type of terrorist developments occurring overseas. No change was made to the Arms Act.

In 2018 my research found that, apart from a small number of specialist practitioners who recognised the existence of terrorist risk in New Zealand, there was a general bureaucratic complacency about it, as well as political and legislative inertia in addressing the risks.[24] One practitioner noted the impossibility of convincing anyone that any current or future risk of terrorism existed when no such attack had ever happened.[25] The community agreed. A Muslim speaker at the 2018 Massey University National Security Conference praised New Zealand's commitment to human rights as the reason that no terrorism had occurred here, and why so few New Zealanders had become foreign fighters elsewhere.[26] It was as if the bombings in New Zealand of the 1970s and 1980s had never happened.

Throughout the first two decades of the twenty-first century, terrorism had become a major global security concern. Despite significantly greater intelligence and law enforcement capabilities of the US, UK, France and several other countries, as well as the existence of watchlists, cases of intensive surveillance, significant legislative changes and new powers extended to counterterrorism agencies, terrorist attacks still penetrated those security systems and inflicted dreadful casualties on unsuspecting communities.

New Zealand had experienced almost two decades entirely free of the type of mass killing-based terrorism that had become typical elsewhere. A handful of individuals had been detected with extremist propaganda or intimating desires to commit violent acts, but they had been caught before committing violence, if they ever actually intended to. No need was seen to make any legislative change, alter any security setting, revitalise arms licensing or impose greater regulation or oversight on MSSAs. By the night of 14 March 2019, New Zealand's terrorism threat level had been set at 'low' for several years. New Zealanders went to bed content that they were safe from the type of violence that had only ever occurred elsewhere.

The next day this illusion of safety was shattered. The manifestation of mass-casualty violence was initiated by an isolated individual, Brenton Tarrant. Tarrant had gorged himself on a diet of extremist propaganda. He had exposed the vulnerability of New Zealand's open society, its almost casual acceptance that anyone was a 'fit and proper' person to be licensed for firearms, and the unregulated arsenal that was available for the outlay of a just few thousand dollars. The TV series we had been watching for almost 20 years had suddenly become a dreadful reality.

Initially, there was the understandable concern that something much bigger had gone undetected, and that Tarrant may have been group-based, or group-supported, and others could be awaiting their opportunity to follow suit. But this was soon found not to be the case. There was no well-established and well-organised right-wing extremist community in New Zealand that had drawn Tarrant here. His manifesto even expressed disappointment in New Zealand's National Front, describing them as 'milquetoast'.[27] The scale of the tragedy aside, Tarrant had exhibited the same characteristics of New Zealand's previous individual perpetrators, he was isolated and alone, and New Zealand's domestic terrorism risk — suddenly elevated to 'high' — was probably no more than it had ever been.

Since 2019 our agency watchlists have been expanded in an increased endeavour to find the next attacker, a process akin to looking for a needle in a haystack by making the haystack bigger and increasing the camouflage in which the needle can be hidden. New Zealand Police,

NZSIS and a number of other agencies now commit more resources to the realm of 'counterterrorism' than they did prior to 15 March 2019, and they pay more attention to groups and individuals who they identify as right-wing. Critically, it is highly improbable that anything they do now, had they done it previously, would have detected Brenton Tarrant, and they are unlikely to detect the next person like him. Tarrant carefully avoided groups, he did not relate to other people, he did not break the law and he was careful not to do anything that would put him on a watchlist. He hid perfectly in the haystack. He was not just dangerous because he was a violent extremist — he was dangerous because he was extremely careful.

Moreover, as noted above, many other countries had experienced far worse attacks more frequently throughout the first two decades of the twenty-first century. Those countries had a much longer history of dealing with terrorism (the UK had 30 years dealing with the IRA before most people had ever heard of Al Qaeda). They had greater resources, intelligence capabilities and law enforcement powers than New Zealand has. But attackers still got through undetected to strike time and again.

A strong and well-resourced security system maximises available resources to mitigate recognised risks, but it cannot provide any guarantee that all risks will be detected or stopped. New Zealand's earlier mistake was not that it failed to look in the right places — the absence of any attack, prior to 2019, indicates that wherever our security agencies were looking they either found and neutralised any threat there was, or there was nothing to find whether they looked or not. Our mistake was rather in assuming that this state of affairs would necessarily continue to be the case, and that we did not need to prepare for the moment when it suddenly wasn't.

In the days after the Christchurch attacks, the sale of semi-automatic weapons was banned and possession of them outlawed. This ban was presented as an immediate and proactive governmental response, but frankly, if the 1990 Aramoana mass killing had not been sufficient warning of MSSA risks, the Thorp Report and Operation Eight incontrovertibly were. Nothing had been done, and the permissive environment, in which licensed gun owners were free to possess MSSAs, had been allowed to develop. Responsibility for this situation lies squarely with successive governments who had opportunities to act but didn't. At the cost of 51 lives, significant social damage, $120 million in buy-back payments and $35 million in administrative costs by mid-2020 alone, the ability for a single individual with sinister intent to arm themselves legally and lethally with multiple weapons and quantities of ammunition had finally been eliminated — 29 years after that risk was first exposed at Aramoana.[28]

THE CHRISTCHURCH CALL WAS PRIME MINISTER Jacinda Ardern's attempt to impose voluntary regulation over social media platforms. It appealed to a few international leaders, and interest was expressed on certain platforms. But cyberspace remains an effectively unpoliceable domain, and the spread of criminal, malicious, misleading, harmful and extremist content continues despite attempts to suppress it. The Christchurch Call, then, remains largely symbolic, offering a well-intentioned and optimistically focused endeavour to deny the internet to those who seek to use it for the dissemination of harmful content. Terrorist motivation had not needed the internet throughout the greater part of the era of modern terrorism. The significant number of terrorist acts that took place during the 1970s 'days of rage' in the US,[29] or during the 30 years of the Troubles in Ireland, had all occurred without it. If, by some miracle of modern technology, the censorship of harmful content becomes possible, it is unlikely to stop the spread of dangerous ideologies.

In April 2019 Prime Minister Ardern announced the establishment of a Royal Commission of Inquiry (RCOI) into the Christchurch attacks. Its terms of reference were narrowly focused on what security agencies knew prior to 15 March 2019, what action they took, what action they could have taken in relation to what they knew, and what measures could be taken to prevent such attacks in the future.[30] The Royal Commission report, when it was finally completed, strayed outside these terms in many respects — dwelling on victims' experiences and advancing broader social policy solutions, although in no great detail.

The commissioners had sought vast amounts of detail from officials across various agencies, but largely overlooked any external independent practitioner or academic expertise. Critically, they treated terrorism in New Zealand as a solely recent and ideological phenomenon and did not consider clearly relevant antecedents, such as those described above. They should have observed that New Zealand has typically experienced political violence by individual perpetrators, or occasionally by very small groups. Such violence has tended to be non-sequential, infrequent and ideologically diverse, making those who seek to commit terrorist violence very difficult to detect.

There is no sign that this is changing. Tarrant fitted the mould entirely. New Zealanders have tended to observe overseas events occurring while being unable to anticipate that such things could occur here. We are still doing so. For example, without convenient access to explosives or firearms, overseas terrorists use commercially available chemicals to improvise explosives.[31] Such chemicals are currently available in New Zealand, unregulated and unmonitored. The Russian-Ukrainian war has demonstrated the destructive power of cheap, commercially available drones, and these have already been used by terrorists.[32] New Zealand currently has no effective regulation of drones, or any ability to intercept them.[33] The RCOI did not advance anything like these concerns, despite the fact that they are key lessons drawn from our past and foreseeable risks in our future.

GLOBALLY, AND FOR DECADES, EVERY identifiable counterterrorism campaign has been profoundly influenced by the terrorists it has sought to defeat. Therefore, to examine New Zealand's counterterrorism effort, the nature of our terrorist risk must be understood in terms of established historical trends, contemporary overseas developments that could be replicated here, and the local potential of those who have harmful intent, capability and opportunity. New Zealand terrorism has shown itself to be generally infrequent, improvised and disconnected. This has been misread as equating to the absence of such risk and has fed the assumption that there was no necessity to consider what could be done to mitigate it, or to prepare for the aftermath of an attack should one occur. If some years pass before another such attack occurs, we must guard against this complacency recurring.

New Zealand allowed legal access to, and neglected prudent administration of, MSSAs, their battlefield capacity magazines and ammunition. This long-standing loophole has finally been closed. But the next terrorist will adapt to these conditions, and our challenge now is to envisage how these adaptions might occur in the future. Over the past 50 years there were observable indicators, weaknesses in legislation and in the powers of agencies to act, and general complacency in the face of overseas developments and the long-standing risk associated with MSSAs. For the future, we need to take steps to avoid making these same mistakes again. Critically, we must be vigilant in observing events overseas and ask ourselves: Could that happen here tomorrow?

Expectations, however, need to be managed. The detection of genuine threats will remain a highly demanding challenge. New Zealand's law enforcement and intelligence agencies are small, and they have finite resources. They deploy those resources in an endeavour to keep us safe and secure from those who intend us harm. It is an endeavour that will succeed; but it is also an endeavour that will inevitably fail. We need to plan for that failure. At the time of writing, New Zealand's terrorism threat level has been assessed as 'low', where it was on the morning of 15 March 2019.[34] We are as safe now as we were then.

13.

BEHIND THE FLORAL AESTHETIC

▌ Women in right-wing extremism

Donna Carson

Right-wing extremism (RWE) is largely assumed to be a male domain. Retaining a default 'male as extremist' lens allows women's contributions to go unseen and effectively erases them as extremists.[1] Gender stereotyping in this context gives women a cloak of plausible deniability, which some strategically manipulate to disguise their involvement. Prominent right-wing spokeswoman Lana Lokteff is highly skilled at this tactic and once boasted, 'since we aren't physically intimidating, we can get away with saying big things.[2]

Women within RWE movements are enduring and complex characters.[3] The attraction the ideologies hold for some 'white activist' women presents an untapped security consideration. RWE groups know that a 'soft female face' peddling RWE beliefs is a more acceptable gateway into society. In New Zealand, as in the rest of the world, it is important that we recognise how this tactic presents itself.

What are the core RWE beliefs, and how does the extreme right utilise gender for recruitment, optics and motivation? Although RWE is male dominated, there is power and purpose in RWE for women, even as idealised white wives. The imagery of RWE 'Traditional Wife' ('Trad Wife') subculture encourages external labelling of these women as subservient, further obscuring their contributions.[4] To comprehend this worldview more clearly, readers are encouraged to buffer any tendency to umbrella mainstream Western feminist norms over RWE women.

Extremist women from majority populations often gain traction before onlookers recognise the truth about their beliefs.[5] These women can become experts at repackaging traditionalism, using crafted vocabulary and imagery of content families as deliberate normalisation tactics for RWE themes. A major oxymoron exists because, despite the promotion of soft femininity, these women are just as capable as men are of embracing toxic organised hate and endorsing violence in all its forms to further the cause.[6]

As Australian researcher Kristy Campion emphasises, RWE women range from facilitators to shooters, arsonists and murderers.[7] As evidence of that diversity, the following snapshots of women linked to right-wing violent extremism demonstrate how pastel imagery can downplay women's true potential within extremist contexts. Although these are international examples, I also provide brief insights into two examples from my research to show that New Zealand women are not immune to RWE.

RWE women have been missing from New Zealand's extremist discourse for decades, despite ample evidence that they have long existed.[8] However, although I advocate for the inclusion of women into New Zealand's RWE threatscape, I caution against overzealous approaches that ostracise or demonise these women, as that nourishes RWE victimhood narratives and cements extremist ideals.[9] Any informative risk analysis is lost if we do not consider these women with the correct ideological perspective.

Security practitioners, researchers and general readers must consider the possible risks if New Zealand continues to overlook RWE women as distinct extremist participants. Women are equally capable as right-wing extremists, and their increased presence makes it irresponsible not to analyse their complex participation more accurately.[10] If we do not include women, we are arguably ill-equipped to identify all RWE presentations, even those of men.

MANY RWE IDEOLOGICAL VARIATIONS EXIST today, allowing enthusiasts to navigate variations or 'pick'n'mix' beliefs into an ideology that suits them. Additionally, RWE can cross-pollinate with others (such as conspiracy theorists and anti-government entities), creating ideological chaos that further weakens recognition of RWE groups. While it is outside the scope of this chapter to present the nuances of each variation, commonalities do exist.

True believers reject feminism, multiculturalism and immigration and argue that progressive politics have detrimentally eroded traditional patriarchal society and family structures.[11] Devotees typically support 'accelerationism' — the notion that chaos and violence are necessary to collapse states through a race war that will reset society to its 'natural' racial and gender hierarchies (a white ethnostate).[12] This theme provides a racist sense of victimhood and a call to action which sends the disenfranchised the message that joining will reconnect them with their racial entitlements and birthright authority.[13]

This grievance package endorses the conspiracy of 'The Great Replacement' (TGR), designed by global elites, frequently depicted as Jews, to eradicate and replace white races with non-white ethnicities.[14] This belief alone reveals that white women are fundamental to the survival of RWE movements, given that the movements want more white children as a countermeasure to this replacement. As well as motherhood, however, white female engagement and activism help to promote RWE's veneered racist 'family values' and renewed traditionalism to the mainstream. Julia Ebner warns that this traditional packaging appeals to women as it is emotionally manipulative and influential.[15]

As far back as 2003, researcher Kayla Cunningham reported an upsurge in modern RWE women due to the amplification of global online platforms supporting their participation.[16] In 2017 Kathleen Blee's analysis of Western RWE found that women joining clean-cut white nationalist groups outnumbered those joining traditional race-centric movements (such as neo-Nazis).[17] White nationalism specifically attracts women disappointed with feminism; typically, they support the male argument that feminist advances have undermined Western civilisation.[18]

These women believe white nationalism has their best interests at heart, and they encourage other women to revolt against the mainstream by presenting a romantic portrayal of the RWE cultural fabric.[19] They actively seek to dampen down RWE's misogynist reputation by depicting the movement as a 'refuge', where white women can embrace racial heritage and femininity without shame.[20] This can be seen, for example, in online memes that advertise 'white women are worth preserving' and 'dying for'.[21] Gender symbology and purity notions push the false optics of the white population as righteous and superior and under existential threat.

Dreama Moon and Michelle Holling explain that white victimhood portrayals allow white women to build ranks through feminist resentment and use 'white women's tears to sideline women of color so they can epitomise [white] victimhood'.[22] Kathleen Blee observes that today's female recruits hold expectations of themselves as 'comrades in the struggle for white supremacism'.[23] Calls to action against perceived injustice have the same draw to men and women alike, especially as guardians of cultural, social and religious values.[24]

Trojan horse campaigns about human rights are one example of RWE's selective advocacy under the guise of values and justice. Examples include the Wellington anti-mandate and anti-lockdown occupation of the grounds of Parliament in 2022, 'Let Women Speak' anti-transgender rallies,[25] or the free speech campaigns that erupted after Auckland venues refused to host RWE speakers Lauren Southern and Stefan Molyneux in 2018.[26] Trojan horse campaigns are powerful recruitment calls for both men and women, especially if they feature children. After all, what type of person are you if you do not protect women and children?

RWE women like Wolfie James (aka Anna Vuckovic) and Lokteff are well-versed in defensive social diatribes, right-wing semantics, and 'white is right' narratives that call on women and men to defend their culture and families.[27] James once commented, 'Although men are better suited to the cause' (due to their masculinity, strength and capacity for violence), it was women who could 'boost it to the next level'.[28] Lokteff proclaimed, 'Lionesses and shield maidens and Valkyries would inspire men to fight political battles for the future of the white civilization.'[29] Importantly, not all RWE individuals are Christians; for instance, some utilise Norse mythology to justify their agenda.

Solidarity on RWE ideals does not equate to females' participation in violence; still, they can undoubtedly endorse it. When women engage in concerning rhetoric and amplify RWE propaganda but do not break the law, their behaviour is challenging for democratic legal systems.[30] The RWE manipulation of white womanhood is a long-standing strategy that exploits free speech by crafting bigotry to make it more palatable, especially when women lead the charge with 'floral aesthetics'.

RWE DEPICTS FEMINISM AS A corrupt movement that has demonised and invalidated white men through gender equality. This anti-feminism is primarily a vehement retrospective pushback against the historical advances of Western feminists and feeds a strong victimhood narrative. Some women find attraction in themes that depict them as 'shieldmaidens of whiteness',[31] 'endangered womanhood' and the 'key to racial salvation', and which allow them to choose their model of RWE femininity.[32] Many women enter the RWE ecosystem through anti-feminism and evolve to adopt more pro-white views despite any internal RW group sexism they experience.

These women may remain deeply committed to representing and endorsing RWE movements despite gender infighting.[33] For example, in 2018, the linked manosphere[34] — a collection of blogs, online forums and websites promoting masculinity and misogyny — harassed high-profile RWE woman 'Bre Faucheux' online because of their strong dislike for women. As a result, she discontinued her RWE online series, *This Week on the Alt-Right*, which promoted a racist white nationalist ideology. One follower's comment on Faucheux's farewell video stated, 'Noooooo, you're supposed to be the gateway drug for other women!'[35] Months later, Faucheux returned to her social media accounts as a married woman, a status that appears to have protected her against further internal harassment.[36]

Lokteff proclaims that women have taken on too many male responsibilities and, in doing so, have erased men's natural role as protectors and providers. In other words, women's political and sexual freedoms have been detrimental to men and the traditional family.[37] To sideline right-wing male critiques of her crusading, Lokteff tells women that if their home is in order, their children cared for and their husband happy, they should engage in 'pro-white activism'.[38]

At her peak, Canadian White Nationalist Lauren Southern campaigned publicly against feminism (#TheTriggering) and helped to cement anti-feminism as an overt right-wing counter-culture.[39] Anti-feminism affords women a sense of power and agency that aims to detoxify patriarchy and allows them to reframe male authority as chivalry, protection and biological order.[40] In the process, feminism gets defined as a cultural diversion and promotes that white women should be feminine, not feminist. Femininity is fundamental because when women look innocent, 'hip' but 'sexually pristine',[41] this helps RWE appear legitimate. Attractiveness also lets women downplay their views and deflect criticism by using general gender stereotypes, such as Lokteff's statement, 'Pretty white girls get a bad rap.'[42] These deflections and depictions of womanhood aim to normalise anti-feminism, right-wing maternalism and 'civil' racism while romanticising a patriarchal lifestyle.

FAUCHEUX, KNOWN ONLINE AS 'Wife with a Purpose', asserted that a white woman's primary duty is to have children and support her husband. As another woman declared in an online RW platform, 'Having three or five or eight white children is probably the most "pro-White" thing a person can do, and the most resistant to any charge of "racism". How about that?'[43]

This worldview is sold online through pastel, low-threat images of dutiful children, crafts, cooking and pristine homes. The women, sometimes referred to as 'traditional wives' (Trad Wives) tote purity and fertility and endorse a lack of sexual promiscuity. Promoting pro-white lifestyles in this way implies to others that a RWE man can provide everything a woman needs. Lokteff often reassures RWE men that if they do provide, the 'women will fall into line'.[44]

RWE Trad Wives is a retro subculture, often promoted as representing the preferred white female identity within a patriarchal family structure. A significant emphasis is placed on 'white mothers, white children' to increase white birth rates and fortify a white nation.[45] RWE women can push white pride at the dinner table, during their children's playdates and through personal messages. Seyward Darby warns that this promotion of traditionalism is a charismatic message for mainstream conservatives: not all trad wives are necessarily racist.[46]

A contrast to RWE low-threat imagery is a wife's role in home-schooling children, often emphasising heritage, race and culture. In February 2023 an Ohio couple was outed for their pro-Nazi telegram channel 'Dissent Homeschool', which broadcast lesson plans to 2400 members that contained Hitler quotes, anti-Semitism and white supremacy.[47] Founder Katja Lawrence later defended the telegram channel (now deleted) as wholesome. In a neo-Nazi podcast, she admitted to starting the online school in 2021 because she could not find 'Nazi-approved school material' and wanted to ensure a child could become 'a wonderful Nazi'.[48]

The mainstream school system itself may contain pro-white teachers as well. In 2018 teacher Dayanna Volitich resigned from a Florida school after she was found to be the host of a RWE podcast.[49] Volitich submitted her resignation, and Lokteff later stated, 'Two girls do a simple podcast, talking about leftism and how we need to take schools back and it's national news.'[50] Her comments epitomise how such women use irony and ambiguity to offset criticism.

A SNAPSHOT OF SEVERAL WOMEN connected to right-wing violent extremism reveals the complex spectrum of women's engagement. Past female martyrs like Kathy Ainsworth (KKK, 1968) and the death of Vicky Weaver (Ruby Ridge Siege, 1992) created a pathway for today's right-wing women.[51] Today a global network of RWE women exists, including a young online cohort who call themselves the Brentonettes and express their admiration for the 2019 Christchurch terrorist Brenton Tarrant.[52]

The first of these examples, Lauren Southern, in July 2017 released a YouTube video entitled 'The Great Replacement'; this was also the title of the Christchurch terrorist's manifesto. Southern dismissed its potential influence, but on the first anniversary of the attacks, despite proclaiming that she had abandoned political activism in June 2019, she joked on Twitter about writing a manifesto. By June 2020 Southern had returned to social media platforms, refuting the RWE label, and in April 2023 she appeared on Fox News described as a Canadian Freedom Fighter.[53]

The second, pro-RWE Proud Girl Tara LaRosa, has a history of using physical violence against counter-protestors during right-wing rallies. In 2020 the white nationalist Proud Girls marched alongside their peers, the Proud Boys, and a video captured LaRosa (a mixed martial arts star) joining physical clashes alongside the Proud Boys.[54] Proud Girl social media often discusses 'civil war' and advises people to 'buy guns now'.[55] In June 2022 New Zealand designated the Proud Boys as a terrorist organisation.[56] As with other nations, however, the female Proud Girl offshoot is missing from such designations.

The third, Erica Alduino, is an example of RWE women skirting the legal radar. In November 2021 a total of 24 American RWE men and groups[57] were found liable in a civil trial for 'engaging in conspiracy' relating to the Charlottesville 2017 Unite the Right (UTR) rally, which ended with the murder of a female counter-protestor. Missing from this line-up was then 30-year-old Alduino, the 'quiet architect' who collected levies, managed logistics, connected groups, verified identities and created a private server for UTR planning.[58] Soon after the UTR rally she moved interstate, joined a new movement, and remains missing from broader discussions about Charlottesville.

More recently, right-wing social media have glorified veteran Ashli Babbitt, who was shot and killed as a 'patriot' during the 6 January 2021 insurrection in Washington DC's Capitol Building. The insurrection saw 102 women arrested (as at mid-March 2022) for offences ranging from misdemeanours to felonies, accounting for 13 per cent of cases. Ten per cent of the women were accused of violence or conspiracy to commit violence. Professor Cynthia Miller-Idriss describes these women as 'the new normal of right-wing extremism'.[59]

These women are not unusual outliers; many examples exist and can be found if exploring extremist ecosystems or actions with a lens that accepts the variations of women's non-violent and violent participation. Any such exploration must also consider how women and children serve as symbols to justify male RWE actions globally and within New Zealand.

IN HER 2018 COMMENTARY *The Housewives of White Supremacy* Annie Kelly warned that the presence of RWE women made it irresponsible not to analyse their participation.[60] Comments like Kelly's initiated my master's research into women and extremism in New Zealand (2021).[61] My research concluded that New Zealand literature has not explicitly considered RWE women despite them being visible; for example, wearing the uniform and attending rallies in online images of the New Zealand National Front.[62] I discovered awareness of RWE female diversity at a security practitioner level. Yet the overarching strategic frameworks often overlooked them or took a 'genderless' approach that lost the vital nuances of women's involvement.

One New Zealand woman I discovered online stated explicitly that white supremacy was 'pro-Western values', that 'Western Anglo-Saxon' values are superior, and asked, 'What is wrong with superiority when it comes to culture?'[63] This rhetoric was a consistent theme as she excused discrimination as a personal choice, claiming 'there was nothing wrong' with that.[64] She complained, 'We have been so dominated by multiculturalism that we are losing our culture, losing our values.'[65]

Looking further back, I located a 2012 incident in which an 18-year-old female punched a Vietnamese man and encouraged her dog to 'kill him' while she stomped on his groceries. A few months later she and her male partner set their dogs onto a Filipino man, forcing him to seek refuge inside a building. They then encouraged their dogs to attack a Japanese woman. In court, the couple pleaded guilty, admitted their attacks were racially motivated, and told the judge they had stopped 'associating with right-wing groups after the attacks'.[66]

These are not the only examples of female RWE in New Zealand. Given that we have RWE men (Action Zealandia, for example) and that the broader movement needs women to help boost the white population, RWE recruiting of women in New Zealand needs assessment. We must look through low-threat presentations, such as Trad Wives, to analyse calls to protect women and children and consider gender bias in order to understand their participation rationally.

I completed my research before the Covid-19 pandemic, which has altered the New Zealand threatscape through dissent, discontent and polarisation over various social and political issues. Globally, researchers have linked the pandemic to a rise in extremism as multiple groups use it for propaganda and mobilisation. To modernise our strategies and understanding, research is needed to objectively analyse instigators, movements and protests, in order to identify how extremist right-wing women have featured in this environment in New Zealand, in a considered approach that does not overestimate or underestimate their influence.

HISTORY AND RESEARCH SHOW THAT women have long participated in RWE's male-dominated ecosystem and have promoted or conducted non-violence and violence to advance the RWE agenda.[67] Whether they choose to be Trad Wives or opt for another RWE subculture, women can blend ideological values and doctrine into their everyday lives effortlessly and overtly under feminine conservative themes that obfuscate their extremism.

Anti-feminism creates multiple pathways for white women's activism, and onlookers need to recognise it as a backlash against historical gains in gender equality, liberal values and progressive politics. Understanding this backlash makes RWE gender constructs recognisable as vehicles for their multiple themes rather than just about patriarchal hierarchy. In reality, these women are influential caretakers of RWE ideologies and can connect to mainstream social issues more quickly than their male peers, and often without question.

Various presentations, such as RWE Trad Wives, are not subcultures to be ridiculed; they serve to normalise and soften white supremacy in sinister and ironic ways.[68] Seyward Darby recognises these women as the 'hate movement's dulcet voices and its standard bearers' and 'hate's secret weapons'.[69] Unfortunately, when outsiders depict extremist women in sexualised or infantilised ways (as brides or pawns, for example), they motivate public, security, political and legal responses to do the same.[70]

While RWE activism can be peaceful, women have the potential to engage in political violence or promote cultural hate, including utilising their 'white woman' status to motivate their male peers. Additionally, some individuals are willing and able to employ violent tactics. Despite the sexism and misogyny of the extreme right, women are not passive accessories without self-agency.

The world of RWE and female involvement is diverse and nuanced. A clouded view will persist in New Zealand in the short term because our local scholarly research on women's complex involvement is deficient. At the time of my research in 2021, I was unable to locate any literary work that was solely dedicated to women and extremism in New Zealand.

Nonetheless, the floral aesthetics of RWE are receiving growing attention and hopefully encouraging future research on this demographic. By working to eliminate RWE women's diversity as a blind spot, New Zealand can begin to offer and implement practical recommendations for a gender-inclusive (not genderless) security approach to enhance counterterrorism frameworks, cross-government collaboration and public engagement.

Part 4

FUTURE SECURITY CHALLENGES

Ultimately, we need to think about our national identity. Who are we? What sort of nation do we aspire to be?

14.

RUSSIA'S INVASION OF UKRAINE

What is the strategic challenge for New Zealand?

Justyna Eska-Mikołajewska

One of the current and future challenges for global security is the ongoing war in Ukraine. This is not a new conflict but an escalation of armed aggression initiated by the Russian invasion of Crimea in February 2014. The entry of Russian troops into Ukraine territory again after eight years naturally has the greatest impact on neighbouring countries such as Poland; however, its importance to the regional balance of power cannot be underestimated. The defence of Ukraine would not be possible without the military, financial and humanitarian aid that is being offered primarily by the European Union (EU), other members of G7, countries such as New Zealand, Australia and South Korea and multilateral organisations such as the International Monetary Fund (IMF), the World Bank, the United Nations (UN) as well as the European Bank of Reconstruction and Development (EBRD).[1]

The war in Ukraine, which — surprisingly for Russia — did not end in the blitzkrieg-style victory Russia expected, has become a war of attrition.[2] Its range of influence now extends far beyond the theatre of war and has resulted in a highly complex refashioning of global security architecture as a key element for international order.

With no particular close ties to Russia, New Zealand has become aware of the importance of thinking strategically and reacting early in this attempt to reshape the international order by force. As a small island nation and some distance from most of its trading partners, New Zealand is particularly vulnerable to significant disruptions in trade. The weaknesses in the international system revealed by Russia's invasion of Ukraine affect New Zealand's national security.

The ongoing conflict raises a number of concerns, including the prospect of a global nuclear war. Increased tensions between the major powers, centred around the United States and the strategic alliance led by Russia and China, complicate New Zealand's position. The challenge for New Zealand is to maintain its reputation as a balanced international actor promoting a rules-based order.

How can New Zealand retain an independent foreign and security policy and support for a rules-based order in the face of Russian aggression in Ukraine? The changing global context in which this war is taking place forces New Zealand to rethink what an independent moral foreign policy actually looks like. The analysis of the means to achieve the objectives of this policy will allow New Zealand to assess its ability to adapt to changing conditions and face strategic challenges in a way that enables it to continue to benefit from the dynamically changing world order.

UNDERSTANDING THE EVOLVING DISTRIBUTION OF power in the Asia-Pacific region requires an examination of the global security architecture as it existed in a period of a bipolar structure, such as in the Cold War, which ran from 1947–91. It concerned a state of tension and rivalry in ideological, political, military and economic dimensions, which existed between the Eastern Bloc (also known as the Communist or Soviet Bloc), formed by the USSR, its satellite and allied non-European states, and the Western Bloc, non-communist states gathered in NATO and other defence pacts such as SEATO or CENTO under the leadership of the US. Tense US-Soviet relations were accompanied by an arms race, which from 1957 also took place in outer space; the ability to send rockets into space demonstrated the capability to do the same with nuclear weapons.

During the Cold War, the status and functional hierarchy of two superpowers, and the ability to play international roles and to shape and enforce global security imperatives reflected the real balance of power. The objective position of both powers, together with the awareness of the importance of maintaining mutual supremacy relations within global interests, resulted from the logic of the bipolar system. It was a stable system, giving a better guarantee of maintaining peace than the multilateral system. The stability of the Cold War order was a consequence of the superpowers' awareness of the prospects of a nuclear confrontation and the satisfaction felt by the US and the USSR with the existing status quo.[3] This prompted both countries to formulate their concepts and plans for international action.

One of these was the Soviet propaganda and disinformation activities which seriously undermined the moral prestige of the US. They were associated with the World Peace Council (WPC), established in Warsaw in 1950. Attempting to present itself as an independent movement accredited by the UN, the WPC actually functioned as a cover organisation sponsored by the USSR. The leadership of the Kremlin, without a doubt, was very effective when its own concern for peace, reflected in numerous peace campaigns in the 1970s by the WPC, was juxtaposed with the public impression of indifference, or even opposition, of the US to various peace initiatives.[4]

According to Russia, the global security architecture that emerged after the dismantling of the Eastern Bloc led to the creation of an unfair construction of the international order in which the US became the sole superpower. Thus, all alternative paths of development — such as those involving selective acceptance of democratic principles or the consolidation of authoritarianism — as well as opportunities for countries that do not fit into this new reality are unacceptable to the US.

Meanwhile, Russia has continued to aspire to build a global architecture of security and international order with its significant participation and in accordance with the standards it accepted. Russia is still a trans-regional player with the ability to project power in its immediate vicinity, but, as the armed confrontation in Ukraine proves, also in much more distant areas. Apart from convincing international public opinion about its military strength, the Kremlin builds its potential by applying raw material pressure against the former Soviet republics and through gas expansion in Europe.

The main premise of President Franklin Delano Roosevelt's political concepts — that satisfying Soviet territorial and political aspirations would guarantee political order in Europe — has not been confirmed.

What's more, Russia's thinking in terms of spheres of influence is still alive. Geopolitical rivalry combined with the clash of spheres of influence was an important element of the Cold War. The collapse of the Soviet Union implied the emergence of a kind of 'geopolitical vacuum', which in turn resulted in increased competition between world powers to expand their spheres of influence.

As a condition for maintaining its superpower status, Russia recognised its presence in the post-Soviet area, understood as its imperial heritage.[5] Its activity in this area includes exerting strong political, economic and military pressure, through which it reveals the questioning of a number of norms in the field of global governance, maritime law and international diplomacy, as well as overtly violating principles of international law, including the principle of non-aggression and non-intervention.[6] It is indisputable that all military operations of the Russian Federation are a de facto repetition of the colonial pattern: Russia is waging wars to regain lost influence and possessions over which it lost control after the collapse of the USSR.

The next stage of the rebirth of the Russian superpower after the Russian-Georgian conflict in 2008 was the annexation of Crimea in 2014. This was a response to imperial sentiments still alive in Russia and the already established thinking in terms of spheres of influence. The official recognition of the Crimean Peninsula as a temporarily occupied territory and the conflict in eastern Ukraine actually began the Ukrainian-Russian war.[7]

The Russian aggression against Ukraine and the illegal annexation of Crimea became a catalyst for changes in the Euro-Atlantic security environment. The countries of this area reacted accordingly to the violations committed by Russia on the territory of democratic and sovereign Ukraine.

The US and its allies are consistently showing support for Ukraine by imposing severe sanctions against Russia, but also Belarus and Iran. The sanctions are a set of restrictive measures, including bans on the export and import of certain goods (such as natural gas and crude oil), as well as services and technologies that may be used by the Russian defence industry. It is the tenth most powerful package of sanctions in history, and sends a clear signal to Russia that the West does not intend to limit its aid to Kyiv.[8]

Western attempts to deprive Russia of its oil or coal revenue have reduced the distance between Moscow and Beijing, with China continuing and even deepening trade ties with Russia. China is loudly repeating Russia's wish for a closer energy partnership. The Russian resources of oil, natural gas, coal and electricity meet the needs of China as the largest energy consumer in the world. It is significant that Beijing has never publicly condemned Russia's invasion of Ukraine; instead, President Xi Jinping's regime has taken a stance that can be described as pro-Russian neutrality.[9]

The Russian-Ukrainian war fits into the broader context of the new rivalry between old adversaries — the US and Russia — that has been developing for over a decade. This creates a highly tense security situation which to some extent is similar to the unpredictability of the Cold War bipolar system. However, the current rivalry is taking place in a multipolar world in which the US is the only superpower, while Russia, which cannot come to terms with the loss of its superpower position, is trying to secure the most appropriate geostrategic position for itself.

Since the US's greatest strategic challenge is the rise of China, Russia has started intensive economic cooperation, especially in the field of energy resources and military armaments, with this emerging Asian power. The unquestionable rapprochement between China and Russia has increased fears that, in the future, other countries may dare to take actions as dangerous as those currently being taken by Russia, including China towards Taiwan.

THE RISE OF MAJOR POWERS and the constant tension between them has a negative impact on New Zealand's security environment. New Zealand has, for many years, based its security on the conviction that it is protected by its isolation. Over the past 30 years, since the end of the Cold War, New Zealand has used its strengths effectively in relations with other countries that are much more exposed to various security threats. These strengths include political stability, a strong economy, cultural diversity and, above all, a good reputation as a country involved in a number of initiatives to solve global problems in the field of environmental protection, human rights and supporting regional security.

In the twentieth century, the basic instrument of New Zealand's security policy was bilateral and multilateral cooperation. New Zealand developed allied relations, first with Great Britain, then with the US, along with other Western countries. Its choice of allies was dictated by successful historical experiences.[10]

Since the 1970s, New Zealand has also realised the economic strength of Asia. In order to strengthen its influence, New Zealand expanded its traditional network of bilateral partnerships and multilateral cooperation formats to include like-minded Western countries, countries of Southeast Asia and the emerging powers of East Asia. Its attempts for membership in various alliances has been motivated by many factors.[11] Allied relations with different countries at different times were recognised as beneficial, and this concerned not only those agreements that corresponded to New Zealand's national values, such as the Commonwealth, Close Defence Relations (CDR) or Five Power Defence Arrangements (FPDA), but also those that emphasised the fear of a specific threat not necessarily direct, but at least potentially harmful. This was illustrated by New Zealand's accession to the Southeast Asia Treaty Organization (SEATO), the aim of which was to create a collective security system against external aggression, with an emphasis on preventing communism from gaining ground in the Southeast Asia region.

The stability of cooperation and regional initiatives remained an important aspect of New Zealand's international relations. As one of the main actors shaping the security situation in the South Pacific, over the years New Zealand has built a reputation as a committed player, strengthening its international position through influence expansion and by providing development assistance to the small island states in Oceania. These relations are based on New Zealand's unique position and result from strong historical, geographical and cultural ties.

The range of means used in its foreign policy on a sub-regional scale proves that New Zealand's potential influence is sufficient to further strengthen the independence and wellbeing of South Pacific countries and their resilience to crises. Undoubtedly, New Zealand also benefits from long-term stability in its immediate security environment; a peaceful and prosperous Pacific helps to protect New Zealand's interests and influence.[12] This balance reflects a pragmatic approach, according to the model of 'globally motivated regional policy'. According to this new paradigm, 'the region of the twenty-first century must be an effective actor on the global stage'.[13]

One of the fundamental assumptions of New Zealand's foreign policy has been the pursuit of greater independence in security matters. Both New Zealand and Australia were bound by the 1985 South Pacific Nuclear Free Zone (SPNFZ) Treaty. Being much larger, however, Australia took a more moderate approach to nuclear issues.[14] Its goal was to maintain allied guarantees from the US and to conduct disarmament diplomacy based on multilateralism.[15]

Meanwhile, a fully independent New Zealand foreign policy, led by the country's anti-nuclear stance, was an important element of its defence posture.[16] The New Zealand Nuclear Free Zone, Disarmament, and Arms Control Act 1987, banning nuclear-powered ships and nuclear weapons from entering the country, confirmed that even small states are able to achieve their own political goals without being dependent on larger players dominating the international arena.[17]

As Amy Catalinac argues, New Zealand's position should be seen from the perspective of gains, in particular for exercising moral leadership in the conduct of an ethical foreign policy, also sometimes referred to as exercising potentially effective symbolic power.[18] Riding the post-Cold War wave of the global movement for nuclear disarmament, New Zealand was able to advance its own initiative. It used various multilateral forums for this purpose and, by exerting pressure and persuasion against nuclear-weapon states, acted as a kind of catalyst for changes in nuclear disarmament diplomacy. This action was consistent with New Zealand's commitment to multilateral cooperation and also strengthened its position as an increasingly independent country.[19]

THE ASIAN DIRECTION IN NEW ZEALAND'S foreign policy gained importance in the 1970s, while in the first decade of the twenty-first century contacts with Asia became critical for the functioning of this country in the international arena. New Zealand has benefited from many opportunities mainly resulting from economic exchange, but also political relations, which influenced its greater interest in maintaining regional security. With this in mind, New Zealand modified its national security strategy. As its basic security and economic needs began to diverge, one of the country's new goals was to maintain a balance in relations with the US and China. By adopting this 'asymmetric hedging strategy', which assumes that a small state makes efforts to maintain positive relations with two rival powers without choosing one over the other, New Zealand took a neutral position without directly advocating for either party.[20]

Being a partner to everyone in the region required good diplomacy. New Zealand emphasised repeatedly that, as a responsible member of the international community, it would advocate consistently for multilateralism and strengthening of the rules-based international system. For a small country like New Zealand, this approach has been the only way to promote and protect its own interests in a largely power-based system, as evidenced by examples of greater aggression from authoritarian regimes such as Russia.[21] That is why New Zealand has tried both to maintain ties with traditional allies — for instance, it has managed to rebuild its security relationship with the US without having to abandon its anti-nuclear policy — and benefit from strengthening trade and defence relations with Asian states.[22]

By maintaining an equal distance between economic and geopolitical imperatives, New Zealand has sought to preserve its reputation as a neutral state that eases tensions and contributes to building trust between antagonised parties. Observance of the principle of independence in foreign policy has included neutrality towards armed conflicts and non-intervention in the internal affairs of other states. New Zealand, unlike most Western countries, did not have its own formal sanctions mechanism. It could only support UN sanctions based on the United Nations Act 1946. This made it easier for New Zealand to manoeuvre between different partners and avoid pressure to take sides.

The international rules-based order is fundamental to New Zealand's national security because it supports the country's independent policy, allowing it to contribute to international peace and security. There are benefits to be gained from sticking up for multilateral institutions and collective arrangements. It means, however, that New Zealand is obliged to be at constant readiness to take action to prevent or resolve any problems that may disturb this order.

NEW ZEALAND HAS ALREADY POINTED out that Russia's approach of discrediting the values and norms of traditional advocates of the rules-based international order, using undemocratic and dangerous methods, is unacceptable. The New Zealand government expressed its critical stance towards Russia after the annexation of Crimea in 2014, in part by withdrawing from free trade negotiations with Russia, Belarus and Kazakhstan.

New Zealand has also imposed some travel restrictions on Russians and Ukrainians that are linked to the events in Ukraine. In the *2014 Defence Assessment*, the New Zealand Ministry of Defence presented Russia as a leading challenger of the international order; the *2016 Defence White Paper* drew attention to Russia's violation of the rules of sovereignty in its annexation of Crimea and intervention in the territory of Ukraine.[23] Due to a lack of binding legislation allowing the government to impose autonomous sanctions, however, New Zealand's responses remained limited.[24]

The outbreak of war in Ukraine marked a significant shift in the approach to defining New Zealand's independence. Until now, New Zealand had relied on multilateralism to pursue its own security interests and had employed only lower-level retaliatory measures, which are not formal sanctions. Several important factors, including the conviction that the United Nations Security Council (UNSC) was powerless to respond to the Russian invasion, the Russian veto over a resolution condemning its actions, as well as increasing pressure from Western allies, led New Zealand to implement an independent sanctions mechanism. The government passed the Russia Sanctions Act 2022 as a direct response to Russia's military action in sovereign Ukraine; it can also be extended to any other country where action by the UNSC is unlikely.[25]

INITIALLY WITH SOME CAUTION, REFERRING to the effects of a 'flagrant breach of fundamental international rules', New Zealand strongly condemned the 'unprovoked attack', for which it said Russia should bear the consequences.[26] New Zealand did not become an active participant in the war but also did not remain indifferent, considering the implications of this conflict for a rules-based world. It has shown its solidarity with the Ukrainian people by offering defence force personnel to assist with training, intelligence, logistics, liaison and command, and administration support at a cost of over NZ$22 million. Although proportionally less than aid provided by other Western countries, this clearly shows New Zealand's commitment to ending the ongoing conflict.[27]

New Zealand focuses on diplomacy, the effectiveness of which is now more desirable than ever. Russia's illegal invasion of Ukraine has potentially undermined New Zealand's stance of neutrality. The introduction of an autonomous sanctions regime can be seen as the country's return to its traditional security relations.[28] Using the current situation to confirm how efficiently it can adapt to changing geopolitical conditions and face challenges, while still maintaining its independent foreign policy, is now crucial.

Since the end of the Second World War, New Zealand has unfailingly supported the rules-based system of international relations as well as the principle of multilateralism.[29] That hasn't changed. It still primarily emphasises the importance of and supports all the resolutions condemning Russia adopted by UN bodies such as the General Assembly and the Human Rights Council. In the absence of the Security Council's ability to apply globally binding sanctions on its permanent members, who — as in the case of Russia — will no doubt veto them, UN member countries have designed and imposed sanctions of their own. The enaction of a stand-alone law imposing sanctions on Russia, with the intention of limiting Russia's ability to finance and equip the war in Ukraine, strengthens New Zealand's presence in the collective condemnation of Russian aggression. In doing so, New Zealand reaffirms its unequivocal defence of fundamental democratic values.

In July 2022, Prime Minister Jacinda Ardern, in her speech at the Lowey Institute in Sydney, drew attention to the need to reform the UNSC so Russia can be held properly to account for its attack on Ukraine. The prime minister described Russia's position in the UN as 'morally bankrupt', and highlighted the importance of equipping the International Criminal Court to investigate and prosecute war crimes and crimes against humanity committed during the war in Ukraine.[30]

New Zealand maintains that the UN multilateral system is the basis for preserving and promoting the rules-based order; if it has ceased to fulfil its functions properly, it should be reformed. What is more, New Zealand insists that the international community should not be allowed to rely solely on autonomous sanctions imposed by individual countries.

Consistently advocating multilateralism, New Zealand recognises that leaving the right to assess the legitimacy of imposing sanctions to any individual country, regardless of whether a similar judgement is issued by the UN, could result in a number of risks. These are related to the weakening of the importance of international bodies and institutions, whose role is to set rules and enforce states' conduct to maintain peace and security, such as through 'refraining in their international relations from the threat or use of force' against any other sovereign nation.[31]

A consistent response from states to threats to the rules-based order, resulting from the implementation of common obligations, both strengthens the practical effectiveness of international law and increases the influence of individual countries. This applies especially to small countries, for whom participation in global forums and international networks is an opportunity to increase their capacity to influence in a world dominated by major powers.

The outbreak of a war that contributes to the transformation of New Zealand's security environment has caused changes to the country's foreign and security policy. However, it does not mean a change in assumptions; New Zealand is not moving away from its independent status. First, New Zealand has established itself as a trusted partner, valued for its ongoing commitment to protecting democratic institutions, principles and values.

Second, New Zealand contributes to stability and development both in its narrower and wider home region. In the South Pacific it uses a range of soft-power measures to give it an advantage against Chinese expansion in this area. In the Indo-Pacific region, however, it benefits from economic and security cooperation with the US and China, as two sides of global competition in the 'multipolar world', characterised by a shift from rules to power,[32] and in which New Zealand is becoming increasingly assertive. It avoids entering into alliances with any of the major powers, has strengthened its ties with its Five Eyes partners, and adopts a cautious approach to challenges posed by authoritarian regimes.[33]

Third, New Zealand remains a steadfast promoter of peace and rules-based order in terms of maintaining global stability. It shows pragmatism and adaptability more typical of a minor power than a small state, as seen in the introduction of an autonomous sanctions regime when it became apparent that the action of multilateral institutions in the face of Russia's invasion was futile.

Fourth, New Zealand focuses on strengthening diplomacy as its most effective tool to address global challenges and conflicts. With the current increased risk of an escalation of security threats — including towards uncontrolled conflict with the use of nuclear weapons — the issues of non-proliferation of weapons of mass destruction and disarmament, which in 2017 were already at the top of the government's foreign policy agenda, take on a whole new meaning.[34] Known for its uncompromising stance on limiting the proliferation of weapons of mass destruction, New Zealand is well placed to cooperate with other like-minded states and, moreover, to promote initiatives to control compliance with the rules for the possession and production of nuclear weapons.

RUSSIA'S INVASION OF UKRAINE HAS changed the global balance of power irrevocably, and the West is united in its concerns about the serious threat posed by Russia.

New Zealand's unequivocal condemnation of the invasion in all regional and international forums is consistent with the country's strategic narrative. Advocating compliance with commonly established rules and international legal accountability, New Zealand has consistently built its global reputation as a credible team player, respected for its neutrality and multilateral stance.

In the wake of the invasion, New Zealand was forced to use all available means to achieve its foreign and security policy goals, both for moral reasons and, above all, to stop Russia's revisionist actions. Russia's brutal attack on Ukraine provided the incentive to reflect on an independent moral foreign policy and adapt it to the new reality.

New Zealand has joined the united front of states imposing sanctions and providing military support, humanitarian, economic and diplomatic assistance to Ukraine.[35] In doing so it has become stronger, able not only to face strategic challenges but also to fulfil international expectations regarding its contribution to maintaining the global security architecture. Along with focusing on the issue of the nuclear threat, which is the cornerstone of New Zealand's identity, the essential issues remain: to be consistent in its international activities, both diplomatically — in fulfilling its traditional role as a peace-promoting intermediary — and in using the tools of multilateralism.

15.

DIGITAL CURRENCIES

Their potential role in New Zealand's economic statecraft

José Miguel Alonso-Trabanco

Digital currencies are virtual monetary items. This high-tech innovation was born in an age shaped by the growing digitalisation of finance and the worldwide rise of monetary pluralism. They offer various technical, strategic, economic, financial and political opportunities for the transformative renewal of money in the twenty-first century. As is often the case with game-changing breakthroughs and currencies throughout history, they entail both potential threats and advantages for nation states that are not self-evident at first glance. In fact, the extent of their disruptive potential includes multifaceted implications for the increasingly complex field of national security.

Therefore, it is pertinent to clarify the larger significance of virtual currencies for contemporary economic statecraft in order to develop preparedness to achieve favourable outcomes, map risks, manage threats and harness opportunities, and to provide a sharper understanding of this matter from the perspective of New Zealand's national interests.

In order to offer strategic clarity about the long-term implications of this complex phenomenon, this chaper addresses the overall nature of digital currencies, New Zealand's current experience with these currencies, prospective risks for the country's national security related to them, opportunities to engage in the world of digital currencies to increase national power, and the potential to position a digital version of the New Zealand dollar as a minor regional reserve currency.

DIGITAL CURRENCIES ARE PURELY VIRTUAL items created to perform all the roles of money: as a medium of exchange, a unit of account and a store of value. Access to their systems is granted through cryptographic keys. They were born in the wake of the 2008 global financial crisis, a turning point that stimulated debates about the legitimacy of fiat money issued by central banks, the global position of the US dollar as the dominant reserve currency, unsound monetary policies and the unchecked power of high finance. The arrival of digital currencies — in the context of the ongoing innovative wave known as the Fourth Industrial Revolution — represents the latest chapter in the evolutionary history of money. Their technological engine is the automatic record-keeping system known as blockchain, which enables the collective verification of transactions. It is relevant to note that the existence of cybercurrencies is not confined to the digital world. Their environments are anchored to material reality since they involve computational hardware, an accompanying infrastructure and the energy grids that power them.[1]

The first generation of cryptocurrencies — which includes Bitcoin and its offshoots — was disruptive for several reasons. As stateless, unregulated and unofficial money, they are not issued or backed by governmental entities. Rather than being controlled by a centralised source of authority, they have a dispersed horizontal architecture underpinned by the networks of their virtual communities. As digital cash that flows through unsupervised channels, they enable transactions that conceal users' identities. Thanks to algorithmic programming, their operational systems resemble self-sustaining, reliable and inalterable clockwork mechanisms whose perpetual motion behaves predictably.

Initially, cybercurrency started as a marginal phenomenon that gained traction only in small niches. However, despite the drawbacks of these virtual currencies — including volatile exchange rates — they have now reached a substantial international projection. They have attracted the attention of start-up companies, high-tech corporations, libertarians, outlaws, large financial firms and governmental agencies. In other words, they have become mainstream. Moreover, the universe of digital currencies is becoming increasingly plural and complex, as evidenced by the rise of 'stablecoins' designed by transnational companies, and central bank digital currencies (CBDCs) developed by governments as a new form of state-backed legal tender.

NEW ZEALAND'S EXPERIENCE WITH CYBERCURRENCIES has been limited, but mixed. Contrasting examples show their nature as a double-edged sword that entails both risks and benefits for this South Pacific state. In other words, they have ambivalent implications for the country's national interests.

New Zealand's most direct contact with these monetary innovations is seen in the thriving business of cryptocurrency exchanges. These are virtual platforms in which said currencies can be bought and sold for profit, mostly as speculative assets. Both domestic and foreign firms offer this service in New Zealand.[2] Yet, the government warns that investing in unregulated cryptoassets comes with the risks of financial volatility, hacking, scams and fraud.[3] In addition, the borderless dynamics of cryptoassets makes them hard to track and to determine if an exchange has been compromised by illicit activity.[4]

In 2021 a cyberattack targeted Waikato District Health Board. The orchestrators, whose identities remain unclear, demanded payment in cryptocurrency. Healthcare services were disrupted and confidential information — medical, administrative and financial — was stolen and then shared through the so-called dark web (as a likely retaliation for the refusal to comply with the hackers' demands).[5] The situation required the involvement of the National Cyber Security Centre. The event demonstrated the disruptive potential of cybercrime facilitated through unofficial cybercurrencies. In fact, some experts argue that ransomware as a criminal phenomenon is enabled by the existence of cryptocurrencies.[6]

Perhaps the most troubling aspect of this episode is that it is part of a larger trend of growing cyberattacks reported in New Zealand.[7] Although this incident was likely motivated by the economic interests of non-state actors,[8] it indirectly raised concerns about preparedness to face the hypothetical prospect of similar acts either sponsored by hostile states or launched against strategic economic sectors or critical infrastructure. Such a precedent highlights that New Zealand cannot afford to ignore the plausible involvement of non-state cybercurrencies in acts of hybrid warfare.

ACCORDING TO *THE ECONOMIST*, more than 50 national states are developing their own official versions of digital money.[9] Specifically, the Reserve Bank of New Zealand has been studying the possibility of launching a CBDC as part of the country's journey towards a cashless economy. This exploration — motivated by the rising traction of virtual forms of money — includes feedback from the public, deliberations, consultations, and the assessment of both advantages and drawbacks.[10] Although research continues, no conclusive decision has yet been made.[11] Nevertheless, these ongoing debates are mostly framed in accordance with economic, financial, regulatory and technical criteria. A broader and deeper perspective is needed to define a course of action based on the strategic criteria of economic statecraft.

Not unlike multinational corporations, transnational organised crime networks are non-state actors that harness innovations to increase the profitability of their illicit businesses, conquer new markets and diversify their sources of wealth.[12] The New Zealand government indicates that phenomena like cybercrime, the illicit commercial exploitation of natural resources, drug smuggling, wildlife trafficking, fraud and tax evasion represent threats for national security, law enforcement and societal wellbeing. The authorities also warn about local motorcycle gangs, and foreign criminal organisations from Mexico, China and Southeast Asia.[13] In this respect, unofficial cybercurrencies provide unsupervised financial channels that are suitable to engage in illicit transactions — especially through the lawless cyber domain known as the dark web — and to launder money.[14]

New Zealand is vulnerable to the growth of both illicit businesses and money-laundering activities of transnational criminal networks due to being perceived as a wealthy nation, its attractive consumer market, its developed financial system (including cryptocurrency exchanges) and the openness of its economy. Hence, stateless cryptocurrencies can represent enablers that facilitate the operations of criminal organisations in New Zealand or against New Zealand targets.

In 2021 the theft by unknown perpetrators of Bitcoin worth NZ$45,000 from a cryptocurrency wallet of the New Zealand Police — a sum meant to be used in an undercover operation against money laundering — is a strong reminder of these risks.[15] This example generates reasonable doubts about the preparedness of New Zealand to address the national security implications of the cryptocurrency landscape. Another concern is the possibility that, as the RAND Corporation has warned, virtual currencies could be co-opted, manipulated, exploited and maybe even launched by terrorist, separatist and insurgent forces for political reasons.[16]

The eventual proliferation of unofficial and private cryptocurrencies represents a potential economic, political, technical and symbolic challenge for the preservation of the monopolistic control held by states over the issuance of money.[17] Monetary policy is not only an expression of territorial national sovereignty. It is an instrument for states to strategically direct the performance of their economies — including the management of trade, taxation and debts — in accordance with their national interests and to underwrite governmental expenses.[18] Therefore, central banks are often reluctant to accept the legitimacy of cryptoassets because they could weaken national currencies. Likewise, their widespread adoption and/or circulation could encourage speculative attacks motivated by economic or political interests.[19]

Yet, the prospect that these virtual currencies could overtake state-backed legal tender seems unlikely due to their instability, limited projection and lack of support by a great power. These considerations must also be weighted in the deliberations of New Zealand policymakers, experts and scholars.

THE DOMAIN OF MONEY IS one of the chessboards in which great power competition is currently manifested. The hegemonic role held by the United States dollar since the second half of the twentieth century is being contested by states like China, Russia and Iran. These challengers are encouraging a de-dollarisation campaign on a global scale through various asymmetric measures.[20] There is a strong incentive for states interested in a multipolar world to seek alternatives to the American dollar. These alternatives include the accumulation of gold holdings and other hard assets with intrinsic value, bilateral deals conceived to increase de-dollarised transactions and the promotion of a rising monetary pluralism. In this regard, the involvement of digital currencies in such manoeuvres is expected because they offer strategic advantages worth harnessing.[21]

Iran has engaged the Bitcoin ecosystem to deflect the impact of Western sanctions and to find backchannels which bypass circuits connected to the dollar.[22] Russia is contemplating the use of non-state cybercurrencies as alternatives to undertake international economic and financial exchanges through parallel arteries and also as a counter-hegemonic vector of a grand strategy whose purpose is to diminish the greenback's dominance.[23] China — the world's leader in the development of FinTech platforms — is launching the e-CNY as a state-backed sovereign currency, an innovation that will likely accelerate the process of renminbi (RMB) internationalisation and strengthen the projection of Chinese influence, leadership and prestige.[24]

In the meantime, Washington's increasing reliance on the weaponisation of the dollar against its rivals[25] is a trend that offers incentives to create parallel financial and monetary systems.[26] Moreover, the BRICS countries (Brazil, India, Russia, China, South Africa) — all of which support a multipolar balance of power — are interested in the design of a shared multilateral currency.[27] Considering both its security partnerships and the orientation of its economic interests, the eventual bifurcation or fragmentation of the global financial and monetary system has challenging implications for New Zealand. Accordingly, the country needs to address cautiously the complex geoeconomic rivalry between Washington and Beijing, manage the evolving currency landscape, adapt to the changing correlation of forces in the Indo-Pacific and hedge its strategic bets.

As nascent innovations, there can be other unanticipated or unknown risks associated with non-state cybercurrencies. From a long-range perspective, their introduction is fairly recent and they have proved to be resilient and reliable, but the impact of emerging phenomena could threaten the stability of their systems or even unleash deeper unexpected consequences.[28] For instance, quantum computing could compromise their cryptographic protection.[29]

NEW ZEALAND CAN ENGAGE THE world of cybercurrencies in various ways to bolster its national power, understood as the ability to pursue its interests, harness advantages, enhance its security, strengthen its strategic position and further its influence.

As a report written by former CIA executives explains, a better knowledge of blockchain-based environments can improve the analytical, operational and technical capabilities of governmental agencies responsible for financial intelligence (FININT).[30] Unsurprisingly, both official statements and open sources confirm the involvement of the United States intelligence community in the domain of stateless cybercurrencies.[31] Particularly, a sharper understanding of cryptocurrency ecosystems can help New Zealand track suspicious transfers of wealth — involving potentially problematic behaviours of both state and non-state actors — through their unsupervised circuits. The collection of FININT can uncover actionable data about money flows and hidden connections. However, its usefulness goes beyond surveillance. FININT is also a strategic instrument of economic statecraft which is suitable to target and disrupt enemy financial networks if necessary.[32]

Despite the fluctuations of their exchange rates, non-state cryptocurrencies represent unconventional assets worth considering for the diversification of foreign exchange reserves. They are resilient enough to withstand both spontaneous market disruptions and intentional attempts to undermine them. Moreover, since they are not issued by any national state, they can be leveraged by countries that seek to assume a nonaligned strategic orientation, which makes them helpful to avoid an overreliance on financial systems unilaterally controlled by foreign powers.[33] For New Zealand, adding denationalised cryptoassets to its reserves would be beneficial to manage the problematic financial and monetary ramifications of the growing rivalry between the United States and China, increase its margin of strategic autonomy and avoid taking sides.

IN DECENTRALISED CRYPTOCURRENCY ENVIRONMENTS, the consensual validation of blockchain-based transactions requires the computational performance of mathematical equations to decipher increasingly complex puzzles. The network node which finds the answer first is rewarded by the system with newly minted cryptoassets, an incentive that encourages participation in said competitive endeavour. This pursuit requires advanced computers, optimum internet access and an intensive supply of electricity, as well as cooling systems that mitigate the heat generated as a by-product. The process is known as 'cryptocurrency mining' because it mirrors the difficult extraction of precious metals.[34]

Its strategic benefits include the promotion of technological development, the encouragement of innovative entrepreneurial dynamism and the generation of wealth. As a way to upgrade the industrial profile of its economy, New Zealand has substantial comparative advantages to become a sustainable cryptocurrency mining hub: (1) the cool temperatures of the South Island; (2) the sophistication and openness of its financial system; (3) an affordable and reliable supply of energy generated by renewable sources; (4) flexible legal frameworks; (5) a well-trained workforce; and (6) geographical proximity to the Asian economies which manufacture the high-tech equipment that is needed. So far, individuals, local businesses and virtual communities are independently involved in this activity in New Zealand.[35] As yet, the state has not formulated a directive industrial policy that favours the structural development of economies of scale and maximises gains for the national interest.

FOR SMALL NATIONS LIKE NEW ZEALAND, the domain of non-state cryptocurrencies — especially those that offer high levels of discretion like Bitcoin and Monero — can be leveraged as non-military instruments of power projection against hostile states and non-state actors. Their asymmetric advantages can be harnessed by the country's special forces and intelligence agencies to carry out covert tasks and acts of hybrid warfare overseas. Their specific potential applications to target rivals include the ability to: (1) make clandestine purchases in black markets; (2) reward informants and assets; (3) instigate macroeconomic disruptions in nations with weak currencies; (4) buy hidden influence to wage psychological warfare through social media platforms; and (5) fund militant proxies and political groups whose activities fuel agitation, unrest and turmoil behind enemy lines.[36] In other words, the cryptocurrency landscape offers New Zealand multiple opportunities to hit potential rivals in a stronger way than would be possible through its conventional capabilities.

Blockchain is not only the technological cornerstone of virtual currencies. Since it offers inalterable data records, distributed operational protocols and cryptographic shields, this technology has potential applications in the domain of security. This innovation can be useful to enhance the logistical management of military supply chains, the protection of classified information and the resilience of communication platforms.[37] New Zealand can leverage these attributes in order to bolster its military readiness and to modernise its hard power, especially in an uncertain and dangerous regional context that will likely require a transition towards an assertive grand strategy of 'armed neutrality' in the near future.[38] Likewise, these instrumental applications of blockchain could be helpful to develop the expeditionary capability that Wellington would need to project its presence and protect its strategic interests in the coming geopolitical race to control Antarctica and its deposits of natural resources.[39]

ACCORDING TO SWIFT (Society for Worldwide Interbank Financial Telecommunications), the New Zealand dollar is the world's sixteenth-most used currency in terms of volume in international payments, with a proportional share of 0.29 per cent.[40] This puts it ahead of the national currencies of countries whose economies are far larger, such as Mexico and Chile. The introduction of a sovereign CBDC launched by the Reserve Bank of New Zealand could offer an opportunity to bolster the domestic strength of its official money in an age of monetary pluralism, but also to seek the position of minor regional reserve currency in the Indo-Pacific, similar to the traditional role held by the Swiss franc in Europe. This pursuit is feasible now that the region acts as the top centre of global economic dynamism.[41]

In order to do this, New Zealand can harness Auckland's financial know-how, a legal heritage that upholds both the sanctity of private property and rule of law, the country's involvement in international economic exchanges and its unimpeded access to international capital markets, as well as its membership in frameworks such as the Asian Infrastructure Investment Bank (AIIB), the Regional Comprehensive Economic Partnership (RCEP) and the Digital Economy Partnership Agreement (DEPA). The worldly wisdom of economic statecraft suggests the pertinence of developing the financial infrastructure to connect the digital 'Kiwi' with arteries affiliated with both Western and Asian currencies and maybe even operate as a bridge between them.

Although Wellington cannot remake the global monetary landscape with its own CBDC, it can play an assertive independent role in an emerging scenario of currency multipolarity. Likewise, New Zealand can harness this opportunity to position itself as a neutral world-class financial centre that engages partners with varying geopolitical alignments. Aside from influence and strategic advantages, another benefit of this endeavour would be a stronger projection of the New Zealand national 'soft power'.

LIKE A DOUBLE-EDGED SWORD, THE larger strategic significance of cryptocurrency entails both risks for New Zealand's national security and various opportunities to strengthen its national power in the near future. For the time being, New Zealand economic statecraft is still not fully prepared to address the ambivalent implications of this high-tech monetary invention and its incremental complexity. Such limitation is not just a cognitive shortcoming. An incomplete understanding of the phenomenon can lead to the neglectful proliferation of threats and missed opportunities, especially in an uncertain international environment.

This chapter has sought to widen the spectrum of deliberations and raise awareness about potential challenges of digital currencies. The expectation is that New Zealand can approach this disruptive FinTech innovation in an advantageous way as an increasingly assertive and self-confident state.

16.

THE FUTURE OF THE 'GOOD CITIZEN'

▌ A perspective from the Polish frontline

Marcin Lasoń

The Russian Federation's aggression against Ukraine, which began in 2014, has changed the perception of threats to national and international security in many countries. In Poland, just as in Western Europe, the prevailing belief until then was that the military threat to its existence and development had ceased to exist; international law, including the prohibition of the use of force, was the foundation of world order. Therefore, the annexation of Crimea, the fighting in eastern Ukraine, the establishment by Russia in 2014 of two separatist states (Donetsk and Luhansk People's Republics) and the launch of the offensive against Ukraine on 24 February 2022 came as a shock. Consequently, Polish authorities have accelerated an unprecedented and costly increase to and modernisation of their armed forces, a move for which there is social consent due to the sense of threat experienced by the inhabitants of the state.

Russian policy threatens not only its neighbours and Europeans, however, but also the rules-based international order, and this poses a threat to the existence and sovereignty of small states in particular. Violations of international law are particularly destructive for small states, regardless of their geographical location. Should this provoke a serious reaction from New Zealanders *before* a possible enemy is at their door, as happened in the case of Poland?

The authors of the New Zealand Ministry of Defence's *2016 Defence White Paper* acknowledged that New Zealand's geographical isolation could no longer guarantee security.[1] In diagnosing the international security environment, the authors noted the annexation of Crimea by the Russian Federation, an action that disrupted the principles upon which the international system based on law is built.[2] They argued that, because of changes occurring in the international security environment, as part of building a national security policy it would be necessary to invest in the development and modernisation of the armed forces' capabilities.[3] Thus, the first step towards counteracting the threat to New Zealand's security were taken.

New Zealand must be ready to act: to unequivocally take the side of the West, to participate in international security organisations and agreements, and to bear the associated costs. If the Russians are not stopped, there may be imitators in other parts of the world, including close to New Zealand.

The evolution of the security policy mentioned above, visible after the outbreak of the Russian-Ukrainian war in 2014, took place at the time of major changes in the international security environment. The Russian Federation militarised its foreign policy, the aim of which was to rebuild the empire stretching to the former borders of the USSR, with the area of influence covering the states it controlled in the years 1945–89. The Polish authorities repeatedly warned Western countries that Russia was heading in this direction and that it should be counteracted. However, this concern was not always understood. Those who wanted to conduct lucrative business with Russia accused Poles of Russophobia.[4] Only after 24 February 2022 did many Western politicians, followed by media and public opinion, acknowledge the seriousness of the situation.[5]

Poles did not immediately come to these conclusions about Russian policy. Even after the Russian aggression against Georgia in 2008, Poland still followed the path set by the US and tried for a reset in relations with Russia, symbolised by Polish Prime Minister Donald Tusk's 2009 meeting with Russian President Vladimir Putin on the anniversary of the outbreak of the Second World War. This attempt at renovation failed in 2014 when the Russians invaded Ukraine and annexed Crimea.

A year earlier, the *White Book on National Security of the Republic of Poland* (2013) had presented the principles of the Komorowski Doctrine (named after Bronisław Komorowski, then president of Poland), which emphasised the role of Poland's defence forces in national security. The main principle was the change in the priorities of the Polish security and defence policy: from the abilities of expeditionary armed forces to defending the state's territory.[6] Until then, Poland had played the role of the 'good NATO member', for example by sending military contingents of around 2500 soldiers to Afghanistan. Such activities increased the likelihood that, in the event of an attack on the territory of the Republic of Poland (from the only likely aggressor, Russia), Poland's allies would in turn provide military assistance where needed.

This was related to the differences in how powerful they are and belief in the great strength of the Russian army, a belief present not only in Poland but also among Western politicians, journalists and societies. Yet there were politicians in Poland who warned against the imperial Russian policy, and pointed to the need to develop defence capabilities. The words of President Lech Kaczyński, delivered in Tbilisi during the 2008 Russian aggression against Georgia, are often recalled in this context: 'And we also know very well that today it is Georgia, tomorrow Ukraine, the day after tomorrow the Baltic States, and later maybe it will be time for my country, Poland!'[7]

After Russia's aggression against Ukraine in 2014, in 2015 a change of Polish government saw it launch a new security and defence policy, the aim of which was to strengthen defence capabilities and to prioritise the defence of Poland's own territory over foreign peacekeeping missions. Defence spending increased, and a new type of Polish Armed Forces was created: the Territorial Defence Forces.

The key stimulant of rapid progress in this area was Russia's transition to the next phase of the war with Ukraine on 24 February 2022. After that date, a number of contracts were signed for the purchase of military equipment for the Polish Armed Forces to replace post-Soviet equipment that had been transferred to Ukraine. Table 1 illustrates the enormity of this increased spending.

In 2022, Polish military spending calculated in GDP was the third highest in the North Atlantic Treaty Organization (NATO), exceeded only by Greece and the US. According to the data provided by the Polish government for the entirety of 2022, armament contracts amounted to approximately PLN100 billion.

Table 1: Poland's defence spending, 2014 and 2022

	2014	2022 (e)
Defence expenditure (million PLN)	31,874	73,850
Defence expenditure (million US dollars)	10,107	17,806
Defence expenditure as a share of GDP and annual real change (based on 2015 prices) (%)	1.86	2.42
Military personnel (thousands)	99.0	122.5

e: estimates
Source: Defence Expenditure of NATO Countries (2014/2022), 27 June 2022,
www.nato.int/cps/en/natohq/news_197050.htm

Poland is in the process of buying more weapons, such as the Patriot systems, and there are orders for further equipment. The largest contract so far concerns the Borsuk infantry fighting vehicle produced in Poland (1400 vehicles for PLN11 billion gross).[8] The US authorities agreed to sell Poland almost 500 HIMARS rocket launchers for about US$10 billion.[9] Given the scale of the orders, it should come as no surprise that, both within Poland and across the world, it is claimed that Poland is assembling the largest and strongest land army in Europe.[10]

Finance for this outlay comes from increased defence spending, which in 2023 will amount to approximately PLN100 billion (minimum 3 per cent of GDP) and a special Armed Forces Support Fund of approximately PLN30 billion. The legal basis for increasing expenditures to allow for the simultaneous modernisation and expansion of the Polish Army is the Act on the Defence of the Homeland, adopted on 11 March 2022.[11] The Act also introduces new forms of military service, since Poland, like many other countries, is facing problems of recruiting personnel.

Poland has taken these actions in order to deter Russia if the need arises. As well, it is playing for the West the shielding role adopted by the Federal Republic of Germany during the Cold War. It recognises that helping Ukraine to win the war is the best guarantee of security for the next few years. These actions also ensure the permanent presence of US troops and other allied and partner countries in its territory and strengthens its international position.

The scale of Polish aid for Ukraine is significant. In 2022 Poland spent EUR8.36 billion (equivalent to 1.5 per cent of GDP, and more than any other European country) on humanitarian aid, of which EUR6.2 billion was for accommodation and direct assistance to refugees.[12] EUR1.82 billion went to military support, which put Poland in fourth position behind the US, the UK and Germany. Conversion to GDP shows that Poland ranked fourth in this as well, at 0.3 per cent, behind Estonia (1 per cent), Latvia (0.88 per cent) and Lithuania (0.35 per cent).[13]

Naturally, there are also internal reasons for helping Ukraine and increasing defence spending, and these relate to the 2023 parliamentary elections. Regardless of this, however, the Polish authorities did not want the phrase 'hindsight is always 20/20' to be valid in the case of threats related to the Russian-Ukrainian war and chose instead to be guided by the maxim *Si vis pacem para bellum* ('If you want peace, prepare for war').

New Zealand is far from Poland (about 17,000 kilometres), yet its authorities and inhabitants are, and should be, interested in what is happening in Central and Eastern Europe.

NEW ZEALAND CURRENTLY FACES NO threats of aggression or annexation of its territory. However, if the system based on international law collapses, there may be a state that wishes to make claims against New Zealand, if not for possession of its territory, then for control and deprivation of its sovereignty. Geographical isolation in itself is not an absolute guarantee of safety; in 1917 the German auxiliary cruiser *Wolf* laid sea mines off the coast, which sank two ships, and its on-board seaplane flew over New Zealand territory.[14]

New Zealand is known as a 'small state' or 'small nation', axioms that are frequently present in statements by New Zealand politicians and officials.[15] Anita Wan suggests that the country depends on the international community, particularly larger countries, for its economic and environmental security.[16] As Jeanne Hey suggests, its policy may be characterised, among other things, by an emphasis on moral values in international policy, legal order, the importance of international institutions, and relying on powers for protection.[17]

New Zealand's primary determinant of its international role is its identity, which consists of historical, political, economic, social and cultural factors.[18] As a small state, it describes its role as that of a 'good international citizen'. One of its tools for this role is the New Zealand Defence Force (NZDF), which is tasked with supporting international order based on law. And it is precisely for the observance of this key principle of international order that the Russian-Ukrainian war is being fought. That is why it is also New Zealand's war, not just 'other people's war'. It explains why New Zealanders are helping Ukrainians to defend themselves by training their soldiers and providing other support, and why three New Zealanders (at 21 March 2023) were killed in the war on Ukraine's territory. It is also why the minister of defence paid a visit to Kyiv in July 2022.

In the course of intensifying great-power competition, the New Zealand authorities (and the nation) will have to make a choice about the scale of aid to be provided. It will no longer be possible to be simply a 'good international citizen'. The core values of international order based on law will have to be safeguarded by force, and New Zealand must contribute. We know New Zealand can do this — after all, the country did not shy away from contributing during the First and Second World Wars, as well as at the beginning of the Cold War, when it was to be prepared to field divisions for operations in the Middle East. It did so actively in Southeast Asia, for example during the Vietnam War. It would not be out of the ordinary for New Zealand to once again embark on the path of being a strong, reliable partner, an ally of the West and thus of the United States.

The country's previous efforts secured economic prosperity, a good image on the international stage and strong relations with selected partners. However, New Zealand must now contribute to the defence of the international system based on law in the conditions of global competition for power, in which contenders are willing to undermine the system in order to achieve their goals.

Just as Poland gained importance for the US after 24 February 2022, New Zealand can play the role of the security guardian for the South Pacific and provide strength there when needed. Surely it is better to prepare for this before being forced to do so. In order to contribute to military operations, however, the NZDF needs greater capabilities.

THE SLOGAN 'NEW ZEALAND PUNCHES above its weight' is fashionable in this country and is used in many contexts from politics to sport. It may be revolutionary to say that New Zealand does not need to punch *above* its weight; it can enter a higher weight class and box with others as an equal. As already mentioned, self-perception is key here: if New

Zealand revises its idea of being a 'small nation', the state will have enough resources to cope with the challenge. That this is worthwhile is supported by Greg Alnutt who, in 2012, answered the question of why New Zealand sends troops abroad:[19]

- To be seen as a 'good citizen of the international community' and to protect trade routes;
- To establish relationships with other countries; and
- To protect a democratic centre-right or left-wing government, good infrastructure and social security, education for children and a crisis response system.

Such a state is worth defending, not only for patriotic reasons but also for living standards. There is no better way to defend these values than by stopping the expansion of imperialism that may one day reach New Zealand's borders. Therefore, there is a need to change policy, including strengthening relations with the US, Australia, the UK and other countries, such as those of Central and Eastern Europe. All this requires greater investment in the NZDF.

Can New Zealand afford it? A similar question was asked for many years in Poland until there was no other way out. Pragmatic New Zealanders should not wait until such a situation arises but prepare for it by developing niche defence skills to offer to the West, such as in the field of special operations or image reconnaissance.

Table 2 examines New Zealand's defence spending in comparison with that of other small countries. The countries are selected on the basis of GDP per capita for 2021, according to the World Bank. The comparison is made with the first seven small countries with higher incomes and the next seven with lower incomes than New Zealand (so that the difference each way is about $20,000).

Based on this data, it can be concluded that New Zealand's defence spending is at a similar level to countries with higher per capita incomes, but has the smallest number of soldiers. At the same time, unlike Sweden or the Netherlands, it does not have a combat air force, nor does it maintain conscription or extensive territorial defence, like Finland does. Therefore, if it increases troop numbers and introduces the necessary weapons into service, it will enter a higher weight. Of the countries that

Table 2: New Zealand's defence spending in comparison with other small countries[1]

State	GDP per capita 2021 (US$)	Defence spending 2014–21 (% GDP)	Armed forces personnel 2019 (last published)
Denmark	68,007.8	1.1 → 1.4	15,000
Sweden	61,028.7	1.1 → 1.3	15,000
Netherlands	57,767.9	1.2 → 1.4	41,000
Finland	53,654.8	1.5 → 2	27,000
Austria	53,637.7	0.7 → 0.8	22,000
Belgium	51,247.0	1 → 1.1	26,000
New Zealand	48,781.0	1 → 1.4	9000
Malta	33,486.7	0.5 → 0.5	2000
Cyprus	31,551.8	1.5 → 2	16,000
Slovenia	29,291.4	1 → 1.2	7000
Estonia	27,943.7	1.9 → 2.2	7000
Czech Republic	26,821.2	1 → 1.4	25,000
Portugal	24,567.5	1.8 → 2.1	52,000

are poorer per capita, only two spend less, and three maintain smaller armed forces. Some of them have a combat air force and many have heavy equipment.

Taking this into account, it can be assumed that New Zealand can afford more spending and stronger armed forces, both quantitatively and qualitatively. The remaining problem is the will of the public, who must agree to it. In Poland and Lithuania, such a will materialised when citizens felt themselves in great danger from Russian imperialism. However, the more distant a threat is, the less it is felt; this can be seen in Western European countries, which have been much slower to strengthen their defence capabilities.

However, there are some countries whose nations understand the nature of the threat and the need to pursue a long-term defence strategy. The best examples in Europe are Estonia, Norway and Finland (although in Finland the economic crisis at the turn of the second decade of the twenty-first century led to a reduction in defence spending and a decline in capabilities). These nations maintain a high level of spending and pursue a policy of deterrence based on comprehensive defence.

The mechanism whereby an increased sense of threat engenders consent to an increase in military power, and the costs associated with it, is familiar to New Zealanders from the First and Second World Wars. New Zealanders prepared for the First World War with territorial-based training, and recorded its greatest defence numbers (and strength) in 1943 during the Second World War, when the country had some 60,000 territorial defence soldiers and 700 tanks of various types. This number later decreased in favour of soldiers of the expeditionary corps fighting outside the country.[20]

Prevention of the outbreak of a third world war today may well depend on the approach that the commander of the territorial defence forces in Poland, Brigadier General Maciej Klisz, calls 'R2D2' — 'resilience, resistance and deterrence, defence'.[21] New Zealand can also apply this approach and choose the political path of a Western country whose existence and wealth depends on compliance with the existing principles of the law-based system.

THE FACT THAT THE ONGOING Russian-Ukrainian war, and a coalition of authoritarian states wanting to change the existing international law-based order, threatens New Zealand is best demonstrated by Russian propaganda. In his speech to the United Nations on 14 March 2023, historian Timothy Snyder cited the following examples of the dehumanisation of Ukrainians:

> We see this when Russian state television presents Ukrainians as pigs. We see this when Russian state television presents Ukrainians as parasites. We see this when Russian state television presents Ukrainians as worms. We see this when Russian state television presents Ukrainians as Satanists or as ghouls. We see this when Russian state television proclaims that Ukrainian children should be drowned. We see this when Russian state television proclaims that Ukrainian houses should be burned with the people inside. We see this when people appear on Russian state television and say: 'They should not exist at all. We should execute them by firing squad.' We see this when someone appears on Russian state television and says, 'We will kill 1 million, we will kill 5 million, we can exterminate all of you,' meaning all of the Ukrainians.[22]

One could put Finns, Estonians, Poles, Czechs, Belgians or New Zealanders in place of Ukrainians in this quote. To prevent this, it is necessary to stop the aggressor, and anyone who would like to follow in their footsteps, as quickly as possible. New Zealand is a wise and pragmatic nation, able to draw conclusions from the experience of others — not only Poland, but also Lithuania (which had to catch up in defence policy quickly after 2014) or Estonia (which pursued a balanced defence policy despite the economic crisis).

Poland is a frontline country, a leader in helping Ukraine, who would not be able to continue its defence without this assistance. Poland offers opportunities for beneficial cooperation from New Zealand. One of these is in the field of special operations. Poland's GROM Special Mission Unit, like the New Zealand SAS, is ranked among the best units in the world and is known for its recent evacuation operations in Afghanistan, and for VIP protection in Poland and Ukraine during the Russian-Ukrainian war. Another area of opportunity is territorial defence, developed effectively in Poland since 2017, and which in 2022 grew to 36,000 soldiers despite the recruitment difficulties occurring in Western societies (and well known to New Zealand).

I believe the time has come for New Zealand to become an unequivocal ally of the West, understood as a bloc of democratic countries facing authoritarian and dictatorial governments that are trying to change the world for the worse. With all its flaws, the US-led order gives us better opportunities for development than the Russian or Chinese order. New Zealand should be able to take responsibility for the security of the South Pacific; make a significant contribution to operations in Europe and South-East Asia; and act as responsibly as it did during the First and Second World Wars, with the difference now of having the power to prevent another 'great war'. The decision to take this responsibility is a natural consequence of New Zealand's actions to support Ukraine in 2022–23.

17.

SELF-DETERMINATION OR TERRITORIAL INTEGRITY?

▌ Mixed messages from the Ukraine war

Rouben Azizian

Russia's invasion of Ukraine has sparked the largest conflict in Europe since the Second World War, and its repercussions continue to reverberate around the world.[1] A recent Chatham House report lists seven ways Russia's war on Ukraine has changed the world. These include shifting alliances, security redrawing, nuclear risks, energy and food challenges, questions about Russia's survival and future Ukraine, as well as international legal consequences.[2]

These issues are having an immediate impact on international security and are regularly discussed and debated by experts and scholars. What has been receiving less attention, however, but which is starting to loom on the horizon, is the effect of the war in Ukraine on historical tensions between the principles of self-determination and territorial integrity, both in the post-Soviet space and beyond.

Initially, before and immediately after the Russian invasion, the issues of sovereignty and self-determination were very much the focus of international attention, including in New Zealand. Speaking to Parliament's Foreign Affairs, Defence and Trade Select Committee on 17 February 2022, a week before the full-scale Russian attack, Chris Seed, the Ministry of Foreign Affairs and Trade (MFAT) chief executive, stated that at the heart of the Russia-Ukraine confrontation were the issues of sovereignty and self-determination.

'There is no question in our mind that this is one of the most significant security challenges and risks to international peace and security since the end of the Cold War,' he told the members of New Zealand Parliament. 'As a small state we cannot abide the idea that large countries assert their interest by invading small ones or indeed, any country invading any other.'[3] 'Aotearoa New Zealand strongly supports Ukraine's sovereignty and territorial integrity,' tweeted Minister of Foreign Affairs Nanaia Mahuta two days before the invasion.[4] The Ukrainian struggle also resonates with the self-determination aspirations of some Māori. The Green Party's co-leader, Marama Davidson, expressed confidence that 'Māori will rally behind the people of Ukraine as they face up to the Russian invasion'. 'Māori understand what it is to be forced to defend whenua,' she added.[5]

Despite their mutual hostilities and confrontational relations, both Russia and Ukraine consider self-determination as the key driving force of the conflict, even if they disagree about the subjects of their individual self-determination struggle. In his declaration of war, President Putin stated that 'circumstances require us to take decisive and immediate action. The People's Republics of Donbass turned to Russia with a request for help. I decided to conduct a special military operation. Its goal is to protect people who have been subjected to bullying and genocide by the Kyiv regime for eight years.'[6]

According to Ukrainian scholar Yuliya Yurchenko, 'reducing this war to conflict between the West and Russia overlooks Ukraine and treats it as a mere pawn between powers. That analysis denies Ukrainians our subjectivity and our agency in the conflict. It also suppresses discussion of our right to self-determination and our fight for national liberation.'[7]

WHILE SOME NATIONAL GOVERNMENTS AND interested parties view the Ukraine conflict as a legitimate anti-imperialist and anti-colonial struggle against Russia in the context of self-determination, others consider Ukraine's response to Russia's invasion as a reassertion of territorial integrity. This is interpreted by some as a justified response to separatist tendencies and by others as an unwelcome violation of legitimate ethnic Russian rights. Self-determination and territorial integrity are often seen as opposites, but it is different in Ukraine as the country claims both rights — of territorial integrity and self-determination.[8] At the same time, Russia denies self-determination for Ukraine but insists on self-determination of Russians in Crimea and Donbas.[9]

This ambiguity and the interwovenness have sent mixed messages across the globe, with various parties using them to advance their narrow political interests. In some cases, this has even led to splits and disagreements within political movements. For example, Benny Wenda, the interim president of the United Liberation Movement of West Papua (ULMWP), claimed that West Papuans feel a special affinity with the Ukrainian people; he accused the international community of remaining silent about more than half a century of conflict in West Papua.[10]

At the same time, spokesperson for ULMWP, Sebby Sambom, criticised Indonesia for joining 140 other countries in condemning Russia and demanding that Russian forces in Ukraine withdraw immediately. According to Sambom, both Indonesia and Ukraine are 'evil countries' and 'stooges of American capitalists': 'Russia's attack on Ukraine is natural and reasonable because the Ukrainian government, through its military and police forces, carried out genocide against indigenous people [likely referring to the Russian minorities] in two regions that wanted their own independence.'[11]

The definition and exercise of the right to national self-determination, sovereignty and territorial integrity have always been problematic. In the early 2020s, there are approximately 200 sovereign states in the world. Most have achieved sovereign status as a result of the collapse of empires. As a consequence, a new geopolitical world order was established on the basis of state sovereignty and territorial integrity. The United Nations reinforced this consensus through a series of resolutions.[12]

The UN Charter clarifies two meanings of the term 'self-determination'. First, a state is said to have the right of self-determination in the sense of having the right to choose freely its political, economic, social and cultural systems. Second, the right to self-determination is defined as the right of a people to constitute itself in a state or otherwise freely determine the form of its association with an existing state. Both meanings have their basis in the Charter (Article 1, paragraph 2; and Article 55, paragraph 1).[13]

In practice, self-determination has ranged from secession and granting independence to a people from the parent state (external self-determination) through to granting a people — a national minority — the right to self-government or autonomy within the confines of their parent state (internal self-determination). Although there is no official stance on what self-determination entails, the right to secession has been strongly discouraged under international law to protect the territorial integrity and political unity of existing states.[14]

The right of 'self-determination of the people' is a double-edged sword. It has been used by postcolonial nations to reclaim their territories and economy. The idea has also been exploited by powerful countries to divide the world on ethnic and religious lines to advance their influence through humanitarian interventions.[15]

While the Ukraine war reminds us that state-to-state conflict is a phenomenon that continues to be present, the majority of conflicts have occurred internally within existing states. Empirical studies demonstrate that since 1945, more than 70 per cent of wars have been intrastate rather than interstate in origin; moreover, intrastate wars have comprised more than 90 per cent of all international conflicts since the early 1990s.[16]

Separating the intra-state and state-to-state conflicts is, however, becoming more problematic as we are witnessing the rise of geopolitics and major power rivalry. According to Uppsala Conflict Data Program (2020), internal conflicts are increasingly taking on international dimensions, as regional and international powers back different sides and directly contribute troops and materiel.[17]

THE RUSSIAN INVASION OF UKRAINE triggers a spectrum of worldwide scenarios in which the intersection of self-determination ambitions and external geopolitical interests could spark a new wave of conflict, civil unrest and instability. Apart from the Baltic states, the post-Soviet nation-building is still incomplete. Most of the former Soviet republics experience significant economic or strategic dependence on Russia. While attempting to free themselves from Russia's dominance based on their aspiration for self-determination, three of them, namely Moldova, Georgia and Azerbaijan, are in the process of dealing with self-determination movements from their own minorities. Russia itself has a federal system that includes more than 20 autonomous ethnic regions.

There is a list of active separatist movements in Asia-Pacific, too. Myanmar is one, where ethnic self-determination, political confrontation and geopolitical rivalry are interwoven. The geopolitical factor enabled Sri Lanka to suppress the separatist Tamil Tigers, but the Tamil self-determination problem hasn't been resolved. West Papua's independence movement in Indonesia remains active and is increasingly supported by the Melanesian states. The Association of Southeast Asian Nations' (ASEAN) very cautious position on the war in Ukraine is dictated not only by the members' geopolitical balancing but also by the fear of opening the 'Pandora's box' of numerous separatist movements.

According to the Chatham House report, all ASEAN countries value the principle of national sovereignty above almost everything, but they see the best way to protect that sovereignty is to avoid entanglements in wider international affairs. For ASEAN, sovereignty is much easier to defend at home than abroad.[18]

These examples demonstrate how vulnerable and fragile many states in the post-Soviet space — as well as the Asia-Pacific region — are when it comes to fulfilling the dual mission of the state: to protect national sovereignty and territorial integrity and, at the same time, ensure the rights of ethnic minorities.

THE RUSSIAN CONCEPT OF SELF-DETERMINATION for the regions it has annexed in Ukraine suggests a forceful path forward for other territories claiming self-determination. It can be argued that the Russian moves may effectively steer international law in a new direction that equates self-determination with secession. According to Loqman Radpey, Russia's challenge could spur various national groups and incite the re-emergence of historical conflicts rooted in language, race and religion.[19] This could aggravate existing conflicts between and within states.

Post-Soviet Central Asia could become one of the regions most affected by Moscow's actions. There is still a large Russian population in northern Kazakhstan along the border with Russia. During the 1990s, a small but vocal group of them called for the Russian annexation of areas in northern Kazakhstan, similar to the situation in Donetsk and Luhansk in Ukraine.[20] Russian officials, including President Putin, have said publicly that there never was such a thing as a Kazakh state.[21] Another potential hotbed for separatism in Central Asia is Karakalpakstan in western Uzbekistan, where some have been calling for independence for 30 years; and Tajikistan's far eastern Gorno-Badakhshan region, where many would at least like greater autonomy from the Tajik government.[22]

The West's selective approach to the notion of self-determination has also become the subject of concern and criticism. Alexander Hill argues that in the recent past the West has proven willing to support the 'right' to self-determination of minorities within larger entities where there has been a degree of Western hostility towards the larger of the two. However, where the 'big' guy is deemed to be the 'good' guy, self-determination for the smaller entity can often be all but thrown out of the window, as in the case of Israel and the Palestinians. According to Hill, such double standards have already undermined Western credibility in the Middle East, but the double standards at play over the war in Ukraine threaten to undermine it even further.[23]

VLADIMIR PUTIN'S ATTACK ON UKRAINE has revived discussions about whether Russia needs to be 'decolonised', or perhaps 'defederalised', to bury its imperialist ambitions and subdue its military threat. A break-up of today's Russia is seen as a possible — for some even the most desirable — outcome of a failed Ukraine invasion.[24] Putin's authoritarianism and centralisation have created real tensions between the regions and Moscow — tensions that have become magnified by the war in Ukraine. Soldiers with roots in poorer regions are disproportionately represented among Russian casualties in the war.[25]

In a 2023 Atlantic Council report 40 per cent of experts surveyed 'expect Russia to break up internally by 2033 because of revolution, civil war, political disintegration, or some other reason'. Twenty-one per cent, the largest number of respondents, believed that Russia was the country 'most likely to become a failed state within the next ten years'.[26]

A small but growing lobby in Europe and the United States is making the case for the break-up of the Russian Federation. Advocates of this position also draw the analogy with the collapse of the Soviet Union. They argue the same thing could happen to the Russian Federation, which occupies 60 per cent of the territory of the Soviet Union and governs over 190 ethnic groups inside the federation. Such arguments were advanced at a meeting in Brussels on 31 January 2023, convened by the European Conservatives and Reform group in the European Parliament. They called for the creation of 34 new states on the territory of the Russian Federation.[27]

However, there are no signs of the Russian Federation breaking up in the foreseeable future. While Russians accounted for only 51 per cent of the Soviet population, they make up over 80 per cent of the Russian Federation's inhabitants. They constitute the majority ethnic group in most of the 21 ethnically designated republics.[28]

Finally, parallels between the Soviet collapse and the supposed imminent end of Russia are legally incompatible. For one thing, the USSR fell apart because its constitution granted the country's constituent republics a formal right to secede from the union, which they chose to exercise when the political winds made it possible in the late 1980s. One of the reasons why Moscow could not prevent the USSR dissolving was because when the Soviet republics declared independence, they were applying a legal power they clearly possessed. By contrast, Russia's federal subjects don't have a comparable constitutional right to secession.[29]

But if the spark does come, would a likely Russian collapse be destabilising and violent, and perhaps involve civil war? Former US Secretary of State Henry Kissinger has argued that 'the dissolution of Russia or destroying its ability for strategic policy could turn its territory encompassing 11 time zones into a contested vacuum'. Russian groups might turn on each other and use violence, while outside powers could use force to expand their claims. 'All these dangers would be compounded by the presence of thousands of nuclear weapons,' Kissinger wrote. The best course of action, he advised, would be to avoid rendering Russia 'impotent by the war', instead including Russia in a 'peace process'.[30]

Other realist thinkers in the West believe that even if Russia fractured without a nuclear catastrophe along the way, there's little reason to think this would be to the geostrategic benefit of the United States, which faces a far more formidable challenge in a rising China.[31]

THE MIXED MESSAGES AND INTERPRETATIONS from the war in Ukraine have not only triggered renewed calls for self-determination but have also enhanced attempts by several governments and regimes to reclaim territorial integrity. Some of the responses and actions in that regard have raised an alarm. China's 12-point plan for political settlement of the Ukraine crisis demonstrates sympathy for Russia and accuses the West of triggering the Ukraine crisis. Its first point, however, urges respect for the 'territorial integrity of all countries'.[32] Obviously, Beijing has been using the Ukraine war to increase its pressure on Taiwan, which has led to international fears of an invasion of the island by the Chinese People's Liberation Army.

In Myanmar, Russia's Ukraine campaign and international reactions are being watched closely. Democracy activists and ethnic groups see parallels between the Russian invasion and their own oppression and lack of self-determination. Countries such as Japan, Singapore and South Korea, which support sanctions against Russia and Belarus but have not adopted sanctions against Myanmar, are coming under increasing criticism.[33]

At the United Nations General Assembly emergency session on Ukraine on 2 March 2022, the Philippines condemned the 'use of separatism and secession as a weapon of diplomacy' — in part a reference to its own difficulties with ongoing insurgency in Mindanao.[34]

As Russia's military power and prestige collapse due to losses and defeats in Ukraine, Russia's ability to control frozen conflicts and tensions elsewhere in the lands of the former Soviet Union is also deteriorating, and there is a serious danger that these conflicts will reignite. Russia's influence in the former Soviet space has not been as uniformly negative as the invasion of Ukraine has suggested; in parts of that region Russia has acted to maintain peace and stability. The effects of this can already be seen in the flare-up of fighting between Azerbaijan and Armenia, now inadequately kept in check by Russian peacekeepers.[35]

In his speech to the Armenian National Assembly, the country's prime minister, Nikol Pashinyan, admitted that having lost faith in Russia's protection and under pressure from the international community Armenia was prepared to recognise the territorial integrity of Azerbaijan.[36] He warned, however, that a lack of strict international guarantees to protect the Armenian population in Nagorno-Karabakh, which would be ruled by authoritarian Azerbaijan, could lead to a new wave of violence. Unfortunately, and tragically, that is what ensued during September 2023. From December 2022, Azerbaijan started progressively closing the Lachin corridor, the only crossing point between Armenia and Nagorno-Karabakh, cutting off access to food, medicine and fuel for the population of the enclave.[37]

On 19 September 2023, Azerbaijan launched a so called 'anti-terrorist operation' in the disputed region in order to 'restore constitutional order'.

At the same time, it opened the Lachin corridor, essentially forcing a mass deportation of the demoralised and physically exhausted Armenian population who feared possible atrocities from the invading Azerbaijani military. In a matter of a week, almost the entire Armenian population of around 120,000 had fled Nagorno-Karabakh to Armenia, creating a huge humanitarian crisis. Russian peacekeepers who were present around the enclave took no action to prevent the restart of the hostilities.[38] While the Western leaders described Azerbaijan's strangulation strategy, aimed at provoking mass emigration of Armenians from Nagorno-Karabakh as illegal and immoral, they took no concrete action to stop it, most likely not to endanger Azerbaijan's energy supplies to Europe at a time when Europe is reducing its energy dependence on Russian energy. This inaction by the EU was recognised and condemned in the resolution of the European Parliament of 5 October 2023.[39]

Radical groups in Georgia, emboldened by the Ukrainian struggle for its territorial integrity, are urging the government to retake by force the territories of South Ossetia and Abkhazia, lost in the 2008 war with Russia. Some of these voices belong to Georgian volunteers fighting with the Ukrainians. '[W]e Georgians who have been fighting for freedom in Ukraine are also ready to fight for the freedom of Georgia,' stated a spokesperson for the Georgian fighting unit. 'Therefore, we urge you to take up arms and strike at the enemy. We will never have such a chance again.'[40] Such statements not only provoke Russia but also neglect the damaging impact of earlier Georgian nationalism towards the two breakaway regions.

The Quincy Institute for Responsible Statecraft Report urges the Biden administration not to drive Russian influence from the southern Caucasus and, in particular, not to encourage Georgia to resume war for the reconquest of Abkhazia and South Ossetia.[41]

WHERE THEN DOES NEW ZEALAND stand in this? The Ukraine war has driven a revival of debates on sovereignty and self-determination and requires a reassessment of New Zealand's perspectives and role in these matters. There are several tiers and mechanisms of New Zealand's involvement in self-determination matters, both internally and externally. They include obligations under the Treaty of Waitangi, the UN Charter, the Biketawa Declaration of the Pacific Islands Forum, and

New Zealand's declared support for rules-based order and protection of international human rights.

New Zealand is accountable to the United Nations for exercising the self-determination rights of its indigenous population. The United Nations Declaration on the Rights of Indigenous Peoples was adopted by the General Assembly in September 2007 after many years of negotiation. The New Zealand government's support for the declaration was announced in April 2010. In its statement of support, the government recognised the 'long involvement of Māori in the elaboration of the declaration and the extent of their investment in its development'. Importantly, for the arguments in this chapter, the declaration is clear that the right to self-determination does not compromise the territorial integrity of member states.[42] The lack of public awareness in New Zealand of the country's obligations under the United Nations Declaration on the Rights of Indigenous Peoples is unfortunate, given the heated debate on co-governance in New Zealand, and the concerns raised in some political circles that co-governance could effectively lead to Māori take-over or separatism.[43]

New Zealand also has obligations under Article 73 of the UN Charter to develop Tokelau's self-government. Tokelau has been on the United Nations list of non-self-governing territories, following the declaration of the intention by New Zealand to transmit information on the Tokelau Islands under Article 73 of the Charter.[44] In accordance with its obligations, New Zealand has progressively devolved its administrative powers to Tokelau over the past three decades, supporting the territory's development of its own governance institutions. The key priority of MFAT's Tokelau Four Year Plan (October 2021) is to strengthen the territory's effective governance 'because transparent, accountable, capable, inclusive and democratic government systems are important enablers of positive, resilient development'.[45]

The debate about the status of Tokelau as a non-self-governing territory of New Zealand has been revived by its Parliament, the Tokelau General Fono, and plans are afoot to mark 100 years of colonial supervision by finally deciding its future by 2025/26. In Tokelau's case, the three options for becoming 'decolonised' would be: full independence (which Sāmoa achieved in 1962); in free association with New Zealand (which Niue gained in 1974 and the Cook Islands in 1965); or fully integrating with New Zealand (like the Chatham Islands).[46]

NEW ZEALAND HAS BEEN ACTIVELY involved in mitigating conflicts in the Pacific driven by ethnic strife and self-determination through efforts such as the Regional Assistance Mission to the Solomon Islands (RAMSI) and the Lincoln Agreement on Peace Security and Development on Bougainville. The situation both in the Solomon Islands and Papua New Guinea continues to be contentious and could require New Zealand's participation again in the future. The recent injection of the geopolitical factor indicated in the controversial China-Solomon Islands security agreement confirms the earlier-mentioned findings of the Uppsala Conflict Data Program 2020 in terms of the externalisation of internal conflicts.

The situation in New Caledonia requires significant attention, too. After the rejection of full sovereignty in three referendums and the expiry of the Nouméa Accord, a new statute for New Caledonia has to be created. While the pro-independence parties want Paris to give a timetable to full independence, the anti-independence parties want Paris to realign the territory with France.[47]

There is also a growing national and regional criticism of the New Zealand government's stance on self-determination of West Papua. In the 1950s New Zealand supported the self-determination for the former Dutch colony, but in 1962 opted to back Indonesia as it took over the territory. A number of Pacific governments have taken up the cause and made strong representations at the UN General Assembly, but New Zealand has so far refused to be part of this advocacy.

In her book *See No Evil: New Zealand's betrayal of the people of West Papua*, Maire Leadbeater writes that the consequences of repressive Indonesian rule have been tragic for the West Papuan people, who are experiencing 'slow genocide'. Although West Papua remains largely closed to foreign journalists, its story is now beginning to be heard. A growing number of Pacific Island nations are calling for change, but so far New Zealand has opted for caution and collusion to preserve a 'business as usual' relationship with Indonesia.[48]

As well, the New Zealand government has been under increasing pressure both domestically and from international allies to take a stronger stance on the situation in China's Xinjiang region. While the government has expressed 'grave concerns about the growing number of credible reports of severe human rights abuses against ethnic Uyghurs and other Muslim minorities in Xinjiang', it refused to join Britain, Canada and the US in calling the abuses a 'genocide'.[49] So far, the New Zealand government has been attempting to balance its human rights commitments with the demands of its largest trade partner — China.

And finally, New Zealand's treatment of its indigenous people and ethnic minorities has historically been inconsistent and problematic. Although in international public opinion the country ranks higher than some of its Western partners in that regard, New Zealand's ability to successfully manage its own internal cultural and ethnic challenges would make its international moral standing even stronger.[50]

RUSSIAN PRESIDENT VLADIMIR PUTIN'S USE of military force against Ukraine has attacked sovereignty and self-determination, the twin pillars of post-war liberal international order.[51] Hopefully, Ukraine's legitimate struggle to assert its sovereignty and regain territorial integrity will not have a one-dimensional international effect through prioritisation of territorial integrity without the recognition of legitimate self-determination rights. An absolutist position on territorial integrity is as dangerous and damaging as a self-determination narrowly defined as secession. The recent tragic developments in Nagorno-Karabakh, discussed earlier, should become a strong warning sign in that context. Looking at the situation with nuance is often the only real way to approach a true solution or more often a mitigation.[52]

The tension between territorial integrity and self-determination is likely to increase due to the existence of authoritarian regimes and increased global geopolitical rivalry. The threat to international peace and security will continue as long as the sovereignty of states is not considered equal in practice as well as in law. New Zealand has a responsibility and opportunity to promote good national and international governance based on respect for both the rules-based order and human rights. A consistent informed thinking about the tension between sovereignty and self-determination must be a part of our approach to both domestic and international politics.

Conclusion

CONSTRUCTING RESILIENCE AND HOPE

How can we challenge the feeling of insecurity?

Deidre Ann McDonald & Wil Hoverd

In the introduction we proposed that over the last five years Aotearoa New Zealand has shifted from a benign national security environment to a threatening one. Now that we have assessed the volume's evidence, let us examine that proposition. The Ukraine war provides strong evidence that there has been a shift from a rules-based international order to an order forming around great power blocs, some of which are authoritarian. Global free-market capitalism is being complicated by a turn to economic blocs, trade wars, sanctions, inflation and supply chain issues. Economic security is a significant issue, suggesting that trade will shift from efficient globalism to a focus on resilience.

We see seven rationales underpinning the proposition that a shift has occurred. First, we begin with the assumption that we need to be careful around voices of security because they can easily slip into a language of hyperbole that may exaggerate threat. However, the book's essays resoundingly see threat and the need for Aotearoa to secure itself carefully to contribute proactively as an international rules-based player. Second, war has come and NATO is supporting Ukraine. Third, the spectre of war, stemming from China, Aotearoa's largest trading partner, looms over Taiwan. Fourth, New Zealand is perhaps being asked to take a side by joining AUKUS as a Pillar 2 member state. Fifth, our institutions (particularly the NZDF) and economy are currently degraded; shortages and poverty are potential drivers of conflict. Sixth, the Christchurch mosque attacks and the Wellington protest, while very different events, both demonstrate that, domestically, we are not immune from violence and require significant internal policing, intelligence and counter-terrorism apparatus with effective oversight to keep us safe. Seventh, our geographic isolation and border do not protect us from biosecurity threats, terrorism, cyberattacks and pandemics.

An important aspect of security that this book touches upon indirectly is the reality of climate change for Aotearoa. We know that climate change is an existential threat to life on Earth, and that this meteorological wildcard will amplify other security conundrums. The climate itself is already becoming a global threat actor (of the non-malicious variety), manifesting in violent storms, floods, fires and droughts. The consequences are homelessness, loss of life, industry and property, widespread destruction and long-term community ruptures. We can only expect more, and more intense, climatic events in the near future. For a country that relies heavily on agricultural, horticultural and forestry exports for its economic security, climate change directly challenges our environmental and economic resilience.

Together, these factors suggest that Aotearoa's national security environment has changed, and not for the better. Our view is not necessarily that the world is more threatening: this hyperbolic statement suggests a fight or flight option is the only sane response. There are distinct differences between how the public perceives threat and how governments calculate threat. The chapters outline evolving security complexities in which threat language and the feeling of being threatened are part of that landscape.

In the introduction we mentioned that public national security discourse tells us what we should be concerned about. It evokes emotion. In this vein, we suggest that Aotearoa feels less secure than it did in 2018. The questions then become for all of us: 'What can we do to be more resilient in the face of this feeling?' and 'Where and how do we best invest scarce resources to build our resilience?' In an evolving security environment, there is a need for more public discussion on how we spend on defence and national security, why we need to spend, and what we want to generate from that spend.

Those questions lead us to ask what we value, as a society and as individuals, because collective social values often inform what individuals are willing to protect. These values also help set the government's financial priorities, such as how much money the NZDF receives or where to focus covert surveillance activities. Time and again we have seen that New Zealanders will act to uphold their country's values, both on and offshore. They will protest when they feel it matters, whether against racial apartheid, nuclear testing in the Pacific or the illegal confiscation of indigenous whenua. Some will risk their lives to support people overseas whom they have never met, and others will mobilise to form human chains outside mosques to protect worshippers from harm. New Zealanders have a long history of standing up when they think it is right to do so.

Of course, there are steps we can take to invest in Aotearoa and make it resilient. We can work on closing the socioeconomic gaps between the richest and the poorest. We can invest in diplomacy, particularly preventative diplomacy — the strengthening of our regional and global institutions — and we can continue to invest in the Pacific and be a trustworthy partner. We can act honestly and in good faith with all our international partners.

Domestically, we need to recognise and affirm freedom of speech, with the understanding that when that speech turns to hatred, misogyny or violence it is no longer acceptable. We must be able to converse with each other about civics and have safe conversations about difficult topics. Our populations need to be able to see multiple sides of arguments and be able to put themselves in the shoes of the other. All of these actions create possibilities to bridge conflict and create solutions that focus on making all parties feel more secure, included and accepted.

Ultimately, too, we need to think about our national identity. Who are we? What sort of nation do we aspire to be? What does it mean to be a postcolonial nation? Are we the West? Are we a Pacific or an Asia-Pacific nation, or both? And how does or should that identity influence our security priorities? To reiterate, it matters who speaks about national security.

At the beginning of this book, readers were introduced to national security as a political and social construct made and understood through language, politics and people's lived experiences. If national security is constructed through these things, then it can be influenced and changed. We know that those constructing the meaning and value of security remain overwhelmingly white, educated and male, and that this elevated minority has both public and private platforms from which to speak about security on behalf of others. We have argued that there should be significant discomfort about leaving it up to a few to speak for the many, particularly about the security values of a socially and ethnically diverse nation that has grown up over layers of colonisation and loss. As if our own socio-political situation were not complex enough, it is imperative for national security that any community discomfort and/or disquiet be encouraged to surface. We already know that silence can be dangerous, even deadly, and that invisibility cannot be relied on to evidence an absence of threat.

The essays in this book have illustrated that national security is impactful for all New Zealanders, irrespective of whether they are involved in discussions about its priorities or not. A challenge for all is to identify the values that we will hold fast to in troubled times. Free speech, free movement, food security, democracy and the rule of law are some obvious democratic values, but what will you speak up for? And what will you stand against? Is it a growing disinformation subculture? Maybe the most pressing concern for your community is the presence of neo-racism or the perpetuation of online hatred. What can each of us do to keep this country socially and politically secure? We can commit to having ongoing and open conversations about the growing threats to our humanity.

This book contributes to that national security conversation by delving deeply into selected socio-political and geopolitical crises, whether they manifest as offshore or domestic threats to our security. We hope the essays offered will spark further discussions about national security, because these matters vitally encompass so many aspects of what it means to live in Aotearoa New Zealand, and indeed the world.

Notes

Introduction

1   William Hoverd, 'The Changing New Zealand National Security Environment: New threats, new structures, and new research', *National Security Journal* 1, no. 1 (2019): 17–34; William Hoverd, Nick Nelson & Carl Bradley (eds), *New Zealand National Security: Challenges, trends and issues* (Auckland: Massey University Press, 2017).

2   In 2014 Sir John Key argued that 'ISIL was a game-changer for New Zealand' and used this speech to rationalise the deployment of the NZDF to Iraq. See www.beehive.govt. nz/speech/speech-nz-institute-international-affairs; recent media commentary from experts with commercially related business owners engages regularly in hyperbole. Bryce Edwards discusses the Disinformation Project's Sanjana Hattotuwa's ongoing hyperbolic claims in Bryce Edwards, 'The need to take disinformation seriously', Democracy Project, 12 April 2023, https://democracyproject.nz/2023/04/12/bryce-edwards-the-need-to-take-disinformation-seriously/; Paul Buchanan owns 36th Parallel and is a regular media commentator on RNZ. Paul Buchanan, 'New Zealand must own this terrorist attack', *RNZ*, 20 March 2019, www.rnz.co.nz/news/on-the-inside/385167/paul-buchanan-new-zealand-must-own-this-terrorist-attack; 'Buchanan says he sounded alarm over disinformation in NZ', *RNZ*, 13 June 2023, www.rnz.co.nz/national/programmes/morningreport/audio/2018894129/buchanan-says-he-sounded-alarm-over-disinformation-in-nz

3   Edwards, 'The need to take disinformation seriously'.

4   Media coverage of the consequences of war or violence rarely shows the graphic nature of the implementation of power and violence.

5   See www.dpmc.govt.nz/our-business-units/national-security-group

6   Department of Prime Minister and Cabinet, 'Aide-Memoire to the Incoming Minister for National Security Intelligence', 25 January 2023, www.beehive.govt.nz/sites/default/files/2023-03/BIM%20-%20Minister%20for%20National%20Security%20and%20Intelligence.pdf

7   Ibid.

8   Ibid; Andrew Little, 'Intelligence and security in our changing world: Speech to the Victoria University of Wellington Centre for Strategic Studies', 4 November 2021, www.beehive.govt.nz/speech/intelligence-and-security-our-changing-world-speech-victoria-university-wellington-centre; Andrew Hampton, 'Understanding and Preparing for Cyber Threats relating to the Russian invasion of Ukraine: Speech by Director-General of the Government Communications Security Bureau Andrew Hampton to the Wairarapa branch of the New Zealand Institute of International Affairs', 19 May 2022, www.gcsb.govt.nz/news/the-cybersecurity-implications-of-the-russian-invasion-of-ukraine/

9   Andrew Little, 'New Zealand condemns malicious cyber activity by Chinese state-sponsored actors', 19 July 2021, www.beehive.govt.nz/release/new-zealand-condemns-malicious-cyber-activity-chinese-state-sponsored-actors; Patrick Wintour, 'New Zealand's stance on China has deep implications for the Five Eyes alliance', www.theguardian.com/world/2021/apr/23/new-zealands-stance-on-china-has-deep-implications-for-the-five-eyes-alliance; Stacey Kirk, 'Russia dominates PM Jacinda Ardern's talks in London, with UK calling Five Eyes meeting', www.stuff.co.nz/national/politics/103223973/prime-minister-jacinda-ardern-talks-security-trade-with-uks-theresa-may

10 Department of Prime Minister and Cabinet, *Aotearoa's National Security Strategy: Secure Together Tō Tātou Korowai Maanaki*, 4 August 2023.

11 Ibid., 1–4.

12 Anecdotally, there are always concerns that soundbites might be taken out of context by the Fourth Estate to sell a story. Certainly, this is the experience of one of the editors. Often media engagement is at odd hours, and/or academic experts feel uncomfortable speaking outside their area of expertise. Examples would be when specific opinion is requested on matters such as whether the NZSIS or police could have acted differently. This can lead to headlines that say 'Academic says that NZSIS/NZ Police should have . . .', which can be deeply unsettling. Sometimes there are consequences for being an expert. In the case of Professor Anne Marie Brady, there may have been consequences for being a critic

of Chinese policy. See Leith Huffadine, 'Professor Anne Marie Brady who warned about China interference, says car was sabotaged', *Stuff*, 16 November 2018, www.stuff.co.nz/national/108649435/professor-annemarie-brady-who-warned-about-china-interference-says-car-was-sabotaged. Quite simply, those who do talk to media are the ones who feel motivated to pick up the phone, which is why certain voices are heard and others are not.

13 Education Act 1987.

14 Steve Elers, Phoebe Elers & Mohan Dutta, 'Responding to White Supremacy: An analysis of Twitter messages by Māori after the Christchurch terrorist attack', in *Indigenous Peoples Rise Up*, Bronwyn Carlson & Jeff Berglund (New Brunswick: Rutgers University Press, 2021), 65–79.

15 Harley Williamson & Kristina Murphy, 'Animus Toward Muslims and Its Association with Public Support for Punitive Counter-terrorism Policies: Did the Christchurch terrorist attack mitigate this association?', *Journal of Experimental Criminology* (2020): 1–21.

16 Chris Wilson, 'Beating up the "Alt-Right"', *Newsroom*, 16 February 2023, www.newsroom.co.nz/beating-up-the-alt-right; Katie Scotcher, 'As police call-outs for mental health issues rise, the commissioner wants a new approach', *RNZ*, 19 November 2021, www.rnz.co.nz/news/national/456062/as-police-call-outs-for-mental-health-issues-rise-the-commissioner-wants-a-new-approach

17 See William Hoverd, 'Peace Action Protest and the NZDIA Annual Forum: Is it irreconcilable?', *Line of Defence*, 20 February 2019, https://defsec.net.nz/2019/02/20/nzdia-forum-protest

18 Pinar Temocin, 'From Protest to Politics: The effectiveness of civil society in shaping the nuclear-free policy in Aotearoa New Zealand', *Interface Journal of Social Movement* 13 (2021): 174–92.

19 'NZ-China Free Trade Agreement', Ministry of Foreign Affairs and Trade, www.mfat.govt.nz/en/trade/free-trade-agreements/free-trade-agreements-in-force/nz-china-free-trade-agreement/

20 Henry Cooke, 'New Zealand extends Iraq and Afghanistan deployments', *Stuff*, 17 September 2018, www.stuff.co.nz/national/politics/107149082/new-zealand-extends-iraq-and-afghanistan-deployments; Maj. Thomas D. Arnold & Maj. Nicolas Fiore, 'Five Operational Lessons from the Battle for Mosul', *Military Review*, January–February 2019, www.armyupress.army.mil/Journals/Military-Review/English-Edition-Archives/Jan-Feb-2019/Arnold-Mosul/; https://operationburnham.inquiry.govt.nz

21 Ben Leahy, 'Details of Kiwi Isis hostage Louisa Akavi's ordeal heard in US court', *New Zealand Herald*, 2 April 2022, www.nzherald.co.nz/nz/details-of-kiwi-isis-hostage-louisa-akavis-ordeal-heard-in-us-court/RCHDO23D62X5NWPRZZG35KEOGY; Bevan Hurley, 'Police build case against "bumbling Jihadi" Mark Taylor, but outdated anti-terrorism laws could see him walk free', *Stuff*, 13 October 2019, www.stuff.co.nz/national/116471644/police-build-case-against-bumbling-jihadi-mark-taylor-but-outdated-antiterrorism-laws-could-see-him-walk-free

22 Danielle Chubb, 'Perceptions of Terrorism in Australia: 1978–2019', *Australian Journal of International Affairs* 74, no. 3 (2020): 264–81.

23 Andrew Little, 'Government accepts findings of LynnMall supermarket rerror attack review', 14 December 2022, www.beehive.govt.nz/release/government-accepts-findings-lynnmall-supermarket-terror-attack-review

24 Cabinet External Relations and Security Committee, 'The Pacific Reset: The first year', 4 December 2018, www.mfat.govt.nz/assets/OIA/R-R-The-Pacific-reset-The-First-Year.PDF

25 Henryk Szadziewski, 'Converging Anticipatory Geographies in Oceania: The belt and road initiative and look north in Fiji', *Political Geography* 77 (2020): 102119.

26 Maria Giannacopoulos & Claire Loughnan, "Closure" at Manus Island and Carceral Expansion in the Open Air Prison', *Globalizations* 17, no. 7 (2020): 1118–35, https://doi.org/10.1080/14747731.2019.1679549

27 Henrietta McNeill & Marinella Marmo, 'Past–Present Differential Inclusion: Australia's targeted deportation of Pacific Islanders, 1901 to 2021', *International Journal for Crime, Justice and Social Democracy* 12, no. 1 (2023): 42–55, https://doi.org/10.5204/ijcjsd.2743; Gregory D. Breetzke et al., 'Gang Membership and Gang Crime in New Zealand: A national study identifying spatial risk factors', *Criminal Justice and Behaviour* 49, no. 8 (2022): 1154–72.

28 Jose Sousa-Santos & Loene M. Howes, 'Policing Illicit Drugs in the Pacific: The role of culture and community on the frontline', *Journal of Contemporary Criminal Justice* 38, no. 3 (2022): 364–79; Breetzke et al., 'Gang membership and gang crime in New Zealand'; Carl Bradley, 'Hells Angels, Head Hunters and the Filthy Few: The history of outlaw bikers in Aotearoa New Zealand', *Deviant Behavior* 43, no. 3 (2022): 271–84.

29 'Andrew Little addresses Massey University national security conference', *Line of Defence*, 20 July 2018, https://defsec.net.nz/2018/07/20/andrew-little-addresses-massey-university-national-security-conference/

30 Ministry of Defence, 'Responding to the climate crisis: An implementation plan', December 2019, www.defence.govt.nz/publications/publication/responding-to-the-climate-crisis

31 Ministry for Primary Industries, 'Phased eradication of *Mycoplasma bovis*', June 2018, www.mpi.govt.nz/dmsdocument/29303/send

32 Thomas O'Brien & Nicholas Huntington, '"Vaccine Passports Equal Apartheid": Covid-19 and parliamentary occupation in Aotearoa New Zealand', *Social Movement Studies* (2022): 1–7; 'Threats against Prime Minister Jacinda Ardern triple, according to report', *New Zealand Herald*, 12 June 2022, www.nzherald.co.nz/nz/threats-against-prime-minister-jacinda-ardern-triple-according-to-report/ESKHAL4HNASO6HQZ2IPPBEK3HA

33 Department of Prime Minister and Cabinet, *Aotearoa's National Security Strategy: Secure Together Tō Tātou Korowai Maanaki*, p. ii.

34 Christine Helen Elers & Pooja Jayan, '"This Is Us": Free speech embedded in whiteness, racism and coloniality in Aotearoa, New Zealand', *First Amendment Studies* 54, no. 2 (2020): 236–49.

35 Royal Commission of Inquiry into the Terrorist Attack on Christchurch Mosques on 15 March 2019, 'Part 2: Context', 8 December 2022, https://christchurchattack.royalcommission.nz/the-report/part-2-context/overview-of-the-national-security-system-intelligence-function-and-the-counter-terrorism-effort

36 New Zealand Government, 'New Zealand's Countering Terrorism and Violent Extremism Strategy', 2020, www.dpmc.govt.nz/sites/default/files/2021-10/New%20Zealands%20Countering%20Terrorism%20and%20Violent%20Extremism%20Strategy.pdf; H. Vanderberg & W. Hoverd, 'The Inconsistent Usage of the Terms "Extremism" and "Terrorism" around the Christchurch Mosque Attacks', *National Security Journal* 2, no. 1 (2020): 1–13, https://nationalsecurityjournal.nz/latest-issues-2021/the-inconsistent-usage-of-the-terms-extremism-and-terrorism-around-the-christchurch-mosque-attacks

37 Royal Commission of Inquiry into the Terrorist Attack on Christchurch Mosques on 15 March 2019.

38 William James Hoverd, Leon Salter & Kevin Veale, 'The Christchurch Call: Insecurity, democracy and digital media — can it really counter online hate and extremism?', *SN Social Sciences* 1, no. 1 (2020): 2.

39 Hoverd, 'The changing New Zealand national security environment'; Damien Rogers & Shaun Mawdsley, 'Restoring Public Trust and Confidence in New Zealand's Intelligence and Security Agencies: Is a Parliamentary commissioner for security the missing key?', *Policy Quarterly* 8, no. 1 (2022).

40 Andrew Little, 'Ministerial Statements — LynnMall Terror Attack', *Hansard*, 7 September 2021, www.parliament.nz/en/pb/hansard-debates/rhr/combined/HansDeb_20210907_20210907_08

41 Bethan K. Greener, 'The Role of the Military in New Zealand's Response to COVID', *The KCIS*, 7 September 2021, www.thekcis.org/publications/insights/insight-22

42 Jane Patterson, 'Defence force role in MIQ "reduces capability" to deal with major disaster', *RNZ*, 13 August 2021, www.rnz.co.nz/news/political/449077/defence-force-role-in-miq-reduces-capability-to-deal-with-major-disaster

43 Laura Walters, 'Defence force struggling with high attrition, low morale after MIQ duties', *Stuff*, 9 April 2022, www.stuff.co.nz/national/128305132/defence-force-struggling-with-high-attrition-low-morale-after-miq-duties

44 'Opposition claims NZDF facing "workforce crisis"', *RNZ*, 8 December 2022, www.rnz.co.nz/national/programmes/checkpoint/audio/2018870456/opposition-claims-nzdf-facing-workforce-crisis; Russell Palmer, 'New Zealand increases defence force pay rates, funding', *RNZ*, 8 May 2023, www.rnz.co.nz/news/political/489510/new-zealand-increases-defence-force-pay-rates-funding

45 Charlotte Cook, 'NZ Defence Force ongoing staff shortage affected Cyclone Gabrielle response', RNZ, 3 April 2023, www.rnz.co.nz/national/programmes/morningreport/audio/2018884377/nz-defence-force-ongoing-staff-shortage-affected-cyclone-gabrielle-response

46 Ibid.

47 Ibid.

48 Alexander Gillespie & Claire Breen, 'Parliament protest report shows NZ Police have come a long way since 1981', *RNZ*, 2 May 2023, www.rnz.co.nz/news/on-the-inside/489125/parliament-protest-report-shows-nz-police-have-come-a-long-way-since-1981

49 Ibid.

50 Thomas & Huntington, 'Vaccine passports equal Apartheid'.

51 Jamie Ensor, 'Threats against politicians, Jacinda Ardern jump massively over past year, peaked during parliament protest', *Newshub*, 28 February 2023, www.newshub.co.nz/home/politics/2023/02/threats-against-politicians-jacinda-ardern-jump-massively-over-past-year-peaked-during-parliament-protest.html

52 Nik Dirga, 'Yesterday was New Zealand's January 6. What happens now?', *RNZ*, 4 March 2022, www.rnz.co.nz/news/on-the-inside/462681/yesterday-was-new-zealand-s-january-6-what-happens-now

53 'Misinformation, scams and online harm', New Zealand Government, 16 December 2021, https://covid19.govt.nz/prepare-and-stay-safe/misinformation-scams-and-online-harm

54 Anthony R. DiMaggio, 'Conspiracy Theories and the Manufacture of Dissent: QAnon, the "Big Lie", Covid-19, and the rise of rightwing propaganda', *Critical Sociology* 48, no. 6 (2022): 1025–48.

55 www.ipca.govt.nz/Site/parliament-protest

56 Nigel Hemmington & Lindsay Neill, 'Hospitality Business Longevity under COVID-19: The impact of COVID-19 on New Zealand's hospitality industry', *Tourism and Hospitality Research* 22, no. 1 (2022): 102–14.

57 Ian Seymour Yeoman, Heike A. Schänzel & Elisa Zentveld, 'Tourist Behaviour in a COVID-19 World: A New Zealand perspective', *Journal of Tourism Futures* 8, no. 2 (2022); Tina Morrison, 'A2 milk at "peak uncertainty" after Covid-19 hits key Daigou trade', *Stuff*, 1 October 2021, www.stuff.co.nz/business/the-monitor/126279298/a2-milk-at-peak-uncertainty-after-covid19-hits-key-daigou-trade; www.educationcounts.govt.nz/publications/80898/the-impact-of-covid-19-on-tertiary-education-in-new-zealand-initial-impact-on-participation

58 Peterson K. Ozili & Thankom Arun, 'Spillover of COVID-19: Impact on the global economy', in *Managing Inflation and Supply Chain Disruptions in the Global Economy* (Hershey, PA: IGI Global, 2023), 41–61. https://doi.org/10.4018/978-1-6684-5876-1

59 Tom Stannard, Gregorious Steven & Chris McDonald, 'Economic Impacts of COVID-19 Containment Measures', No. AN2020/04 (Wellington: Reserve Bank of New Zealand, 2020).

60 Chung Yim Yiu, 'A Natural Quasi-Experiment of the Monetary Policy Shocks on the Housing Markets of New Zealand during COVID-19', *Journal of Risk and Financial Management* 16, no. 2 (2023): 73.

61 Brandon M. Boylan, Jerry McBeath & Bo Wang, 'US–China Relations: Nationalism, the trade war, and COVID-19', *Fudan Journal of the Humanities and Social Sciences* 14 (2021): 23–40.

62 Warren Smart, 'The Impact of COVID-19 on Tertiary Education in New Zealand: Initial impact on participation', *Education Counts*, December 2021, www.educationcounts.govt.nz/publications/80898/the-impact-of-covid-19-on-tertiary-education-in-new-zealand-initial-impact-on-participation

63 Sandeep Jagtap et al., 'The Russia-Ukraine Conflict: Its implications for the global food supply chains', *Foods* 11, no. 14 (2022): 2098.

64 Peter A. Petri & Michael G. Plummer, 'East Asia decouples from the United States: Trade war, COVID-19, and East Asia's new trade blocs', Peterson Institute for International Economics, Working Papers 20-9, June 2020, www.piie.com/publications/working-papers/east-asia-decouples-united-states-trade-war-covid-19-and-east-asias-new

65 Taylor Collins, 'Inflation Targeting in New Zealand: Does policy match practice?', *Journal of Applied Business & Economics* 24, no. 1 (2022): 122–32.

66 Department of Prime Minister and Cabinet, *Aotearoa's National Security Strategy*.

67 'Russian Invasion of Ukraine', Ministry of Foreign Affairs and Trade; Michael T. Klare, 'China Reacts Aggressively to Pelosi's Taiwan Visit', *Arms Control Today* 52, no. 7 (2022): 31–32.

68 Paul Haenle & Nathaniel Sher, 'How Pelosi's Taiwan visit has set a new status quo for US-China tensions', Carnegie Endowment for International Peace, 17 August 2022, https://carnegieendowment.org/2022/08/17/how-pelosi-s-taiwan-visit-has-set-new-status-quo-for-u.s-china-tensions-pub-87696

69 Bonny Lin, *US Allied and Partner Support for Taiwan: Responses to a Chinese attack on Taiwan and potential US Taiwan policy changes* (Santa Monica, CA: Rand Project Air Force, 2021).

70 'Australian Submarine Agency', Australian Government, 1 July 2023, www.defence.gov.au/about/taskforces/aukus#:~:text=The%20AUKUS%20nuclear%2Dpowered%20submarine,Kingdom%20and%20the%20United%20States, 6.

71 Amy Hawkins & Rhoda Kwan, 'China says Aukus submarines deal embarks on "path of

error and danger"', *The Guardian*, 14 March 2023, www.theguardian.com/world/2023/mar/14/china-aukus-submarines-deal-embarks-path-error-danger

72 'New Zealand may join Aukus pact's non-nuclear component', *The Guardian*, 28 March 2023, www.theguardian.com/world/2023/mar/28/new-zealand-may-join-aukus-pacts-non-nuclear-component

73 Thomas Manch, 'Chinese debt a concern in Tonga's post-eruption rebuild', *Stuff*, 21 January 2022, www.stuff.co.nz/national/politics/127547778/chinese-debt-a-concern-in-tongas-posteruption-rebuild; Koroi Hawkins, 'Concerns voiced on security pact between China and Solomons', *RNZ*, 26 April 2022, www.rnz.co.nz/international/pacific-news/465925/concerns-voiced-on-security-pact-between-china-and-solomons

1. US-China Great-Power Competition

1 Graham Allison, 'The Thucydides Trap: Are the US and China headed for war?', *The Atlantic*, 24 September 2015, www.theatlantic.com/international/archive/2015/09/united-states-china-war-thucydides-trap/406756

2 Jonathan M. DiCicco & Tudor A. Onea, 'Great-Power Competition', *Oxford Research Encyclopedia of International Studies*, 31 January 2023, 1, https://oxfordre.com/internationalstudies/view/10.1093/acrefore/9780190846626.001.0001/acrefore-9780190846626-e-756

3 S. Tang, 'The Security Dilemma: A conceptual analysis', *Security Studies* 18, no. 3 (2009): 587–62.

4 Joseph S. Nye, *Bound to Lead: The changing nature of American power* (New York: Basic Books, 1990).

5 Van Jackson, 'Understanding Spheres of Influence in International Politics', *European Journal of International Security* 5, no. 3 (2020): 255–73; D. Kaur, 'The US-Japan-Netherlands chip export restrictions are leaving China uneasy: Here's why', *Techwire Asia*, 17 February 2023, https://techwireasia.com/2023/02/the-us-japan-netherlands-chip-export-restrictions-are-leaving-china-uneasy-heres-why

6 John Lewis Gaddis, *Strategies of Containment: A critical appraisal of American national security policy during the Cold War* (New York: Oxford University Press, 2005).

7 Malcolm McKinnon, *Independence and Foreign Policy: New Zealand in the world since 1935* (Auckland: Auckland University Press, 1993).

8 F. Fukuyama, 'The End of History', *The National Interest*, Summer 1989, www.wesjones.com/eoh.htm

9 H. Brands & M. Beckley, *Danger Zone: The coming conflict with China* (New York: W.W. Norton & Company, 2022).

10 Ibid.

11 World Bank, search 'United States' and 'China', 2023, https://data.worldbank.org/indicator/NY.GDP.MKTP.CD; Q. Zhou, 'China's GDP grew by 3 percent in 2022, population declined 0.85 million', 17 January 2023, www.china-briefing.com/news/chinas-gdp-grew-by-3-percent-in-2022-population-declined-0-85-million; 'Gross Domestic Product, fourth quarter and year 2022 (advance estimate)', *Bureau of Economics Analysis*, 26 January 2023, www.bea.gov/news/2023/gross-domestic-product-fourth-quarter-and-year-2022-advance-estimate

12 Jasper Jolly, 'China cuts key interest rate amid economic slowdown', *The Guardian*, 21 August 2023, www.theguardian.com/world/2023/aug/21/china-cuts-interest-rate-economy-central-bank-rate

13 Wikimedia, 'Indo-Pacific map outlines with ASEAN overlay', 2020, https://commons.wikimedia.org/wiki/File:Indo-Pacific_map_outlines_with_ASEAN_overlay.jpg

14 K. Chung, 'South Korea's Perspective on Quad Plus and Evolving Indo-Pacific Security Architecture', *Journal of Indo-Pacific Affairs*, Special Issues 2020, https://media.defense.gov/2021/Mar/12/2002599866/-1/-1/0/8-CHUNG.PDF/TOC.pdf; 'Philippines agrees to allow US wider access to military bases', *Reuters*, 2 February 2023, www.aljazeera.com/news/2023/2/2/philippines-set-to-allow-wider-us-access-to-military-bases. The latter includes the QUAD (a grouping of the US, Japan, India and Australia); updating US alliances with Japan, the Philippines and Australia, and encouraging deeper military ties between all of them.

15 Rebecca Kuku, 'US and Papua New Guinea sign pact amid Pacific militarisation concerns', *The Guardian*, 22 May 2023, https://www.theguardian.com/world/2023/may/22/us-png-defence-security-agreement-papua-new-guinea-china-india-modi-pacific-militarisation-concerns

16 E. Anderson & S. Obeng, 'Globalisation and Government Spending: Evidence for the "hyper-globalisation" of the 1990s and 2000s', *The World Economy* 44 (2021): 1144–76.

17 E. Wishnick, 'The China–Russia "no limits" partnership is still going strong with regime security as top priority', 12 October 2022, CNA, www.cna.org/our-media/indepth/2022/10/the-china-russia-no-limits-partnership-is-still-going-strong

18 New Zealand government, *Defence Policy and Strategy Statement 2023*, August 2023, www.defence.govt.nz/assets/publication/file/23-0195-Defence-Policy-and-Strategy-Statement-WEB.PDF

19 D. Zhang, 'China's military engagement with Pacific Island countries', 17 August 2020, Asia and the Pacific Policy Society Policy Forum, www.policyforum.net/chinas-military-engagement-with-pacific-island-countries; Jonathan Pryke, 'The risks of China's ambitions in the South Pacific', Brookings, 20 July 2020, www.brookings.edu/articles/the-risks-of-chinas-ambitions-in-the-south-pacific

20 David Hurst, 'Chinese state company wins contract to redevelop Solomon Islands port, prompting cautious response', *The Guardian*, 22 March 2023, www.theguardian.com/world/2023/mar/22/chinese-state-company-wins-contract-to-redevelop-solomon-islands-honiara

21 S. B. Cohen, *Geopolitics: The geography of international relations* (Maryland: Rowman & Littlefield, 2015).

22 A. Panda, 'International court issues unanimous award in Philippines v. China case on South China Sea', *The Diplomat*, 12 July 2016, https://thediplomat.com/2016/07/international-court-issues-unanimous-award-in-philippines-v-china-case-on-south-china-sea

23 New Zealand Defence Force, 'NZDF joins RIMPAC exercise in waters around Hawaii', 2 July 2022, www.nzdf.mil.nz/media-centre/news/nzdf-joins-rimpac-exercise-in-waters-around-hawaii; CIA Factbook, 'New Zealand', 26 April 2023, www.cia.gov/the-world-factbook/countries/new-zealand

24 New Zealand China Council, 'In perspective: The New Zealand–China trade and business relationship 2022 update', https://nzchinacouncil.org.nz/wp-content/uploads/2022/04/China-trade-report-2022-update.pdf

25 DiCicco & Onea, 'Great-Power Competition'.

26 Reuben Steff & Francesca Dodd-Parr, 'Examining the Imminent Dilemma of Small States in the Asia-Pacific: The strategic triangle between New Zealand, the US and China', *The Pacific Review* 32, no. 1 (2019): 90–112; Reuben Steff, 'The Biden Administration and New Zealand's Strategic Options: Asymmetric hedging, tight Five Eyes alignment, and armed neutrality,' *National Security Journal* 3, no. 2 (March 2021): 1–22, https://nationalsecurityjournal.nz/the-biden-administration-and-new-zealands-strategic-options-asymmetric-hedging-tight-five-eyes-alignment-and-armed-neutrality; N. R. Smith, 'New Zealand's Grand Strategic Options as the Room for Hedging Continues to Shrink', *Comparative Strategy* 41, no. 3 (2022): 314–27.

27 Reuben Steff, 'Great Power Politics and Security: The US-China balance of power in transition', in *Global Security in an Age of Crisis*, ed. Aiden Warren (UK: Edinburgh University Press, 2023).

28 Svetla Ben-Itzhak, 'Space Blocs: The future of international cooperation in space is splitting along lines of power on Earth', *The Space Review*, www.thespacereview.com/article/4373/1

29 Ministry of Foreign Affairs and Trade, 'China market update — December 2022', www.mfat.govt.nz/en/trade/mfat-market-reports/market-reports-asia/china-market-update-december-2022/#:~:text=China%20remains%20Aotearoa%20New%20Zealand's,imports%20(NZ%2417.6%20billion)

30 Nicholas Ross Smith, 'New Zealand's Grand Strategic Options as the Room for Hedging Continues to Shrink', *Comparative Strategy* 41, no. 3 (2022): 314–27.

31 Note that these options are not mutually exclusive — parts of them could be merged in New Zealand's strategy, and if one were to be fully adopted it could give way, in time, to another based upon external and internal circumstances. Furthermore, the value of considering even unlikely proposals, such as aspects of armed neutrality, is that it offers ideas that could complement the other strategies.

32 Stats NZ, 'New Zealand International Trade', 2023, https://statisticsnz.shinyapps.io/trade_dashboard

33 White House, 'FACT SHEET: Implementation of the Australia–United Kingdom–United States Partnership (AUKUS)', 5 April 2022, www.whitehouse.gov/briefing-room/statements-releases/2022/04/05/fact-sheet-implementation-of-the-australia-united-kingdom-united-states-partnership-aukus

34 'New Zealand may join AUKUS pact's non-nuclear component', *The Guardian*, 28 March 2023, www.theguardian.com/world/2023/mar/28/new-zealand-may-join-aukus-pacts-non-nuclear-component

35 Steff, 'The Biden Administration and New Zealand's Strategic Options'.

36 'Switzerland military strength', Global Firepower, 2023, www.globalfirepower.com/country-military-strength-detail.php?country_id=switzerland#:~:text=For%202023%2C%20 Switzerland%20is%20ranked,0.0000%20is%20considered%20'perfect

37 Search 'Switzerland GDP' or 'New Zealand GDP', Trading Economics.

38 'New Zealand military strength', Global Firepower, 2023, www.globalfirepower.com/country-military-strength-detail.php?country_id=new-zealand#:~:text=For%202023%2C%20 New%20Zealand%20is,on%2001%2F09%2F2023

2. Conventional warfare today

1 Mykhaylo Zabrodskyi et al., *Preliminary Lessons in Conventional Warfighting from Russia's Invasion of Ukraine: February–July 2022* (London: Royal United Services Institute for Defence and Security Studies, 2022).

2 The term 'little green men' refers to masked soldiers wearing unmarked green army uniforms who appeared during Russia's 2014 annexation of Crimea. These soldiers were armed with Russian weapons and equipment yet were void of any identifying insignia. John R. Haines, 'E-Notes: How, why, and when Russia will deploy little green men — and why the US cannot', Foreign Policy Research Institute, March 2016, www.fpri.org/article/2016/03/how-why-and-when-russia-will-deploy-little-green-men-and-why-the-us-cannot/; Stephen Pifer, 'Commentary OP-ED: Watch out for little green men', Brookings, July 2014, www.brookings.edu/articles/watch-out-for-little-green-men/

3 Frank Hoffman offers the following definitions for the concepts of hybrid and grey-zone warfare. Hybrid warfare is 'the purposeful and tailed violent application of advanced conventional military capabilities with irregular tactics, with terrorism and criminal activities, or combination of regular and irregular forces, operating as part of a common design in the same battlespace'. Grey-zone warfare is the use of 'those covert or illegal activities of non-traditional statecraft that are below the threshold of armed organized violence; including disruption of order, political subversion of government or non-government organizations, psychological operations, abuse of legal processes, and financial corruption as part of an integrated design to achieve strategic advantage'. The primary difference between these concepts is the deliberate application of organised violence within the hybrid approach and the attempt to avoid attribution in the grey zone. Frank G. Hoffman, 'Examining Complex Forms of Conflict: Gray zone and hybrid challenges', *PRISM* (National Defence University) 7, no. 4 (2018): 30–47; Michael Kofman et al., *Lessons from Russia's Operations in Crimea and Eastern Ukraine* (Santa Monica: RAND Corporation, 2017).

4 Zabrodskyi et al., *Preliminary Lessons in Conventional Warfighting*.

5 Ibid.; Seth G. Jones, 'Russia's Ill-fated Invasion of Ukraine: Lessons in modern warfare', CSIS Briefs, Washington DC: Center for Strategic and International Studies, 1 June 2022.

6 Antulio J. Echevarria II, *Clausewitz and Contemporary War* (Oxford: Oxford University Press, 2007).

7 Ibid.

8 T. Edmunds & M. Malesic (eds), *Defence Transformation in Europe: Evolving military roles*, NATO Programme for Security through Science Series vol. 2 (Amsterdam: IOS Press, 2005).

9 United Nations, 'United Nations Register of Conventional Arms, April 2023', www.unroca.org/about; Theo Farrell, *The Norms of War: Cultural beliefs and modern conflict* (Lynne Rienner Publishers 2005).

10 Thomas C. Bruneau & Scott D. Tollefson, *Who Guards the Guardians and How: Democratic civil-military relations* (Austin: University of Texas Press, 2006); Christopher Dandeker, 'New Times for the Military: Some sociological remarks on the changing role and structure of the armed forces of the advanced societies', *British Journal of Sociology* (1994): 637–54; M. Edmonds, *Armed Services and Society* (Leicester: Leicester University Press, 1988); T. Edmunds, 'What are Armed Forces for?' *International Affairs* (2006): 1059–75; A. Forster, *Armed Forces and Society in Europe* (New York: Palgrave Macmillan, 2005).

11 Edmunds & Malesic, *Defence Transformation in Europe*.

12 Emile Simpson, *War from the Ground Up: Twenty-first-century combat as politics* (Oxford: Oxford University Press, 2012).

13 Ibid.

14 Ibid.

15 Zabrodskyi et al., 'Preliminary Lessons in Conventional Warfighting'; Jones, 'Russia's Ill-fated Invasion of Ukraine'.

16 Ibid.

17 The Minsk II agreements were brokered by France and Germany to halt the conflict between Ukraine and Russian-backed separatists in the Donbas Region. Duncan Allan, *The Minsk Conundrum: Western policy and Russia's war in eastern Ukraine* (London: Royal Institute of International Affairs, 2020).

18 Zabrodskyi et al., 'Preliminary Lessons in Conventional Warfighting'.

19 Ibid.

20 Ibid.

21 Ibid.

22 Ibid.

23 Ibid.

24 Ibid.

25 Ibid.

26 Ibid.

27 Zabrodskyi et al., 'Preliminary Lessons in Conventional Warfighting'; Jones, 'Russia's Ill-fated Invasion of Ukraine'.

28 Ibid.

29 Ibid.

30 T. Garden, 'Iraq: The military campaign', *International Affairs* 79. no. 4 (2003): 701–18; Lawrence Freedman & Efraim Karsh, 'How Kuwait was Won: Strategy in the Gulf War', *International Security* (1991): 5–41.

31 E. Knott, 'Existential Nationalism: Russia's war against Ukraine', *Nations and Nationalism* (2023): 45–52; 'Verkhovna Rada approves decree on mobilisation in Ukraine', Ukrinform, 3 March 2022, www.ukrinform.net/rubric-ato/3419149-verkhovna-rada-approves-decree-on-mobilization-in-ukraine.html

32 Kerry Chavez, 'Learning to Fly: Drones in the Russian-Ukrainian war', *Arms Control Today* (2023): 6–11.

33 Zabrodskyi et al., 'Preliminary Lessons in Conventional Warfighting'; Jones, 'Russia's Ill-fated Invasion of Ukraine'; Niklas Masuhr & Benno Zogg, 'The War in Ukraine: First lessons', *CSS Analyses in Security Policy* 301 (April 2022), https://doi.org/10.3929/ethz-b-000540121

34 Ibid.

35 Zabrodskyi et al., 'Preliminary Lessons in Conventional Warfighting'.

36 Ibid.

37 Seth G. Jones, *Empty Bins in a Wartime Environment: The challenge to the US defense industrial base* (CSIS Reports: 2023).

38 T. Garden, 'Iraq: The military campaign'; Nicolas Fiore, 'The 2003 Battle of Baghdad', *Military Review* (Sept–Oct 2020): 127–39.

39 New Zealand Defence Force, 'Support to Ukraine', 1 May 2023, www.nzdf.mil.nz/nzdf/significant-projects-and-issues/support-to-ukraine

40 Hal Brands & Zack Cooper, 'Getting Serious about Strategy in the South China Sea', *Naval War College Review* 71, no. 1 (2018): 12–32; Bernard D. Cole, 'Conflict in the South China Sea', in *Great Decisions 2017* (New York: Foreign Policy Association, 2017), 39–50; Madeline McLaughlin, 'US Strategy in the South China Sea' (Washington DC: American Security Project Report, 2020).

41 Brands & Cooper, 'Getting Serious about Strategy in The South China Sea'; McLaughlin, 'US Strategy in the South China Sea'.

42 T. M. Bonds et al., *What Role Can Land-Based, Multi-Domain Anti-Access/Area-Denial Forces Play in Deterring or Defeating Aggression?* (Santa Monica, CA: RAND Corporation, 2017).

43 Platform-centric focus refers to the specific effects particular vessels or aircraft deliver in the environment they were designed for, e.g. submarines, frigates and aircraft carriers all have unique capabilities they bring to naval task groups, therefore the use of these vessels is guided by the particular capabilities they bring to an operation.

44 New Zealand Defence Force, 'Our equipment', 1 May 2023, www.nzdf.mil.nz/nzdf/our-equipment

3. Retaining a national security workforce

1   Charlotte Cook, 'NZ Defence Force ongoing staff shortage affected Cyclone Gabrielle response', *RNZ*, 3 April 2023, www.rnz.co.nz/national/programmes/morningreport/audio/2018884377/nz-defence-force-ongoing-staff-shortage-affected-cyclone-gabrielle-response

2   Ministry of Defence, *Strategic Defence Policy Statement 2018* (Wellington: New Zealand Government, 2018), www.defence.govt.nz/assets/Uploads/8958486b29/Strategic-Defence-Policy-Statement-2018.pdf

3   Ministry of Defence, *Strategic Defence Policy Statement*, 5, clause 6.

4   Clifford Geertz, 'Deep Hanging Out', *The New York Review of Books* 45, no. 16 (1998).

5   United Nations Development Programme, *Human Development Report 1994: New dimensions of human security* (New York: UN, 1994), https://hdr.undp.org/content/human-development-report-1994

6   George Block, 'Three years until army at pre-Covid strength as MIQ drives military resignations', *Stuff*, 27 November 2021, www.stuff.co.nz/national/300463411/three-years-until-army-at-precovid-strength-as-miq-drives-military-resignations; New Zealand Defence Force, *New Zealand Defence Force Capability and Readiness Update as at June 2022,* www.nzdf.mil.nz/assets/Uploads/DocumentLibrary/OIA-2022-4503_NZDF-Capability-Readiness-Update-June-2022.pdf, 2; Cook, 'NZ Defence Force ongoing staff shortage'.

7   George Block, '"Massively concerning" — 338 military personnel who served in MIQ quit', *Stuff*, 4 December 2021, www.stuff.co.nz/national/300469780/massively-concerning–338-military-personnel-who-served-in-miq-quit

8   New Zealand Defence Force, *Capability and Readiness Update*, 2; Thomas Manch, 'Army attrition above 15% as units and ranks depleted by quitting soldiers', *Stuff*, 11 November 2022, www.stuff.co.nz/national/politics/130440514/army-attrition-above-15-as-units-and-ranks-depleted-by-quitting-soldiers; Thomas Manch, 'Defence Force launches recruitment blitz to battle tight labour market', *Stuff*, 7 October 2022, www.stuff.co.nz/national/politics/130022707/defence-force-launches-recruitment-blitz-to-battle-tight-labour-market; 'Defence Force struggling to recruit in a tight job market', *RNZ*, 8 May 2022, www.rnz.co.nz/national/programmes/afternoons/audio/2018842446/defence-force-struggling-to-recruit-in-a-tight-job-market; Brosnan Perich, 'NZ Army experiencing "spike in attrition" as soldiers leave', *1 News*, 26 November 2022, www.1news.co.nz/2021/11/26/nz-army-experiencing-spike-in-attrition-as-soldiers-leave

9   Laura Walters, 'Defence Force struggling with high attrition, low morale after MIQ duties', *Stuff*, 9 April 2022, www.stuff.co.nz/national/128305132/defence-force-struggling-with-high-attrition-low-morale-after-miq-duties

10 New Zealand Defence Force, *Capability and Readiness Update*, 5.

11 Ibid., 4.

12 Ibid.

13 Cook, 'NZ Defence Force ongoing staff shortage'.

14 Ibid.

15 Ibid.

16 Block, 'Three Years'; Cook, 'NZ Defence Force Ongoing Staff Shortage'.

17 Block, 'Three Years'; Block, 'Massively Concerning'; Walters, 'Defence Force Struggling'; New Zealand Defence Force, *Capability and Readiness Update*, i.

18 Ministry of Defence, *Strategic Defence Policy Statement*, 6, clause 10.

19 See, for example, Natalie Jester, 'Army Recruitment Video Advertisements in the US and UK Since 2002: Challenging ideals of hegemonic military masculinity?', *Media, War and Conflict* 14, no. 1 (2021): 58, https://doi.org/10.1177/1750635219859488; Malte Riemann & Norma Rossi, 'From Subject to Project: Crisis and the transformation of subjectivity in the armed forces', *Globalizations* (2022): 5, https://doi.org/10.1080/14747731.2022.2104017; John Capon, Oleksandr S. Chernyshenko & Stephen Stark, 'Applicability of Civilian Retention Theory in the New Zealand Military,' *New Zealand Journal of Psychology* 36, no. 1 (2007): 50.

20 Danya Levy, 'Military morale remains very low', *Dominion Post*, 28 September 2012, www.stuff.co.nz/dominion-post/news/7743502/Military-morale-remains-very-low

21 Charles Moskos, 'From Institution to Occupation: Trends in military organization', *Armed Forces and Society* 4, no. 1 (1977): 42.

22 Riemann & Rossi, 'From Subject', 2; Fabrizio Battistelli, 'Peacekeeping and the Postmodern Soldier', *Armed Forces and Society* 23, no. 3 (1997): 469, 471.

23 Moskos, 'From institution', 43.

24 Capon, Chernyshenko & Stark 'Applicability', 50; M. Guesgen, 'Closing the Door on Military

25 Geoffrey W. Rice, 'A Revolution in Social Policy, 1981–1991', in *The Oxford History of New Zealand*, ed. Geoffrey W. Rice, 2nd edn (Oxford: Oxford University Press, 2002), 483.

26 Rice, 'A Revolution', 482; Jane Kelsey, *Rolling Back the State: Privatisation of power in Aotearoa/New Zealand* (Wellington: Bridget Williams Books, 1993), 11.

27 Jane Kelsey, *The New Zealand Experiment: A world model for structural adjustment?* (Auckland: Auckland University Press, 1997).

28 Karen Nairn, Jane Higgins & Judith Sligo, *Children of Rogernomics: A neoliberal generation leaves school* (Dunedin: Otago University Press, 2012), 11.

29 Dana Grosswirth Kachtan & Eve Binks, 'Soldiers' Perceptions and Expectations of Converting Military Capital: The cases of Israeli and British militaries', *Sociological Inquiry* 91, no. 4 (2021): 851, https://doi.org/10.1111/soin.12397; Felicity Ware, Mary Breheny & Margaret Forster, 'The Politics of Government "Support" in Aotearoa/New Zealand: Reinforcing and reproducing the poor citizenship of young Māori parents', *Critical Social Policy* 37, no. 4 (2017): 501, https://doi.org/10.1177/0261018316672111

30 Peter Roberts, 'A New Patriotism? Neoliberalism, citizenship and tertiary education in New Zealand', *Educational Philosophy and Theory* 41, no. 4 (2009): 412, 416, https://doi.org/10.1111/j.1469-5812.2008.00437.x

31 Nairn, Higgins & Sligo, *Children of Rogernomics*.

32 Karen Nairn & Jane Higgins, 'New Zealand's Neoliberal Generation: Tracing discourses of economic (ir)rationality,' *International Journal of Qualitative Studies in Education* 20, no. 3 (2007): 264, https://doi.org/10.1080/09518390701281819

33 Kachtan & Binks, 'Soldier's Perceptions'; Riemann & Rossi, 'From Subject'; Sanna Strand & Joakim Berndtsson, 'Recruiting the "Enterprising Soldier": Military recruitment discourses in Sweden and the United Kingdom,' *Critical Military Studies* 1, no. 3 (2015), https://doi.org/10.1080/23337486.2015.1090676; Frank A. Stengel & David Shim, 'Militarizing Antimilitarism? Exploring the gendered representation of military service in German recruitment videos on social media', *International Feminist Journal of Politics* 24, no. 4 (2022), https://doi.org/10.1080/14616742.2021.1935289

34 Nina Harding, 'Thwarted Selves: Neoliberal boredom among Aotearoa New Zealand peacekeepers', *Critical Military Studies* (2022), https://doi.org/10.1080/23337486.2022.2143676

35 Eileen Oak, 'Methodological Individualism for the Twenty-first Century? The neoliberal acculturation and remoralisation of the poor in Aotearoa New Zealand', *Sites* 12, no. 1 (2015), http://dx.doi.org/10.11157/sites-vol12iss1id271

36 'Christopher Luxon explains his "bottom feeding" comments', *1 News*, 23 March 2023, www.1news.co.nz/2022/03/22/christopher-luxon-explains-his-bottom-feeding-comments

37 Manch, 'Defence force launches recruitment blitz'.

38 Nairn, Higgins & Sligo, *Children of Rogernomics*, 13–14.

39 Any discussion of a return to conscription in this neoliberal context — that is, potential loss of control over the career and economic stability everyone is individually responsible for — would only increase daily insecurity for all citizens.

40 Amelia Wade, 'Budget 2023: Defence boost to stop personnel leaving as "geostrategic competition in our region" intensifies', *Newshub*, 8 May 2023, www.newshub.co.nz/home/politics/2023/05/budget-2023-defence-boost-to-stop-personnel-leaving-as-geostrategic-competition-in-our-region-intensifies.html

41 Thomas Manch, 'Defence force spends $60m to stop its staff walking out the door', *Stuff*, 5 April 2023, www.stuff.co.nz/national/politics/131693673/defence-force-spends-60m-to-stop-its-staff-walking-out-the-door

42 'Cyclone Gabrielle: CHB soldiers get stuck into disaster response', *Hawke's Bay Today*, 3 March 2023, www.nzherald.co.nz/hawkes-bay-today/news/cyclone-gabrielle-chb-soldiers-get-stuck-in-to-disaster-response/KRVIZVHTVFCSZMNNQXY2NKKW7E

43 Block, 'Massively Concerning'.

44 'Two years since NZ first locked down — expert reaction', *Science Media Centre*, 21 March 2022, www.sciencemediacentre.co.nz/2022/03/21/two-years-since-nz-first-locked-down-expert-reaction

45 Walters, 'Defence Force Struggling'.

46 Ibid.

47 Block, 'Three Years'.

48 Perich, 'NZ Army'; Block, 'Massively Concerning'.
49 Ministry of Defence, *Strategic Defence Policy Statement*.
50 William J. Fish et al., 'The Limits of the Military Instrument', in *Army Fundamentals: From making soldiers to the limits of the military instrument*, ed. B. K. Greener (Auckland: Massey University Press, 2017); Rouben Azizian et al., *The 2018 Strategic Defence Statement: Ten different views from Massey scholars*, Security, Politics and Development Network Massey University, 1 August 2018, https://mro.massey.ac.nz/bitstream/handle/10179/13613/SPDN%202018.pdf?sequence=1&isAllowed=y
51 Walters, 'Defence Force Struggling'.

4. Maritime trade security threats

1 Adam Smith, *The Wealth of Nations* (1776); David Ricardo, *Principles of Political Economy and Taxation* (1815).
2 'Review of Maritime Transport 2018', United Nations Conference on Trade and Development (UNCTAD), https://unctad.org/publication/review-maritime-transport-2018#:~:text=Maritime%20transport%20is%20the%20backbone,upswing%20in%20the%20world%20economy
3 UNCTAD statistics as interpreted and presented by Felix Richter, 'The steep rise in global seaborne trade', *Statista*, 26 March 2021, https://www.statista.com/chart/24527/total-volume-of-global-sea-trade
4 The Naval Register cites the number of commissioned US Navy ships at 238. This omits the reserve fleet and ships coming on line, https://en.wikipedia.org/wiki/List_of_current_ships_of_the_United_States_Navy#Fleet_totals
5 Jan Hoffman & Julia Hoffman, 'Ports in the global liner shipping network: Understanding their position, connectivity, and changes over time', UNCTAD, 10 August 2020, https://unctad.org/news/ports-global-liner-shipping-network-understanding-their-position-connectivity-and-changes-over
6 Andrew Davies, 'Graph of the week: Why (fleet) size matters', Australian Strategic Policy Institute, 1 February 2013, www.aspistrategist.org.au/graph-of-the-week-why-fleet-size-matters
7 According to George Driver writing in *The Spinoff*, 'Shipping companies, however, have been making record profits out of the crisis and there have been accusations of price gouging. Some have pointed the finger at the three major shipping alliances that control 80% of the market. In New Zealand, importers have claimed the price of freight for a shipping container has increased four-fold and that has largely been passed on to consumers', https://thespinoff.co.nz/business/24-11-2021/whats-causing-the-shipping-crisis-and-when-will-it-end
8 UNCTAD, https://unctadstat.unctad.org/wds/TableViewer/tableView.aspx?ReportId=93; *The Economist*, 17 October 2015, www.economist.com/economic-and-financial-indicators/2015/10/17/merchant-fleets
9 Gerald Chan, *China's Maritime Silk Road: Advancing global development?* (Cheltenham: Edward Elgar, 2020).
10 'Merchant fleets', *The Economist*, 17 October 2015, www.economist.com/economic-and-financial-indicators/2015/10/17/merchant-fleets
11 John Xie, 'China's global network of shipping ports reveal Beijing's strategy', *Voice of America*, 13 September 2021, https://www.voanews.com/a/6224958.html
12 'China to inspect ships in Taiwan Strait, Taiwan says won't cooperate', *Reuters*, 6 April 2023, www.reuters.com/world/asia-pacific/china-inspect-ships-taiwan-strait-taiwan-says-wont-cooperate-2023-04-06/#:~:text=The%20maritime%20safety%20authority%20in,operation%20of%20key%20projects%20on
13 UNCTAD, 'Review of Marine Transport 2022: Navigating stormy waters', https://unctad.org/publication/review-maritime-transport-2022
14 https://www.transport.govt.nz/assets/Uploads/Report/MSS-Summary_V6_U.pdf
15 Hugo Grotius, *Mare Liberum* (1609) and *On the Rights of War and Peace* (1625).
16 www.transport.govt.nz/assets/Uploads/Report/MaritimeSecurityStrategy.pdf
17 The following passages paraphrase the Maritime Security Strategy public document found at www.transport.govt.nz/assets/Uploads/Report/MaritimeSecurityStrategy.pdf
18 www.maritimenz.govt.nz/content/about/what-we-do/history-of-MNZ/default.asp; this agency traces its origin back to the Marine Board, established in 1862 to construct and manage lighthouses. The Marine Board, succeeded by the Marine Department in 1866, was incorporated into the Ministry of Transport in 1972 and renamed the Marine Division, then the Maritime Transport Division. In 1993 it was recast as the Maritime Safety Authority, an autonomous Crown agency, and in 2005 was renamed Maritime New Zealand.

19 Counterpart Agencies of Maritime New Zealand: Ministry of Transport; New Zealand Transport Agency; Civil Aviation Authority; Ministry of Business, Innovation and Employment; WorkSafe; Environmental Protection Authority; regional councils; New Zealand SAR Secretariat; New Zealand Police; LandSAR; Coastguard; Surf Life Saving New Zealand; Fire and Emergency NZ; New Zealand Defence Force; Amateur Radio Emergency Communications; Customs; US Coast Guard; Australian Maritime Safety Authority; Asia-Pacific Heads of Maritime Safety Agencies Forum; International Maritime Organization; New Zealand intelligence agencies; Ministry of Foreign Affairs and Trade.

20 International Maritime Agreements to which New Zealand has acceded: International convention for the safety of life at sea, 1974 and the 1978 and 1988 protocols; Convention on the International regulations for preventing collisions at sea 1972; International convention on load lines 1966 and the 1988 protocol; International convention on tonnage measurement of ships 1969; International convention for safe containers 1972; International convention on standards of training, certification and watchkeeping for seafarers 1978 as amended in 1995; International convention on maritime search and rescue 1979; International convention relating to intervention on the high seas in cases of oil pollution casualties 1969 and its 1973 protocol; Convention on the international maritime satellite organisation 1976; International convention on civil liability for oil pollution damage 1969 and its 1992 protocol; International convention on limitation of liability for maritime claims 1976, and its 1996 protocol; International convention on the establishment of an international fund for compensation for oil pollution damage 1971 and its 1992 protocol; International convention for the prevention of pollution from ships 1973 and the 1978 protocol Annexes I, II, III and V; International convention on oil pollution preparedness, response and co-operation 1990; International convention on civil liability for bunker oil pollution damage 2001; International convention for the control and management of ships' ballast water and sediments 2004; Maritime Labour Convention, 2006.

21 These include: Maritime Security Act; Maritime Transport Act; Ship Register Act; Health and Safety at Work Act; Hazardous Substances and New Organisms Act; Civil Aviation Act; Submarine Cables and Pipeline Protection Act.

22 www.maritimenz.govt.nz/content/about/annual-reports/documents/MNZ-annual-report-2021-2022.pdf

23 www.police.govt.nz/news/release/operation-hydros-police-customs-and-nzdf-recover-half-billion-dollars%E2%80%99-worth-cocaine

24 https://nzhistory.govt.nz/politics/plant-and-animal-quarantine

25 'By 2004 it had accredited 12,000 people to unpack containers at 5000 facilities, massively expanding the border security force', https://nzhistory.govt.nz/politics/plant-and-animal-quarantine

26 Driver, cited above, noted that Chris Edwards, president of the Customs Brokers and Freight Forwarders of New Zealand in 2021 said, 'NZ has been one of the countries most impacted by the crisis — not only are we an island nation heavily dependent on shipping, but we are at the very end of shipping routes, meaning we experience all of the delays further up the line', https://thespinoff.co.nz/business/24-11-2021/whats-causing-the-shipping-crisis-and-when-will-it-end

27 www.beehive.govt.nz/release/livestock-exports-sea-cease

28 www.smh.com.au/world/oceania/idle-ships-staff-shortages-low-salaries-hit-new-zealand-navy-20221208-p5c4wp.html

29 Three hundred 'strategically significant' defence force personnel with critical skills have recently been awarded salary bonuses. The May 2023 budget allocated $419 million to increase servicepersons' pay. From 1 July, most servicepersons will get additional annual salary payments ranging from $4000 to $15,000 depending on rank and role.

5. Supply chain disruptions and deep uncertainty

1 My thanks go to the Multi-Agency Research Network for granting funding for interview transcription and workshops for this project.

2 T. Birtchnell, S. Savitzky & J. Urry, *Cargomobilities: Moving materials in a global age* (New York: Routledge, 2015).

3 Supply chain disruptions were well known prior to the pandemic. See, for example, M. Heins, 'Globalizing the nation-state: The shipping container and American infrastructure', *Mobilities* 10, no. 3 (2015): 345–62.

4 K. Chellel, M. Campbell & K. O. Ha, 'Six days in Suez: The inside story of the ship that broke

global trade', *Bloomberg*, 24 June 2021, www.bloomberg.com/news/features/2021-06-24/how-the-billion-dollar-ever-given-cargo-ship-got-stuck-in-the-suez-canal

5   D. Ivanov & A. Dolgui, 'Stress Testing Supply Chains and Creating Viable Ecosystems', *Operations Management Research: Advancing practice through theory* 1 (2021), https://doi.org/10.1007/s12063-021-00194-z; J. M. Lawrence et al., 'Leveraging a Bayesian Network Approach to Model and Analyze Supplier Vulnerability to Severe Weather Risk: A case study of the U.S. pharmaceutical supply chain following Hurricane Maria', *International Journal of Disaster Risk Reduction* 49 (2020): 101607, https://doi.org/10.1016/j.ijdrr.2020.101607; M. M. Queiroz et al., 'Impacts of Epidemic Outbreaks on Supply Chains: Mapping a research agenda amid the COVID-19 pandemic through a structured literature review', *Annals of Operations Research* (2020), https://doi.org/10.1007/s10479-020-03685-7; E. Solingen, *Geopolitics, Supply Chains, and International Relations in East Asia* (Cambridge: Cambridge University Press, 2021).

6   K. F. Davis, S. Downs & J. A. Gephart, 'Towards Food Supply Chain Resilience to Environmental Shocks', *Nature Food* 2, no. 1 (2021): 54–65, https://doi.org/10.1038/s43016-020-00196-3; Lawrence et al., 'Leveraging a Bayesian Network Approach'; N. P. T. Le, 'The Application of Social Network Analysis to Study Supply Chain Resilience' (PhD thesis, Massey University, 2019); S. Matthewman, 'Mobile Disasters: Catastrophes in the age of manufactured uncertainty', *Transfers* 7, no. 3 (2017): 6–22, https://doi.org/10.3167/TRANS.2017.070303

7   The Royal Society, 'How does climate change affect the strength and frequency of floods, droughts, hurricanes, and tornadoes?', March 2020, https://royalsociety.org/topics-policy/projects/climate-change-evidence-causes/question-13

8   Ivanov & Dolgui, 'Stress Testing Supply Chains'.

9   A. Boin, A. McConnell & P. 't Hart, 'Pathways to Resilience', in A. Boin, A. McConnell & P. 't Hart (eds), *Governing the Pandemic: The politics of navigating a mega-crisis* (New York: Springer International Publishing, 2021), 107–20, https://doi.org/10.1007/978-3-030-72680-5_6

10 'Parliament protest: Plan to commemorate occupation one year on', *RNZ*, 10 February 2023, www.rnz.co.nz/news/covid-19/484015/parliament-protest-plan-to-commemorate-occupation-one-year-on

11 S. Goldfinch, 'Economic Reform in New Zealand', *The Otemon Journal of Australian Studies* 30 (2004): 75–98; L. Humpage (ed.), 'Social Citizenship, Neoliberalism and Attitudinal Change', in *Policy Change, Public Attitudes and Social Citizenship: Does neoliberalism matter?* (Bristol: Bristol University Press, 2014), 17–52, https://doi.org/10.46692/9781847429667.002

12 R. Handfield et al., 'A Commons for a Supply Chain in the Post-COVID-19 Era: The case for a reformed strategic national stockpile', *The Milbank Quarterly* 98, no. 4 (2020), 1058–90: https://doi.org/10.1111/1468-0009.12485

13 Ministry of Foreign Affairs and Trade, *New Zealand's Covid-19 Trade Recovery Strategy*, www.mfat.govt.nz/en/trade/trade-recovery-strategy/trade-recovery-strategy-overview

14 A.-M. Kennedy, C. McGouran & J. A. Kemper, 'Alternative Paradigms for Sustainability: A relational worldview', *European Journal of Marketing* 54, no. 4 (2020): 825–55, https://doi.org/10.1108/EJM-01-2018-0043

15 Hon. D. Parker, 'Covid-19 Response: New Zealand and Singapore launch initiative to ensure free flow of essential goods', The Beehive, 15 April 2020, www.beehive.govt.nz/release/covid-19-response-new-zealand-and-singapore-launch-initiative-ensure-free-flow-essential

16 L. Thornley et al., 'Building Community Resilience: Learning from the Canterbury earthquakes', *Kōtuitui: New Zealand Journal of Social Sciences Online* 10, no. 1 (2015): 23–35, https://doi.org/10.1080/1177083X.2014.934846

17 M. Kawharu, 'Reinterpreting the Value Chain in an Indigenous Community Enterprise Context', *Journal of Enterprising Communities: People and places in the global economy* 13, no. 3 (2019): 242–62, https://doi.org/10.1108/JEC-11-2018-0079

18 A. Wilkinson & E. Eidinow, 'Evolving Practices in Environmental Scenarios: A new scenario typology', *Environmental Research Letters* 3, no. 4 (2008): 045017, https://doi.org/10.1088/1748-9326/3/4/045017

19 *Taranaki Climate Resilience: Te Tirohanga o ngā Tohu*, The Deep South National Science Challenges, 3 March 2022, https://deepsouthchallenge.co.nz/research-project/taranaki-climate-resilience-te-tirohanga-o-nga-tohu

20 *Improving Economic Resilience: Issues paper*, New Zealand Productivity Commission, 2023, www.productivity.govt.nz/assets/Inquiries/resilience/Resilience_Issues_Paper_Final_17-Feb-2023.pdf

6. Out of sight and out of mind

1   Lionel Carter et al., *Submarine Cables and the Oceans: Connecting the world* (Cambridge & Lymington: United Nations Environmental Programme World Conservation Monitoring Centre and the International Cable Protection Committee, 2009), 3; Frank Rose, 'Emerging threats: Outer space, cyberspace, and undersea cables', *Arms Control Today*, January/February 2017, www.armscontrol.org/act/2017-01/news/remarks-emerging-threats-outer-space-cyberspace-undersea-cables

2   Christian Bueger & Tobias Liebetrau, 'Protecting Hidden Infrastructure: The security politics of the global submarine data cable network', *Contemporary Security Policy* 42, no. 3 (2021): 392, https://doi.org/10.1080/13523260.2021.1907129

3   Ibid., 393–94.

4   Utpal Kumar Raha & K. D. Raja, *Submarine Cables Protection Regulation: A comparative analysis and model framework* (Singapore: Springer, 2021), 1.

5   Rishi Sunak, *Undersea Cables: Indispensable, insecure* (London: Policy Exchange, 2017).

6   Roland Wenzlhuemer, *Connecting the Nineteenth-century World: The telegraph and globalization* (Cambridge: Cambridge University Press, 2012), 30–58.

7   David R. Headrick & Pascal Griset, 'Submarine Telegraph Cables: Business and politics, 1838–1939', *The Business History Review* 75, no. 3 (Autumn 2001): 544.

8   Simone M. Müller, *Wiring the World: The social and cultural creation of global telegraph networks* (New York: Columbia University Press, 2016), 19–47.

9   P. M. Kennedy, 'Imperial Cable Communications and Strategy, 1870–1914', *The English Historical Review* 86, no. 341 (1971): 729–31.

10 Tara Davenport, 'Submarine Cables, Cybersecurity and International Law: An intersectional analysis', *Catholic University Journal of Law and Technology* 24, no. 1 (2017): 6–67.

11 Jeffrey K. Lyons, 'The Pacific Cable, Hawaii, and Global Communication', *The Hawaiian Journal of History* 39 (2005): 35–42.

12 Keith Lewis, 'Engineering on the Sea Floor — Submarine cables', *Te Ara: The Encyclopedia of New Zealand*, https://teara.govt.nz/en/engineering-on-the-sea-floor; Carter et al., *Submarine Cables and the Oceans*, 14–15.

13 Ministry for Culture and Heritage, 'Warkworth Satellite Earth Station', NZ History, https://nzhistory.govt.nz/media/photo/warkworth-satellite-earth-station

14 Keith Newman, *Connecting the Clouds: The internet in New Zealand* (Auckland: Activity Press, 2008), https://www.nethistory.co.nz/Chapter_6_-_Craving_for_Connection

15 Carter et al., *Submarine Cables and the Oceans*, 16.

16 Bueger & Liebetrau, 'Protecting Hidden Infrastructure', 405.

17 Douglas R. Burnett & Lionel Carter, *International Submarine Cables and Biodiversity of Areas Beyond National Jurisdiction: The cloud beneath the sea* (Leiden and Boston: Brill, 2017), 54–55, https://doi.org/10.1163/24519359-12340002

18 Hilary McGeachy, 'The Changing Strategic Significance of Submarine Cables: Old technology, new concerns', *Australian Journal of International Affairs* 76, no. 2 (2022): 164–66; Bueger & Liebetrau, 'Protecting hidden infrastructure', 405.

19 Ministry for Culture and Heritage, 'Warkworth Satellite Earth Station'.

20 George H. Seltzer et al., 'New Zealand's Aqualink Network: A submarine solution for domestic high-speed infrastructure', 2001, https://cdn.b12.io/client_media/n8KzZTRM/59d857a4-d2e9-11eb-945e-0242ac110003-Aqualink_01.pdf; TeleGeography, 'Submarine cable map', www.submarinecablemap.com/; Winston Qui, 'Raglan Cable Landing Station', Submarine Cable Networks, 30 September 2020, www.submarinenetworks.com/en/stations/oceania/new-zealand/raglan

21 Daniel Smith, 'Oceanic cable to double New Zealand's internet capacity launches from Auckland', *Stuff*, 29 June 2021, www.stuff.co.nz/business/300344613/oceanic-cable-to-double-new-zealands-internet-capacity-launches-from-auckland

22 Hong Shen, 'Building a Digital Silk Road? Situating the internet in China's Belt and Road Initiative', *International Journal of Communication* 12 (2018): 3683.

23 Christof Gerlach & Richard Seitz, *Economic Impact of Submarine Cable Disruptions* (Singapore: APEC Policy Support Unit, 2013), 9.

24 'Boe Declaration on Regional Security', Pacific Islands Forum, 2018, www.forumsec.org/2018/09/05/boe-declaration-on-regional-security

25 Karen Scott, 'Laws governing undersea cables have hardly changed since 1884 — Tonga is a reminder they need modernising', *The Conversation*, 21 January 2022, https://

theconversation.com/laws-governing-undersea-cables-have-hardly-changed-since-1884-tonga-is-a-reminder-they-need-modernising-175312

26 'Protecting New Zealand's undersea cables', Te Manatū Waka Ministry of Transport, www.transport.govt.nz/about-us/what-we-do/queries/protecting-new-zealands-undersea-cables

27 Scott, 'Laws governing undersea cables have hardly changed since 1884'.

28 Carter et al., *Submarine Cables and the Oceans*, 39.

29 Kennedy, 'Imperial Cable Communications and Strategy', 729–31; Elizabeth Bruton, 'The Cable Wars: Military and state surveillance of the British telegraph cable network during World War One', in Andreas Marklund & Mogens Rüdiger (eds), *Historicizing Infrastructure* (Aalborg: Aalborg University Press, 2017), 5–6.

30 Congressional Research Service, 'Undersea Telecommunication Cables: Technology overview and issues for Congress', CRS Report R47237 (Washington, DC: Congressional Research Service, 2022), 11–13.

31 Philip Dorling, 'Edward Snowden reveals tapping of major Australia–New Zealand undersea telecommunications cable', *Sydney Morning Herald*, 15 September 2014, www.smh.com.au/technology/edward-snowden-reveals-tapping-of-major-australianew-zealand-undersea-telecommunications-cable-20140915-10h96v.html

32 Congressional Research Service, 'Undersea Telecommunication Cables', 13.

33 Sunak, *Undersea Cables*, 19.

34 Dennis E. Harbin III, 'Targeting Submarine Cables: New approaches to the law of armed conflict in modern warfare', *Military Law Review* 229, no. 3 (2021): 351.

35 TeleGeography, 'Submarine cable map'.

36 Sebastian Moss, 'Fortune on the High Seas — DCD', Datacenter Dynamic, 2016, www.datacenterdynamics.com/en/analysis/fortune-on-the-high-seas

37 Jonathan E. Hillman, *The Digital Silk Road: China's quest to wire the world and win the future* (London: Profile Books, 2021), 107.

38 TeleGeography, 'Submarine cable map'.

39 Carter et al., *Submarine Cables and the Oceans*, 9.

40 Ulrich Speidel, 'The Hunga Tonga Hunga Ha'apai Eruption — a Postmortem: What happened to Tonga's internet in January 2022, and what lessons are there to be learned?', *AINTEC 2022* (Association for Computing Machinery: 18–21 December 2022), 75; Tom Bateman, 'Tonga is finally back online: Here's why it took 5 weeks to fix its volcano-damaged internet cable', *Euronews*, 23 February 2022, www.euronews.com/next/2022/02/23/tonga-is-finally-back-online-here-s-why-it-took-5-weeks-to-fix-its-volcano-damaged-interne

41 Ulrich Speidel, 'Cyclone Gabrielle broke vital communication links when people needed them most — what happened and how do we fix it?', *New Zealand Herald*, 3 March 2023, www.nzherald.co.nz/nz/cyclone-gabrielle-broke-vital-communication-links-when-people-needed-them-most-what-happened-and-how-do-we-fix-it/22NDWWPKMZEKDIQWCP6566X2UQ

42 Ramakrishnan Durairajan, Carol Barford & Paul Barford, 'Lights Out: Climate change risk to internet infrastructure', *ANRW 2018* (Association for Computing Machinery: 16 July 2018), 9–15.

43 Deloitte Access Economics, *New Zealand Space Economy: Its value, scope and structure* (Wellington: Ministry of Business, Innovation and Employment, November 2019), www.beehive.govt.nz/sites/default/files/2019-11/Deloitte NZ Space Economy Report.pdf

44 Speidel, 'Cyclone Gabrielle broke vital communication links when people needed them most'.

7. Outlaw motorcycle gangs and the illegal drug trade

1 Jarrod Gilbert, *Patched: The history of gangs in New Zealand* (Auckland: Auckland University Press, 2013); Gregory D. Breetzke et al., 'Gang Membership and Gang Crime in New Zealand: A national study identifying spatial risk factors,' *Criminal Justice and Behavior* (2021): 1154–72; Anusha Bradley, 'Gangs of New Zealand: Explosion of violence prompts fears police have lost control', 23 March 2020, *The Guardian*, www.theguardian.com/world/2020/mar/23/gangs-of-new-zealand-explosion-of-violence-prompts-fears-police-have-lost-control; New Zealand Parliamentary Services, 'New Zealand gang membership: A snapshot of recent trends', July 2022, www.parliament.nz/media/9557/gangs-in-nz-snapshot-july-2022.pdf

2 Anna Leask, 'Organised crime evolving "rapidly" in NZ as borders become "porous" to illicit trade', 15 October 2019, *New Zealand Herald*, www.nzherald.co.nz/nz/news/article.cfm?c_id=1&objectid=12276597; Breetzke et al., 'Gang membership', 1154;

'Methamphetamine in New Zealand: What is currently known about the harm it causes?', New Zealand Police, July 2021, www.police.govt.nz/sites/default/files/publications/methamphetamine-in-new-zealand.pdf; Jared Savage, *Gangland: New Zealand's underworld of organised crime* (Auckland: HarperCollins, 2020); Gilbert, *Patched*, 9.

3   Breetzke et al, 'Gang Membership', 1154; Leask, 'Organised crime evolving rapidly'.
4   'Methamphetamine in New Zealand'.
5   Carl Bradley, 'Outlaw Bikers and Patched Street Gangs: The nexus between violence and shadow economy,' *National Security Journal* (2020), https://doi.org/10.36878/nsj20200201.02
6   Gilbert, *Patched*.
7   Bradley, 'Outlaw Bikers'.
8   'Methamphetamine in New Zealand.'
9   Breetzke et al, 'Gang membership', 1154; Chris Wilkins et al., 'Determinants of High Availability of Methamphetamine, Cannabis, LSD and Ecstasy in New Zealand: Are drug dealers promoting methamphetamine rather than cannabis?', *International Journal of Drug Policy* (2018): 15–22; Chris Wilkins et al., 'Determinants of the Retail Price of Illegal Drugs in New Zealand', *International Journal of Drug Policy* (2020), https://doi.org/10.1016/j.drugpo.2020.102728
10 New Zealand Parliamentary Services, 'New Zealand gang membership.'
11 Ibid.
12 Ibid.
13 Rachel Maher, 'New Zealand records highest ever number of gang members, grew by 338 in two months', *New Zealand Herald*, 22 November 2022, www.nzherald.co.nz/nz/new-zealand-records-highest-ever-number-of-gang-members-grew-by-338-in-two-months/RZZOGMWYENDEJEXMK44IWURA64
14 New Zealand Parliamentary Services, 'New Zealand gang membership'.
15 Ibid.
16 Gilbert, *Patched*; 'Methamphetamine in New Zealand'; Wilkins et al., 'Determinants of High Availability', 15; Wilkins et al., 'Determinants of the Retail Price'; Greg Newbold, *Crime in New Zealand* (Palmerston North: Dunmore Press, 2000); Chris Wilkins & Sally Casswell, 'Organized Crime and Cannabis Cultivation in New Zealand: An economic analysis', *Contemporary Drug Problems* 30, no. 4 (2003): 757–77.
17 'Methamphetamine in New Zealand'.
18 UNODC, 'World Drug Report 2022', 2022, www.unodc.org/res/wdr2022/MS/WDR22_Booklet_4.pdf
19 Leask, 'Organised crime evolving rapidly'.
20 'Evidence to inform a regulated cannabis market', BERL, June 2020, https://berl.co.nz/sites/default/files/2020-09/Evidence-to-inform-a-regulated-cannabis-market-June-2020-PROACTIVE-FINAL.pdf
21 'The war on meth', New Zealand Police Association, 1 March 2017, https://www.policeassn.org.nz/news/the-war-on-meth#/; Mike Houlahan, 'Meth is "everywhere"', *Otago Daily Times*, www.odt.co.nz/news/dunedin/meth-everywhere; Florence Kerr, 'Gangs go to social media to push brand and recruit', *Stuff*, 6 March 2016, www.stuff.co.nz/national/crime/77484541/Gangs-go-to-social-media-to-push-brand-and-recruit; Florence Kerr, 'Gang warfare coming to a town near you', *Stuff*, 22 January 2016, www.stuff.co.nz/national/crime/75445578/gang-warfare-coming-soon-to-a-town-near-you?rm=m
22 Kerr, 'Gang warfare'.
23 Wilkins et al., 'Determinants of the Retail Price', 15.
24 Ibid.
25 Ibid.
26 Ibid.
27 Jonathan P. Caulkins, 'Local Drug Markets' Response to Focused Police Enforcement', *Operations Research* (2003): 848–63.
28 New Zealand Gang Intelligence Centre, 'The New Zealand Organised Crime Governance Group insights report update' (Wellington: New Zealand Police internal report: unpublished, 2019).
29 '501s mean business', New Zealand Police Association, 1 November 2019, www.policeassn.org.nz/news/501s-mean-business
30 Ibid.
31 New Zealand Gang Intelligence Centre, 'The New Zealand Organised Crime Governance Group'.
32 Ibid.
33 Ibid.

34 Chris Wilkins et al., *Recent Trends in Illegal Drug Use in New Zealand, 2006–2016: Findings from the Illicit Drug Monitoring System* (Auckland: SHORE & Whariki Research Centre, Massey University, 2017); Chris Wilkins et al., *New Zealand Arrestee Drug Use Monitoring (NZ-ADUM) 2010–2016* (Auckland: SHORE & Whariki Research Centre, Massey University, 2017).

35 Tina Van Havere et al., 'Drug Use and Nightlife: More than just dance music', *Substance Abuse Treatment Prevention and Policy* 6, no. 18 (2011), https://doi.org/10.1186/1747-597X-6-18

36 Those less than 15 per cent complete (i.e. only the demographic and 'drugs ever tried during life' sections answered) and responses in which age was unspecified or outside the age range 16–100 years were removed. To avoid compromising anonymity, respondent IP addresses were not stored; instead, a custom software solution was used to convert IP addresses into non-reversible numbers. Survey responses with the same numbers were flagged as potential duplicates and then checked for demographic similarities and extent of completion to determine if they had been submitted by the same person. In cases where demographics matched, the most complete survey response was kept. If demographics differed, both responses were kept (i.e. two separate people had completed the survey on the same device). Following this quality control process, a total of 1395 responses were removed, 85 of which were duplicates, 1273 were insufficiently completed, and 37 were outside the age range. The median time taken to complete the survey was 12 minutes. The NZDTS was approved by the Massey University Human Ethics Committee (application code: SOA 17/43).

37 Monica J. Barratt et al., 'Lessons from Conducting Trans-national Internet-Mediated Participatory Research with Hidden Populations of Cannabis Cultivators', *International Journal of Drug Policy* 26, no. 3 (2014): 238–49.

38 'Internet Service Provider Survey', Stats NZ, 10 October 2017.

39 Andy Fyers & Henry Cooke, 'Facebook is New Zealand's second-favourite leisure activity', *Stuff*, 23 March 2017, www.stuff.co.nz/technology/90005751/Facebook-is-New-Zealands-second-favourite-leisure-activity

40 Ivar Krumpal, 'Determinants of Social Desirability Bias in Sensitive Surveys: A literature review', *Quality & Quantity* 47 (2013): 2025–47.

41 'Data hub table builder,' Stats NZ, 2018, http://nzdotstat.stats.govt.nz/wbos/Index.aspx?ga=2.91779928.391607928.1536553580-1016169874.1533096415

42 'Data hub table builder'.

43 Leask, 'Organised crime evolving rapidly'.

44 Breetzke et al, 'Gang membership', 1154; Bradley, 'Outlaw Bikers'.

45 Breetzke et al, 'Gang membership'.

46 Wilkins et al., 'Determinants of High Availability', 15; Wilkins et al., 'Determinants of the Retail Price'.

47 Ibid.

8. Biosecurity intelligence in Aotearoa

1 Timothy R. Millar et al., 'Spatial Distribution of Species, Genus and Phylogenetic Endemism in the Vascular Flora of New Zealand, and Implications for Conservation', *Australian Systematic Botany* 30, no. 2 (2017): 134–47, https://doi.org/10.1071/sb16015; Briar Taylor-Smith, Mary Morgan-Richards & Steven A. Trewick, 'Patterns of Regional Endemism Among New Zealand Invertebrates', *New Zealand Journal of Zoology* 47, no. 1 (2020): 1–19, https://doi.org/10.1080/03014223.2019.1681479

2 Rebecca S. Epanchin-Niell, 'Economics of Invasive Species Policy and Management', *Biological Invasions* 19 (2017): 3333–54, https://doi.org/10.1007/s10530-017-1406-4; Benjamin D. Hoffman & Linda M. Broadhurst, 'The Economic Cost of Managing Invasive Species in Australia', *NeoBiota* 31 (2016): 1–18, http://dx.doi.org/10.3897/neobiota.31.6960

3 Ministry of Agriculture and Forestry, 'Management of biosecurity risks', https://oag.parliament.nz/2002/biosecurity

4 Kanako Itagaki, 'Evaluating the Role of Public Opinion in the New Zealand Biosecurity Act 1993' (PhD dissertation, Lincoln University, 2013), 3–4; Jorma Kajava, Reijo Savola & Rauno Varonen, 'Weak Signals in Information Security Management', in *Computational Intelligence and Security: International Conference, CIS 2005, Xi'an, China, December 15–19, 2005, Proceedings, Part II* (Berlin: Springer, 2005): 508–17, https://doi.org/10.1007/11596981_75

5 Evan Brenton-Rule, Susy Frankel & Phil Lester, 'Improving Management of Invasive Species: New Zealand's approach to pre- and post-border pests', *Policy Quarterly* 12, no. 1 (2016), https://doi.org/10.26686/pq.v12i1.4582

6   Philip E. Hulme, 'Biosecurity: The changing face of invasion biology', in *Fifty Years of Invasion Ecology: The legacy of Charles Elton* (Oxford: Blackwell Publishing, 2011): 73–88; Philip E. Hulme, 'One Biosecurity: A unified concept to integrate human, animal, plant, and environmental health', *Emerging Topics in Life Sciences* 4, no. 5 (2020): 539–49, https://doi.org/10.1042/ETLS20200067

7   Randolph Pherson & Richard Heuer Jr., 'The Role of Structured Techniques', in *Structured Analytic Techniques for Intelligence Analysts* (Thousand Oaks, CA: CQ Press, 2020), 17–32.

8   Peter Gill & Mark Phythian, *Intelligence in an Insecure World* (3rd edn) (Cambridge: Polity Press, 2018).

9   Eric G. Little & Galina L. Rogova, 'An Ontological Analysis of Threat and Vulnerability', in *9th International Conference on Information Fusion* (2006), https://doi.org/ 10.1109/ICIF.2006.301716

10 Michela Nardo et al., 'Handbook on Constructing Composite Indicators: Methodology and user guide', *Organisation for Economic Co-operation and Development* (2005), https://dx.doi.org/10.1787/533411815016; David Niemeijer & Rudolf S. de Groot, 'A Conceptual Framework for Selecting Environmental Indicator Sets', *Ecological Indicators* 8, no. 1 (2008): 14–25, https://doi.org/10.1016/j.ecolind.2006.11.012; Cecilia Wong, 'Indicator Selection Criteria', *Encyclopedia of Quality of Life and Well-Being Research* 32 (2021), https://doi.org/10.1007/978-3-319-69909-7_1428-2

11 Jerry Ratcliffe, 'Intelligence Research', in *Strategic Thinking in Criminal Intelligence*, ed. J. Ratcliffe (Alexandria, NSW: Federation Press, 2009).

12 Anissa Frini & Anne-Claire Boury-Brisset, 'An Intelligence Process Model Based on a Collaborative Approach' (Quebec: Defense Research and Development Canada, 2011).

13 Ibid.; Elisa Shahbazian, 'Intelligence Analysis: Needs and solutions', in *Meeting Security Challenges Through Data Analytics and Decision Support*, eds E. Shahbazian & G. Rogova (Amsterdam: IOS Press, 2016), https://doi.org/10.3233978-1-61499-716-0-18

14 National Academies of Sciences, Engineering, and Medicine, 'The Work of an Intelligence Analyst', in *A Decadal Survey of the Social and Behavioral Sciences: A research agenda for advancing intelligence analysis* (Washington, DC: The National Academies Press, 2019), https://doi.org/10.17226/25335

9.   Does AI dream of protecting sheep?

1   The opinions expressed in this work are the authors' own and should not be taken as reflecting those of their respective organisations. We thank the reviewers for their generous feedback, which as usual has made this chapter infinitely better than it first appeared.

2   V. Higgins et al., 'Harmonising Devolved Responsibility for Biosecurity Governance: The Challenge of competing institutional logics', *Environment and Planning A* (2016): 48, 1133–51; H. Buller, 'Safe from the Wolf: Biosecurity, biodiversity, and competing philosophies of nature', *Environment and Planning A: Economy and Space* 40, no. 7 (2008): 1583–97, https://doi.org/10.1068/a4055; K. Barker, 'Flexible Boundaries in Biosecurity: Accommodating gorse in Aotearoa New Zealand', *Environment and Planning A* 40, no. 7 (2008): 1598–1614. In Aotearoa, biosecurity is a term defined by public policy as 'the exclusion, eradication or management of pests and diseases that pose a risk to the economy, environment, cultural and social values, including human health' (Ministry for Primary Industries, *Biosecurity 2025 Direction Statement for New Zealand's Biosecurity System*, 2016).

3   See generally A. Dobson, K. Barker & S. Taylor (eds), *Biosecurity: The socio-politics of invasive species and infectious diseases* (New York: Routledge, 2013).

4   Steve Hinchliffe & Kim Ward, 'Geographies of Folded Life: How immunity reframes biosecurity', *Geoforum* 53 (2014): 136–44, https://doi.org/10.1016/j.geoforum.2014.03.002

5   Exports of primary products earned the country more than NZ$53 billion in the 12 months prior to June 2022, and this figure is forecast to reach NZ$55 billion by June 2023 (Ministry for Primary Industries, *Situation and Outlook for the Primary Industries*, December 2022). Biosecurity is economically important for Aotearoa in large part because the country exports over 90 per cent of all the food it produces.

6   M. Achtnich, 'Mobile Livings: On the bioeconomies of mobility', *Cultural Anthropology* 37, no. 1 (2022): 1–8, https://doi.org/10.14506/ca37.1.01

7   'Foot and Mouth Disease' (Queensland Government, 2023), www.business.qld.gov.au/industries/farms-fishing-forestry/agriculture/biosecurity/animals/diseases/guide/foot-mouth

8   Evangeline Corcoran & Grant Hamilton, 'The Future of Biosecurity Surveillance', in *The Handbook of Biosecurity and Invasive Species*, eds Kezia Barker & Robert A. Francis (New York: Routledge, 2021), 261–75.

9   F. Tirado, E. Baleriola & S. Moya, 'The Emergency Modality: From the figures to the mobilisation of affects', in *The Handbook of Invasive Species*, eds Kezia Barker & Robert A. Francis (London: Routledge, 2021), 290.

10 D. Campbell & R. Lee, 'Carnage by Computer: The blackboard economics of the 2001 Foot and Mouth epidemic', *Social and Legal Studies* 12, no. 3 (2003), https://doi.org/10.1177/0964663903012004002

11 OECD (*Recommendation of the Council on Artificial Intelligence*). New Zealand adheres to this recommendation, which sets out principles for responsible use of AI, including ethics, transparency and fairness.

12 Colin Gavaghan et al., *Government Use of Artificial Intelligence in New Zealand* (Wellington: New Zealand Law Foundation, 2019), www.cs.otago.ac.nz/research/ai/AI-Law/NZLF%20 report.pdf

13 Big data predictive analytics seeks to find and share meaningful patterns in what is most often unstructured (raw) data sets too large, too dynamic and too spread out for traditional processing technologies, for example, social media, device data, or remote sensor data. 'Big' is distinguished from other data by claims of superior qualities in volume, velocity, variety, veracity and value. IBM Corporation, 2023, 'Big Data and Analytics Support', www.ibm.com/docs/en/spectrum-scale-bda?topic=big-data-analytics-support

14 While artificial intelligence remains an elusive term, it is accepted that machine learning is included in its scope (see S. Sapienza, *Big Data, Algorithms and Food Safety: A legal and ethical approach to data ownership and data governance* [New York: Springer, 2020]). A well-known platform is Chat-GPT, which employs 'a combination of multilingual natural language and programming language to provide comprehensive and adaptable answers' (T. Zhou, Y. Huang, C. Chen & Z. Xing, 'Exploring AI Ethics of ChatGPT: A diagnostic analysis' [arXiv:2301.12867v4 [cs.CL], 29 May 2023, https://arxiv.org/pdf/2301.12867.pdf])

15 See, for instance, https://aws.amazon.com/machine-learning/accelerate-machine-learning-P3 and https://coral.ai/industries/agriculture; Ministry for Primary Industries, 'Drone monitoring project gains "beyond visual line of sight" aviation approval to help protect Māui dolphins' (media release, 18 January 2023, www.mpi.govt.nz/news/media-releases/drone-monitoring-project-gains-beyond-visual-line-of-sight-aviation-approval-to-help-protect-maui-dolphins; N. J. Bloomfield et al., 'Automating the Assessment of Biofouling in Images Using Expert Agreement as a Gold Standard', *Scientific Reports* 11, no. 2739 (2021), https://doi.org/10.1038/s41598-021-81011-2; D. Parker, 'Rollout of cameras on fishing vessels to begin' (media release, The Beehive, 25 May 2022), www.beehive.govt.nz/release/rollout-cameras-fishing-vessels-begin

16 Andrea Wild, 'AI-powered app helps keep Australia free from stink bug pests', *CSIRO*, 15 March 2022, www.csiro.au/en/news/news-releases/2022/ai-powered-app-helps-keep-australia-free-from-stink-bug-pests; Bob Edlin, 'Researchers launch artificial intelligence app to identify NZ's wildlife', *New Zealand Institute of Agricultural & Horticultural Science Inc.*, 23 January 2023, www.agscience.org.nz/researchers-launch-artificial-intelligence-app-to-identify-nzs-wildlife; 'Data company brings "intelligent eye" to managing herd health', *RNZ*, 18 June 2021, www.rnz.co.nz/national/programmes/ninetonoon/audio/2018800309/data-company-brings-intelligent-eye-to-managing-herd-health; Krishna Moorthy Babu et al., 'Computer Vision in Aquaculture: A case study of juvenile fish counting', *Journal of the Royal Society of New Zealand* 53 (2023): 52–68, https://doi.org/10.1080/03036758.2022.210 1484; Tim Callanan, 'New artificial intelligence technology used to protect bees from Varroa Destructor mite,' *ABC*, 29 March 2021, www.abc.net.au/news/2021-03-29/ai-technology-used-to-protect-bees-from-pests/100035134; Neelesh Rampal et al., 'High-resolution Downscaling with Interpretable Deep Learning: Rainfall extremes over New Zealand', *Weather and Climate Extremes* 38 (2022), https://doi.org/10.1016/j.wace.2022.100525

17 Angus J. Carnegie et al., 'Airborne Multispectral Imagery and Deep Learning for Biosecurity Surveillance of Invasive Forest Pests in Urban Landscapes', *Urban Forestry and Urban Greening* 81 (2023), https://doi.org/10.1016/j.ufug.2023.127859; see, for example, G. Nistala, K. Murakoshi & M. Jamieson, 'How researchers at UC Davis support the swine industry with data analytics on AWS', *AWS Public Sector Blog*, 18 March 2022, https://aws.amazon.com/blogs/publicsector/how-researchers-uc-davis-save-swine-data-analytics-aws-cloud; Jim Eadie, 'Novel machine-learning tool can predict PRRSV outbreaks and biosecurity effectiveness', *Swine Web*, 24 May 2021, https://swineweb.com/

novel-machine-learning-tool-can-predict-prrsv-outbreaks-and-biosecurity-effectiveness; Konstantinos Demertzis, Lazaros S. Iliadis & Vardis-Dimitris Anezakis, 'Extreme Deep Learning in Biosecurity: The Case of machine hearing for marine species identification', *Journal of Information and Telecommunication* 2, no. 4 (2018): 492–510, https://doi.org/10.1080/24751839.2018.1501542

18 Jun Bao & Qiuju Xie, 'Artificial Intelligence in Animal Farming: A systematic literature review', *Journal of Cleaner Production* 331 (January 2022), https://doi.org/10.1016/j.jclepro.2021.129956

19 C. Lazaro & M. Rizzi, 'Predictive Analytics and Governance: A New sociotechnical imaginary for uncertain futures', *International Journal of Law in Context* 19 (2023): 70–90, https://doi.org/10.1017/S1744552322000477

20 Corcoran & Hamilton, 'The Future of Biosecurity Surveillance', 261–75.

21 Ibid., 266; see also A. Rhem, 'AI Ethics and its Impact on Knowledge Management', *AI and Ethics* 1 (2021): 33–37, https://doi.org/10.1007/s43681-020-00015-2. Though, in one piece of research, the performance and accuracy of machine learning models developed from livestock databases in Aotearoa have been shown to vary widely (C. P. Jewell, M. van Andel, W. D. Vink & A. M. J. McFadden, 'Compatibility Between Livestock Databases Used for Quantitative Biosecurity Response in New Zealand', *New Zealand Veterinary Journal* 64 [2016]: 158–64, https://doi.org/10.1080/00480169.2015.1117955).

22 The International Plant Protection Convention defines a quarantine pest as 'A pest of potential economic importance to the area endangered thereby and not yet present there, or present but not widely distributed and being officially controlled'; and a regulated pest as 'A non-quarantine pest whose presence in plants for planting affects the intended use of those plants with an economically unacceptable impact and which is therefore regulated within the territory of the importing contracting party' (United Nations Food and Agriculture Organization, 'International Plant Protection Convention' [1997], https://assets.ippc.int/static/media/files/publication/en/2019/02/1329129099_ippc_2011-12-01_reformatted.pdf); 'Terrestrial Animal Health Code', World Organisation for Animal Health, 2022, www.woah.org/en/what-we-do/standards/codes-and-manuals/terrestrial-code-online-access; 'Aquatic Animal Health Code', World Organisation for Animal Health, 2022, www.woah.org/en/what-we-do/standards/codes-and-manuals/aquatic-code-online-access

23 Section 2 of the Biosecurity Act 1993 defines an unwanted organism as 'any organism that a chief technical officer believes is capable or potentially capable of causing unwanted harm to any natural and physical resources or human health', www.legislation.govt.nz/act/public/1993/0095/latest/DLM314623.html; see section 45 of the Biosecurity Act 1993, www.legislation.govt.nz/act/public/1993/0095/latest/DLM315346.html; see Schedule 2 of the Hazardous Substances and New Organisms Act 1996, www.legislation.govt.nz/act/public/1996/0030/latest/DLM386556.html#DLM386556; effectively 29 July 1998 for many organisms. See section 2A of the Hazardous Substances and New Organisms Act 1996, www.legislation.govt.nz/act/public/1996/0030/93.0/DLM382982.html

24 'Biosecurity 2025 Direction Statement for New Zealand's biosecurity system', Ministry for Primary Industries, 2016, www.mpi.govt.nz/dmsdocument/14857-Biosecurity-2025-Direction-Statement-for-New-Zealands-biosecurity-system

25 Such as the Official New Zealand Pest Register, https://pierpestregister.mpi.govt.nz/pests-of-concern

26 Juliet Fall, 'What is an Invasive Alien Species? Discord, dissent and denialism', in *The Handbook of Biosecurity and Invasive Species*, eds Kezia Barker & Robert A. Francis (London: Routledge, 2021), https://doi.org/10.4324/9781351131599. For example, kiore (*Rattus exulans*) is both 'pest' and a taonga species (S. Lambert & M. Mark-Shadbolt, 'Indigenous Biosecurity: Past, present and future', in *The Handbook of Biosecurity and Invasive Species*, 55–65).

27 The concept of an assemblage is borrowed from the theory of G. Deleuze & F. Guattari, *A Thousand Plateaus*, trans. Brian Massumi (Minneapolis: University of Minnesota Press, 1987). Thomas Nail (2017) describes an assemblage as 'an arrangement or layout of heterogenous elements': Thomas Nail, 'What Is an Assemblage?', *SubStance* 46 (2017): 22, http://doi.org/10.1353/sub.2017.0001

28 Donna Haraway, 'Situated Knowledges: The science question in feminism and the privilege of partial perspective', *Feminist Studies* 14 (1988): 575–99, https://doi.org/10.2307/3178066

29 Meike Wolf, 'Urbanisation and Globally Networked Cities', in *The Handbook of Invasive Species*, 215–25.

30 A. Stirling, 'Comment: Keep it complex', *Nature* 468 (December 2010): 1029–30.
31 B. Latour (ed.), *The Pasteurization of France* (Cambridge, MA: Harvard University Press, 1991), 153–236.
32 R. Pesonen, 'Argumentation, Cognition, and the Epistemic Benefits of Cognitive Diversity', *Synthese* 200 (2022): 295, https://doi.org/10.1007/s11229-022-03786-9
33 Geoffrey C. Bowker, 'All Knowledge is Local', *Learning Communities* 138 (2008): 142.
34 Ministry for Business Innovation and Employment, Digital Technologies Draft Industry Transformation Plan 2022–2032 (2022), www.mbie.govt.nz/dmsdocument/18603-draft-digital-technologies-industry-transformation-plan-2022-2032-pdf
35 Susan Leigh Star, 'This is not a Boundary Object: Reflections on the origin of a concept', *Science, Technology, and Human Values* 5 (2010): 601–17, http://www.jstor.org/stable/25746386
36 Ibid.
37 For example, by setting character limits, or mandating processes and formats.
38 Lazaro & Rizzi, 'Predictive Analytics'.
39 Arun Agrawal, 'Indigenous Knowledge and the Politics of Classification', *International Social Science Journal* 54 (2002): 287–97, https://doi.org/10.1111/1468-2451.00382
40 Jane E. Fountain, 'The Moon, the Ghetto and Artificial Intelligence: Reducing systemic racism in computational algorithms', *Government Information Quarterly* 39 (April 2022): 2, 9, https://doi.org/10.1016/j.giq.2021.101645
41 This is especially problematic given a need to determine 'the facts' (objectivity).
42 Zhou et al. calls these 'exclusionary norms' (Zhou, Huang, Chen & Xing, 'Exploring AI Ethics of ChatGPT').
43 J. Fellenor, J. Barnett & G. Jones, 'User-generated Content: What can the forest health sector learn?', in *The Human Dimensions of Forest and Tree Health: Global perspectives*, eds J. Urquhart, M. Marzano & C. Potter (New York: Palgrave MacMillan, 2018).
44 Stuart Reeves, 'Navigating Incommensurability Between Ethnomethodology, Conversation Analysis, and Artificial Intelligence', *Medium*, 18 June 2022, https://5tuartreeves.medium.com/navigating-incommensurability-between-ethnomethodology-conversation-analysis-and-artificial-e99c29867242
45 D. Chandler, 'A World Without Causation: Big data and the coming of age of posthumanism', *Millennium: Journal of International Studies* (2015): 836.
46 Slippage or leakage can be broadly understood as the rate at which contamination travels through borders undetected, equivalent to the residual risk of an organism entering Aotearoa New Zealand. 'Biosecurity System Achievements, 2003–2015', Ministry for Primary Industries, https://mpi.govt.nz/dmsdocument/13185/direct
47 Benjamin N. Jacobsen, 'Machine Learning and the Politics of Synthetic Data', *Big Data and Society* (17 January 2023), https://doi.org/10.1177/20539517221145372
48 Wendy Hui Kyong Chun, 'Crisis, Crisis, Crisis, or Sovereignty and Networks', *Theory, Culture & Society* 28, no. 6 (2011): 91–112.
49 R. Montasari, *Countering Cyberterrorism: The confluence of artificial intelligence, cyber forensics and digital policing in US and UK national cybersecurity* (New York: Springer, 2023).
50 Ibid.
51 Fountain, 'The Moon, the Ghetto and Artificial Intelligence'.
52 Montasari, *Countering Cyberterrorism*.
53 Lauren C. Richardson et al., 'Cyberbiosecurity: A call for cooperation in a new threat landscape', *Frontiers in Bioengineering and Biotechnology* 7 (June 2019), https://doi.org/10.3389/fbioe.2019.00099
54 Charles L. Briggs, 'Communicating Biosecurity', *Medical Anthropology* 30 (2011): 6–29, https://doi.org/10.1080/01459740.2010.531066
55 Montasari, *Countering Cyberterrorism*.
56 Lazaro & Rizzi, 'Predictive Analytics'.
57 Susan Erikson, 'Cell Phones ≠ Self and Other Problems with Big Data Detection and Containment during Epidemics', *Medical Anthropology Quarterly*, 32 (2018): 315–39, https://anthrosource.onlinelibrary.wiley.com/doi/full/10.1111/maq.12440
58 Dan Milmo & Alex Hern, 'UK and US intervene amid AI industry's rapid advances', *The Guardian,* 4 May 2023, www.theguardian.com/technology/2023/may/04/uk-and-us-intervene-amid-ai-industrys-rapid-advances
59 P. Drahos, '"Trust me": Patent Offices in developing countries', Working Paper, Centre for Governance of Knowledge and Development, November 2007, http://ssrn.com/abstract=1028676

60 Colin Gavighan et al., 'Government Use of Artificial Intelligence in New Zealand', The New Zealand Law Foundation, 2019, www.otago.ac.nz/caipp/otago711816.pdf

61 Ibid.

62 American Civil Liberties Union et al., 'Predictive Policing Today: A shared statement of civil rights concerns', 31 August 2016, http://civilrightsdocs.info/pdf/FINAL_JointStatementPredictivePolicing.pdf

63 Robert K. Merton, 'The Self-fulfilling Prophecy', *The Antioch Review* 8 (1948): 193–210, https://doi.org/10.2307/4609267

64 Gavighan et al., 'Government Use of Artificial Intelligence in New Zealand'.

65 See Montasari, *Countering Cyberterrorism*; Fountain, 'The Moon, the Ghetto and Artificial Intelligence'.

66 'AI Alliance for Biodiversity submission to Department of Conservation and Toitū Te Whenua Land Information New Zealand on use of information and emerging technologies to enhance biodiversity', AI Forum New Zealand, January 2023, https://aiforum.org.nz/wp-content/uploads/2023/01/AI-Forum-submission-on-the-use-of-information-and-emerging-technologies-to-enhance-biodiversity.docx.pdf

67 Mariella Marzano et al., 'The Role of the Social Sciences and Economics in Understanding and Informing Tree Biosecurity Policy and Planning: A global summary and synthesis', *Biological Invasions* 19 (2017): 3317–32, https://doi.org/10.1007/s10530-017-1503-4

68 See, for example, G. Enticott, C. M. Gates & A. Hidano, '"It's Just the Luck of the Draw": Luck, good farming and the management of animal disease in Aotearoa New Zealand', *Geoforum* 119 (2021): 143–51. See also M. McEntee et al., 'Park Rangers and Science-public Expertise: Science as care in biosecurity for kauri trees in Aotearoa/New Zealand', *Minerva* 61 (2023): 117–40, https://doi.org/10.1007/s11024-022-09482-9

69 Lazaro & Rizzi, 'Predictive Analytics'.

70 Fellenor, Barnett & Jones, 'User-generated Content'.

71 'Ko Tātou: This is Us: Biosecurity 2025', Biosecurity New Zealand, www.thisisus.nz

72 Thibault Laugel et al., 'The Dangers of Post-Hoc Interpretability: Unjustified counterfactual explanations', *IJCAI '19: Proceedings of the 28th International Joint Conference on Artificial Intelligence*.

73 Charles D. Raab, 'Regulating Surveillance: The importance of principles', *Routledge Handbook of Surveillance Studies* (London: Routledge, 2012), 377–85.

74 Corcoran & Hamilton, 'The Future of Biosecurity Surveillance', 261–75.

75 Ibid.

76 Will Douglas Heaven, 'Artificial Intelligence: GPT-4 is bigger and better than ChatGPT — but OpenAI won't say why,' *MIT Technology Review*, 14 March 2023, www.technologyreview.com/2023/03/14/1069823/gpt-4-is-bigger-and-better-chatgpt-openai; Ministry for Business Innovation and Employment, *Digital Technologies Draft Industry Transformation Plan 2022–2032*; Lawrence Carter, 'CIA looking into Possible Uses of Generative AI in Agency Operations', *Potomac Officers Club*, 17 February 2023, https://potomacofficersclub.com/news/cia-looking-into-possible-uses-of-generative-ai-in-agency-operations

77 Timnit Gebru et al., 'Statement from the listed authors of Stochastic Parrots on the "AI pause' letter"', *DAIR*, 31 March 2023, www.dair-institute.org/blog/letter-statement-March2023

78 Alex Engler, 'Fighting deepfakes when detection fails', Brookings, 14 November 2019, www.brookings.edu/research/fighting-deepfakes-when-detection-fails

79 Corcoran & Hamilton, 'The Future of Biosecurity Surveillance'.

80 T. Gillespie, *Custodians of the Internet Platforms: Content moderation, and the hidden decisions that shape social media* (Yale: Yale University Press, 2018), https://tarletongillespie.org/Gillespie_CUSTODIANS_print.pdf

10. Accountability and oversight

1 See paragraphs 3.7 and 3.14, respectively.

2 See Government Communications Security Bureau and the New Zealand Security Intelligence Service, *Briefing to the Incoming Minister* (2017); and Government Communications Security Bureau and the New Zealand Security Intelligence Service, *Incoming Minister's Briefing* (2020).

3 See Doug Martin & Simon Mount, *Inquiry into the Use of External Security Consultants by Government Agencies* (State Services Commission, 2018).

4 This includes New Zealand Police and the New Zealand Defence Force as well as

Immigration New Zealand within the Ministry for Business, Innovation and Employment, the New Zealand Custom Service, the Ministry for Primary Industries, Department of Internal Affairs and the Inland Revenue Department, among others.

5 *Cabinet Manual*, para 3.27.

6 See Andrew Defty, '"Familiar but Not Intimate": Executive oversight of the UK intelligence and security agencies', *Intelligence and National Security* 37, no. 1 (2022): 57–72; Andrew Defty, 'Coming in from the Cold: Bringing the intelligence and security committee into Parliament', *Intelligence and National Security* 34, no. 1 (2019): 22–37; Andrew W. Neal, 'The Parliamentarianism of Security in the UK and Australia', *Parliamentary Affairs* 74, no. 2 (2021): 464–82; Andrew W. Neal, *Security as Politics: Beyond the state of exception* (Edinburgh: Edinburgh University Press, 2019).

7 Department of the Prime Minister and Cabinet, *Briefing to Incoming Minister for National Security and Intelligence* (2017), 12.

8 S. 193 of the Intelligence and Security Act 2017.

9 Ibid., 23.

10 S.156 of the Intelligence and Security Act 2017.

11 *Ko tō tātou kāinga tēnei: Report of the Royal Commission of Inquiry into the terrorist attack on Christchurch masjidain on 15 March 2019* (2020), 737.

12 S. 235 of the Intelligence and Security Act 2017.

13 Ibid.

14 Sir Terence Arnold & Matanuku Mahuika, 'Taumaru: Protecting Aotearoa New Zealand as a free, open and democratic society. Review of the Intelligence and Security Act 2017' (Wellington: Ministry of Justice, 2023), 256–57.

15 That is, the New Zealand Defence Force and the New Zealand Police.

16 Cheryl Gwyn, *Report into the Release of Information by the New Zealand Security Intelligence Service in July and August 2011* (Office of the Inspector-General of Intelligence and Security, 2014).

17 Cheryl Gwyn, 'Speech to the New Zealand Centre for Public Law Public Officeholders' Lecture Series "Spotlight on Security" (Victoria University of Wellington Faculty of Law, 4 May 2016).

18 *Ko tō tātou kāinga tēnei*, 24–25.

19 Terence Arnold & Geoffrey Palmer, *Report of the Government Inquiry into Operation Burnham*, 33.

20 The term 'public unease' is taken from Didier Bigo, 'Security and Immigration: Towards a critique of the governmentality of unease', *Alternatives* 27 (2002): 63–92.

21 Independent Police Conduct Complaints Authority, *Operation Eight: The report of the Independent Police Conduct Authority*, www.ipca.govt.nz/site/publications-and-media/2013-re-ports-on-investigations

22 William Young & Jacqui Caine, Summary of Submissions (28 November 2020), 140.

23 See, respectively: *Office of the Inspector-General of Intelligence and Security Work Programme 2022–23*; Arnold & Palmer, *Report of the Government Inquiry into Operation Burnham and Related Matters* (2020); Madeleine Laracy, *Report of inquiry into the role of the GCSB and the NZSIS in relation to certain specific events in Afghanistan* (Office of the Inspector-General of Intelligence and Security, 2020); Cheryl Gwyn, *Inquiry into possible New Zealand intelligence and security agencies' engagement with the CIA detention and interrogation programme 2001–2009* (Office of the Inspector-General of Intelligence and Security, 2019); Office of the Inspector-General of Intelligence and Security, Independent Police Conduct Complaints Authority, and the Office of the Inspectorate, *Coordinated review of the management of the LynnMall supermarket attacker* (December 2022).

24 See, for instance, John Key, 'Speech to the New Zealand Institute of International Affairs', Wellington, 6 November 2014; Andrew Little, 'Opening Address to the Massey University National Security Conference 2018', Auckland, 5 April 2018.

25 *Ko tō tātou kāinga tēnei*, 23, 24.

26 Ibid., 25, 26, 27.

27 Minister Andrew Little, 'Press Release: Arihia Bennett to chair Royal Commission Ministerial Advisory Group', 12 June 2021.

28 See, for instance, Didier Bigo, Arnaud Kurze, Elspeth Guild & Sophia Soares, *The Question of the Legitimacy of Secret Services Coalition Among Democracies: For transnational oversight* (copy on file with the author but available at request from Didier Bigo).

29 United Nations, *The Right to Privacy in a Digital Age* (2014).

30 Didier Bigo, Arnaud Kurze, Elspeth Guild & Sophia Soares, *Executive Summary: For a*

transnational oversight of secret services coalitions (copy on file with the author but available at request from Didier Bigo).

31 For an explanation explaining why this is the case, see Damien Rogers, 'The Anatomy of Political Impunity in New Zealand', forthcoming.

32 S.17(d) of the Intelligence and Security Act 2017.

33 Damien Rogers & Shaun Mawsdsley, 'Reconfiguring the Relationship between Intelligence Professionals and the Public: A first step towards democratising New Zealand's national security?', *National Security Journal* 3, no. 3 (2021), https://doi.org/10.26686/pq.v18i1.7504

34 Damien Rogers & Shaun Mawdsley, 'Restoring Public Trust and Confidence in New Zealand's Intelligence and Security Agencies: Is a parliamentary commissioner for security the missing key?', *Policy Quarterly* 18, no. 1 (2022): 59–66.

35 Damien Rogers, 'Public Submission on the Inspector-General of Defence Bill' (6 January 2023), www.parliament.nz/resource/en-NZ/53SCFD_EVI_128620_FD1752/e6a9c2d830c3724693a335d846e4deaabf42687c

11. Leading New Zealand's security system

1 'National security and intelligence role created', *Scoop*, 6 October 2014, www.scoop.co.nz/stories/PA1410/S00026/national-security-and-intelligence-role-created.htm

2 D. Rogers, 'Extraditing Kim Dotcom: A case for reforming New Zealand's intelligence community?', *Kōtuitui: New Zealand Journal of Social Sciences Online* 10, no. 1 (2015): 46–57, https://doi.org/10.1080/1177083X.2014.992791

3 Government Communications and Security Bureau, 'PM releases report into GCSB compliance', 9 April 2013, www.gcsb.govt.nz/news/pm-releases-report-into-gcsb-compliance; Hon Sir Michael Cullen & Dame Patsy Reddy, 'Intelligence and Security in a Free Society: Report of the first independent review of intelligence and security in New Zealand', 29 February 2016, https://igis.govt.nz/assets/Review-report-Part-1.pdf; Intelligence and Security Act 2017.

4 Department of Prime Minister and Cabinet, 'Briefing to the Incoming Minister of National Security and Intelligence,' 20 October 2017.

5 Department of the Prime Minister and Cabinet, 'National Security System Handbook Update, August 2021', www.dpmc.govt.nz/sites/default/files/2021-10/National%20Security%20Systems%20Handbook%20Factsheet%20Update%20October%202021.pdf

6 Department of Prime Minister and Cabinet, 'Briefing to the Incoming Minister of National Security and Intelligence', 20 October 2017, 5.

7 Wil Hoverd, 'Introduction', in *New Zealand National Security: Challenges, trends and issues*, eds W. Hoverd, N. Nelson & C. Bradley (Auckland: Massey University Press, 2017), 30.

8 Department of Prime Minister and Cabinet, 'Briefing to the Incoming Minister of National Security and Intelligence', 20 October 2017, 5.

9 Department of Prime Minister and Cabinet, 'Brief to the Incoming Minister of National Security and Intelligence', 2 November 2020, 10.

10 Department of the Prime Minister and Cabinet, 'The Officials Committee for Domestic and External Security Coordination (ODESC)', 27 October 2020, www.dpmc.govt.nz/our-programmes/national-security-and-intelligence/new-zealands-national-security-system-during-a-crisis/governance-during-crisis/odesc

11 Department of Prime Minister and Cabinet, 'Briefing to the Incoming Minister of National Security and Intelligence', 20 October 2017, 5.

12 Department of Prime Minister and Cabinet, 'Brief to the Incoming Minister of National Security and Intelligence', 2 November 2020, 7.

13 Ibid., 2.

14 *Ko tō tatou kāinga tēnei: Royal Commission of Inquiry into the terrorist attack on Christchurch masjidain on 15 March 2019* (2020), https://christchurchattack.royalcommission.nz

15 Department of Prime Minister and Cabinet, 'Brief to the Incoming Minister of National Security and Intelligence', 2 November 2020, 10–12.

16 Ibid.

17 '2. Recommendations to Improve New Zealand's Counterterrorism Effort', *Ko tō tatou kāinga tēnei*.

18 A BIM 2023b will be produced after the 2023 general election. Department of Prime Minister and Cabinet, 'Aide Memoire — Briefing to the Incoming Minister of National Security and Intelligence', 1 January 2023.

19 '2022 Review of the Intelligence and Security Act 2017', Department of the Prime Minister

and Cabinet 29 May 2023, www.dpmc.govt.nz/our-programmes/national-security/intelligence-and-security-act-2017/2022-review-intelligence-and

20 Department of Prime Minister and Cabinet, 'Aide Memoire — Briefing to the Incoming Minister of National Security and Intelligence, 1 January 2023, 3.

21 Ibid., 4.

22 Ibid., 3.

23 Ibid.

24 Ibid., 3, 9.

25 Ibid.

26 Department of Prime Minister and Cabinet, *Aotearoa's National Security Strategy: Secure Together Tō Tātou Korowai Maanaki*, 4 August 2023.

27 Ibid., ii.

28 Ibid., i.

29 The author has attended both speeches and the release of the 2023 National Security Strategy.

30 John Key, 'Speech to NZ Institute of International Affairs', 6 November 2014, www.beehive.govt.nz/speech/speech-nz-institute-international-affairs-0

31 Ibid.

32 Ibid.

33 Ibid.

34 Ibid.

35 Ibid.

36 'National Security Long-term Insights Briefing', Department of Prime Minister and Cabinet, 25 May 2023, www.dpmc.govt.nz/our-programmes/national-security/national-security-long-term-insights-briefing#:~:text=What%20is%20a%20Long%2Dterm,least%20once%20every%20three%20years

37 Rt Hon Jacinda Ardern, 'Speech to New Zealand's Hui on Countering Terrorism and Violent Extremism — He Whenua Taurikura', 1 November 2022, www.beehive.govt.nz/speech/speech-new-zealand%E2%80%99s-hui-countering-terrorism-and-violent-extremism-%E2%80%93-he-whenua-taurikura

38 Ibid.

39 Ibid.

40 Ibid.

41 Department of Prime Minister and Cabinet, *Aotearoa's National Security Strategy: Secure Together Tō Tātou Korowai Maanaki*, 12.

12. As safe now as we were then

1 The precise number of bombings, bomb threats, or improvised explosive devices discovered in New Zealand in the course of the 1970s has never been tabulated. The historical sequence of 'terrorist' type events using a range of sources to get an idea of the relative frequency and severity of them was attempted in 2019. There were at least a dozen bombings prompted by opposition to the Vietnam War in 1970; there may have been more. See John Battersby, 'The Ghost of New Zealand's Terrorism Past and Present', *National Security Journal* 1, no. 1 (2019): 40, https://doi.org/10.36878/NSJ201901.35

2 John Battersby, 'Can Old Lessons Inform Current Directions: Australia, New Zealand, and Ananda Marga's trans-Tasman "terrorism" 1975–1978', *Studies in Conflict & Terrorism* 44, no. 8 (2021): 686–700, https://doi.org/10.1080/1057610X.2019.1575031

3 Battersby, 'The Ghost of New Zealand's Terrorism Past and Present', 35–47.

4 Ibid., 38.

5 Hamish McNeilly, 'The snowman and the queen: The story of a Kiwi teen terrorist and would-be assassin', *Stuff*, 8 January 2018, www.stuff.co.nz/national/crime/99760154/the-snowman-and-the-queen-the-story-of-a-kiwi-teen-terrorist-and-wouldbe-assassin

6 Vaughan Yarwood, 'A Bomb for Big Brother: One man takes on the state', *New Zealand Geographic*, www.nzgeo.com/stories/7335

7 Sam Sherwood, 'Trades Hall bombing: Chief suspect dies in cold case, police interview revealed', *New Zealand Herald*, 19 March 2023, www.nzherald.co.nz/nz/trades-hall-bombing-nearly-40-years-on-chief-suspect-dies-in-cold-case-police-interview-released/WG4UYV2Z7ZDY3E7MALW64GHC7I

8 John Battersby, 'There is No Terrorism Here!: New Zealand's long-standing gulf between perception and reality', submitted and accepted, Konrad Adenauer Stiftung. Publication pending.

9   Sheridan Webb, 'From Hijackings to Right-Wing Extremism: The drivers of New Zealand's counter-terrorism legislation 1977–2020', *National Security Journal* 3, no. 1 (2021): 101–24, https://doi.org/10.36878/nsj20210409.04

10 See Michael King, *Death of the Rainbow Warrior* (Auckland: Penguin, 1986), 152.

11 Webb, 'From Hijackings to Right-Wing Extremism', 107–08.

12 John Battersby, 'The Ghost of New Zealand's Terrorism Past and Present', 40.

13 John Battersby & Rhys Ball, 'Christchurch in the Context of New Zealand Terrorism and Right-wing Extremism', *Journal of Policing, Intelligence and Counter Terrorism* 14, no. 3 (2019): 191–207, https://doi.org/10.1080/18335330.2019.1662077

14 'Remembering the deadly Aramoana massacre 30 years on', *Stuff*, 13 November 2020, www.stuff.co.nz/national/crime/123390946/remembering-the-deadly-aramoana-massacre-30-years-on

15 Prior to the Arms Act 1983, all weapons were legally required to be registered. The 1983 Act removed the register and licensed the firearms owners instead. Sir Thomas Thorp, *Review of Firearms Control in New Zealand, 30 June 1997*, https://colfo.org.nz/images/files/review-of-firearms-control-in-new-zealand-recommendations.pdf

16 Leith Huffadine, Brad Flahive & Megan Gattey, 'Tiger Woods, the NZ Gold Open and the terrorist cyanide threat', *Stuff*, 30 March 2018, www.stuff.co.nz/national/102697753/tiger-woods-the-nz-golf-open-and-the-terrorist-cyanide-threat; Patrick Gower, Paula Oliver & Alan Perrott, 'Cyanide letter threat to Cup', *New Zealand Herald*, 26 February 2003, www.nzherald.co.nz/nz/cyanide-letter-threat-to-cup/EXHWJDFZUWXJWRJZRPMBT4AOYE

17 'Act too complex to use, says Collins', *Stuff*, 31 January 2009, www.stuff.co.nz/national/17681/Act-too-complex-to-use-says-Collins

18 Affidavit of Detective Sergeant Aaron Lee Pascoe, released under OIA request, 2018.

19 'Review of terror laws stopped', *Sunday Star-Times*, 15 September 2013, www.stuff.co.nz/national/politics/9166763/Review-of-terror-laws-stopped

20 Interview with former officer, name withheld, 22 August 2022.

21 'The Terrorism Files' and 'Watched at every step', *Dominion Post*, 14 November 2007.

22 'Review of terror laws stopped'.

23 References to radicalisation and deradicalisation are numerous. An excellent discussion is provided in Richard Jackson & Damien Rogers, 'Trans-disciplinary Dialogue on New Zealand's Counter Terrorism Approach: A call to action for researchers', *National Security Journal* 5, no. 1 (2023): 1–21; https://doi.org/10.36878/nsj20230319.01

24 John Battersby, 'Security Sector Practitioner Perceptions of the Terror Threat Environment Before the Christchurch Attacks', *Kōtuitui: New Zealand Journal of Social Sciences Online* 15, no. 2 (2020):295–309; doi.org/10.1080/1177083X.2019.1701049

25 Ibid., 297.

26 Aliya Danzeisen, 'New Zealand as Model for Governments Connecting with Muslim Communities', *Line of Defence* (Winter 2018): 52–54, https://indd.adobe.com/view/2ec2dced-3b72-4e45-9261-28ddf0da58f3

27 Brenton Tarrant's manifesto 'The Great Replacement', viewed with permission of the Chief Censor.

28 Collette Devlin, 'How effective was the $120m firearms buyback scheme? We don't know', *Stuff*, 7 May 2020, www.stuff.co.nz/national/politics/121445278/how-effective-was-the-120m-firearms-buyback-scheme-we-dont-yet-know

29 'Days of Rage' refers to the 1970s-era terrorism largely in the US. The term was used as a book title by Brian Burrough, *The Days of Rage: America's radical underground, the FBI, and the forgotten age of revolutionary violence* (Harmondsworth: Penguin, 2017).

30 Royal Commission of Inquiry into the Terrorist Attack on Christchurch Mosques on 15 March 2019, Order 2019, 8 April 2019, www.legislation.govt.nz/regulation/public/2019/0072/latest/LMS183988.html

31 Paul Cruickshank, 'Source: Early assessment finds TATP at Barcelona attackers' bomb factory', *CNN*, 19 August 2017, https://edition.cnn.com/2017/08/18/europe/spain-terror-attacks-tatp/index.html

32 Nick Paton Walsh et al., 'Inside the August plot to kill Maduro with drones', *CNN*, 21 June 2019, https://edition.cnn.com/2019/03/14/americas/venezuela-drone-maduro-intl/index.html

33 Andrew Shelley, 'A Counter-drone Strategy for New Zealand', *National Security Journal* 4, no. 1 (2022): 63–91; https://doi.org/10.36878/nsj201901.17

34 Thomas Manch, 'New Zealand's terror threat level drops from "medium" to "low",' *Stuff*, 30 November 2022, https://www.stuff.co.nz/national/politics/130625081/new-zealands-terror-threat-level-drops-from-medium-to-low

13. Behind the floral aesthetic

1. Extremism as defined in New Zealand's Counter Terrorism Strategy 2021 (DPMC): 'Religious, social, political belief systems that exist substantially outside of more broadly accepted belief systems in large parts of society, and are often seen as objectionable to large parts of society. Extreme ideologies may seek radical changes in the nature of government, religion, or society to create a community based on their ideology.'
2. Seyward Darby, 'The Rise of the Valkyries', *Harper's Magazine: Report*, September 2017, https://harpers.org/archive/2017/09/the-rise-of-the-valkyries
3. See work by Kathleen Blee, Kathleen Belew, Kristy Campion, Cynthia Miller-Idriss and Julia Ebner.
4. There is nothing wrong with a traditional family/wife lifestyle, however RWE 'Trad Wife' versions blend in racism and other forms of bigotry over time.
5. Donna Carson, 'Breaking the Masculine Looking Glass: Women as co-founders, nurturers, and executors of extremism in New Zealand' (Master's thesis, Massey University, 2021), 73.
6. Kathleen M. Blee, *Inside Organised Racism: Women of the hate movement* (Los Angeles: University of California Press, 2002), 136.
7. Kirsty Campion, 'Women in the Extreme and Radical Right: Forms of participation and their implications', *Social Sciences* 9, no. 149 (August 2020): 12.
8. Carson, 'Breaking the Masculine Looking Glass'.
9. Ibid., 140.
10. Annie Kelly, 'The Housewives of White Supremacy', *New York Times*, 1 June 2018, www.nytimes.com/2018/06/01/opinion/sunday/tradwives-women-alt-right.html
11. This excludes Jewish men, who are often isolated as a specific enemy population by RWE. Other targets are LGBTQA+ communities or anyone they deem to be the enemy, such as the media, academics and authorities.
12. Counter Extremism Project, 'Accelerationism' (2023), www.counterextremism.com/content/accelerationism
13. Darby, 'The Rise of the Valkyries'.
14. Other terms can be used by believers, such as White Genocide; Daniel Byman, *Spreading Hate* (Oxford: Oxford University Press, 2022): 105–06.
15. Michelle Duff, 'How women are being weaponised by the freedom movement', *Stuff*, 3 July 2023, www.stuff.co.nz/national/300621092/how-women-are-being-weaponised-by-the-freedom-movement
16. Karla Cunningham, 'Cross Regional Trends in Female Terrorism', *Studies in Conflict and Terrorism* 26 (2003): 173.
17. Kathleen Blee, 'Similarities/Differences in Gender and Far Right Politics in Europe and the USA', in *Gender and the Far-Right Politics in Europe*, eds Michaela Kottig, Renata Bitzan & Andrea Peto (London: Palgrave Macmillian, 2017), 195.
18. Darby, 'Rise of the Valkyries'.
19. Ibid.
20. Ibid.
21. Carson, 'Breaking the Masculine Looking Glass', 158.
22. Dreama G. Moon & Michelle A. Holling, 'White Supremacy in Heels: (White) feminism, white supremacy, and discursive violence', *Communication and Critical/Cultural Studies* 17, no. 2 (June 2020): 255.
23. Blee, 'Similarities/Differences', 195.
24. Major Marne L. Sutten, 'The Rising Importance of Women in Terrorism and the Need to Reform Counterterrorism Strategy', *School of Advanced Military Studies Monographs* (Kansas, USA, 2009), 27.
25. 'Posie Parker: Anti-trans rally attracted a range of far-right groups, researchers say', *New Zealand Herald*, 28 March 2023, www.nzherald.co.nz/nz/posie-parker-anti-trans-rally-attracted-a-range-of-far-right-groups-researchers-say/T6AMCXNMUFGDPBIT5SY5ALBR5U
26. Nikki Preston, 'High Court rules Auckland Council within rights to cancel Lauren Southern, Stefan Molyneux event', *New Zealand Herald*, 30 September 2019, www.nzherald.co.nz/nz/high-court-rules-auckland-council-within-rights-to-cancel-lauren-southern-stefan-molyneux-event/BY4MX0Q7P5AJD3G7C2LYAWEHUE
27. Ashley Mattheis, 'Shieldmaidens of Whiteness: (Alt) maternalism and women recruiting for the Far/Alt Right', *Journal for Deradicalization* 17 (Winter 2018/2019): 128–29.
28. Monica Hesse, 'Wolfie James and the insidious role of female white nationalists', *Washington Post*, 14 August 2019, www.washingtonpost.com/lifestyle/style/wolfie-james-

274

and-the-horrifying-softer-side-of-white-supremacy/2019/08/14/19c86a68-babe-11e9-b3b4-2bb69e8c4e39_story.html

29 Lana Lokteff as quoted by Darby, 'The Rise of the Valkyries'.

30 Rebecca Turkington & Audrey Alexander, 'Treatment of Terrorists: How does gender affect justice?', *CTC Sentinel* 11, no. 8 (2018): 24–29.

31 Mattheis, 'Shieldmaidens of Whiteness', 128–29.

32 Kirsty Campion, 'Women in the Extreme and Radical Right: Forms of participation and their implications', *Social Sciences* 9, no. 149 (2020): 15.

33 Carson, 'Breaking the Masculine Looking Glass', 70.

34 The manosphere consists of specific groups such as involuntary celibates (incels), MGTOW (men going their own way), PUAs (pick up artists) and extreme MRAs (men's rights activists).

35 Alexandra Minna Stern, *Proud Boys and the White Ethnostate: How the alt-right is warping the American imagination* (Boston: Beacon Press, 2019), 93–94.

36 Ibid.

37 Carson, 'Breaking the Masculine Looking Glass', 80.

38 Anti-Defamation League (ADL), 'When women are the enemy: The intersection of misogyny and white supremacy', www.adl.org/resources/report/when-women-are-enemy-intersection-misogyny-and-white-supremacy

39 Julie Ebner & Jacob Davey, 'How Women Advance the Internationalization of the Far Right', in *Perspectives on the Future of Women, Gender, & Violent Extremism*, ed. Audrey Alexander (Washington, DC: George Washington University, 2019), 34.

40 Ibid.

41 Julia Ebner, *Going Dark: The secret social lives of extremists* (London: Bloomsbury, 2020), 54–57.

42 Seyward Darby, *Sisters in Hate: American women and white extremism* (New York: Back Bay Books, 2021), 219.

43 Stern, *Proud Boys and the White Ethnostate*, 93–94.

44 ADL, 'When Women are the Enemy', 10.

45 Patrik Hermansson, David Lawrence, Joe Mulhal & Simon Murdoch, *The International Alt-Right: Fascism for the 21st century?* (London: Routledge, 2020), 185.

46 Darby, *Sisters in Hate*, 155. Telegram is a popular encrypted, largely unmoderated, global social media platform that allows for private messaging, data sharing (videos, images, documents) and group discussions.

47 David Gilbert, 'Inside a US neo-Nazi home-school network with thousands of members', *Vice News*, 20 January 2023, www.vice.com/en/article/z34ane/neo-nazi-homeschool-ohio

48 Ibid.

49 Jessica T. DeCuir-Gunby, Elizabeth M. Allen & Janet K. Boone, 'Examining Pre-service Teachers' Color-blind Racial Ideology, Emotion Regulation, and Inflexibility with Stigmatizing Thoughts about Race', *Contemporary Educational Psychology* 60 (2020): 1.

50 Ebner, *Going Dark*, 227.

51 Carson, 'Breaking the Masculine Looking Glass', 93.

52 Ebner, *Going Dark*, 240.

53 YouTube, 'Lauren Southern on Tucker Carlson Tonight/Fox News 4/14/2023', www.youtube.com/watch?v=Q6dNO_fP-ig

54 Karim Zidan, 'Tara LaRosa: The worrying case of MMA's Proud Girl', *The Guardian*, 21 January 2021, www.theguardian.com/sport/2021/jan/21/tara-larosa-mma-far-right-proud-boys

55 Ibid.

56 New Zealand Police, 'Statement of case to designate the American Proud Boys as a terrorist entity', 20 June 2022, www.police.govt.nz/sites/default/files/publications/statement-of-case-the-american-proud-boys-terrorist-entity-20-june-2022.pdf

57 Fourteen people and ten white supremacist-nationalist groups.

58 Magna Legal Services, Exhibit 2: Deposition of Erica Alduino, 3 December 2018, www.courtlistener.com/recap/gov.uscourts.vawd.109120/gov.uscourts.vawd.109120.457.2.pdf; Darby, *Sisters in Hate*, 171–72.

59 Cynthia Miller-Idriss, 'Women among the Jan 6th attackers are the new normal of right-wing extremism', *MSNBC*, 8 January 2022, www.msnbc.com/opinion/women-among-jan-6-attackers-are-new-normal-right-wing-n1287163

60 Kelly, 'The Housewives of White Supremacy'.

61 Carson, 'Breaking the Masculine Looking Glass'.

62 It is of note that the National Front disbanded entirely after the 2019 Christchurch mosque attacks and members have re-emerged in different movements.

63 Carson, 'Breaking the Masculine Looking Glass', 159–63.
64 Ibid.
65 Ibid.
66 Ibid, 89–90.
67 See work by Kathleen Blee, Kathleen Belew, Kristy Campion, Cynthia Miller-Idriss and Julia Ebner.
68 Other presentations are known as White Power Barbies, Flashy Femmes, Shield Maidens and Valkyries; Nancy S. Love, 'Shield Maidens, Flashy Femmes and Tradwives: Feminism, patriarchy and right-wing populism', *Frontiers in Sociology* 5 (December 2020): 1.
69 Darby, *Sisters in Hate*, 257.
70 Carson, 'Breaking the Masculine Looking Glass', 2.

14. Russia's invasion of Ukraine

1 Christoph Trebesch et al., 'The Ukraine support tracker: Which countries help Ukraine and how?', *Kiel Working Paper* 2218 (February 2023): 1–77, www.ifw-kiel.de/fileadmin/Dateiverwaltung/IfW-Publications/-ifw/Kiel_Working_Paper/2022/KWP_2218_Which_countries_help_Ukraine_and_how_/KWP_2218_Trebesch_et_al_Ukraine_Support_Tracker.pdf
2 Hans P. Midttun, 'Why did the Russian "Blitzkrieg" fail?', *Stratagem*, 8 July 2022, www.stratagem.no/why-did-the-russian-blitzkrieg-fail
3 Rafał Kopeć, *Strategie nuklearne w okresie pozimnowojennym* (Kraków: UP Scientific Publishing House, 2014), 10–11.
4 Andrew O. Gordijewski, *KGB*, transl. R. Brzeski (Warszawa: Bellona Publishing House, 1997), 442–43.
5 Andrzej Wawrzusiszyn, 'Neoimperializm w polityce bezpieczeństwa Federacji Rosyjskiej', *Cybersecurity and Law* 8, no. 2 (2022): 265–77.
6 K. Rydel, 'Przyłączenie Krymu przez Rosję w świetle prawa międzynarodowego', *Historia da Teoria* 1, no. 7 (2018): 225–37.
7 In 2014 Unkraine passed the Law of Ukraine 'On the Protection of Citizen Rights and Freedoms on Temporarily Occupied Territory of Ukraine', which defines the status of the Crimea Peninsula as temporarily occupied as a result of Russia's military aggression; the so-called law on the reintegration of Donbass, in 2018, while not recognising Russian aggression as a state of war, de facto confirmed the existence of the conflict in eastern Ukraine. See Daniel Szeligowski, 'Ukraińska ustawa o okupowanych terytoriach Donbasu', *Biuletyn PISM* 12, no. 1585 (24 January 2018): 1–2.
8 'EU sanctions against Russia explained', Council of the European Union, www.consilium.europa.eu/en/policies/sanctions/restrictive-measures-against-russia-over-ukraine/sanctions-against-russia-explained
9 Jason Li, 'Ukraine at one year: Has China supported Russia?', *Stimson*, 13 February 2023, www.stimson.org/2023/ukraine-at-one-year-has-china-supported-russia
10 Amy L. Catalinac, 'Why New Zealand took itself out of ANZUS: Observing "opposition for autonomy" in asymmetric alliances', *Foreign Policy Analysis* 6 (2010): 317–38.
11 James Rolfe, 'New Zealand's security: Alliances and other military relationships', Centre for Strategic Studies, Victoria University of Wellington, Working Paper 10 (1997): 1–23.
12 Ministry of Foreign Affairs and Trade, *Strategic Intentions 2021–2025* (Wellington: New Zealand Government, 2016), 13, www.mfat.govt.nz/assets/About-us-Corporate/MFAT-strategies-and-frameworks/MFAT-Strategic-Intentions-2021-2025.pdf
13 A. Kukliński, 'O nowym modelu polityki regionalnej — artykuł dyskusyjny', *Studia Regionalne i Lokalne* 4, no. 4 (2003): 5–14.
14 Naoki Kamimura, 'Civil society, nuclear disarmament and the U.S. alliance: The cases of Australia, New Zealand, and Japan', *East-West Centre Working Papers, Politics and Security Series* 8 (October 2004): 1–29.
15 This attitude resulted in the signing of the AUKUS agreement in September 2021 between Australia, the United States and Great Britain, under which Australia will ultimately receive five submarines. However, any concerns about the increasing nuclearisation of Australia, and in particular accusations from China of AUKUS non-compliance with the SPNFZ Treaty, are not justified. All submarines delivered under this agreement will be nuclear-powered, but not nuclear-armed. See Lauren Sanders, 'If AUKUS is all about nuclear submarines, how can it comply with nuclear non-proliferation treaties? A law scholar explains', *The Conversation*, 15 March 2023, https://theconversation.com/if-aukus-is-all-about-nuclear-

276

submarines-how-can-it-comply-with-nuclear-non-proliferation-treaties-a-law-scholar-explains-201760

16 David Capie, 'Nuclear-free New Zealand: Contingency, contestation and consensus in public policymaking', in *Successful Public Policy: Lessons from Australia and New Zealand*, eds J. Luetjens, M. Mintrom & P. 't Hart (Acton: ANU Press, 2019), 390.

17 Kevin P. Clements, 'New Zealand paying for nuclear ban', *Bulletin of the Atomic Scientists* 43, no. 6 (July/August 1987): 41–44.

18 Catalinac, 'Why New Zealand took itself out of ANZUS'.

19 Kamimura, 'Civil society', 814.

20 Reuben Steff, 'The Biden administration and New Zealand's strategic options: Asymmetric hedging, tight Five Eyes alignment, and armed neutrality', *National Security Journal* 3, no. 2 (2021): 1–22.

21 Robert G. Patman, 'New Zealand's multilateralism and the challenge of an international system in transition', in *Multilateralism in a Changing World Order*, eds C. Echle et al. (Singapore: Konrad-Adenauer Stiftung, 2018), 99.

22 'NZ "ally" and close friend of US — Rice', *New Zealand Herald*, 26 July 2008, www.nzherald.co.nz/nz/nz-ally-and-close-friend-of-us-rice/PDXIJQENQRKG5ZTXEMIYYINFNE

23 Ministry of Defence, *2014 Defence Assessment* (Wellington: New Zealand Government, 2014), 55, www.defence.govt.nz/assets/Uploads/802ce528c8/defence-assessment-2014-public.pdf; Ministry of Defence, *2016 Defence White Paper* (Wellington: New Zealand Government, 2016), 32, www.defence.govt.nz/assets/Uploads/daac08133a/defence-white-paper-2016.pdf

24 Robert Ayson, 'New Zealand and the great irresponsible: Coping with Russia, China and the US', *Australian Journal of International Affairs* 74, no. 4 (2020): 455–78.

25 Ministry of Foreign Affairs and Trade, 'Russia sanctions', www.mfat.govt.nz/en/countries-and-regions/europe/ukraine/russian-invasion-of-ukraine/sanctions

26 Neil Reid, 'Russia invades Ukraine: Putin's "full-scale war" strike condemned by NZ politicians', *New Zealand Herald*, 24 February 2022, www.nzherald.co.nz/nz/russia-invades-ukraine-putins-full-scale-war-strike-condemned-by-nz-politicians/I5ZDO4LJZDVIMCVXXCTG7DS3IU

27 Alexander Gillespie, 'Ukraine a year on: The invasion changed NZ foreign policy — as the war drags on, cracks will begin to show', *The Conversation*, 23 February 2023, https://theconversation.com/ukraine-a-year-on-the-invasion-changed-nz-foreign-policy-as-the-war-drags-on-cracks-will-begin-to-show-200524

28 Geoffrey Miller, 'Russia's invasion of Ukraine will change New Zealand's foreign policy', *The Diplomat*, 1 March 2022, https://thediplomat.com/2022/03/russias-invasion-of-ukraine-will-change-new-zealands-foreign-policy

29 Ministry of Defence, *Strategic Defence Policy Statement 2018* (Wellington: New Zealand Government, 2018), 13, www.defence.govt.nz/assets/Uploads/8958486b29/Strategic-Defence-Policy-Statement-2018.pdf

30 'Jacinda Ardern calls for reform of united Nations, urges "friendship" in climate challenge', *SBS News*, 7 July 2022, www.sbs.com.au/news/article/jacinda-ardern-calls-for-reform-of-united-nations-urges-friendship-in-climate-challenge/uhhkfpxab

31 The United Nations (UN), *Charter of the United Nations and Statute of the International Court of Justice* (San Francisco: UN, 1945), https://treaties.un.org/doc/publication/ctc/uncharter.pdf

32 The latest Strategic Foreign Policy Assessment highlights three 'Big Shifts' in the international order that will define New Zealand's position in the world in the period to 2035. See Ministry of Foreign Affairs and Trade, *Navigating a Shifting World* (Wellington: New Zealand Government, 2023), 6, www.mfat.govt.nz/assets/About-us-Corporate/MFAT-strategies-and-frameworks/MFATs-2023-Strategic-Foreign-Policy-Assessment-Navigating-a-shifting-world-June-2023.pdf

33 Austin Gee & Robert G. Patman, 'Small state or minor power? New Zealand's Five Eyes membership, intelligence reforms, and Wellington's response to China's growing Pacific role', *Intelligence and National Security* 36, no. 1 (2021): 34–50.

34 Robert Ayson, 'The Ardern government's foreign policy challenges', *Policy Quarterly* 14, no. 2 (May 2018): 18–24.

35 Ministry of Foreign Affairs & Trade, 'Russian Invasion of Ukraine', www.mfat.govt.nz/en/countries-and-regions/europe/ukraine/russian-invasion-of-ukraine

15. Digital currencies

1 Saifedean Ammous, *The Bitcoin Standard: The decentralized alternative to central banking* (New Jersey: Wiley, 2018); James Bridle, 'Bitcoin and the Money Myth', *New Statesman* 148, no. 5479 (2019): 32–37; Benjamin Fichera, 'La Guerre des Cryptomonnaies', *Ecole de Guerre Economique*, 19 December 2022, https://tinyurl.com/4xjscmuw; Bill Maurer, Taylor Nelms & Lana Swartz, 'When Perhaps the Real Problem is Money Itself! The practical materiality of bitcoin', *Social Semiotics* 23, no. 2 (2013): 261–77; David Orell & Roman Chlupty, *The Evolution of Money* (New York: Columbia University Press, 2016); James Rickards, *Cryptocurrency Wars* (Baltimore: Agora Financial, 2018); Zac Zimmer, 'Bitcoin and Potosí Silver: Historical perspectives on cryptocurrency', *Technology and Culture* 58, no. 2 (2017): 307–34.

2 Alex Sims, 'Cryptocurrency and cryptocurrency exchanges explained', University of Auckland, 19 December 2022, https://tinyurl.com/49uz72ek; 'Australian-based cryptocurrency exchange Swyftx launches in New Zealand', *RNZ*, 31 August 2021, https://tinyurl.com/yck8cvu4

3 'Cryptocurrencies', Financial Markets Authority, 28 November 2022, https://tinyurl.com/yckh58jk

4 'Crypto a double-edged sword, MPs told', *Sunday Star-Times*, 21 November 2021.

5 'Waikato DHB ransomware cyberattack: Documents released online', *RNZ*, 29 June 2021, https://tinyurl.com/5xjzuh8e

6 'Crypto a double-edged sword, MPs told'; Inphysec, *Waikato District Health Board (WDHB) Incident Response Analysis*, Wellington, 2022.

7 Tom Pullar-Strecker, 'Ransomware attacks and crypto-currency scams on the rise', *Stuff*, 16 September 2021, https://tinyurl.com/f8jspe9r

8 'Waikato DHB data breach likely "seven . . . eight figure" cryptocurrency ransom — expert', *RNZ*, 28 May 2021, https://tinyurl.com/3m3brb3x; Miriam Burrell, 'NZ spy agency assisting Waikato DHB after attack/ransom demand', *New Zealand Herald*, 18 May 2021, https://tinyurl.com/mwta5frt

9 'The rise of e-money: Why govcoins matter', *The Economist* 439, no. 9244 (2021): 11.

10 Amber Wadsworth, *The Pros and Cons of Issuing a Central Bank Digital Currency* (Wellington: Reserve Bank of New Zealand, 2018); *The Future of Money: Central bank digital currency* (Wellington: Reserve Bank of New Zealand, 2021).

11 'RBNZ says no decision yet on central bank digital currency', *Reuters*, 28 April 2022, https://tinyurl.com/5n7pwh9w

12 Jean-François Gayraud, *Le Nouveau Capitalisme Criminel* (Paris: Odile Jacob, 2014).

13 *Transnational Organised Crime in New Zealand: Our strategy 2020–2025* (Wellington: New Zealand Police, 2020).

14 Jared Kleiman, 'Beyond the Silk Road: Unregulated decentralized virtual currencies continue to endanger US national security', *National Security Law Brief* 4, no. 1 (2013): 59–78.

15 David Fisher, 'Criminals steal $45,000 in Bitcoin during NZ police money-laundering operation', *New Zealand Herald*, 9 July 2021, https://tinyurl.com/y6j3besm

16 Joshua Baron et al., *National Security Implications of Virtual Currency: Examining the potential for non-state actor deployment* (Santa Monica, CA: RAND Corporation, 2015).

17 Simon Butler, 'The Philosophy of Bitcoin and the Question of Money', *Theory, Culture & Society* 39, no. 5 (2021): 1–22.

18 Strategic Forecasting Inc., *Examining the Future of Bitcoin* (Austin: STRATFOR, 2015); Donncha Kavanagh & Gianluca Miscione, 'Bitcoin and blockchain: A coup d'état in digital heterotopia', research paper, Humanistic Management Network, 2015.

19 Ryan Frebowitz, 'Cryptocurrency and State Sovereignty' (Master's thesis, Naval Postgraduate School, 2018).

20 James Rickards, *Currency Wars: The making of the next global crisis* (Princeton: Portfolio/Penguin, 2012).

21 Gal Luft & Anne Korin, *De-dollarization: The revolt against the dollar and the rise of a new financial world order* (Independently published, 2019).

22 Tom Robinson, 'How Iran uses Bitcoin to evade sanctions and "export" millions of barrels of oil', *Elliptic*, 21 May 2021, www.elliptic.co/blog/how-iran-uses-bitcoin-mining-to-evade-sanctions

23 Nicholas Ross Smith, 'Could Russia Utilize Cryptocurrencies in its Foreign Policy Grand Strategizing?', *Russia in Global Affairs* 17, no. 2 (2019): 143–52; Annabelle Liang, 'Russia considers accepting Bitcoin for oil and gas', *BBC*, 23 March 2022, https://tinyurl.com/27zhvn4r

24 Sam Davidson, 'Digital Dynasties: How China's cryptocurrency could unseat the dollar', *Harvard International Review*, 29 August 2022, https://tinyurl.com/3fjad7km; Robert

Greene, 'Beijing's global ambitions for central bank digital currencies are growing clearer', Carnegie Endowment for International Peace, 6 October 2021, https://carnegieendowment.org/2021/10/06/beijing-s-global-ambitions-for-central-bank-digital-currencies-are-growing-clearer-pub-85503

25 The dollar's hegemonic position as the top reserve currency gives Washington the unrivalled power to monitor dollar-denominated transactions, freeze assets held in dollars and isolate enemies from international financial platforms and capital markets controlled directly or indirectly by American entities. For instance, US geopolitical analyst George Friedman holds that, in the context of the retaliatory measures implemented as a response to the Russian invasion of Ukraine, 'the United States has demonstrated that perhaps the most powerful weapon in the world is the weaponized dollar'. See: George Friedman, 'Learning lessons from the war in Ukraine', *Geopolitical Futures*, 15 March 2022, https://tinyurl.com/tf8uctea

26 Juan Zarate, *Treasury's War: The unleashing of a new era of financial warfare* (New York: Public Affairs, 2013).

27 Zongyuan Zoe Lie & Mihaela Papa, *Can BRICS De-Dollarize the Global Financial System?* (Cambridge: Cambridge University Press, 2022).

28 Matthew Pine, *Bitcoin and US National Security* (Bitcoin Policy Institute, 2022).

29 Rickards, *Cryptocurrency Wars*.

30 Michael Morell, Josh Kirsher & Thomas Schoenberger, *An Analysis of Bitcoin's Use in Illicit Finance* (Crypto Council for Innovation, 2021).

31 Sam Biddle, 'The NSA worked to "track down" Bitcoin users, Snowden documents reveal', *The Intercept*, 18 March 2018, https://tinyurl.com/34huppfz; Morgen Peck, 'Let's destroy bitcoin', *MIT Technology Review* 121, no. 3 (2018): 72–77; Leah Goodman, 'No paper tigers: The US government wants to know if bitcoin and other virtual currencies are a threat to national security', *Newsweek* 167, no. 23 (2016): 22–24; William Burns, 'A World of Risk', *Wall Street Journal*'s CEO Summit (conference), 6 December 2021, https://tinyurl.com/2jvzkfmu

32 Zarate, *Treasury's War*, 46–49.

33 Ashwath Komath, 'Bancor Comes of Age: A case for an Indian bitcoin reserve', *India Quarterly* 78, no. 1 (2021): 121–42.

34 Rickards, *Cryptocurrency Wars*.

35 Inland Revenue, 'Mining cryptoassets for a profit-making scheme', *Inland Revenue*, 28 April 2021, https://tinyurl.com/2vjekbxw; 'Cryptocurrency Mining NZ: New Zealand's bitcoin guide', Cryptocurrency NZ, 2023, https://tinyurl.com/4fu4kb52.

36 Megan McBride & Zack Gold, *Cryptocurrency: Implications for special operations forces* (Arlington: CNA Analysis and Solutions, 2019); Chris Telley, 'A Coin for the Tsar: The two disruptive sides of cryptocurrency', *Small Wars Journal*, 6 January 2018, https://tinyurl.com/2tp9masu; Alexander Losev, 'Regulating the Unregulated: What is the future of crypto assets', *Valdai Discussion Club*, 2 March 2022, https://tinyurl.com/bbnfeyh8

37 Neil Barnas, 'Blockchains in National Defense: Trustworthy systems in a trustless world' (research report, Air University, 2016).

38 Reuben Steff, 'The Biden Administration and New Zealand's Strategic Options: Asymmetric hedging, tight Five Eyes alignment, and armed neutrality', *National Security Journal* 3, no. 2 (2021): 27–48.

39 José Miguel Alonso-Trabanco, 'Reformulating New Zealand's Grand Strategy', *New Zealand International Review* 48, no. 3 (2023): 11–14.

40 Society for Worldwide Interbank Financial Telecommunication (SWIFT), *RMB Tracker* (La Hulpe: SWIFT, 2022).

41 Parag Khanna, *The Future is Asian* (New York, Simon & Schuster, 2019).

16. The future of the 'good citzen'

1 New Zealand Ministry of Defence, *2016 Defence White Paper*, June 2016, 18–19.

2 Ibid., 32.

3 Ibid., 5, 17.

4 Oliver Bullough, 'Are you a "Russophobe"?', *Politico Magazine*, 3 April 2014, www.politico.com/magazine/story/2014/04/just-who-is-a-russophobe-105292

5 Andrew Higgins, 'No one in Europe is telling Poland to "shut up" now', *New York Times*, 21 February 2023, www.nytimes.com/2023/02/21/world/europe/poland-russia-ukraine.html

6 National Security Bureau, *White Paper on National Security of the Republic of Poland*, 2013, www.bbn.gov.pl/ftp/dokumenty/Biala_Ksiega_inter_mm.pdf

7   'Visit of the President of the Republic of Poland to Georgia', The official website of the President of the Republic of Poland, 12 August 2008, www.president.pl/archive/news-archive-2000-2010/news-2008/president-of-rp-sets-off-to-visit-georgia,37405

8   Wojciech Huk, 'The largest order in the history of the Polish arms industry: 1400 new vehicles for the army', *Polish Press Agency*, 1 March 2023, www.pap.pl/aktualnosci/news%2C1543168%2Cnajwieksze-zamowienie-w-historii-polskiego-przemyslu-zbrojeniowego-1400

9   Mariusz Błaszczak (@mblaszczak), 'The great reinforcement of the Polish artillery is getting closer. The US State Department has approved the sale of almost 500 Himars launchers to Poland', *Twitter*, 7 February 2023, https://tinyurl.com/yue4u3cr

10 Matthew Day, 'Poland builds Europe's largest land force to counter Russian threat', *The Telegraph*, 11 March 2023, www.telegraph.co.uk/world-news/2023/03/11/revolution-polish-army-builds-europes-largest-land-force

11 Law of 11 March 2022 on Homeland Defence (Journal of Laws of 2022, Item 655), https://sip.lex.pl/akty-prawne/dzu-dziennik-ustaw/obrona-ojczyzny-19220069

12 OECD Report, *Responding to the Ukrainian Refugee Crisis*, International Migration Outlook 2022, 46th edn., 95–115, https://read.oecd-ilibrary.org/social-issues-migration-health/international-migration-outlook-2022_23898d5a-en#page1

13 'Ukraine Support Tracker', Kiel Institute for the World Economy, www.ifw-kiel.de/topics/war-against-ukraine/ukraine-support-tracker/?cookieLevel=not-set

14 Christopher Pugsley et al., *Kiwis in Conflict: 200 years of New Zealanders at war* (Auckland:David Bateman in association with Auckland Museum, 2008).

15 Audrey Young & Claire Trevett, 'NZ wins seat on security council: Victory for the small states', *New Zealand Herald*, 16 October 2014, www.nzherald.co.nz/nz/nz-wins-seat-on-security-council-victory-for-the-small-states/2AC43UL3YEWCZRAUFRBIAOZ3B4

16 Anita Wan, *The Importance to Small States of International Cooperation through the United Nations: An annotated bibliography* (Wellington: The United Nations Association of New Zealand, 2011).

17 Jeanne A. K. Hey, 'Introducing Small State Foreign Policy', in *Small States in World Politics: Explaining foreign policy behavior*, ed. Jeanne A. K. Hey (London: Boulder London, 2003), 3–5.

18 Justyna Zając, 'International Roles of Medium-Sized State — Theoretical Aspects', *National Studies* 10, no. 4 (2013): 15–27.

19 Ibid., 184–85.

20 Peter D. F. Cooke & John Crawford, *The Territorials: The History of the territorial and volunteer forces of New Zealand* (Auckland: Random House, 2011), 246–83.

21 Maciej Klisz, 'The Polish Territorial Defence Forces (POL TDF): A significant component in national resilience and resistance', *The KCIS*, 2 August 2022, www.thekcis.org/publications/insights/insight-28

22 Timothy Snyder, 'Playing the victim: Testimony to the United Nations Security Council on Russian hate speech', 15 March 2023, https://snyder.substack.com/p/playing-the-victim

1   World Bank: GDP per capita (current US$), 2021, https://data.worldbank.org/indicator/NY.GDP.PCAP.CD?most_recent_value_desc=true; World Bank, Military expenditure (% of GDP), 2014–21, https://data.worldbank.org/indicator/MS.MIL.XPND.GD.ZS; World Bank, Armed Forces personnel, total, https://data.worldbank.org/indicator/MS.MIL.TOTL.P1

17. Self-determination or territorial integrity?

1   Scott Neuman and Alyson Hurt, 'The ripple effects of Russia's war in Ukraine continue to change the world', *NPR*, 22 February 2023, www.npr.org/2023/02/22/1157106172/ukraine-russia-war-refugees-food-prices

2   'Seven ways Russia's war on Ukraine has changed the world', *Chatham House*, 20 February 2023, www.chathamhouse.org/2023/02/seven-ways-russias-war-ukraine-has-changed-world

3   'Ukraine crisis one of most "significant risks to international peace" since Cold War with potential impact on NZ, MFAT boss says', *Newshub*, 17 February 2022, www.newshub.co.nz/home/politics/2022/02/ukraine-crisis-one-of-most-significant-risks-to-international-peace-since-cold-war-with-potential-impact-on-nz-mfat-boss-says.html

4   'Ukraine: NZ says recognition of breakaway republics is "pretext for invasion"', *Stuff*, 22 February 2022, www.stuff.co.nz/national/politics/300523317/ukraine-nz-says-recognition-of-breakaway-republics-is-pretext-for-invasion

5   'Ukraine struggle for whenua resonates with Māori', *Waatea News*, 28 February 2022, https://waateanews.com/2022/02/28/ukraine-struggle-for-whenua-resonates-with-maori

6   Andrea Maria Pelliconi, 'Self-determination as faux remedial secession in Russia's annexation policies: When the Devil wears justice', *Völkerrechtsblog*, 26 January 2023, https://voelkerrechtsblog.org/self-determination-as-faux-remedial-secession-in-russias-annexation-policies

7   'Fighting for Ukrainian self-determination', *International Viewpoint,* 13 April 2023, https://internationalviewpoint.org/spip.php?article7611

8   'Ukraine says talks with Russia hinge on "territorial integrity"', *Aljazeera*, 22 November 2022, www.aljazeera.com/news/2022/11/8/ukraine-says-talks-with-russia-hinge-on-territorial-integrity

9   'Putin denies Ukraine's historic legitimacy, recognises Donetsk and Luhansk independence', *Nationalia*, 29 May 2023, www.nationalia.info/new/11460/putin-denies-ukraines-historic-legitimacy-recognises-donetsk-and-luhansk-independence

10   'Wenda likens Ukraine crisis to that of West Papua', *RNZ*, 7 March 2022, www.rnz.co.nz/international/pacific-news/462731/wenda-likens-ukraine-crisis-to-that-of-west-papua

11   'Papuan rebels succumb to Kremlin war propaganda', *Polygraph*, 15 March 2022, www.polygraph.info/a/fact-check-paupa-indonesia-war-ukraine/6743316.html

12   Brian Girvin, 'Putin, national self-determination and political independence in the twenty-first century', *Nations and Nationalism*, 26 September 2022, https://onlinelibrary.wiley.com/doi/full/10.1111/nana.12876

13   'Self-determination', *Britannica*, www.britannica.com/topic/self-determination

14   Sofia Cavandoli & Gary Wilson, 'Distorting Fundamental Norms of International Law to Resurrect the Soviet Union: The international law context of Russia's invasion of Ukraine', *Netherlands International Law Review* 69 (July 2022): 383–410, https://link.springer.com/article/10.1007/s40802-022-00219-9

15   Atul Bhardwaj, 'Ukraine war and the perils of "self-determination"', *Strategic Affairs*, 30 July 2022, www.epw.in/journal/2022/31/strategic-affairs/ukraine-war-and-perils-%E2%80%98self-determination%E2%80%99.html

16   Richard Jackson, 'Towards an Understanding of Contemporary Intrastate War', *Government and Opposition* 42, no. 1 (2007): 121–28, www.cambridge.org/core/journals/government-and-opposition/article/abs/towards-an-understanding-of-contemporary-intrastate-war/06AC70DB2F57025995068DB2F5B97D96

17   Uppsala Conflict Data Program, 2020, https://ucdp.uu.se

18   Bill Hayton, 'ASEAN is slowly finding its voice over Ukraine', *Chatham House*, 4 March 2022, www.chathamhouse.org/2022/03/asean-slowly-finding-its-voice-over-ukraine

19   Loqman Radpey, 'Remedial peoplehood: Russia's new theory on self-determination in international law and its ramifications beyond Ukraine', *Ejil: Talk*, 7 October 2022, www.ejiltalk.org/remedial-peoplehood-russias-new-theory-on-self-determination-in-international-law-and-its-ramifications-beyond-ukraine

20   'Majlis Podcast: Putin, Ukraine, and why there's uneasiness in Central Asia', *RFE/RL*, 27 February 2022, www.rferl.org/a/majlis-podcast-putin-central-asia-ukraine/31726290.html

21   'Putin downplays Kazakh independence, sparks angry reaction,' *RFE/RL*, 3 September 2014, www.rferl.org/a/kazakhstan-putin-history-reaction-nation/26565141.html

22   'Majlis Podcast: Putin, Ukraine, and why there's uneasiness in Central Asia'.

23   Alexander Hill, 'Self-determination in Ukraine should cut both ways', *Canadian Dimension*, 1 March 2023, https://canadiandimension.com/articles/view/self-determination-in-ukraine-should-cut-both-ways

24   Leonid Bershidsky, 'Is breaking up Russia the only way to end its imperialism?', *Washington Post*, 1 June 2022, www.washingtonpost.com/business/energy/is-breaking-up-russia-the-only-way-to-end-its-imperialism/2022/06/01/e1962c3e-e170-11ec-ae64-6b23e5155b62_story.html

25   John Dobson, 'How Putin's Russia will collapse', *Sunday Guardian*, 14 January 2023, https://sundayguardianlive.com/world/putins-russia-will-collapse

26   Taras Byk, 'Is Putin's Russia heading for collapse like its Czarist and Soviet predecessors?', *Atlantic Council*, 9 February 2023, www.atlanticcouncil.org/blogs/ukrainealert/is-putins-russia-heading-for-collapse-like-its-czarist-and-soviet-predecessors

27   Peter Rutland, 'Why pushing for the breakup of Russia is absolute folly', *Responsible Statecraft*, 23 March 2023, https://responsiblestatecraft.org/2023/03/24/why-pushing-for-the-break-up-of-russia-is-absolute-folly

28   Ibid.

29   Ido Vock, 'No Russia isn't about to break apart,' *New Statesman*, 14 February 2023, www.newstatesman.com/world/europe/ukraine/2023/02/russia-federation-break-up

30 Alexander Motyl, 'It's high time to prepare for Russia's collapse', *Foreign Policy*, 7 January 2023, https://foreignpolicy.com/2023/01/07/russia-ukraine-putin-collapse-disintegration-civil-war-empire

31 Christopher McCallion, 'Russian disintegration is a dangerously dumb delusion', *The Hill*, 3 February 2023, https://thehill.com/opinion/national-security/3837672-russian-disintegration-is-a-dangerously-dumb-delusion

32 'China's position on the political settlement of the Ukraine crisis', *Ministry of Foreign Affairs of the People's Republic of China*, 24 February 2023, www.fmprc.gov.cn/mfa_eng/zxxx_662805/202302/t20230224_11030713.html

33 Shalini Yog Shah & Jost Pachaly, 'The Ukraine war: Perspectives and reactions in Asia', *Heinrich Böll Foundation*, 19 May 2022, www.boell.de/en/2022/05/11/ukraine-war-perspectives-and-reactions-in-asia

34 Hayton, 'ASEAN is slowly finding its voice over Ukraine'.

35 Anatol Lieven & Artin DerSimonian, 'The threat of new wars in the Caucasus: A good case for U.S. restraint', *Quincy Brief*, no. 36, 8 December 2022, https://quincyinst.org/report/the-threat-of-new-wars-in-the-caucasus-a-good-case-for-u-s-restraint

36 Alexa Fults & Paul Stronski, 'The Ukraine war is reshaping the Armenia-Azerbaijan conflict', Carnegie Endowment for International Peace, https://carnegieendowment.org/2022/04/25/ukraine-war-is-reshaping-armenia-azerbaijan-conflict-pub-86994

37 'Tensions over Karabakh rise after Azerbaijan blocks land route from Armenia,' *Reuters*, 24 April 2023, www.reuters.com/world/asia-pacific/azerbaijan-puts-checkpoint-lachin-corridor-bridge-leading-karabakh-2023-04-23

38 'Russian peacekeepers stand inactively by as Azerbaijan renews attack on Nagorno-Karabakh,' *ItelliNews*, 19 September 2023, www.intellinews.com/russian-peacekeepers-stand-inactively-by-as-azerbaijan-renews-attack-on-nagorno-karabakh-293347

39 'European Parliament condemns Azerbaijan and EU over Nagorno-Karabakh attack', *Politico*, 5 October 2023, www.politico.eu/article/european-parliament-condemns-azerbaijan-eu-over-nagorno-karabakh-attack

40 'In Georgia, calls emerge to retake South Ossetia, Abkhazia', *RFE/RL's Georgian Service*, 10 March 2022, www.rferl.org/a/georgia-abkhazia-south-ossetia-russia-ukraine/31746764.html

41 Lieven & DerSimonian, 'The threat of new wars in the Caucasus'.

42 'Supporting UN declaration restores NZ's mana,' *Beehive.govt.nz*, 20 April 2010, www.beehive.govt.nz/release/supporting-un-declaration-restores-nzs-mana

43 New Zealand First Party, 'Co-governance and separatism', *Scoop*, 25 September 2022, www.scoop.co.nz/stories/PA2209/S00130/co-governance-and-separatism.htm

44 United Nations, 'The United Nations and decolonization, Tokelau', www.un.org/dppa/decolonization/en/nsgt/tokelau

45 Ministry of Foreign Affairs and Trade, 'Tokelau Four Year Plan', October 2021, www.mfat.govt.nz/assets/Aid/4YPs-2021-24/Tokelau-4YP.pdf

46 Samson Samasoni, 'New Zealand's new far, Far North? Tokelau set to decide its future', *The Spinoff,* 27 July 2022, https://thespinoff.co.nz/politics/27-07-2022/new-zealands-new-far-far-north-tokelau-set-to-decide-its-future

47 'Tensions mount in New Caledonia as Kanaks insist on decolonisation,' *RNZ*, 26 April 2023, www.rnz.co.nz/international/pacific-news/488622/tensions-mount-in-new-caledonia-as-kanaks-insist-on-decolonisation

48 Maire Leadbeater, *See No Evil: New Zealand's betrayal of the people of West Papua* (Dunedin: Otago University Press, 2018).

49 'New Zealand draws back from calling Chinese abuses of Uyghurs genocide', *The Guardian*, 4 May 2021, www.theguardian.com/world/2021/may/04/new-zealand-draws-back-from-calling-chinese-abuses-of-uyghurs-genocide

50 'Indigenous well-being in four countries: An application of the UNDP'S Human Development Index to Indigenous Peoples in Australia, Canada, New Zealand, and the United States', *BMC International Health and Human Rights* 7 (2007), www.ncbi.nlm.nih.gov/pmc/articles/PMC2238768

51 Atul Bhardwaj, 'Ukraine war and the perils of "self-determination"'.

52 Ian Siegert, 'Self-determination is more nuanced than you might think', *TNR,* 3 October 2022, www.newsrecord.org/opinion/opinion-self-determination-is-more-uanced-than-you-might-think/article_92dc9d8a-431d-11ed-987c-17dcb72b5f6c.html

Bibliography

Achtnich, M. 'Mobile Livings: On the bioeconomies of mobility'. *Cultural Anthropology* 37, no. 1 (2022): 1–8, https://doi.org/10.14506/ca37.1.01

'Act too complex to use, says Collins'. *Stuff*, 31 January 2009, www.stuff.co.nz/national/17681/Act-too-complex-to-use-says-Collins

Agrawal, Arun. 'Indigenous Knowledge and the Politics of Classification'. *International Social Science Journal* 54 (2002): 287–97. https://doi.org/10.1111/1468-2451.00382

Ahmed, Zahid Shahab. 'Impact of the China–Pakistan Economic Corridor on Nation-Building in Pakistan'. *Journal of Contemporary China* 28, no. 117 (2019): 400–14. https://doi.org/10.1080/10670564.2018.1542221

'AI Alliance for Biodiversity submission to Department of Conservation and Toitū Te Whenua Land Information New Zealand on use of information and emerging technologies to enhance biodiversity'. AI Forum New Zealand, January 2023, https://aiforum.org.nz/wp-content/uploads/2023/01/AI-Forum-submission-on-the-use-of-information-and-emerging-technologies-to-enhance-biodiversity.docx.pdf

Allan, Duncan. *The Minsk Conundrum: Western policy and Russia's war in eastern Ukraine*. London: Royal Institute of International Affairs, 2020.

Allison, Graham. 'The Thucydides Trap: Are the U.S. and China headed for war?' *The Atlantic*, 24 September 2015, www.theatlantic.com/international/archive/2015/09/united-states-china-war-thucydides-trap/406756

Allnutt, Greg. *Keeping the Peace: A Kiwi's modern conflict experience*. Christchurch: John Douglas Publishing, 2012.

Alonso-Trabanco, José Miguel. 'Reformulating New Zealand's Grand Strategy'. *New Zealand International Review* 48, no. 3 (2023): 11–14.

American Civil Liberties Union et al. 'Predictive Policing Today: A shared statement of civil rights concerns'. 31 August 2016, http://civilrightsdocs.info/pdf/FINAL_JointStatementPredictivePolicing.pdf

Ammous, Saifedean. *The Bitcoin Standard: The decentralized alternative to central banking*. New Jersey: Wiley, 2018.

Anderson, E., & S. Obeng. 'Globalisation and Government Spending: Evidence for the "hyper-globalisation" of the 1990s and 2000s'. *The World Economy* 44, no. 5 (2021): 1144–76.

Andriole, S. J. 'Basic Intelligence'. In *The Military Intelligence Community*, edited by Gerald W. Hopple & Bruce W. Watson. New York: Routledge, 1986.

Anti-Defamation League. 'When women are the enemy: The intersection of misogyny and white supremacy'. www.adl.org/resources/report/when-women-are-enemy-intersection-misogyny-and-white-supremacy

Ardern, Jacinda. 'Speech to New Zealand's hui on countering terrorism and violent extremism — He Whenua Taurikura'. The Beehive, 1 November 2022, www.beehive.govt.nz/speech/speech-new-zealand%E2%80%99s-hui-countering-terrorism-and-violent-extremism-%E2%80%93-he-whenua-taurikura

Arnold, Major Thomas D., & Major Nicholas Fiore. 'Five Operational Lessons from the Battle for Mosul'. *Military Review* (January–February 2019). www.armyupress.army.mil/Journals/Military-Review/English-Edition-Archives/Jan-Feb-2019/Arnold-Mosul

Arnold, Sir Terence, & Matanuku Mahuika. 'Taumaru: Protecting Aotearoa New Zealand as a free, open and democratic society. Review of the Intelligence and Security Act 2017'. Wellington: Ministry of Justice, 2023.

Arnold, Terrence, & Geoffrey Palmer. *Report of the Government Inquiry into Operation Burnham and Related Matters*. 2020, https://operationburnham.inquiry.govt.nz/inquiry-report

Austin, B. 'How China came to dominate South Sudan's oil: China's appetite for risk-taking cemented its presence in the conflict-torn young country'. *The Diplomat*, 11 February 2019, https://thediplomat.com/2019/02/how-china-came-to-dominate-south-sudans-oil

'Australian-based cryptocurrency exchange Swyftx launches in New Zealand'. *RNZ*, 31 August 2021, www.rnz.co.nz/news/business/450434/australian-based-cryptocurrency-exchange-swyftx-launches-in-new-zealand

Ayson, Robert. 'New Zealand and the Great Irresponsible: Coping with Russia, China and the US'. *Australian Journal of International Affairs* 74, no. 4 (2020): 455–78.

—— 'The Ardern Government's Foreign Policy Challenges'. *Policy Quarterly* 14, no. 2 (2018): 18–24.

Azizian, Rouben, et al. *The 2018 Strategic Defence Statement: Ten different views from Massey scholars*. Security, Politics and Development Network, Massey University, 1 August 2018, https://mro.massey.ac.nz/bitstream/handle/10179/13613/SPDN%20 2018.pdf?sequence=1&isAllowed=y

Baker, R., R. Cannon, P. Bartlett & I. Barker. 'Novel Strategies for Assessing and Managing the Risks Posed by Invasive Alien Species to Global Crop Production and Biodiversity'. *Annals of Applied Biology* 146, no. 2 (2005): 177–91. https://doi.org/10.1111/j.1744-7348.2005.040071.x

Bao, Jun, & Qiuju Xie. 'Artificial Intelligence in Animal Farming: A systematic literature review'. *Journal of Cleaner Production* 331 (January 2022). https://doi.org/10.1016/j. jclepro.2021.129956

Barratt, Monica J., Gary R. Potter, Marije Wouters, Chris Wilkins et al. 'Lessons from Conducting Trans-national Internet-mediated Participatory Research with Hidden Populations of Cannabis Cultivators'. *International Journal of Drug Policy* 26, no. 3 (2014): 238–49.

Bateman, Tom. 'Tonga is finally back online: Here's why it took 5 weeks to fix its volcano-damaged Internet cable'. *Euronews*, 23 February 2022, www.euronews.com/ next/2022/02/23/tonga-is-finally-back-online-here-s-why-it-took-5-weeks-to-fix-its-volcano-damaged-interne

Barker, K. 'Flexible Boundaries in Biosecurity: Accommodating gorse in Aotearoa New Zealand'. *Environment and Planning A: Economy and Space* 40, no. 7 (2008): 1598–1614.

Barnas, Neil. 'Blockchains in National Defense: Trustworthy systems in a trustless world'. Research report, Air University, 2016.

Baron, Joshua, Angela O'Mahony, David Manheim & Cynthia Dion-Schwarz. *National Security Implications of Virtual Currency: Examining the potential for non-state actor deployment*. Santa Monica, CA: RAND Corporation, 2015.

Battersby, John. 'Security Sector Practitioner Perceptions of the Terror Threat Environment Before the Christchurch Attacks'. *Kotuitui: New Zealand Journal of Social Sciences Online* 15, no. 2 (2019): 295–309. https://doi.org/10.1080/1177083X.2019.1701049

—— 'The Ghost of New Zealand's Terrorism Past and Present'. *National Security Journal* 1, no. 1 (2019). https://doi.org/10.36878/NSJ201901.35

—— 'Can Old lessons Inform Current Directions: Australia, New Zealand, and Ananda Marga's trans-Tasman "terrorism" 1975–1978'. *Studies in Conflict and Terrorism* 44, no. 8 (2021): 686–700. https://doi.org/10.1080/1057610X.2019.1575031

—— 'There Is no Terrorism Here!: New Zealand's long-standing gulf between perception and reality'. Submitted and accepted, Konrad Adenauer Stiftung, publication pending.

—— & Rhys Ball. 'Christchurch in the Context of New Zealand Terrorism and Right-wing Extremism'. *Journal of Policing, Intelligence and Counter Terrorism* 14, no. 3 (2019): 191–207. https://doi.org/10.1080/18335330.2019.1662077

Battistelli, Fabrizio. 'Peacekeeping and the Postmodern Soldier'. *Armed Forces and Society* 23, no. 3 (1997): 467–84.

Ben-Itzhak, Svetla. 'Space Blocs: The future of international cooperation in space is splitting along lines of power on Earth', The Space Review, www.thespacereview.com/article/4373/1

Bershidsky, Leonid. 'Is breaking up Russia the only way to end its imperialism?'. *Washington Post*, 1 June 2022, www.washingtonpost.com/business/energy/is-breaking-up-russia-the-only-way-to-end-its-imperialism/2022/06/01/e1962c3e-e170-11ec-ae64-6b23e5155b62_story.html

Bhardwaj, Atul. 'Ukraine War and the perils of "self-determination"'. *Strategic Affairs*, 30 July 2022, www.epw.in/journal/2022/31/strategic-affairs/ukraine-war-and-perils-%E2%80%98self-determination%E2%80%99.html

Biddle, Sam. 'The NSA worked to "track down" Bitcoin users, Snowden documents reveal'. *The Intercept*, 18 March 2018, https://theintercept.com/2018/03/20/the-nsa-worked-to-track-down-bitcoin-users-snowden-documents-reveal

Bigo, Didier. 'Security and Immigration: Towards a critique of the governmentality of unease'. *Alternatives* 27 (2002): 63–92.

——, Arnaud Kurze, Elspeth Guild & Sophia Soares. *The Question of the Legitimacy of Secret Services Coalition Among Democracies: For transnational oversight*. Copy on file with the author but available at request from Didier Bigo.

Birtchnell, Thomas, Satya Savitzky & John Urry (eds). *Cargomobilities: Moving materials in a global age*. New York: Routledge, 2015.

Blee, Kathleen. *Inside Organised Racism: Women of the hate movement*. Los Angeles: University of California Press, 2002.

—— 'Similarities/Differences in Gender and Far Right Politics in Europe and the USA'. In *Gender and the Far-right Politics in Europe*, edited by Michaela Kottig, Renata Bitzan & Andrea Peto. London: Palgrave Macmillan, 2017.

Block, George. 'Three years until army at pre-Covid strength as MIQ drives military resignations'. *Stuff*, 27 November 2021, www.stuff.co.nz/national/300463411/three-years-until-army-at-precovid-strength-as-miq-drives-military-resignations

—— '"Massively concerning" — 338 military personnel who served in MIQ quit'. *Stuff*, 4 December 2021, www.stuff.co.nz/national/300469780/massively-concerning--338-military-personnel-who-served-in-miq-quit

Bloomfield, N. J., S. Wei, B. Woodham et al. 'Automating the Assessment of Biofouling in Images Using Expert Agreement as a Gold Standard'. *Scientific Reports* 11, no. 2739 (2021). https://doi.org/10.1038/s41598-021-81011-2

Boin, A., A. McConnell & P. 't Hart. 'Pathways to Resilience'. In *Governing the Pandemic: The politics of navigating a mega-crisis*, edited by A. Boin, A. McConnell, & P. 't Hart, 107–20. New York: Springer International Publishing, 2021. https://doi.org/10.1007/978-3-030-72680-5_6

Bonds, T. M., J. B. Predd, T. R. Heath, M. S. Chase, M. Johnson, M. J. Lostumbo, J. Bonomo, M. Mane & P. S. Steinberg. *What Role can Land-based, Multi-domain Anti-access/Area-denial Forces Play in Deterring or Defeating Aggression?*. Santa Monica. CA: RAND Corporation, 2017.

Bowker, Geoffrey C. 'All Knowledge is Local'. *Learning Communities* 138 (2008).

Boylan, Brandon M., Jerry McBeath & Bo Wang. 'US–China Relations: Nationalism, the trade war, and COVID-19'. *Fudan Journal of the Humanities and Social Sciences* 14 (2021): 23–40.

Bradley, Anusha. 'Gangs of New Zealand: Explosion of violence prompts fears police have lost control'. *The Guardian*, 23 March 2020, www.theguardian.com/world/2020/mar/23/gangs-of-new-zealand-explosion-of-violence-prompts-fears-police-have-lost-control

Bradley, Carl. 'Outlaw Bikers and Patched Street Gangs: The nexus between violence and shadow economy'. *National Security Journal* (2020), https://doi.org/10.36878/nsj20200201.02

—— 'Hells Angels, Head Hunters and the Filthy Few: The history of outlaw bikers in Aotearoa New Zealand'. *Deviant Behavior* 43, no. 3 (2022): 271–84.

Brands, Hal, & Michael Beckley. *Danger Zone: The coming conflict with China*. New York: W.W. Norton and Company, 2022.

Brands, Hal & Zack Cooper. 'Getting Serious about Strategy in the South China Sea'. *Naval War College Review* 71, no. 1 (2018): 12–32.

Breetzke, Gregory D., Sophie Curtis-Ham, Jarrod Gilbert & Che Tibby. 'Gang Membership and Gang Crime in New Zealand: A national study identifying spatial risk factors'. *Criminal Justice and Behaviour* 49, no. 8 (2022): 1154–72.

Brenton-Rule, Evan, Susy Frankel & Phil Lester. 'Improving Management of Invasive Species: New Zealand's approach to pre- and post-border pests'. *Policy Quarterly* 12, no. 1 (2016). https://doi.org/10.26686/pq.v12i1.4582

Bridle, James. 'Bitcoin and the Money Myth', *New Statesman* 148, no. 5479 (2019): 32–37.

Briggs, Charles L. 'Communicating Biosecurity'. *Medical Anthropology* 30 (2011): 6–29. https://doi.org/10.1080/01459740.2010.531066

Bruneau, Thomas C., & Scott D. Tollefson. *Who Guards the Guardians and How: Democratic civil-military relations*. Austin: University of Texas Press, 2006.

Bruton, Elizabeth. 'The Cable Wars: Military and state surveillance of the British telegraph cable network during World War One'. In *Historicizing Infrastructure*, edited by Andreas Marklund & Mogens Rüdiger. Aalborg: Aalborg University Press, 2017.

Buchanan, Paul. 'New Zealand must own this terrorist attack'. *RNZ*, 20 March 2019, www.rnz.co.nz/news/on-the-inside/385167/paul-buchanan-new-zealand-must-own-this-terrorist-attack

'Buchanan says he sounded alarm over disinformation in NZ'. *RNZ*, 13 June 2023, www.rnz.co.nz/national/programmes/morningreport/audio/2018894129/buchanan-says-he-sounded-alarm-over-disinformation-in-nz

Bueger, Christian, & Tobias Liebetrau. 'Protecting Hidden Infrastructure: The security politics of the global submarine data cable network'. *Contemporary Security Policy* 42, no. 3 (2021): 392. DOI:10.1080/13523260.2021.1907129

Buller, H. 'Safe from the Wolf: Biosecurity, biodiversity, and competing philosophies of nature'. *Environment and Planning A: Economy and Space* 40, no. 7 (2008): 1583–97. https://doi.org/10.1068/a4055

Bullough, Oliver. 'Are you a "Russophobe"?'. *Politico Magazine*, 3 April 2014, www.politico.com/magazine/story/2014/04/just-who-is-a-russophobe-105292

Bureau of Economics Analysis. 'Gross Domestic Product, Fourth Quarter and Year 2022 (Advance Estimate)'. 26 January 2023, www.bea.gov/news/2023/gross-domestic-product-fourth-quarter-and-year-2022-advance-estimate

Burnett, Douglas R., & Lionel Carter. *International Submarine Cables and Biodiversity of Areas Beyond National Jurisdiction: The cloud beneath the sea.* Leiden and Boston: Brill, 2017. https://doi.org/10.1163/24519359-12340002

Burns, William. 'A World of Risk'. *Wall Street Journal*'s CEO Summit (conference), 6 December 2021, www.ceocouncil.wsj.com/event/ceo-council-summit-2/

Burrell, Miriam. 'NZ spy agency assisting Waikato DHB after attack/ransom demand'. *New Zealand Herald*, 18 May 2021, www.nzherald.co.nz/nz/nz-spy-agency-assisting-waikato-dhb-after-cyber-attackransom-demand/V2Q3ESGHZC3KPHUUQ7R7PNNRWU

Burrough, Brian. *The Days of Rage: America's radical underground, the FBI, and the forgotten age of revolutionary violence.* Harmondsworth: Penguin, 2017.

Business and Economic Research Limited. 'Evidence to inform a regulated cannabis market'. BERL, June 2020, https://berl.co.nz/sites/default/files/2020-09/Evidence-to-inform-a-regulated-cannabis-market-June-2020-PROACTIVE-FINAL.pdf

Butler, Simon. 'The Philosophy of Bitcoin and the Question of Money'. *Theory, Culture & Society* 39, no. 5 (2021): 1–22. https://doi.org/10.1177/026327642110498

Byk, Taras. 'Is Putin's Russia heading for collapse like its Czarist and Soviet predecessors?'. *Atlantic Council*, 9 February 2023, www.atlanticcouncil.org/blogs/ukrainealert/is-putins-russia-heading-for-collapse-like-its-czarist-and-soviet-predecessors

Byman, Danial. *Spreading Hate.* Oxford: Oxford University Press, 2022.

Callanan, Tim. 'New artificial intelligence technology used to protect bees from Varroa Destructor mite'. *ABC*, 29 March 2021, www.abc.net.au/news/2021-03-29/ai-technology-used-to-protect-bees-from-pests/100035134

Campbell, D., & R. Lee. 'Carnage by Computer: The blackboard economics of the 2001 Foot and Mouth epidemic'. *Social and Legal Studies* 12, no. 3 (2003). https://doi.org/10.1177/0964663903012004002

Campion, Kirsty. 'Women in the Extreme and Radical Right: Forms of participation and their implications'. *Social Sciences* 9, no. 149 (2020): 12.

Capie, David. 'Nuclear-free New Zealand: Contingency, contestation and consensus in public policymaking'. In *Successful Public Policy: Lessons from Australia and New Zealand*, edited by J. Luetjens, M. Mintrom & P. 't Hart. Acton: ANU Press, 2019.

Capon, John, Oleksandr S. Chernyshenko & Stephen Stark. 'Applicability of Civilian Retention Theory in the New Zealand Military'. *New Zealand Journal of Psychology* 36, no. 1 (2007): 50.

Carnegie, Angus J., Harry Eslick, Paul Barber, Matthew Nagel & Christine Stone. 'Airborne Multispectral Imagery and Deep Learning for Biosecurity Surveillance of Invasive Forest Pests in Urban Landscapes'. *Urban Forestry and Urban Greening* 81 (2023). https://doi.org/10.1016/j.ufug.2023.127859

Carson, Donna. 'Breaking the Masculine Looking Glass: Women as co-founders, nurturers and executors of extremism in New Zealand'. Master's thesis, Massey University, 2021, https://mro.massey.ac.nz/handle/10179/17024

Carter, Lawrence. 'CIA looking into Possible Uses of Generative AI in Agency Operations'. *Potomac Officers Club*, 17 February 2023, https://potomacofficersclub.com/news/cia-looking-into-possible-usesof-generative-ai-in-agency-operations

Carter, Lionel, et al. *Submarine Cables and the Oceans: Connecting the world.* Cambridge & Lymington: United Nations Environmental Programme World Conservation Monitoring Centre & International Cable Protection Committee, 2009.

Catalinac, Amy L. 'Why New Zealand Took Itself out of ANZUS: Observing 'opposition for autonomy' in asymmetric alliances'. *Foreign Policy Analysis* 6 (2010): 317–38.

Caulkins, Jonathan P. 'Local Drug Markets' Response to Focused Police Enforcement'. *Operations Research* (2003).

Cavandoli, Sofia, & Gary Wilson. 'Distorting Fundamental Norms of International Law to Resurrect the Soviet Union: The international law context of Russia's invasion of Ukraine'. *Netherlands International Law Review* 69 (2022): 383–410, https://link.springer.com/article/10.1007/s40802-022-00219-9

Chan, Gerald. *China's Maritime Silk Road: Advancing global development?* Cheltenham: Edward Elgar, 2020.

Chandler, D. 'A World Without Causation: Big data and the coming of age of posthumanism'. *Millennium: Journal of International Studies* (2015): 836.

Chavez, Kerry. 'Learning to Fly: Drones in the Russian-Ukrainian war'. *Arms Control Today* (2023): 6–11.

Chellel, K., M. Campbell & K. O. Ha. 'Six days in Suez: The inside story of the ship that broke global trade', *Bloomberg*, 24 June 2021, www.bloomberg.com/news/features/2021-06-24/how-the-billion-dollar-ever-given-cargo-ship-got-stuck-in-the-suez-canal

'China to inspect ships in Taiwan Strait, Taiwan says won't cooperate'. *Reuters*, 6 April 2023, www.reuters.com/world/asia-pacific/china-inspect-ships-taiwan-strait-taiwan-says-wont-cooperate-2023-04- 06/#:~:text=The%20maritime%20safety%20authority%20 in,operation%20of%20key%20projects%20on

'Christopher Luxon explains his "bottom feeding" comments,' *1 News*, 23 March 2023, www.1news.co.nz/2022/03/22/christopher-luxon-explains-his-bottom-feeding-comments

Chubb, Danielle. 'Perceptions of Terrorism in Australia: 1978–2019'. *Australian Journal of International Affairs* 74, no. 3 (2020): 264–81.

Chun, Wendy Hui Kyong. 'Crisis, Crisis, Crisis, or Sovereignty and Networks'. *Theory, Culture & Society* 28, no. 6 (2011): 91–112.

Chung, K. 'South Korea's Perspective on Quad Plus and Evolving Indo-Pacific Security Architecture'. *Journal of Indo-Pacific Affairs*, Special Issue 2020, https://media.defense.gov/2021/Mar/12/2002599866/-1/-1/0/8-CHUNG.PDF/TOC.pdf

CIA Factbook. 'New Zealand', 26 April 2023, www.cia.gov/the-world-factbook/countries/new-zealand

Clements, Kevin P. 'New Zealand Paying for Nuclear Ban'. *Bulletin of the Atomic Scientists* 43, no. 6 (1987): 41–44.

Cohen, S. B. *Geopolitics: The geography of international relations*. Maryland: Rowman & Littlefield, 2015.

Cole, Bernard D. 'Conflict in the South China Sea'. In *Great Decisions 2017*. New York: Foreign Policy Association, 2017.

Collins, Taylor. 'Inflation Targeting in New Zealand: Does policy match practice?'. *Journal of Applied Business & Economics* 24, no. 1 (2022): 122–32.

Congressional Research Service. 'Undersea Telecommunication Cables: Technology overview and issues for Congress'. CRS Report R47237. Washington, DC: Congressional Research Service, 2022.

Cook, Charlotte. 'NZ Defence Force ongoing staff shortage affected Cyclone Gabrielle response'. *RNZ*, 3 April 2023, www.rnz.co.nz/national/programmes/morningreport/audio/2018884377/nz-defence-force-ongoing-staff-shortage-affected-cyclone-gabrielle-response

Cook, David C., Matthew B. Thomas, Saul A. Cunningham, Denis L. Anderson & Paul J. De Barro. 'Predicting the Economic Impact of an Invasive Species on an Ecosystem Service'. *Ecological Applications* 17, no. 6 (2007): 1832–40. https://doi.org/10.1890/06-1632.1

Cooke, Henry. 'New Zealand extends Iraq and Afghanistan deployments'. *Stuff*, 17 September 2018, www.stuff.co.nz/national/politics/107149082/new-zealand-extends-iraq-and-afghanistan-deployments

Cooke, Martin, Francis Mitrou, David Lawrence, Eric Guimond & Dan Beavon. 'Indigenous Well-being in Four Countries: An application of the UNDP'S Human Development Index to indigenous peoples in Australia, Canada, New Zealand, and the United States'. *BMC International Health and Human Rights* 7 (2007), www.ncbi.nlm.nih.gov/pmc/articles/PMC2238768

Cooke, Peter D. F., & John Crawford. *The Territorials: The history of the territorial and volunteer forces of New Zealand*. Auckland: Random House, 2011.

Corcoran, Evangeline, & Grant Hamilton. 'The Future of Biosecurity Surveillance'. In *The Handbook of Biosecurity and Invasive Species*, edited by Kezia Barker & Robert A. Francis, 261–75. New York: Routledge, 2021.

Corlett, Eva. 'White Island anniversary passes quietly, with healing — and reckoning'. *The Guardian*, 8 December 2021, www.theguardian.com/world/2021/dec/09/white-island-anniversary-passes-quietly-with-healing-and-reckoning-far-from-over

Council of the European Union. 'EU sanctions against Russia explained'. www.consilium.europa.eu/en/policies/sanctions/restrictive-measures-against-russia-over-ukraine/sanctions-against-russia-explained

Counter Extremism Project. 'Accelerationism'. www.counterextremism.com/content/accelerationism

Crook, D. C., M. B. Thomas, S. A. Cunningham, D. L. Anderson & P. J. De Barro. 'Predicting the Economic Impact of an Invasive Species on an Ecosystem Service'. *Ecological Applications* 17, no. 6 (2007): 1832–40. https://doi.org/10.1890/06-1632.1

Crowl, T. A., T. O. Crist, R. R. Rarmenter, G. Belovsky & A. E. Lugo. 'The Spread of Invasive Species and Infectious Disease as Drivers of Ecosystem Change'. *Frontiers in Ecology and the Environment* 6, no. 5 (2008): 238–46. https://doi.org/10.1890/070151

Cruickshank, Paul. 'Source: Early assessment finds TATP at Barcelona attackers' bomb factory'. *CNN*, 19 August 2017, https://edition.cnn.com/2017/08/18/europe/spain-terror-attacks-tatp/index.html

Cryptocurrency NZ. 'Cryptocurrency Mining NZ — New Zealand's Bitcoin Guide'. 17 July 2023, https://cryptocurrency.org.nz/crypto-mining-nz

Cullen, Michael, & Patsy Reddy. 'Intelligence and Security in a Free Society: Report of the first independent review of intelligence and security'. 29 February 2016, https://igis.govt.nz/assets/Review-report-Part-1.pdf

Cunningham, Karla. 'Cross Regional Trends in Female Terrorism'. *Studies in Conflict and Terrorism* 26 (2003).

Cuthbert, R. N., et al. 'Biological Invasion Costs Reveal Insufficient Proactive Management Worldwide.' *Science of the Total Environment* 819 (2022): 153404. https://doi.org/10.1016/j.scitotenv.2022.153404

'Cyclone Gabrielle: Challenging times for the supply chains'. *RNZ*, 15 February 2023, www.rnz.co.nz/national/programmes/ninetonoon/audio/2018877870/cyclone-gabrielle-challenging-times-for-the-supply-chains

'Cyclone Gabrielle: CHB soldiers get stuck into disaster response'. *Hawke's Bay Today*, 3 March 2023, www.nzherald.co.nz/hawkes-bay-today/news/cyclone-gabrielle-chb-soldiers-get-stuck-in-to-disaster-response/KRVIZVHTVFCSZMNNQXY2NKKW7E

Dandeker, Christopher. 'New Times for the Military: Some sociological remarks on the changing role and structure of the armed forces of the advanced societies'. *British Journal of Sociology* (1994): 637–54.

Danzeisen, Aliya. 'New Zealand as Model for Governments Connecting with Muslim Communities'. *Line of Defence* (Winter 2018): 52–54. https://indd.adobe.com/view/2ec2dced-3b72-4e45-9261-28ddf0da58f3

Darby, Seyward. 'The Rise of the Valkyries'. *Harper's Magazine: Report*, September 2017, https://harpers.org/archive/2017/09/the-rise-of-the-valkyries

'Data company brings "intelligent eye" to managing herd health'. *RNZ*, 18 June 2021, www.rnz.co.nz/national/programmes/ninetonoon/audio/2018800309/data-company-brings-intelligent-eye-to-managing-herd-health

Davenport, Tara. 'Submarine Cables, Cybersecurity and International Law: An intersectional analysis'. *Catholic University Journal of Law and Technology* 24, no. 1 (2017): 6–67.

Davidson, Sam. 'Digital dynasties: How China's cryptocurrency could unseat the dollar'. *Harvard International Review*, 29 August 2022, https://hir.harvard.edu/digital-dynasties-how-chinas-cryptocurrency-could-unseat-the-dollar

Davies, Andrew. 'Graph of the week — why (fleet) size matters'. *The Strategist*, 1 February 2013, www.aspistrategist.org.au/graph-of-the-week-why-fleet-size-matters

Davis, Bob, & Lingling Wei. 'Biden plans to build a grand alliance to counter China. It won't be easy'. *Wall Street Journal*, 6 January 2021, www.wsj.com/articles/biden-trump-xi-china-economic-trade-strategy-policy-11609945027

Davis, K. F., S. Downs & J. A. Gephart. 'Towards Food Supply Chain Resilience to Environmental Shocks'. *Nature Food* 2, no. 1 (2021): 54–65. https://doi.org/10.1038/s43016-020-00196-3

Day, Matthew. 'Poland builds Europe's largest land force to counter Russian threat'. *The Telegraph*, 11 March 2023, www.telegraph.co.uk/world-news/2023/03/11/revolution-polish-army-builds-europes-largest-land-force

DeCuir-Gunby, Jessica T., Elizabeth M. Allen & Janet K. Boone. 'Examining Pre-service Teachers' Color-blind Racial Ideology, Emotion Regulation, and Inflexibility with Stigmatizing Thoughts about Race'. *Contemporary Educational Psychology* 60 (2020).

Defence Security New Zealand. 'Andrew Little addresses Massey University National Security Conference.' *Line of Defence*, 20 July 2018. https://defsec.net.nz/2018/07/20/andrew-little-addresses-massey-university-national-security-conference

Defty, Andrew. 'Coming in from the Cold: Bringing the Intelligence and Security Committee into Parliament'. *Intelligence and National Security* 34, no. 1 (2019): 22–37.

—— '"Familiar But Not Intimate": Executive oversight of the UK intelligence and security agencies'. *Intelligence and National* Security 37, no. 1 (2022): 57–72.

Deleuze, G., & F. Guattari. *A Thousand Plateaus*. Trans. Brian Massumi. Minneapolis: University of Minnesota Press, 1987.

Deloitte Access Economics. 'New Zealand Space Economy: Its value, scope and structure'. Ministry of Business, Innovation and Employment, November 2019, www.beehive.govt. nz/sites/default/files/2019-11/Deloitte NZ Space Economy Report.pdf

Demertzis, Konstantinos, Lazaros S. Iliadis & Vardis-Dimitris Anezakis. 'Extreme Deep Learning in Biosecurity: The Case of machine hearing for marine species identification'. *Journal of Information and Telecommunication* 2, no. 4 (2018): 492–510. https://doi.org/10.1080 /24751839.2018.1501542

Department of the Prime Minister and Cabinet. 'The Officials Committee for Domestic and External Security Coordination (ODESC)'. www.dpmc.govt.nz/our-programmes/national-security-and-intelligence/new-zealands-national-security-system-during-a-crisis/ governance-during-crisis/odesc

—— 'New Zealand's countering terrorism and violent extremism strategy'. 2020, www.dpmc. govt.nz/sites/default/files/2021-10/New%20Zealands%20Countering%20Terrorism%20 and%20Violent%20Extremism%20Strategy.pdf

—— 'National Security System Handbook Update, August 2021'. www.dpmc.govt.nz/ sites/default/files/2021-10/National%20Security%20Systems%20Handbook%20 Factsheet%20Update%20October%202021.pdf

—— 'Royal Commission of Inquiry Response: Progress tracker — January 2022'. www.dpmc. govt.nz/sites/default/files/2022-02/rcoi-response-progress-tracker.pdf

—— '2022 review of the Intelligence and Security Act 2017'. 29 May 2023, www.dpmc.govt. nz/our-programmes/national-security/intelligence-and-security-act-2017/2022-review-intelligence-and

—— 'National security long-term insights briefing'. 25 May 2023, www.dpmc.govt.nz/our-programmes/national-security/national-security-long-term-insights-briefing#:~:text=What%20 is%20a%20Long%2Dterm,least%20once%20every%20three%20years

—— *Aotearoa's National Security Strategy: Secure Together Tō Tātou Korowai Maanaki*. www. dpmc.govt.nz/publications/aotearoas-national-security-strategy-secure-together-tatou-korowai-manaaki

Devlin, Collette. 'How effective was the $120m firearms buyback scheme? We don't yet know'. *Stuff*, 7 May 2020, www.stuff.co.nz/national/politics/121445278/how-effective-was-the-120m-firearms-buyback-scheme-we-dont-yet-know

DiCicco, Jonathan. M., & Tudor A. Onea. 'Great-Power Competition.' *Oxford Research Encyclopedia of International Studies*, 31 January 2023, https://oxfordre.com/ internationalstudies/view/10.1093/acrefore/9780190846626.001.0001/acrefore-9780190846626-e-756

DiMaggio, Anthony R. 'Conspiracy Theories and the Manufacture of Dissent: QAnon, the "Big Lie", Covid-19, and the rise of rightwing propaganda'. *Critical Sociology* 48, no. 6 (2022): 1025–48.

Dirga, Nik. 'Yesterday was New Zealand's January 6: What happens now?'. *RNZ*, 4 March 2022, www.rnz.co.nz/news/on-the-inside/462681/yesterday-was-new-zealand-s-january-6-what-happens-now

Dobson, A., K. Barker & S. Taylor (eds). *Biosecurity: The socio-politics of invasive species and infectious diseases*. New York: Routledge, 2013.

Dobson, John. 'How Putin's Russia will collapse'. *Sunday Guardian*, 14 January 2023, https:// sundayguardianlive.com/world/putins-russia-will-collapse

Dorling, Philip. 'Edward Snowden reveals tapping of major Australia–New Zealand undersea telecommunications cable.' *Sydney Morning Herald*, 15 September 2014, www.smh. com.au/technology/edward-snowden-reveals-tapping-of-major-australianew-zealand-undersea-telecommunications-cable-20140915-10h96v.html

Dover, R., M. S. Goodman & C. Hillebrand. *Routledge Companion to Intelligence Studies*. London: Routledge, 2014.

Drahos, P. '"Trust me": Patent Offices in developing countries'. Working Paper, Centre for Governance of Knowledge and Development, November 2007, http://ssrn.com/ abstract=1028676

Driver, George. 'What's causing the shipping crisis – and when will it end?' *The Spinoff*, 24 November 2021, https://thespinoff.co.nz/business/24-11-2021/whatscausing-the-shipping-crisis-and-when-will-it-end

Duff, Michelle. 'How women are being weaponised by the "freedom" movement'. *Stuff*, 3 July 2023, www.stuff.co.nz/national/300621092/how-women-are-being-weaponised-by-the-freedom-movement

Durairajan, Ramakrishnan, Carol Barford & Paul Barford. 'Lights out: Climate change risk to internet infrastructure'. *ANRW 2018*, Association for Computing Machinery, 16 July 2018.

Eadie, Jim. 'Novel machine-learning tool can predict PRRSV outbreaks and biosecurity effectiveness'. Swine Web, 24 May 2021, https://swineweb.com/novel-machine-learning-tool-can-predict-prrsvoutbreaks-and-biosecurity-effectiveness

Ebner, Julia. *Going Dark: The secret social Lives of extremists*. London: Bloomsbury, 2020.

—— & Jacob Davey. 'How Women Advance the Internationalization of the Far Right'. In *Perspectives on the Future of Women, Gender, & Violent Extremism*, edited by Audrey Alexander. Washington, DC: George Washington University, 2019.

Edwards, Bryce. 'The need to take disinformation seriously'. Democracy Project, 12 April 2023, https://democracyproject.nz/2023/04/12/bryce-edwards-the-need-to-take-disinformation-seriously

Echevarria, Antulio J. II. *Clausewitz and Contemporary War*. Oxford: Oxford University Press, 2007.

Edlin, Bob. 'Researchers launch artificial intelligence app to identify NZ's wildlife'. New Zealand Institute of Agricultural & Horticultural Science Inc., 23 January 2023, www.agscience.org.nz/researchers-launch-artificial-intelligence-app-to-identify-nzs-wildlife

Edmonds, M. *Armed Services and Society*. Leicester: Leicester University Press, 1988.

Edmunds, T., & M. Malesic (eds). *Defence Transformation in Europe: Evolving military roles*. NATO Programme for Security through Science Series vol. 2. Amsterdam: IOS Press, 2005.

—— 'What are Armed Forces for?' *International Affairs* (2006): 1059–75.

Ehrenfeld, David. 'Globalisation: Effects on biodiversity, environment and society'. *Conservation and Society* 1, no. 1 (2003): 99–111. http://www.jstor.org/stable/26396456

Elers, Christine Helen, & Pooja Jayan. '"This Is Us": Free speech embedded in whiteness, racism and coloniality in Aotearoa, New Zealand'. *First Amendment Studies* 54, no. 2 (2020): 236–49.

Elers, Steve, Phoebe Elers & Mohan Dutta. 'Responding to White Supremacy: An analysis of Twitter messages by Māori after the Christchurch terrorist attack'. In *Indigenous Peoples Rise Up*, by Bronwyn Carlson & Jeff Berglund, 65–79. New Brunswick: Rutgers University Press, 2021.

Engler, Alex. 'Fighting deepfakes when detection fails'. Brookings, 14 November 2019, www.brookings.edu/research/fightingdeepfakes-when-detection-fails

Ensor, Jamie. 'Threats against politicians, Jacinda Ardern, jump massively over past year, peaked during Parliament protest'. *Newshub*. 28 February 2023, www.newshub.co.nz/home/politics/2023/02/threats-against-politicians-jacinda-ardern-jump-massively-over-past-year-peaked-during-parliament-protest.html

Enticott, G., C. M. Gates & A. Hidano. '"It's Just the Luck of the Draw": Luck, good farming and the management of animal disease in Aotearoa New Zealand'. *Geoforum* 119 (2021): 143–51.

Epanchin-Niell, Rebecca S. 'Economics of Invasive Species Policy and Management'. *Biological Invasions* 19 (2017): 3333–54. https://doi.org/10.1007/s10530-017-1406-4

Erikson, Susan. 'Cell Phones ≠ Self and Other Problems with Big Data Detection and Containment during Epidemics'. *Medical Anthropology Quarterly* 32 (2018): 315–39. https://anthrosource.onlinelibrary.wiley.com/doi/full/10.1111/maq.12440

Fall, Juliet. 'What is an Invasive Alien Species? Discord, dissent and denialism'. In *The Handbook of Invasive Species*, edited by Kezia Barker & Robert A. Francis. London: Routledge, 2021.

Farrell, Theo. *The Norms of War: Cultural beliefs and modern conflict*. Lynne Rienner Publishers 2005.

Fellenor, J., J. Barnett & G. Jones. 'User-generated Content: What can the forest health sector learn?'. In *The Human Dimensions of Forest and Tree Health: Global perspectives*, edited by J. Urquhart, M. Marzano & C. Potter. New York: Palgrave MacMillan, 2018.

Fichera, Benjamin. 'La Guerre des Cryptomonnaies'. *Ecole de Guerre Economique*, 19 December 2022, https://tinyurl.com/4xjscmuw

Financial Markets Authority. 'Cryptocurrencies'. 28 November 2022, https://www.fma.govt.nz/consumer/investing/types-of-investments/cryptocurrencies

Fiore, Nicolas. 'The 2003 Battle of Baghdad'. *Military Review* (Sept–Oct 2020): 127–39.

Fish, William J., et al. 'The Limits of the Military Instrument'. In *Army Fundamentals: From making soldiers to the limits of the military instrument*, edited by B. K. Greener. Auckland: Massey University Press, 2017.

Fisher, David. 'Criminals steal $45,000 in Bitcoin during NZ police money-laundering operation'. *New Zealand Herald*, 9 July 2021, www.nzherald.co.nz/nz/criminals-steal-45000-in-bitcoin-during-nz-police-money-laundering-operation/YENNGLCWMGUNM4T7IR6BIFCQVY

Food and Agriculture Organization of the United Nations. 'Fisheries and Aquaculture'. www.fao.org/fishery/en/aquaculture

'Foot and Mouth Disease'. Queensland Government, 2023, www.business.qld.gov.au/industries/farms-fishing-forestry/agriculture/biosecurity/animals/diseases/guide/foot-mouth

Forster, A. *Armed Forces and Society in Europe*. New York: Palgrave Macmillan, 2005.

Fountain, Jane E. 'The Moon, the Ghetto and Artificial Intelligence: Reducing systemic racism in computational algorithms'. *Government Information Quarterly* 39 (April 2022). https://doi.org/10.1016/j.giq.2021.101645

Frebowitz, Ryan. 'Cryptocurrency and State Sovereignty'. Master's thesis, Naval Postgraduate School, 2018.

Freedman, Lawrence, & Efraim Karsh, 'How Kuwait was Won: Strategy in the Gulf War'. *International Security* (1991): 5–41.

Frini, Anissa, & Anne-Claire Boury-Brisset. *An Intelligence Process Model Based on a Collaborative Approach*. Quebec: Defence Research & Development Canada, 2011.

Fukuyama, F. 'The End of History'. *The National Interest*, Summer 1989, www.wesjones.com/eoh.htm

Fults, Alexa, & Paul Stronski. 'The Ukraine war is reshaping the Armenia-Azerbaijan conflict'. Carnegie Endowment for International Peace, https://carnegieendowment.org/2022/04/25/ukraine-war-is-reshaping-armenia-azerbaijan-conflict-pub-86994

Fyers, Andy, & Henry Cooke. 'Facebook is New Zealand's second-favourite leisure activity'. *Stuff*, 23 March 2017, www.stuff.co.nz/technology/90005751/Facebook-is-New-Zealands-second-favourite-leisure-activity

Gaddis, John Lewis. *Strategies of Containment: A critical appraisal of American national security policy during the Cold War*. New York: Oxford University Press, 2005.

Garden, T. 'Iraq: The military campaign'. *International Affairs* (2003): 701–18.

Gavaghan, Colin, Alistair Knott, James Maclaurin, John Zerilli & Joy Liddycoat. *Government Use of Artificial Intelligence in New Zealand*. Wellington: New Zealand Law Foundation, 2019, www.cs.otago.ac.nz/research/ai/AI-Law/NZLF%20report.pdf

Gay, Edward. 'NZ "ally" and close friend of US — Rice'. *New Zealand Herald*, 26 July 2008, www.nzherald.co.nz/nz/nz-ally-and-close-friend-of-us-rice/PDXIJQENQRKG5ZTXEMIYYINFNE

Gayraud, Jean-François. *Le Nouveau Capitalisme Criminel*. Paris: Odile Jacob, 2014.

Gebru, Timnit, Emily M. Bender, Angelina McMillan-Major & Margaret Mitchell. 'Statement from the listed authors of Stochastic Parrots on the "AI pause' letter"'. *DAIR*, 31 March 2023, www.dair-institute.org/blog/letter-statement-March2023

Gee, Austin, & Robert G. Patman. 'Small State or Minor Power? New Zealand's Five Eyes membership, intelligence reforms, and Wellington's response to China's growing Pacific role'. *Intelligence and National Security* 36, no. 1 (2021): 34–50.

Geertz, Clifford. 'Deep Hanging Out'. *The New York Review of Books* 45, no. 16 (1998).

Gerlach, Christof, & Richard Seitz. *Economic Impact of Submarine Cable Disruptions*. Singapore: APEC Policy Support Unit, 2013.

Giannacopoulos, Maria, & Claire Loughnan. '"Closure" at Manus Island and Carceral Expansion in the Open Air Prison'. *Globalizations* 17, no. 7 (2020): 1118–35. https://doi.org/10.1080/14747731.2019.1679549

Gilbert, David. 'Inside a US neo-Nazi home-school network with thousands of members'. *Vice News*, 20 January 2023, www.vice.com/en/article/z34ane/neo-nazi-homeschool-ohio

Gilbert, Jarrod. *Patched: The history of gangs in New Zealand*. Auckland: Auckland University Press, 2013.

Gill, Peter, & Mark Phythian. *Intelligence in an Insecure World*. Third edition. Cambridge: Polity Press, 2018.

Gillespie, Alexander. 'Ukraine a year on: The invasion changed NZ foreign policy – as the war drags on, cracks will begin to show.' *The Conversation*, 23 February 2023, https://theconversation.com/ukraine-a-year-on-the-invasion-changed-nz-foreign-policy-as-the-war-drags-on-cracks-will-begin-to-show-200524

—— & Claire Breen. 'Parliament protest report shows NZ Police have come a long way since

1981'. *RNZ*, 2 May 2023, www.rnz.co.nz/news/on-the-inside/489125/parliament-protest-report-shows-nz-police-have-come-a-long-way-since-1981

Gillespie, T. *Custodians of the Internet Platforms: Content moderation, and the hidden decisions that shape social media*. Yale: Yale University Press, 2018. https://tarletongillespie.org/Gillespie_CUSTODIANS_print.pdf

Girvin, Brian. 'Putin, national self-determination and political independence in the twenty-first century'. *Nations and Nationalism*, 26 September 2022, https://onlinelibrary.wiley.com/doi/full/10.1111/nana.12876

GlobalFirePower. 'Switzerland military strength'. www.globalfirepower.com/country-military-strength-detail.php?country_id=switzerland#:~:text=For%202023%2C%20Switzerland%20is%20ranked,0.0000%20is%20considered%20'perfect

GlobalFirePower. 'New Zealand military strength'. www.globalfirepower.com/country-military-strength-detail.php?country_id=new-zealand#:~:text=For%202023%2C%20New%20Zealand%20is,on%2001%2F09%2F2023

Goldfinch, S. 'Economic Reform in New Zealand'. *The Otemon Journal of Australian Studies* 30 (2004): 75–98.

Goodman, Leah. 'No paper tigers: The U.S. government wants to know if bitcoin and other virtual currencies are a threat to national security'. *Newsweek* 167, no. 23 (2016): 22–24.

Gordijewski, Andrew O. *KGB*. Translation by R. Brzeski. Warszawa: Bellona Publishing House, 1997.

Government Communications and Security Bureau. 'PM releases report into GCSB compliance'. 9 April 2013, www.gcsb.govt.nz/news/pm-releases-report-into-gcsb-compliance

Government Communications Security Bureau and the New Zealand Security Intelligence Service. *Briefing to the Incoming Minister*. 2017.

Government Communications Security Bureau and the New Zealand Security Intelligence Service. *Incoming Minister's Briefing*. 2020.

Gower, Patrick, Paula Oliver & Alan Perrott. 'Cyanide letter threat to Cup'. *New Zealand Herald*, 26 February 2003, www.nzherald.co.nz/nz/cyanide-letter-threat-to-cup/EXHWJDFZUWXJWRJZRPMBT4AOYE

Greene, Robert. 'Beijing's global ambitions for central bank digital currencies are growing clearer.' Carnegie Endowment for International Peace, 6 October 2021, https://carnegieendowment.org/2021/10/06/beijing-s-global-ambitions-for-central-bank-digital-currencies-are-growing-clearer-pub-85503

Greener, Bethan K. 'The role of the military in New Zealand's response to COVID'. *The KCIS*, 7 September 2021, www.thekcis.org/publications/insights/insight-22

Grotius, Hugo. *Mare Liberum*. 1609.

—— *On the Rights of War and Peace*. 1625.

Guesgen, M. 'Closing the Door on Military Life: The unmaking of officers'. In *Army Fundamentals: From making soldiers to the limits of the military instrument*, edited by B. K. Greener. Auckland: Massey University Press, 2017.

Gwyn, Cheryl. *Report into the Release of Information by the New Zealand Security Intelligence Service in July and August 2011*. Office of the Inspector-General of Intelligence and Security, 2014.

—— *Inquiry into Possible New Zealand Intelligence and Security Agencies' Engagement with the CIA Detention and Interrogation Programme 2001–2009*. Office of the Inspector-General of Intelligence and Security, 2019.

Haenle, Paul, & Nathaniel Sher. 'How Pelosi's Taiwan visit has set a new status quo for U.S.-China tensions'. Carnegie Endowment for International Peace, 17 August 2022, https://carnegieendowment.org/2022/08/17/how-pelosi-s-taiwan-visit-has-set-new-status-quo-for-u.s-china-tensions-pub-87696

Haines, John R. 'E-Notes: How, why, and when Russia will deploy little green men — and why the US cannot', Foreign Policy Research Institute, March 2016, www.fpri.org/article/2016/03/how-why-and-when-russia-will-deploylittle-green-men-and-why-the-us-cannot

Hampton, Andrew. 'Understanding and preparing for cyber threats relating to the Russian invasion of Ukraine: Speech by Director-General of the Government Communications Security Bureau Andrew Hampton to the Wairarapa branch of the New Zealand Institute of International Affairs'. Government Communications Security Bureau, 19 May 2022, www.gcsb.govt.nz/news/the-cybersecurity-implications-of-the-russian-invasion-of-ukraine

Handfield, R., D. J. Finkenstadt, E. S. Schneller, A. B. Godfrey & P. Guinto. 'A Commons for a Supply Chain in the Post-COVID-19 Era: The case for a reformed strategic national stockpile'. *The Milbank Quarterly* 98, no. 4 (2020): 1058–90. https://doi.org/10.1111/1468-0009.12485

Haraway, Donna. 'Situated Knowledges: The science question in feminism and the privilege of partial perspective'. *Feminist Studies* 14 (1988): 575–99. https://doi.org/10.2307/3178066

Harbin, D. E. III 'Targeting Submarine Cables: New approaches to the law of armed conflict in modern warfare'. *Military Law Review* 229, no. 3 (2021).

Harding, Nina. 'Thwarted Selves: Neoliberal boredom among Aotearoa New Zealand peacekeepers'. *Critical Military Studies* (2022), https://doi.org/10.1080/23337486.2022.2143676

Hawkins, Amy, & Rhoda Kwan. 'China says Aukus submarines deal embarks on "path of error and danger"'. *The Guardian*, 14 March 2023, www.theguardian.com/world/2023/mar/14/china-aukus-submarines-deal-embarks-path-error-danger

Hawkins, Koroi. 'Concerns voiced on security pact between China and Solomons'. *RNZ*, 26 April 2022, www.rnz.co.nz/international/pacific-news/465925/concerns-voiced-on-security-pact-between-china-and-solomons

Hayton, Bill. 'ASEAN is slowly finding its voice over Ukraine'. *Chatham House*, 4 March 2022, www.chathamhouse.org/2022/03/asean-slowly-finding-its-voice-over-ukraine

Headrick, David R., & Pascal Griset. 'Submarine Telegraph Cables: Business and politics, 1838–1939'. *The Business History Review* 75, no. 3 (Autumn 2001).

Heaven, Will Douglas. 'Artificial Intelligence: GPT-4 is bigger and better than ChatGPT — but OpenAI won't say why'. *MIT Technology Review*, 14 March 2023, www.technologyreview.com/2023/03/14/1069823/gpt-4-is-bigger-and-better-chatgpt-openai

Heins, M. 'Globalizing the Nation-state: The shipping container and American infrastructure'. *Mobilities* 10, no. 3 (2015): 345–62.

Hemmington, Nigel, & Lindsay Neill. 'Hospitality Business Longevity Under COVID-19: The impact of COVID-19 on New Zealand's hospitality industry'. *Tourism and Hospitality Research* 22, no. 1 (2022): 102–14.

Hermansson, Patrick, David Lawrence, Joe Mulhall & Simon Murdoch. *The International Alt-Right: Fascism for the 21st century?* London: Routledge, 2020.

Hesse, Monica. 'Wolfie James and the insidious role of female white nationalists'. *Washington Post,* 14 August 2019, www.washingtonpost.com/lifestyle/style/wolfie-james-and-the-horrifying-softer-side-of-white-supremacy/2019/08/14/19c86a68-babe-11e9-b3b4-2bb69e8c4e39_story.html

Hey, Jeanne A. K. (ed.) *Small States in World Politics. Explaining foreign policy behavior.* London: Boulder London, 2003.

Higgins, Andrew. 'No one in Europe is telling Poland to "shut up" now'. *New York Times*, 21 February 2023, www.nytimes.com/2023/02/21/world/europe/poland-russia-ukraine.html

Higgins, V., M. Bryant, M. Hernandez-Jover, C. McShane & L. Rast. 'Harmonising Devolved Responsibility for Biosecurity Governance: The Challenge of competing institutional logics'. *Environment and Planning A* (2016): 48, 1133–51.

Hill, Alexander. 'Self-determination in Ukraine should cut both ways'. *Canadian Dimension*, 1 March 2023, https://canadiandimension.com/articles/view/self-determination-in-ukraine-should-cut-both-ways

Hillman, Jonathan E. *The Digital Silk Road: China's quest to wire the world and win the future.* London: Profile Books, 2021.

Hinchliffe, Steve, & Kim Ward. 'Geographies of Folded Life: How immunity reframes biosecurity'. *Geoforum* 53 (2014): 136–44, https://doi.org/10.1016/j.geoforum.2014.03.002

Hoffman, Benjamin D., & Linda M. Broadhurst. 'The Economic Cost of Managing Invasive Species in Australia'. *NeoBiota* 31 (2016): 1–18. http://dx.doi.org/10.3897/neobiota.31.6960

Hoffman, Frank G. 'Examining Complex Forms of Conflict: Gray zone and hybrid challenges', *PRISM* (National Defence University) 7, no. 4 (2018): 30–47.

Hoffman, Jan, & Julia Hoffman. 'Ports in the global liner shipping network: Understanding their position, connectivity, and changes over time'. UNCTAD, 10 August 2020, https://unctad.org/news/ports-global-liner-shipping-network-understanding-their-position-connectivity-and-changes-over

Houlahan, Mike. 'Meth is "everywhere"'. *Otago Daily Times*, 16 December 2017, www.odt.co.nz/news/dunedin/meth-everywhere

Hoverd, William. 'Peace Action Protest and the NZDIA Annual Forum: Is it irreconcilable?'. *Line of Defence*, 20 February 2019, https://defsec.net.nz/2019/02/20/nzdia-forum-protest

—— 'The Changing New Zealand National Security Environment: New threats, new structures, and new research'. *National Security Journal* 1, no. 1 (2019): 17–34.

——, Leon Salter & Kevin Veale. 'The Christchurch Call: Insecurity, democracy and digital media-can it really counter online hate and extremism?' *SN Social Sciences* 1, no. 1 (2020).

——, Nick Nelson & Carl Bradley (eds). *New Zealand National Security: Challenges, trends and issues.* Auckland: Massey University Press, 2017.

Huffadine, Leith. 'Professor Anne Marie Brady who warned about China interference, says car was sabotaged'. *Stuff*, 16 November 2018, www.stuff.co.nz/national/108649435/professor-annemarie-brady-who-warned-aboutchina-interference-says-car-was-sabotaged

——, Brad Flahive & Megan Gattey. 'Tiger Woods, the NZ Gold Open and the terrorist cyanide threat'. *Stuff*, 30 March 2018, www.stuff.co.nz/national/102697753/tiger-woods-the-nz-golf-open-and-the-terrorist-cyanide-threat

Huk, Wojciech. 'The largest order in the history of the Polish arms industry: 1400 new vehicles for the army'. *Polish Press Agency*, 1 March 2023, www.pap.pl/aktualnosci/news%2C1543168%2Cnajwieksze-zamowienie-w-historii-polskiego-przemyslu-zbrojeniowego-1400

Hulme, Philip E. 'One Biosecurity: A unified concept to integrate human, animal, plant, and environmental health'. *Emerging Topics in Life Sciences* 4, no. 5 (2020): 539–49. https://doi.org/10.1042/ETLS20200067

—— 'Biosecurity: The changing face of invasion biology'. In *Fifty Years of Invasion Ecology: The legacy of Charles Elton*, edited by David M. Richardson, 73–88. Oxford: Blackwell Publishing, 2011.

Humpage, L. (ed.). *Policy Change, Public Attitudes and Social Citizenship: Does neoliberalism matter?* Bristol: Bristol University Press, 2014.

Huntley, W. 'The Kiwi that Roared: Nuclear-free New Zealand in a nuclear-armed world'. *The Nonproliferation Review* 4, no. 1 (1996): 1–16.

Hurley, Bevan. 'Police build case against "bumbling Jihadi" Mark Taylor, but outdated anti-terrorism laws could see him walk free'. *Stuff*, 13 October 2019, www.stuff.co.nz/national/116471644/police-build-case-against-bumbling-jihadi-mark-taylor-but-outdated-antiterrorism-laws-could-see-him-walk-free

Hurst, Daniel. 'Chinese state company wins contract to redevelop Solomon Islands port, prompting cautious response'. *The Guardian*, 22 March 2023, https://www.theguardian.com/world/2023/mar/22/chinese-state-company-wins-contract-to-redevelop-solomon-islands-honiara

IBM Corporation. 'Big data and analytics support'. 2023, www.ibm.com/docs/en/spectrum-scale-bda?topic=big-data-analytics-support

'In Georgia, calls emerge to retake South Ossetia, Abkhazia'. *RFE/RL's Georgian Service,* 10 March 2022, www.rferl.org/a/georgia-abkhazia-south-ossetia-russia-ukraine/31746764.html

Independent Police Conduct Authority. 'Parliament protest review'. 20 April 2023, www.ipca.govt.nz/Site/parliament-protest

Inland Revenue. 'Mining cryptoassets for a profit-making scheme'. 28 April 2021, www.ird.govt.nz/cryptoassets/individual/mining/profit-making-scheme

InPhySec. *Waikato District Health Board (WDHB) Incident Response Analysis.* Wellington: InPhySec Security, 2022.

Isik, K. 'Rare and Endemic Species: Why are they prone to extinction?' *Turkish Journal of Botany* 35, no. 4 (2011): 411–417. https://doi.org/10.3906/bot-1012-90

Itagaki, Kanako. 'Evaluating the Role of Public Opinion in the New Zealand Biosecurity Act 1993'. PhD dissertation, Lincoln University, 2013.

Ivanov, D., & A. Dolgui. 'Stress Testing Supply Chains and Creating Viable Ecosystems'. *Operations Management Research: Advancing Practice through Theory* 1 (2021). https://doi.org/10.1007/s12063-021-00194-z

'Jacinda Ardern calls for reform of united Nations, urges "friendship" in climate challenge'. *SBS News*, 7 July 2022, www.sbs.com.au/news/article/jacinda-ardern-calls-for-reform-of-united-nations-urges-friendship-in-climate-challenge/uhhkfpxab

Jackson, Richard. 'Towards an Understanding of Contemporary Intrastate War'. *Government and Opposition* 42, no. 1 (2007): 121–28, www.cambridge.org/core/journals/government-and-opposition/article/abs/towards-an-understanding-of-contemporary-intrastate-war/06AC70DB2F57025995068DB2F5B97D96

—— & Damien Rogers. 'Trans-disciplinary Dialogue on New Zealand's Counter Terrorism

Approach: A call to action for researchers'. *National Security Journal* 5, no.1 (2023): 1–21. https://doi.org/10.36878/nsj20230319.01

Jackson, Van. 'Understanding Spheres of Influence in International Politics'. *European Journal of International Security* 5, no. 3 (2020): 255–73.

Jacobsen, Benjamin N. 'Machine Learning and the Politics of Synthetic Data'. *Big Data and Society* (17 January 2023). https://doi.org/10.1177/20539517221145372

Jagtap, Sandeep, Hana Trollman, Frank Trollman et al. 'The Russia-Ukraine Conflict: Its implications for the global food supply chains.' *Foods* 11, no. 14 (2022).

Jester, N. 'Army Recruitment Video Advertisements in the US and UK since 2002: Challenging ideals of hegemonic military masculinity?'. *Media, War and Conflict* 14, no. 1 (2021). https://doi.org/10.1177/1750635219859488.

Jewell, C. P., M. van Andel, W. D. Vink & A. M. J. McFadden, 'Compatibility Between Livestock Databases Used for Quantitative Biosecurity Response in New Zealand'. *New Zealand Veterinary Journal* 64 (2016): 158–64. https://doi.org/10.1080/00480169.2015.1117955

Jolly, Jasper. 'China cuts key interest rate amid economic slowdown'. *The Guardian*, 21 August 2023, www.theguardian.com/world/2023/aug/21/china-cuts-interest-rate-economy-central-bank-rate

Jones, Seth G. 'Russia's Ill-fated Invasion of Ukraine: Lessons in modern warfare'. CSIS Briefs, Washington DC: Center for Strategic and International Studies, 1 June 2022.

—— 'Empty Bins in a Wartime Environment: The challenge to the US defense industrial base'. CSIS Reports: 2023.

Kachtan, Dana Grosswirth, & Eve Binks. 'Soldiers' Perceptions and Expectations of Converting Military Capital: The cases of Israeli and British militaries'. *Sociological Inquiry* 91, no. 4 (2021). https://doi.org/10.1111/soin.12397

Kajava, Jorma, Reijo Savola & Rauno Varonen. 'Weak Signals in Information Security Management'. *Computational Intelligence and Security: International Conference, CIS 2005, Xi'an, China, 15–19 December 2005, Proceedings, Part II*, 508–17. Berlin: Springer, 2005. https://doi.org/10.1007/11596981_75

Kamimura, Naoki. 'Civil Society, Nuclear Disarmament and the U.S. Alliance: The cases of Australia, New Zealand, and Japan'. *East-West Centre Working Papers, Politics and Security Series* 8 (October 2004): 1–29.

'Karachi attack: China consulate attack leaves four dead'. *BBC*, 23 November 2018, www.bbc.com/news/world-asia-46313136

Kaur, D. 'The US-Japan-Netherlands chip export restrictions are leaving China uneasy. Here's why'. *Techwire Asia*, 17 February 2023, https://techwireasia.com/2023/02/the-us-japan-netherlands-chip-export-restrictions-are-leaving-china-uneasy-heres-why

Kavanagh, Donna, & Gianluca Miscione. 'Bitcoin and Blockchain: A coup d'état in digital heterotopia'. Research paper, Humanistic Management Network, 2015.

Kawharu, M. 'Reinterpreting the Value Chain in an Indigenous Community Enterprise Context'. *Journal of Enterprising Communities: People and Places in the Global Economy* 13, no. 3 (2019): 242–62. https://doi.org/10.1108/JEC-11-2018-0079

Keller, R. P., & C. Perrings. 'International Policy Options for Reducing the Environmental Impacts of Invasive Species'. *BioScience* 61, no. 12 (2011): 1005–12. https://doi.org/10.1525/bio.2011.61.12.10

Kelly, Annie. 'The Housewives of White Supremacy'. *New York Times*, 1 June 2018, www.nytimes.com/2018/06/01/opinion/sunday/tradwives-women-alt-right.html

Kelsey, J. *Rolling Back the State: Privatisation of power in Aotearoa/New Zealand* Wellington: Bridget Williams Books, 1993.

—— *The New Zealand Experiment: A world model for structural adjustment?* Auckland: Auckland University Press, 1997.

Kennedy, A.-M., C. McGouran & J. A. Kemper. 'Alternative Paradigms for Sustainability: A relational worldview'. *European Journal of Marketing* 54, no. 4 (2020): 825–55. https://doi.org/10.1108/EJM-01-2018-0043

Kennedy, P. M. 'Imperial Cable Communications and Strategy, 1870–1914'. *The English Historical Review* 86, no. 341 (1971): 729–31.

Kerr, Florence. 'Gang warfare coming to a town near you'. *Stuff*, 22 January 2016, www.stuff.co.nz/national/crime/75445578/gang-warfare-coming-soon-to-a-town-near-you?rm=m

—— 'Gangs go to social media to push brand and recruit'. *Stuff*, 6 March 2016, www.stuff.co.nz/national/crime/77484541/Gangs-go-to-social-media-to-push-brand-and-recruit

Key, John. 'Speech to New Zealand Institute of International Affairs'. The Beehive, 6 November 2014, www.beehive.govt.nz/speech/speech-nz-institute-international-affairs-0

Khanna, Parag. *The Future is Asian*. New York: Simon & Schuster, 2019.

King, Michael. *Death of the Rainbow Warrior*. Auckland: Penguin, 1986.

Kirk, Stacey. 'Russia dominates PM Jacinda Ardern's talks in London, with UK calling Five Eyes meeting', www.stuff.co.nz/national/politics/103223973/prime-minister-jacinda-ardern-talks-security-trade-with-uks-theresa-may

Kiwi Vine Health. 'The New Zealand biosecurity system and how it operates'. https://kvh.org.nz/assets/documents/Biosecurity-tab/Short_brief_on_how_the_NZ_biosecurity_system_operates.pdf

Klare, Michael T. 'China Reacts Aggressively to Pelosi's Taiwan Visit'. *Arms Control Today* 52, no. 7 (2022): 31–32.

Kleiman, Jared. 'Beyond the Silk Road: Unregulated decentralized virtual currencies continue to endanger US national security'. *National Security Law Brief* 4, no. 1 (2013): 59–78.

Klisz, Maciej. 'The Polish Territorial Defence Forces (POL TDF): A significant component in national resilience and resistance'. *The KCIS*, 2 August 2022, www.thekcis.org/publications/insights/insight-28

Knott, E. 'Existential Nationalism: Russia's war against Ukraine'. *Nations and Nationalism* (2023): 45–52.

Kofman, Michael, Katya Migacheva, Brian Nichiporuk, Andrew Radin, Olesya Tkacheva & Jenny Oberholtzer. *Lessons from Russia's Operations in Crimea and Eastern Ukraine*. Santa Monica, CA: RAND Corporation, 2017.

Komath, Ashwath. 'Bancor Comes of Age: A case for an Indian Bitcoin reserve'. *India Quarterly* 78, no. 1 (2021): 121–42.

Kopeć, Rafał. *Strategie nuklearne w okresie pozimnowojennym*. Kraków: UP Scientific Publishing House, 2014.

Krumpal, Ivar. 'Determinants of Social Desirability Bias in Sensitive Surveys: A literature review'. *Quality & Quantity* 47 (2013): 2025–47.

Kukliński, A. 'O nowym modelu polityki regionalnej — artykuł dyskusyjny'. *Studia Regionalne i Lokalne* 4, no. 4 (2003): 5–14.

Kuku, Rebecca. 'US and Papua New Guinea sign pact amid Pacific militarisation concerns'. *The Guardian*, 22 May 2023, www.theguardian.com/world/2023/may/22/us-png-defence-security-agreement-papua-new-guinea-china-india-modi-pacific-militarisation-concerns

Lambert, S., & M. Mark-Shadbolt. 'Indigenous Biosecurity: Past, present and future'. In *The Handbook of Biosecurity and Invasive Species*, edited by Kezia Barker & Robert A. Francis, 55–65. London: Routledge, 2021.

Laracy, Madeliene. *Report of Inquiry into the role of the GCSB and the NZSIS in relation to certain specific events in Afghanistan*. Wellington: Office of the Inspector-General of Intelligence and Security, 2020.

Latour, B. (ed.). *The Pasteurization of France*. Cambridge, MA: Harvard University Press, 1991.

Laugel, Thibault, Marie-Jeanne Lesot, Christophe Marsala, Xavier Renard & Marcin Detyniecki. 'The Dangers of Post-Hoc Interpretability: Unjustified counterfactual explanations'. *IJCAI '19: Proceedings of the 28th International Joint Conference on Artificial Intelligence.*

Lawrence, J.-M., N. U. Ibne Hossain, R. Jaradat & M. Hamilton. 'Leveraging a Bayesian Network Approach to Model and Analyze Supplier Vulnerability to Severe Weather Risk: A case study of the U.S. pharmaceutical supply chain following Hurricane Maria'. *International Journal of Disaster Risk Reduction* 49 (2020): 101607. https://doi.org/10.1016/j.ijdrr.2020.101607

Lazaro, C., & M. Rizzi. 'Predictive Analytics and Governance: A New sociotechnical imaginary for uncertain futures'. *International Journal of Law in Context* 19 (2023): 70–90. https://doi.org/10.1017/S1744552322000477

Le, N. P. T. 'The Application of Social Network Analysis to Study Supply Chain Resilience'. PhD thesis, Massey University, 2019.

Leadbeater, Maire. *See No Evil: New Zealand's betrayal of the people of West Papua*. Dunedin: Otago University Press, 2018.

Leahy, Ben. 'Details of Kiwi Isis hostage Louisa Akavi's ordeal heard in US court'. *New Zealand Herald*, 2 April 2022, www.nzherald.co.nz/nz/details-of-kiwi-isis-hostage-louisa-akavis-ordeal-heard-in-us-court/RCHDO23D62X5NWPRZZG35KEOGY/

Leask, A. 'Organised crime evolving "rapidly" in NZ as borders become "porous" to illicit trade'. *New Zealand Herald*, 15 October 2019, www.nzherald.co.nz/nz/news/article.cfm?c_id=1&objectid=12276597

Levy, Danya. 'Military morale remains very low'. *Dominion Post*, 28 September 2012, www.stuff.co.nz/dominion-post/news/7743502/Military-morale-remains-very-low

Lewis, Keith. 'Engineering on the sea floor – submarine cables'. *Te Ara: The Encyclopedia of New Zealand*, https://teara.govt.nz/en/engineering-on-the-sea-floor/page-2

Li, Jason. 'Ukraine at one year: Has China supported Russia?'. *Stimson*, 13 February 2023, www.stimson.org/2023/ukraine-at-one-year-has-china-supported-russia

Liang, Annabelle. 'Russia considers accepting Bitcoin for oil and gas'. *BBC*, 23 March 2022, www.bbc.com/news/business-60870100

Lie, Zongyan Zoe, & Mihaela Papa. *Can BRICS De-Dollarize the Global Financial System?* Cambridge: Cambridge University Press, 2022.

Lieven, Anatol, & Artin DerSimonian. 'The Threat of New Wars in the Caucasus: A good case for U.S. restraint'. *Quincy Brief*, no. 36, 8 December 2022, https://quincyinst.org/report/the-threat-of-new-wars-in-the-caucasus-a-good-case-for-u-s-restraint

Lin, Bonnie. *US Allied and Partner Support for Taiwan: Responses to a Chinese attack on Taiwan and potential US Taiwan policy changes*. Santa Monica, CA: Rand Project Air Force, 2021.

Little, Andrew. 'Opening address to the Massey University National Security Conference 2018'. Auckland, 5 April 2018.

—— 'New Zealand condemns malicious cyber activity by Chinese state-sponsored actors'. The Beehive, 19 July 2021, www.beehive.govt.nz/release/new-zealand-condemns-malicious-cyber-activity-chinese-state-sponsored-actors

—— 'Ministerial statements — LynnMall terror attack.' *Hansard*, 7 September 2021, www.parliament.nz/en/pb/hansard-debates/rhr/combined/HansDeb_20210907_20210907_08

—— 'Intelligence and security in our changing world: Speech to the Victoria University of Wellington Centre for Strategic Studies'. The Beehive, 4 November 2021, www.beehive.govt.nz/speech/intelligence-and-security-our-changing-world-speech-victoria-university-wellington-centre

—— 'Government accepts findings of LynnMall supermarket terror attack review'. The Beehive, 14 December 2022, www.beehive.govt.nz/release/government-accepts-findings-lynnmall-supermarket-terror-attack-review

Little, Eric G., & Galina L. Rogova. 'An Ontological Analysis of Threat and Vulnerability'. *2006 9th International Conference on Information Fusion*, https://doi.org/ 10.1109/ICIF.2006.301716

Losev, Alexander. 'Regulating the Unregulated: What is the future of crypto assets?' *Valdai Discussion Club*, 2 March 2022, https://valdaiclub.com/a/highlights/regulation-of-crypto-assets-approaches/?sphrase_id=1489321

Love, Nancy S. 'Shield Maidens, Flashy Femmes and Tradwives: Feminism, patriarchy and right-wing populism'. *Frontiers in Sociology* 5 (December 2020).

Luft, Gal, & Anne Korin. *De-dollarization: The revolt against the dollar and the rise of a new financial world order*. Independently published, 2019.

Lyons, Jeffrey K. 'The Pacific Cable, Hawaii, and Global Communication'. *The Hawaiian Journal of History* 39 (2005): 35–42.

Maher, Rachel. 'New Zealand records highest ever number of gang members, grew by 338 in two months'. *New Zealand Herald*, 22 November 2022, www.nzherald.co.nz/nz/new-zealand-records-highest-ever-number-of-gang-members-grew-by-338-in-two-months/RZZOGMWYENDEJEXMK44IWURA64

'Majlis Podcast: Putin, Ukraine, and why there's uneasiness in Central Asia'. *RFE/RL*, 27 February 2022, www.rferl.org/a/majlis-podcast-putin-central-asia-ukraine/31726290.html

Manch, Thomas. 'Chinese debt a concern in Tonga's post-eruption rebuild'. *Stuff*, 21 January 2022, www.stuff.co.nz/national/politics/127547778/chinese-debt-a-concern-in-tongas-posteruption-rebuild

—— 'Defence Force launches recruitment blitz to battle tight labour market'. *Stuff*, 7 October 2022, www.stuff.co.nz/national/politics/130022707/defence-force-launches-recruitment-blitz-to-battle-tight-labour-market

—— 'Army attrition above 15% as units and ranks depleted by quitting soldiers'. *Stuff*, 11 November 2022, www.stuff.co.nz/national/politics/130440514/army-attrition-above-15-as-units-and-ranks-depleted-by-quitting-soldiers

—— 'New Zealand's terror threat level drops from "medium" to "low"'. *Stuff*, 30 November 2022, www.stuff.co.nz/national/politics/130625081/new-zealands-terror-threat-level-drops-from-medium-to-low

—— 'Defence Force spends $60m to stop its staff walking out the door'. *Stuff*, 5 April 2023, www.stuff.co.nz/national/politics/131693673/defence-force-spends-60m-to-stop-its-staff-walking-out-the-door

Maritime New Zealand. 'Annual Report 2021/22'. www.maritimenz.govt.nz/content/about/annual-reports/documents/MNZ-annual-report-2021-2022.pdf

Martin, Doug, & Simon Mount. *Inquiry into the Use of External Security Consultants by Government Agencies*. State Services Commission, 2018.

Marzano, Mariella et al. 'The Role of the Social Sciences and Economics in Understanding and Informing Tree Biosecurity Policy and Planning: A global summary and synthesis'. *Biological Invasions* 19 (2017): 3317–32. https://doi.org/10.1007/s10530-017-1503-4

Masuhr, Niklas & Benno Zogg. 'The War in Ukraine: First lessons'. *CSS Analyses in Security Policy* 301 (April 2022), https://doi.org/10.3929/ethz-b-000540121

Mattheis, A. 'Shieldmaidens of Whiteness: (Alt) maternalism and women recruiting for the Far/Alt Right'. *Journal for Deradicalization* 17 (Winter 2018/2019).

Matthewman, S. 'Mobile Disasters: Catastrophes in the age of manufactured uncertainty'. *Transfers* 7, no. 3 (2017): 6–22. https://doi.org/10.3167/TRANS.2017.070303

Maurer, Bill, Taylor Nelms & Lana Swartz. 'When Perhaps the Real Problem is Money Itself! The practical materiality of Bitcoin'. *Social Semiotics* 23, no. 2 (2013): 261–77.

McBride, Megan, & Zack Gold. *Cryptocurrency: Implications for Special Operations Forces*. Arlington: CNA Analysis and Solutions, 2019.

McCallion, Christopher. 'Russian disintegration is a dangerously dumb delusion'. *The Hill*, 3 February 2023, https://thehill.com/opinion/national-security/3837672-russian-disintegration-is-a-dangerously-dumb-delusion

McClure, Tess. 'New Zealand draws back from calling Chinese abuses of Uyghurs genocide'. *The Guardian*, 4 May 2021, www.theguardian.com/world/2021/may/04/new-zealand-draws-back-from-calling-chinese-abuses-of-uyghurs-genocide

—— '"A matter of time": New Zealand's foreign minister warns China "storm" could be coming'. *The Guardian*, 24 May 2021, www.theguardian.com/world/2021/may/25/a-matter-of-time-new-zealands-foreign-minister-warns-china-storm-could-be-coming

McEntee, M., F. Medvecky, S. MacBridge-Stewart, V. Macknight & M. Martin. 'Park Rangers and Science-public Expertise: Science as care in biosecurity for kauri trees in Aotearoa/New Zealand'. *Minerva* 61 (2023): 117–40, https://doi.org/10.1007/s11024-022-09482-9

McGeachy, Hilary. 'The Changing Strategic Significance of Submarine Cables: Old technology, new concerns'. *Australian Journal of International Affairs* 76, no. 2 (2022): 164–66.

McKinnon, Malcolm. *Independence and Foreign Policy: New Zealand in the world since 1935*. Auckland: Auckland University Press, 1993.

McLaughlin, Madeline. 'US Strategy in the South China Sea'. Washington DC: American Security Project Report, 2020.

McNeill, Henrietta, & Marinella Marmo. 'Past–Present Differential Inclusion: Australia's targeted deportation of Pacific Islanders, 1901 to 2021'. *International Journal for Crime, Justice and Social Democracy* 12, no. 1 (2023): 42–55. https://doi.org/10.5204/ijcjsd.2743.

McNeilly, H. 'The snowman and the queen: The story of a Kiwi teen terrorist and would-be assassin'. *Stuff*, 8 January 2018, www.stuff.co.nz/national/crime/99760154/the-snowman-and-the-queen-the-story-of-a-kiwi-teen-terrorist-and-wouldbe-assassin

'Merchant fleets'. *The Economist*, 17 October 2015, www.economist.com/economic-and-financial-indicators/2015/10/17/merchant-fleets

Merton, Robert K. 'The Self-fulfilling Prophecy'. *The Antioch Review* 8 (1948): 193–210. https://doi.org/10.2307/4609267

Midttun, H. P. 'Why did the Russian "Blitzkrieg" fail?'. *Stratagem*, 8 July 2022, www.stratagem.no/why-did-the-russian-blitzkrieg-fail

Millar, Timothy R., Peter B. Heenan, Aaron D. Wilton, Rob D. Smissen & Ilse Breitwieser. 'Spatial Distribution of Species, Genus and Phylogenetic Endemism in the Vascular Fora of New Zealand, and Implications for Conservation'. *Australian Systematic Botany* 30, no. 2 (2017): 134–47. https://doi.org/10.1071/sb16015

Miller, Geoffrey. 'Russia's invasion of Ukraine will change New Zealand's foreign policy'. *The Diplomat*, 1 March 2022, https://thediplomat.com/2022/03/russias-invasion-of-ukraine-will-change-new-zealands-foreign-policy

Miller-Idriss, Cynthia. 'Women among the Jan 6th attackers are the new normal of right-wing extremism'. *MSNBC*, 8 January 2022, www.msnbc.com/opinion/women-among-jan-6-attackers-are-new-normal-right-wing-n1287163

Milmo, Dan, & Alex Hern. 'UK and US intervene amid AI industry's rapid advances'. *The*

Guardian, 4 May 2023, www.theguardian.com/technology/2023/may/04/uk-and-us-intervene-amid-ai-industrys-rapid-advances

Miłosz, M. 'The frenzy of arms purchases will not weaken. The year 2023 will be full of large contracts for the army'. *Dziennik Gazeta Prawna*, 29 December 2022, www.gazetaprawna.pl/wiadomosci/kraj/artykuly/8620009,polska-armia-zakupy-kontrakty-zbrojeniowe-satelity-obserwacyjne-patrioty.html

Ministry for Culture and Heritage. 'Warkworth Satellite Earth Station'. NZ History, https://nzhistory.govt.nz/media/photo/warkworth-satellite-earth-station

Ministry for Culture and Heritage. 'Plant and animal quarantine', NZ History, https://nzhistory.govt.nz/politics/plant-and-animal-quarantine

Ministry for Primary Industries. 'Introduction to biosecurity legislation'. www.mpi.govt.nz/legal/legislation-standards-and-reviews/biosecurity-legislation/introduction-to-biosecurity-legislation/#:~:text=MPI%20is%20the%20lead%20agency,goods%20coming%20into%20the%20country

—— 'Biosecurity 2025 Direction Statement for New Zealand's biosecurity system'. 2016, www.mpi.govt.nz/dmsdocument/14857-Biosecurity-2025-Direction-Statement-for-New-Zealands-biosecurity-system

—— 'Biosecurity System Achievements, 2003–2015'. https://mpi.govt.nz/dmsdocument/13185/direct

—— *Biosecurity 2025 Direction Statement for New Zealand's Biosecurity System*. 2016.

—— 'Phased eradication of Mycoplasma bovis'. June 2018, www.mpi.govt.nz/dmsdocument/29303/send

—— *Situation and Outlook for the Primary Industries*. December 2022.

—— 'Drone monitoring project gains "beyond visual line of sight" aviation approval to help protect Māui dolphins'. Media release, 18 January 2023, www.mpi.govt.nz/news/media-releases/drone-monitoring-project-gains-beyond-visual-line-of-sight-aviation-approval-to-help-protect-maui-dolphins

Ministry of Agriculture and Forestry. 'Management of biosecurity risks'. https://oag.parliament.nz/2002/biosecurity

Ministry of Business, Innovation and Employment. *Digital Technologies Draft Industry Transformation Plan 2022–2032*. 2023, www.mbie.govt.nz/dmsdocument/18603-draft-digital-technologies-industrytransformation-plan-2022-2032-pdf

Ministry of Defence. *Defence White Paper 2016*. www.defence.govt.nz/assets/Uploads/daac08133a/defence-white-paper-2016.pdf

—— *Strategic Defence Policy Statement 2018*. www.defence.govt.nz/assets/Uploads/8958486b29/Strategic-Defence-Policy-Statement-2018.pdf

Ministry of Foreign Affairs and Trade. 'NZ-China Free Trade Agreement'. www.mfat.govt.nz/en/trade/free-trade-agreements/free-trade-agreements-in-force/nz-china-free-trade-agreement

—— 'Russia sanctions'. www.mfat.govt.nz/en/countries-and-regions/europe/ukraine/russian-invasion-of-ukraine/sanctions

—— 'Russian invasion of Ukraine'. www.mfat.govt.nz/en/countries-and-regions/europe/ukraine/russian-invasion-of-ukraine

—— 'The Pacific reset: The first year'. Cabinet External Relations and Security Committee, 4 December 2018, www.mfat.govt.nz/assets/OIA/R-R-The-Pacific-reset-The-First-Year.PDF

—— *Strategic Intentions 2021–2025*. www.mfat.govt.nz/assets/About-us-Corporate/MFAT-strategies-and-frameworks/MFAT-Strategic-Intentions-2021-2025.pdf

—— 'New Zealand's Covid-19 trade recovery strategy'. www.mfat.govt.nz/en/trade/trade-recovery-strategy/trade-recovery-strategy-overview

—— 'Tokelau Four Year Plan'. October 2021, www.mfat.govt.nz/assets/Aid/4YPs-2021-24/Tokelau-4YP.pdf

—— 'China market update — December 2022'. www.mfat.govt.nz/en/trade/mfat-market-reports/market-reports-asia/china-market-update-december-2022/#:~:text=China%20remains%20Aotearoa%20New%20Zealand's,imports%20(NZ%2417.6%20billion)

—— *Navigating a Shifting World*. 2023 www.mfat.govt.nz/assets/About-us-Corporate/MFAT-strategies-and-frameworks/MFATs-2023-Strategic-Foreign-Policy-Assessment-Navigating-a-shifting-world-June-2023.pdf

Ministry of Foreign Affairs of the People's Republic of China. 'China's position on the political settlement of the Ukraine crisis'. 24 February 2023, www.fmprc.gov.cn/mfa_eng/zxxx_662805/202302/t20230224_11030713.html

Montasari, R. *Countering Cyberterrorism: The confluence of artificial intelligence, cyber forensics and digital policing in US and UK national cybersecurity*. New York: Springer, 2023.

Moon, M. G., & M. A. Holling. 'White Supremacy in Heels: (White) feminism, white supremacy, and discursive violence'. *Communication and Critical / Cultural Studies* 17, no. 2 (June 2020).

Moorthy, Krishna Babu et al. 'Computer Vision in Aquaculture: A case study of juvenile fish counting'. *Journal of the Royal Society of New Zealand* 53 (2023). https://doi.org/10.1080/03036758.2022.2101484

Morell, Michael, Josh Kirsher & Thomas Schoenberger. *An Analysis of Bitcoin's Use in Illicit Finance.* Crypto Council for Innovation, 2021.

Morrison, Tina. 'A2 milk at "peak uncertainty" after Covid-19 hits key Daigou trade'. *Stuff*, 1 October 2021, www.stuff.co.nz/business/the-monitor/126279298/a2-milk-at-peak-uncertainty-after-covid19-hits-key-daigou-trade

Moskos, Charles. 'From Institution to Occupation: Trends in military organization'. *Armed Forces and Society* 4, no. 1 (1977).

Moss, Sebastian. 'Fortune on the High Seas — DCD'. Datacenter Dynamic, 2016, www.datacenterdynamics.com/en/analysis/fortune-on-the-high-seas

Motyl, Alexander. 'It's high time to prepare for Russia's collapse'. *Foreign Policy*, 7 January 2023, https://foreignpolicy.com/2023/01/07/russia-ukraine-putin-collapse-disintegration-civil-war-empire

Müller, Simone M. *Wiring the World: The social and cultural creation of global telegraph networks.* New York: Columbia University Press, 2016.

Nail, Thomas. 'What Is an Assemblage?'. *SubStance* 46 (2017). http://doi.org/10.1353/sub.2017.0001

Nairn, Karen, & Jane Higgins. 'New Zealand's Neoliberal Generation: Tracing discourses of economic (ir)rationality'. *International Journal of Qualitative Studies in Education* 20, no. 3 (2007). https://doi.org/10.1080/09518390701281819

———, Jane Higgins & Judith Sligo. *Children of Rogernomics: A neoliberal generation leaves school.* Dunedin: Otago University Press, 2012.

Nardo, Michael, Michaela Saisana, Andrea Saltelli, Stefano Tarantola, Anders Hoffman & Enrico Giovannini. 'Handbook on Constructing Composite Indicators: Methodology and user guide'. Organisation for Economic Co-operation and Development, 2005. https://dx.doi.org/10.1787/533411815016.

National Academies of Sciences, Engineering, and Medicine. 'The Work of An Intelligence Analyst'. In *A Decadal Survey of the Social and Behavioral Sciences: A research agenda for advancing intelligence analysis.* Washington, DC: The National Academies Press, 2019. https://doi.org/10.17226/25335

National Security Bureau. *White Paper on National Security of the Republic of Poland.* www.bbn.gov.pl/ftp/dokumenty/Biala_Ksiega_inter_mm.pdf

'National security and intelligence role created'. *Scoop*, 6 October 2014, www.scoop.co.nz/stories/PA1410/S00026/national-security-and-intelligence-role-created.htm

Neal, Andrew W. *Security as Politics: Beyond the state of exception.* Edinburgh: Edinburgh University Press, 2019.

——— 'The Parliamentarianism of Security in the UK and Australia'. *Parliamentary Affairs* 74, no. 2 (2021): 464–82.

Neuman, Scott, & Alyson Hurt. 'The ripple effects of Russia's war in Ukraine continue to change the world'. *NPR*, 22 February 2023, www.npr.org/2023/02/22/1157106172/ukraine-russia-war-refugees-food-prices

New Zealand Defence Force. *New Zealand Defence Force Capability and Readiness Update as at June 2022.* www.nzdf.mil.nz/assets/Uploads/DocumentLibrary/OIA-2022-4503_NZDF-Capability-Readiness-Update-June-2022.pdf

——— 'NZDF joins RIMPAC exercise in waters around Hawaii'. 2 July 2022, www.nzdf.mil.nz/media-centre/news/nzdf-joins-rimpac-exercise-in-waters-around-hawaii

——— 'Support to Ukraine', 1 May 2023, www.nzdf.mil.nz/nzdf/significant-projects-and-issues/support-to-ukraine

——— 'Our Equipment', 1 May 2023, www.nzdf.mil.nz/nzdf/our-equipment

New Zealand First Party. 'Co-governance and Separatism'. *Scoop*, 25 September 2022, www.scoop.co.nz/stories/PA2209/S00130/co-governance-and-separatism.htm

New Zealand Gang Intelligence Centre. 'The New Zealand Organised Crime Governance Group insights report update'. Wellington: New Zealand Police, 2019).

New Zealand Government. 'Misinformation, scams and online harm'. 16 December 2021, https://covid19.govt.nz/prepare-and-stay-safe/misinformation-scams-and-online-harm

——— *Defence Policy and Strategy Statement 2023*, August 2023, www.defence.govt.nz/assets/publication/file/23-0195-Defence-Policy-and-Strategy-Statement-WEB.PDF

'New Zealand may join Aukus pact's non-nuclear component'. *The Guardian*, 28 March 2023, www.theguardian.com/world/2023/mar/28/new-zealand-may-join-aukus-pacts-non-nuclear-component

New Zealand Parliamentary Services. 'New Zealand gang membership: A snapshot of recent trends,' July 2022, www.parliament.nz/media/9557/gangs-in-nz-snapshot-july-2022.pdf

New Zealand Police. 'Methamphetamine in New Zealand: What is currently known about the harm it causes?'. www.police.govt.nz/sites/default/files/publications/methamphetamine-in-new-zealand.pdf

—— *Transnational Organised Crime in New Zealand: Our Strategy 2020 – 2025*. September 2020, https://www.police.govt.nz/about-us/publication/transnational-organised-crime-new-zealand-our-strategy-2020-2025

—— 'Statement of case to designate the American Proud Boys as a terrorist entity'. 20 June 2022, www.police.govt.nz/sites/default/files/publications/statement-of-case-the-american-proud-boys-terrorist-entity-20-june-2022.pdf

—— 'Operation Hydros: Police, Customs and NZDF recover half a billion dollars' worth of cocaine at sea', 8 February 2023, www.police.govt.nz/news/release/operation-hydros-police-customs-and-nzdf-recover-half-billion-dollars%E2%80%99-worth-cocaine

New Zealand Police Association. 'The war on meth'. 1 March 2017, https://www.policeassn.org.nz/news/the-war-on-meth

—— '501s mean business'. 1 November 2019, www.policeassn.org.nz/news/501s-mean-business

New Zealand Productivity Commission. *Improving Economic Resilience: Issues Paper*. 7 February 2023, www.productivity.govt.nz/assets/Inquiries/resilience/Resilience_Issues_Paper_Final_17-Feb-2023.pdf

Newbold, Greg. *Crime in New Zealand*. Palmerston North: Dunmore Press; 2000.

Newman, Keith. *Connecting the Clouds: The internet in New Zealand*. Auckland: Activity Press, 2008.

Niemeijer, David, & Rudolf S. de Groot. 'A Conceptual Framework for Selecting Environmental Indicator Sets'. *Ecological Indicators* 8, no. 1 (2008): 14–25. https://doi.org/10.1016/j.ecolind.2006.11.012

Nistala, G., K. Murakoshi & M. Jamieson. 'How researchers at UC Davis support the swine industry with data analytics on AWS'. AWS Public Sector Blog, 18 March 2022, https://aws.amazon.com/blogs/publicsector/how-researchers-uc-davis-save-swine-data-analytics-aws-cloud

Nye, Joseph S. *Bound to Lead: The changing nature of American power*. New York: Basic Books, 1990.

NZ China Council. 'In Perspective: The New Zealand-China trade and business relationship 2022 update'. https://nzchinacouncil.org.nz/wp-content/uploads/2022/04/China-trade-report-2022-update.pdf

Oak, Eileen. 'Methodological Individualism for the Twenty-first Century? The neoliberal acculturation and remoralisation of the poor in Aotearoa New Zealand'. *Sites* 12, no. 1 (2015). http://dx.doi.org/10.11157/sites-vol12iss1id271

O'Brien, Thomas, & Nicholas Huntington. '"Vaccine passports equal Apartheid": Covid-19 and parliamentary occupation in Aotearoa New Zealand'. *Social Movement Studies* (2022): 1–7.

OECD Report. *Responding to the Ukrainian Refugee Crisis*. International Migration Outlook 2022, 46th edition, 95–115, https://read.oecd-ilibrary.org/social-issues-migration-health/international-migration-outlook-2022_23898d5a-en#page1

Office of the Inspector-General of Intelligence and Security, Independent Police Conduct Complaints Authority, and the Office of the Inspectorate. *Coordinated review of the management of the LynnMall supermarket attacker*. December 2022, https://www.ipca.govt.nz/download/163564/14%20DECEMBER%202022%20-%20Coordinated%20Review%20of%20the%20Management%20of%20the%20LynnMall%20Supermarket%20Attacker.pdf

Official New Zealand Pest Register. https://pierpestregister.mpi.govt.nz/pests-of-concern

'Opposition claims NZDF facing "workforce Crisis"'. *RNZ*, 8 December 2022, www.rnz.co.nz/national/programmes/checkpoint/audio/2018870456/opposition-claims-nzdf-facing-workforce-crisis

Orell, David, & Roman Chlupty. *The Evolution of Money*. New York: Columbia University Press, 2016.

Ozili, Peter K., & Thankom Arun. 'Spillover of COVID-19: Impact on the global economy'. In *Managing Inflation and Supply Chain Disruptions in the Global Economy*, 41–61. Hershey, PA: IGI Global, 2023.

Pacific Islands Forum 2018. 'Boe Declaration on Regional Security'. www.forumsec.org/2018/09/05/boe-declaration-on-regional-security

Palmer, Russell. 'New Zealand increases Defence Force pay rates, funding'. *RNZ*, 8 May 2023, www.rnz.co.nz/news/political/489510/new-zealand-increases-defence-force-pay-rates-funding

Panda, Ankit. 'International court issues unanimous award in Philippines v. China case on South China Sea'. *The Diplomat*, 12 July 2016, https://thediplomat.com/2016/07/international-court-issues-unanimous-award-in-philippines-v-china-case-on-south-china-sea

'Papuan rebels succumb to Kremlin war propaganda'. *Polygraph*, 15 March 2022, www.polygraph.info/a/fact-check-paupa-indonesia-war-ukraine/6743316.html

Parker, David. 'Covid-19 response: New Zealand and Singapore launch initiative to ensure free flow of essential goods'. The Beehive, 15 April 2020, www.beehive.govt.nz/release/covid-19-response-new-zealand-and-singapore-launch-initiative-ensure-free-flow-essential

—— 'Rollout of cameras on fishing vessels to begin'. The Beehive, 25 May 2022, www.beehive.govt.nz/release/rollout-cameras-fishing-vessels-begin

'Parliament protest: Plan to commemorate occupation one year on'. *RNZ*, 10 February 2023, www.rnz.co.nz/news/covid-19/484015/parliament-protest-plan-to-commemorate-occupation-one-year-on

'Pashinyan ready to recognize Azerbaijan's territorial integrity'. *The Armenian Weekly*, 13 April 2022, https://armenianweekly.com/2022/04/13/pashinyan-ready-to-recognize-azerbaijans-territorial-integrity

Patman, Robert G. 'New Zealand's Multilateralism and the Challenge of an International System in Transition'. In *Multilateralism in a Changing World Order*, edited by C. Echle at al. Singapore: Konrad-Adenauer Stiftung, 2018.

Patterson, J. 'Defence Force role in MIQ "reduces capability" to deal with major disaster'. *RNZ*, 13 August 2021, www.rnz.co.nz/news/political/449077/defence-force-role-in-miq-reduces-capability-to-deal-with-major-disaster

Peck, Morgan. 'Let's Destroy Bitcoin'. *MIT Technology Review* 121, no. 3 (2018): 72–77.

Pelliconi, Andrea Maria. 'Self-determination as faux remedial secession in Russia's annexation policies. "When the Devil wears justice"'. *Völkerrechtsblog*, 26 January 2023, https://voelkerrechtsblog.org/self-determination-as-faux-remedial-secession-in-russias-annexation-policies

Perich, B. 'NZ Army experiencing "spike in attrition" as soldiers leave'. *1 News*, 26 November 2022, www.1news.co.nz/2021/11/26/nz-army-experiencing-spike-in-attrition-as-soldiers-leave

Pesonen, R. 'Argumentation, Cognition, and the Epistemic Benefits of Cognitive Diversity'. *Synthese* 200 (2022). https://doi.org/10.1007/s11229-022-03786-9

Petri, Peter A., & Michael G. Plummer. 'East Asia decouples from the United States: Trade war, COVID-19, and East Asia's new trade blocs'. Peterson Institute for International Economics, Working Papers 20-9, June 2020, www.piie.com/publications/working-papers/east-asia-decouples-united-states-trade-war-covid-19-and-east-asias-new

Pherson, Randolph, & Richard Jr. Heuer *Structured Analytic Techniques for Intelligence Analysts.* Thousand Oaks, CA: CQ Press, 2020.

'Philippines agrees to allow US wider access to military bases'. *Aljazeera*, 2 February 2023, www.aljazeera.com/news/2023/2/2/philippines-set-to-allow-wider-us-access-to-military-bases

Pifer, Stephen. 'Commentary OP-ED: Watch out for little green men', Brookings, July 2014, www.brookings.edu/articles/watch-out-for-little-green-men

Pine, Matthew. *Bitcoin and US National Security*. Bitcoin Policy Institute, 2022.

Polish Ministry of National Defence. 'Polish Army as strong as ever'. 30 December 2022, www.gov.pl/web/obrona-narodowa/wojsko-polskie-silne-jak-nigdy

'Posie Parker: Anti-trans rally attracted a range of far-right groups, researchers say', *New Zealand Herald,* 28 March 2023, www.nzherald.co.nz/nz/posie-parker-anti-trans-rally-attracted-a-range-of-far-right-groups-researchers-say/T6AMCXNMUFGDPBIT5SY5ALBR5U

Preston, N. 'High Court rules Auckland Council within rights to cancel Lauren Southern, Stefan Molyneuz event'. *New Zealand Herald*, 30 September 2019. www.nzherald.co.nz/nz/high-court-rules-auckland-council-within-rights-to-cancel-lauren-southern-stefan-molyneux-event/BY4MXOQ7P5AJD3G7C2LYAWEHUE

Pryke, Jonathan. 'The risks of China's ambitions in the South Pacific'. Brookings, 20 July 2020, www.brookings.edu/articles/the-risks-of-chinas-ambitions-in-the-south-pacific

Pugsley, Christopher, et al. *Kiwis in Conflict: 200 years of New Zealanders at war*. Auckland: David Bateman in association with Auckland Museum, 2008.

Pullar-Strecker, Tom. 'Ransomware attacks and crypto-currency scams on the rise'. *Stuff*, 16 September 2021, www.stuff.co.nz/business/126394499/ransomware-attacks-and-cryptocurrency-scams-on-the-rise

'Putin denies Ukraine's historic legitimacy, recognises Donetsk and Luhansk independence'. *Nationalia*, 29 May 2023, www.nationalia.info/new/11460/putin-denies-ukraines-historic-legitimacy-recognises-donetsk-and-luhansk-independence

'Putin downplays Kazakh independence, sparks angry reaction'. *RFE/RL*, 3 September 2014, www.rferl.org/a/kazakhstan-putin-history-reaction-nation/26565141.html

Queiroz, M. M., D. Ivanov, A. Dolgui & S. Fosso Wamba. 'Impacts of Epidemic Outbreaks on Supply Chains: Mapping a research agenda amid the COVID-19 pandemic through a structured literature review'. *Annals of Operations Research* (2020). https://doi.org/10.1007/s10479-020-03685-7

Qui, Winston. 'Raglan Cable Landing Station'. Submarine Cable Networks, 30 September 2020, www.submarinenetworks.com/en/stations/oceania/new-zealand/raglan

Raab, Charles D. 'Regulating Surveillance: The importance of principles'. In *Routledge Handbook of Surveillance Studies*, 377–85. London: Routledge, 2012.

Radpey, Loqman. 'Remedial peoplehood: Russia's new theory on self-determination in international law and its ramifications beyond Ukraine'. *Ejil: Talk*, 7 October 2022, www.ejiltalk.org/remedial-peoplehood-russias-new-theory-on-self-determination-in-international-law-and-its-ramifications-beyond-ukraine

Raha, Uptal K., & K. D. Raja. *Submarine Cables Protection Regulation: A comparative analysis and model framework*. Singapore: Springer, 2021.

Rampal, Neelesh et al. 'High-resolution Downscaling with Interpretable Deep Learning: Rainfall extremes over New Zealand'. *Weather and Climate Extremes* 38 (2022). https://doi.org/10.1016/j.wace.2022.100525

Ratcliffe, Jerry. '*Strategic Thinking in Criminal Intelligence*. Alexandria, NSW: The Federation Press, 2009.

'RBNZ says no decision yet on central bank digital currency'. *Reuters*, 28 April 2022, www.reuters.com/business/finance/rbnz-says-no-decision-yet-central-bank-digital-currency-2022-04-28

Reeves, Stuart. 'Navigating Incommensurability Between Ethnomethodology, Conversation Analysis, and Artificial Intelligence'. Medium, 18 June 2022, https://5tuartreeves.medium.com/navigating-incommensurability-between-ethnomethodologyconversation-analysis-and-artificial-e99c29867242

Reid, Neil. 'Russia invades Ukraine: Putin's "full-scale war" strike condemned by NZ politicians'. *New Zealand Herald*, 24 February 2022, www.nzherald.co.nz/nz/russia-invades-ukraine-putins-full-scale-war-strike-condemned-by-nz-politicians/I5ZDO4LJZDVIMCVXXCTG7DS3IU

'Remembering the deadly Aramoana massacre 30 years on,' *Stuff*, 13 November 2020, www.stuff.co.nz/national/crime/123390946/remembering-the-deadly-aramoana-massacre-30-years-on

Reserve Bank of New Zealand. *The Future of Money: Central bank digital currency*. Wellington: Reserve Bank of New Zealand, 2021.

'Review of terror laws stopped'. *Sunday Star-Times*, 15 September 2013, www.stuff.co.nz/national/politics/9166763/Review-of-terror-laws-stopped

Rhem, A. 'AI Ethics and its Impact on Knowledge Management'. *AI and Ethics* 1 (2021): 33–37. https://doi.org/10.1007/s43681-020-00015-2.

Ricardo, David. *Principles of Political Economy and Taxation*. 1815.

Rice, G. W. 'A Revolution in Social Policy, 1981–1991'. In *The Oxford History of New Zealand*, edited by Geoffrey W. Rice. Oxford: Oxford University Press, 2002.

Richardson, Lauren C., Nancy D. Connell, Stephen M. Lewis, Eleonore Pauwels & Randy S. Murch. 'Cyberbiosecurity: A call for cooperation in a new threat landscape'. *Frontiers in Bioengineering and Biotechnology* 7 (June 2019). https://doi.org/10.3389/fbioe.2019.00099

Richter, Felix. 'The steep rise in global seaborne trade'. Statistica, 26 March 2021, www.statista.com/chart/24527/total-volume-of-global-sea-trade

Rickards, James. *Currency Wars: The making of the next global crisis*. Princeton: Portfolio/Penguin, 2012.

—— *Cryptocurrency Wars*. Baltimore: Agora Financial, 2018.

Riemann, Malte, & Norma Rossi. 'From Subject to Project: Crisis and the transformation of subjectivity in the armed forces'. *Globalizations* (2022). https://doi.org/10.1080/14747 731.2022.2104017

Roberts, Peter. 'A New Patriotism? Neoliberalism, citizenship and tertiary education in New Zealand'. *Educational Philosophy and Theory* 41, no. 4 (2009). https://doi.org/10.1111/j.1469-5812.2008.00437.x

Robinson, Tom. 'How Iran uses Bitcoin to evade sanctions and "export" millions of barrels of oil'. *Elliptic*, 21 May 2021, www.elliptic.co/blog/how-iran-uses-bitcoin-mining-to-evade-sanctions

Rogers, Damien. 'Extraditing Kim Dotcom: A case for reforming New Zealand's intelligence community?'. *Kōtuitui: New Zealand Journal of Social Sciences Online* 10, no. 1 (2015): 46–57. https://doi.org/10.1080/1177083X.2014.992791

—— & Shaun Mawdsley. 'Reconfiguring the Relationship Between Intelligence Professionals and the Public: A first step towards democratising New Zealand's national security?' *National Security Journal* (2021). https://doi.org/10.36878/nsj20210929.02

—— & Shaun Mawdsley. 'Restoring Public Trust and Confidence in New Zealand's Intelligence and Security Agencies: Is a Parliamentary commissioner for security the missing key?' *Policy Quarterly* 18, no. 1 (2022): 59–66.

Rolfe, J., 'New Zealand's Security: Alliances and other military relationships'. Centre for Strategic Studies, Victoria University of Wellington, Working Paper, no. 10 (1997): 1–23.

—— 'Five Eyes: More than technical cooperation, not yet an alliance'. Incline, 3 August 2020, www.incline.org.nz/home/five-eyes-more-than-technical-cooperation-not-yet-an-alliance

Rose, Frank. 'Emerging threats: Outer space, cyberspace, and undersea cables'. Arms Control Today, January/February 2017, www.armscontrol.org/act/2017-01/news/remarks-emerging-threats-outer-space-cyberspace-undersea-cables

Royal Commission of Inquiry into the terrorist attack on Christchurch masjidain on 15 March 2019. *Ko tō tātou kāinga tēnei: Report of the Royal Commission of Inquiry into the terrorist attack on Christchurch masjidain on 15 March 2019*. https://christchurchattack.royalcommission.nz

Rutland, Peter. 'Why pushing for the breakup of Russia is absolute folly'. Responsible Statecraft, 23 March 2023, https://responsiblestatecraft.org/2023/03/24/why-pushing-for-the-break-up-of-russia-is-absolute-folly

Rydel, K. 'Przyłączenie Krymu przez Rosję w świetle prawa międzynarodowego.' *Historia da Teoria* 1, no. 7 (2018): 225–37.

Samasoni, Samson. 'New Zealand's new far, Far North? Tokelau set to decide its future'. *The Spinoff*, 27 July 2022, https://thespinoff.co.nz/politics/27-07-2022/new-zealands-new-far-far-north-tokelau-set-to-decide-its-future

Sanders, Lauren. 'If AUKUS is all about nuclear submarines, how can it comply with nuclear non-proliferation treaties? A law scholar explains'. *The Conversation*, 15 March 2023, https://theconversation.com/if-aukus-is-all-about-nuclear-submarines-how-can-it-comply-with-nuclear-non-proliferation-treaties-a-law-scholar-explains-201760

Sapienza, S. *Big Data, Algorithms and Food Safety: A legal and ethical approach to data ownership and data governance*. New York: Springer, 2020.

Savage, Jared. *Gangland: New Zealand's underworld of organised crime*. Auckland: Harper Collins, 2020.

Science Media Centre. 'Two years since NZ first locked down — expert reaction'. 21 March 2022, www.sciencemediacentre.co.nz/2022/03/21/two-years-since-nz-first-locked-down-expert-reaction

Scotcher, Katie. 'As police call-outs for mental health issues rise, the commissioner wants a new approach'. *RNZ*, 19 November 2021, www.rnz.co.nz/news/national/456062/as-police-call-outs-for-mental-health-issues

Scott, Karen. 'Laws governing undersea cables have hardly changed since 1884: Tonga is a reminder they need modernising'. *The Conversation*, 21 January 2022, https://theconversation.com/laws-governing-undersea-cables-have-hardly-changed-since-1884-tonga-is-a-reminder-they-need-modernising-175312

'Seven ways Russia's war on Ukraine has changed the world'. *Chatham House*, 20 February 2023, www.chathamhouse.org/2023/02/seven-ways-russias-war-ukraine-has-changed-world

Shahbazian, Elisa. 'Intelligence Analysis: Needs and solutions'. In *Meeting Security Challenges Through Data Analytics and Decision Support*. IOS Press, 2016. https:/doi.org/10.3233978-1-61499-716-0-18

Shelley, Andrew. 'A Counter-Drone Strategy for New Zealand', *National Security Journal* 4, no. 1 (2022): 63–91. https://doi.org/10.36878/nsj20220518.02

Shen, Hong. 'Building a Digital Silk Road? Situating the internet in China's Belt and Road Initiative'. *International Journal of Communication* 12 (2018).

Sherwood, S. 'Trades Hall bombing: Chief suspect dies in cold case, police interview revealed'. *New Zealand Herald*, 19 March 2023, www.nzherald.co.nz/nz/trades-hall-bombing-nearly-40-years-on-chief-suspect-dies-in-cold-case-police-interview-released/WG4UYV2Z7ZDY3E7MALW64GHC7I

Siegert, Ian. 'Self-determination is more nuanced than you might think'. *TNR*, 3 October 2022, www.newsrecord.org/opinion/opinion-self-determination-is-more-uanced-than-you-might-think/article_92dc9d8a-431d-11ed-987c-17dcb72b5f6c.html

Simpson, Emile. *War from the Ground Up: Twenty-first-century combat as politics*. Oxford: Oxford University Press, 2012.

Sims, Alex. 'Cryptocurrency and cryptocurrency exchanges explained'. University of Auckland, 19 December 2022, www.auckland.ac.nz/en/news/2022/12/19/cryptocurrency-and-cryptocurrency-exchanges-explained.html

Singh, A. 'Study on the Implications of Autonomous Ships on Maritime Security and Law Enforcement by Reviewing Maritime Security Incidents'. Master's thesis, World Maritime University, 2021.

Smart, W. 'The Impact of COVID-19 on Tertiary Education in New Zealand: Initial impact on participation.' *Education Counts*, December 2021, www.educationcounts.govt.nz/publications/80898/the-impact-of-covid-19-on-tertiary-education-in-new-zealand-initial-impact-on-participation

Smith, Adam. *The Wealth of Nations*. 1776.

Smith, Daniel. 'Oceanic cable to double New Zealand's internet capacity launches from Auckland'. *Stuff*, 29 June 2021, www.stuff.co.nz/business/300344613/oceanic-cable-to-double-new-zealands-internet-capacity-launches-from-auckland

Smith, Nicholas Ross. 'Could Russia Utilize Cryptocurrencies in its Foreign Policy Grand Strategizing?'. *Russia in Global Affairs* 17, no. 2 (2019): 143–52.

—— 'New Zealand's Grand Strategic Options as the Room for Hedging Continues to Shrink'. *Comparative Strategy* 41, no. 3 (2022): 314–27.

Snyder, Timothy. 'Playing the victim, testimony to the United Nations Security Council on Russian hate speech'. 15 March 2023, https://snyder.substack.com/p/playing-the-victim

Solingen, E. *Geopolitics, Supply Chains, and International Relations in East Asia*. Cambridge: Cambridge University Press, 2021.

Sousa-Santos, Jose, & Loene M. Howes. 'Policing Illicit Drugs in the Pacific: The role of culture and community on the frontline'. *Journal of Contemporary Criminal Justice* 38, no. 3 (2022): 364–79.

Speidel, Ulrich. 'The Hung Tonga Hunga Ha'apai eruption — a postmortem: What happened to Tonga's internet in January 2022, and what lessons are there to be learned?' *AINTEC 2022*, Association for Computing Machinery, 18–21 December 2022.

—— 'Cyclone Gabrielle broke vital communication links when people needed them most — what happened and how do we fix it?'. *New Zealand Herald*, 3 March 2023, www.nzherald.co.nz/nz/cyclone-gabrielle-broke-vital-communication-links-when-people-needed-them-most-what-happened-and-how-do-we-fix-it/22NDWWPKMZEKDIQWCP6566X2UQ

Stannard, Tom, Gregorious Steven & Chris McDonald. *Economic Impacts of COVID-19 Containment Measures*. Wellington: Reserve Bank of New Zealand, 2020.

Star, Susan Leigh. 'This is not a Boundary Object: Reflections on the origin of a concept'. *Science, Technology, and Human Values* 5 (2010): 601–17. http://www.jstor.org/stable/25746386

Stats NZ. 'Data hub table builder'. http://nzdotstat.stats.govt.nz/wbos/Index.aspx?ga=2.91779928.391607928.1536553580-1016169874.1533096415

—— 'New Zealand International Trade'. https://statisticsnz.shinyapps.io/trade_dashboard/

Steff, Reuben. 'The Biden Administration and New Zealand's Strategic Options: Asymmetric hedging, tight Five Eyes alignment, and armed neutrality'. *National Security Journal* 3, no. 2 (2021): 1–22.

—— 'For New Zealand, the benefits of joining AUKUS Pillar II outweigh the costs'. *The Diplomat*, 20 April 2023, https://thediplomat.com/2023/04/for-new-zealand-the-benefits-of-joining-aukus-pillar-ii-outweigh-the-costs

—— & F. Dodd-Parr. 'Examining the Imminent Dilemma of Small States in the Asia-Pacific: The strategic triangle between New Zealand, the US and China'. *The Pacific Review* 32, no. 1 (2019): 90–112.

Stengel, Frank A., & David Shim. 'Militarizing Antimilitarism? Exploring the gendered representation of military service in German recruitment videos on social media'. *International Feminist Journal of Politics* 24, no. 4 (2022). https://doi.org/10.1080/146 16742.2021.1935289

Stern, Alexandra M. *Proud Boys and the White Ethnostate: How the alt-right is warping the American imagination*. Boston: Beacon Press, 2019.

Stirling, A. 'Comment: Keep it complex'. *Nature* 468 (December 2010): 1029–30.

Strand, Sanna, & Joakim Berndtsson. 'Recruiting the "Enterprising Soldier": Military recruitment discourses in Sweden and the United Kingdom'. *Critical Military Studies* 1, no. 3 (2015). https://doi.org/10.1080/23337486.2015.1090676

Strategic Forecasting Inc. *Examining the Future of Bitcoin*. Austin: STRATFOR, 2015.

Sunak, Rishi. *Undersea Cables: Indispensable, insecure*. London: Policy Exchange, 2017.

'Supporting UN Declaration restores NZ's mana'. The Beehive, 20 April 2010, www.beehive. govt.nz/release/supporting-un-declaration-restores-nzs-mana

Sutten, Major Marne L. 'The Rising Importance of Women in Terrorism and the Need to Reform Counterterrorism Strategy'. *School of Advanced Military Studies Monographs*. 2009.

Szadziewski, H. 'Converging Anticipatory Geographies in Oceania: The belt and road initiative and look north in Fiji'. *Political Geography* 77 (2020): 102119.

Tang, S. 'The Security Dilemma: A conceptual analysis'. *Security Studies* 18, no. 3 (2009): 587–623.

Taylor-Smith, Briar, Mary Morgan-Richards & Steven A. Trewick. 'Patterns of Regional Endemism Among New Zealand Invertebrates'. *New Zealand Journal of Zoology* 47, no. 1 (2020): 1–19. https://doi.org/10.1080/03014223.2019.1681479

Te Manatū Waka Ministry of Transport. 'Protecting New Zealand's undersea cables'. www. transport.govt.nz/about-us/what-we-do/queries/protecting-new-zealands-undersea-cables

Telley, Chris. 'A coin for the Tsar: The two disruptive sides of cryptocurrency.' *Small Wars Journal*, 6 January 2018, https://smallwarsjournal.com/jrnl/art/coin-tsar-two-disruptive-sides-cryptocurrency

Temocin, Pinar. 'From Protest to Politics: The effectiveness of civil society in shaping the nuclear-free policy in Aoteaora New Zealand'. *Interface* 13 (2021): 174–92.

'Tensions mount in New Caledonia as Kanaks insist on decolonization'. *RNZ*, 26 April 2023, www.rnz.co.nz/international/pacific-news/488622/tensions-mount-in-new-caledonia-as-kanaks-insist-on-decolonisation

The Deep South National Science Challenges. 'Climate change and coastal Māori communities'. https://deepsouthchallenge.co.nz/research-project/climate-change-coastal-maori-communities

The Deep South National Science Challenges. 'Taranaki climate resilience: Te tirohanga o ngā tohu'. https://deepsouthchallenge.co.nz/research-project/taranaki-climate-resilience-te-tirohanga-o-nga-tohu

'The rise of e-money: Why govcoins matter'. *The Economist* 439, no. 9244 (2021).

The Royal Society. 'How does climate change affect the strength and frequency of floods, droughts, hurricanes, and tornadoes?'. https://royalsociety.org/topics-policy/projects/climate-change-evidence-causes/question-13

Thibault, G., L. M. Gareau & F. Le May. 'Intelligence Collation in Asymmetric Conflict: A Canadian armed forces perspective'. In *2007 10th International Conference on Information Fusion*, 1–8. https://doi.org/10.1109/ICIF.2007.4408115

Thornley, L., J. Ball, L. Signal, K. Lawson-Te Aho & E. Rawson. 'Building Community Resilience: Learning from the Canterbury earthquakes'. *Kōtuitui: New Zealand Journal of Social Sciences Online* 10, no. 1 (2015): 23–35. https://doi.org/10.1080/117708 3X.2014.934846

Thorp, T. 'Review of Firearms Control in New Zealand'. 30 June 1997, https://colfo.org.nz/images/files/review-of-firearms-control-in-new-zealand-recommendations.pdf

'Threats against Prime Minister Jacinda Ardern triple, according to report'. *New Zealand Herald*, 12 June 2022, www.nzherald.co.nz/nz/threats-against-prime-minister-jacinda-ardern-triple-according-to-report/ESKHAL4HNASO6HQZ2IPPBEK3HA

Tirado, F., E. Baleriola & S. Moya. 'The Emergency Modality: From the figures to the mobilisation of affects'. In *The Handbook of Biosecurity and Invasive Species*, edited by Kezia Barker & Robert A. Francis. London: Routledge, 2021.

Trebesch, Christoph, et al. 'The Ukraine support tracker: Which countries help Ukraine and how?'. *Kiel Working Paper 2218* (February 2023): 1–77. www.ifw-kiel.de/fileadmin/Dateiverwaltung/IfWPublications/-ifw/Kiel_Working_Paper/2022/KWP_2218_Which_ countries_help_Ukraine_and_how_/KWP_2218_Trebesch_et_al_Ukraine_Support_Tracker.pdf

Turkington, Rebecca, & Audrey Alexander. 'Treatment of Terrorists: How does gender affect justice?'. *CTC Sentinel* 11, no. 8 (2018): 24–29.

'Ukraine crisis one of most "significant risks to international peace" since Cold War with potential impact on NZ, MFAT boss says'. *Newshub*, 17 February 2022, www.newshub.co.nz/home/politics/2022/02/ukraine-crisis-one-of-most-significant-risks-to-international-peace-since-cold-war-with-potential-impact-on-nz-mfat-boss-says.html

'Ukraine: NZ says recognition of breakaway republics is "pretext for invasion"'. *Stuff*, 22 February 2022, www.stuff.co.nz/national/politics/300523317/ukraine-nz-says-recognition-of-breakaway-republics-is-pretext-for-invasion

'Ukraine says talks with Russia hinge on 'territorial integrity''. *Aljazeera*, 22 November 2022, www.aljazeera.com/news/2022/11/8/ukraine-says-talks-with-russia-hinge-on-territorial-integrity

'Ukraine struggle for whenua resonates with Māori'. *Waatea News*, 28 February 2022, https://waateanews.com/2022/02/28/ukraine-struggle-for-whenua-resonates-with-maori

United Nations. *Charter of the United Nations and Statute of the International Court of Justice*. https://treaties.un.org/doc/publication/ctc/uncharter.pdf

—— 'The United Nations and Decolonization, Tokelau'. www.un.org/dppa/decolonization/en/nsgt/Tokelau

—— 'United Nations Register of Conventional Arms'. April 2023, www.unroca.org/about

United Nations Conference on Trade and Development (UNCTAD). 'Review of Maritime Transport 2018'. https://unctad.org/publication/review-maritime-transport-2018#:~:text=Maritime%20transport%20is%20the%20backbone,upswing%20in%20the%20world%20economy

—— 'Review of Marine Transport 2022: Navigating stormy waters'. https://unctad.org/publication/review-maritime-transport-2022

United Nations Development Programme (UNDP). *Human Development Report 1994: New Dimensions of Human Security*. New York: United Nations, 1994. https://hdr.undp.org/content/human-development-report-1994

United Nations Food and Agriculture Organization. 'International Plant Protection Convention'. 1997, https://assets.ippc.int/static/media/files/publication/en/2019/02/1329129099_ippc_2011-12-01_reformatted.pdf

Van der Weijden, W., R. J. Leewis & P. Bol. 'Patterns of Bio-Invasions'. In *Biological Globalisation: Bio-invasions and their impacts on nature, the economy, and public health*, 39–65. KNNV Publishing, 2007.

Van Havere, Tina, Wouter Vanderplasschen, Jan Lammertyn, Eric Broekaert & Mark Bellis. 'Drug Use and Nightlife: More than just dance music'. *Substance Abuse Treatment Prevention and Policy* 6, no. 18 (2011). https://doi.org/10.1186/1747-597X-6-18.

Vanderberg, H., & W. Hoverd. 'The Inconsistent Usage of the Terms "Extremism" and "Terrorism" around the Christchurch Mosque Attacks'. *National Security Journal* 2, no. 1 (2020): 1–13. https://nationalsecurityjournal.nz/latest-issues-2021/the-inconsistent-usage-of-the-terms-extremism-and-terrorism-around-the-christchurch-mosque-attacks

'Verkhovna Rada approves decree on mobilisation in Ukraine'. Ukrinform, 3 March 2022, www.ukrinform.net/rubric-ato/3419149-verkhovna-rada-approves-decreeon-mobilization-in-ukraine.html

Vock, Ido. 'No Russia isn't about to break apart'. *The New Statesman*, 14 February 2023, www.newstatesman.com/world/europe/ukraine/2023/02/russia-federation-break-up

Wade, Amelia. 'Budget 2023: Defence boost to stop personnel leaving as "geostrategic competition in our region" intensifies'. *Newshub*, 8 May 2023, www.newshub.co.nz/home/politics/2023/05/budget-2023-defence-boost-to-stop-personnel-leaving-as-geostrategic-competition-in-our-region-intensifies.html

Wadsworth, Amber. *The Pros and Cons of Issuing a Central Bank Digital Currency*. Wellington: Reserve Bank of New Zealand, 2018.

'Waikato DHB data breach likely "seven . . . eight figure" cryptocurrency ransom – expert'. *RNZ*, 28 May 2021, www.rnz.co.nz/news/national/443589/waikato-dhb-data-breach-likely-seven-eight-figure-cryptocurrency-ransom-expert

'Waikato DHB ransomware cyberattack: Documents released online'. *RNZ*, 29 June 2021, www.rnz.co.nz/news/national/445735/waikato-dhb-ransomware-attack-documents-released-online

Walsh, N. P., et al. 'Inside the August plot to kill Maduro with drones'. *CNN*, 21 June 2019, https://edition.cnn.com/2019/03/14/americas/venezuela-drone-maduro-intl/index.html

Walters, L. 'Defence Force struggling with high attrition, low morale after MIQ duties'. *Stuff*, 9 April 2022, www.stuff.co.nz/national/128305132/defence-force-struggling-with-high-attrition-low-morale-after-miq-duties

Wan, Anita. *The Importance to Small States of International Cooperation through the United Nations: An annotated bibliography*. Wellington: The United Nations Association of New Zealand, 2011.

Ware, Felicity, Mary Breheny & Margaret Forster. 'The Politics of Government "Support" in Aotearoa/New Zealand: Reinforcing and reproducing the poor citizenship of young Māori parents'. *Critical Social Policy* 37, no. 4 (2017). https://doi.org/10.1177/0261018316672111

Wawrzusiszyn, Andrzej. 'Neoimperializm w polityce bezpieczeństwa Federacji Rosyjskiej'. *Cybersecurity and Law* 8, no. 2 (2022): 265–77.

Webb, S. 'From Hijackings to Right-Wing Extremism: The drivers of New Zealand's counter-terrorism legislation 1977–2020'. *National Security Journal* 3, no. 1 (2021): 101–24. https://doi.org/10.36878/nsj20210409.04

'Wenda likens Ukraine crisis to that of West Papua'. *RNZ*, 7 March 2022, www.rnz.co.nz/international/pacific-news/462731/wenda-likens-ukraine-crisis-to-that-of-west-papua

Wenzlhuemer, Roland. *Connecting the Nineteenth-Century World: The telegraph and globalization*. Cambridge: Cambridge University Press, 2012.

Wild, Andrea. 'AI-powered app helps keep Australia free from stink bug pests'. *CSIRO*, 15 March 2022, www.csiro.au/en/news/news-releases/2022/ai-powered-app-helps-keep-australia-free-from-stink-bug-pests

Wilkins, Chris, & Sally Casswell. 'Organized Crime in Cannabis Cultivation in New Zealand: An economic analysis'. *Contemporary Drug Problems* 30, no. 4 (2003).

Wilkins, Chris, Jitesh Prasad, Jose Romeo, & Marta Rychert. *Recent Trends in Illegal Drug Use in New Zealand, 2006–2016: Findings from the Illicit Drug Monitoring System*. Auckland: SHORE & Whariki Research Centre, Massey University; 2017.

——, Jitesh Prasad, Helen Moewaka Barnes, Jose Romeo & Marta Rychert. *New Zealand Arrestee Drug Use Monitoring (NZ-ADUM) 2010–2016*. Auckland: SHORE & Whariki Research Centre, Massey University, 2017.

——, Jose Romeo, Marta Rychert, Jitesh Prasad & Thomas Graydon-Guy. 'Determinants of High Availability of Methamphetamine, Cannabis, LSD and Ecstasy in New Zealand: Are drug dealers promoting methamphetamine rather than cannabis?' *International Journal of Drug Policy* 61 (2018). https://doi.org/10.1016/j.drugpo.2018.09.007

——, Jose Romeo, Marta Rychert, Jitesh Prasad & Thomas Graydon-Guy. 'Determinants of the Retail Price of Illegal Drugs in New Zealand'. *International Journal of Drug Policy* 79 (2020). https://doi.org/10.1016/j.drugpo.2020.102728

Wilkinson, A., & E. Eidinow. 'Evolving Practices in Environmental Scenarios: A new scenario typology'. *Environmental Research Letters* 3, no. 4 (2008): 045017. https://doi.org/10.1088/1748-9326/3/4/045017

Williamson, Harley, & Kristina Murphy. 'Animus Toward Muslims and Its Association with Public Support for Punitive Counter-terrorism Policies: Sid the Christchurch terrorist attack mitigate this association?'. *Journal of Experimental Criminology* (2020): 1–21.

Wilson, Chris. 'Beating up the "alt-right"'. *Newsroom*, 16 February 2023, www.newsroom.co.nz/beating-up-the-alt-right

Wintour, Patrick. 'New Zealand's stance on China has deep implications for the Five Eyes alliance'. www.theguardian.com/world/2021/apr/23/new-zealands-stance-on-china-has-deep-implications-for-the-five-eyes-alliance

Wishnick, E. 'The China-Russia "no limits" partnership is still going strong with regime security as top priority'. CNA, 12 October 2022, www.cna.org/our-media/indepth/2022/10/the-china-russia-no-limits-partnership-is-still-going-strong

Wolf, Meike. 'Urbanisation and Globally Networked Cities'. In *The Handbook of Invasive Species*, edited by Kezia Barker & Robert A. Francis, 215–25. London: Routledge, 2021.

Wong, Cecilia. 'Indicator Selection Criteria.' *Encyclopedia of Quality of Life and Well-Being Research* 32 (2021). https://doi.org/10.1007/978-3-319-69909-7_1428-2

World Organisation for Animal Health. 'Aquatic Animal Health Code'. 2022, www.woah.org/en/what-we-do/standards/codes-and-manuals/aquatic-code-online-access

—— 'Terrestrial Animal Health Code'. 2022, www.woah.org/en/what-we-do/standards/codes-and-manuals/terrestrial-code-online-access

Xie, John. 'China's global network of shipping ports reveal Beijing's strategy'. Voice of America, 13 September 2021, www.voanews.com/a/6224958.html

Yarwood, V. 'A bomb for big brother: One man takes on the state'. *New Zealand Geographic*, https://www.nzgeo.com/stories/7335

Yeoman, Ian Seymour, Heike A. Schänzel & Elisa Zentveld. 'Tourist Behaviour in a COVID-19 World: A New Zealand perspective'. *Journal of Tourism Futures* 8, no. 2 (2022).

Yiu, Chung Yim. 'A Natural Quasi-Experiment of the Monetary Policy Shocks on the Housing Markets of New Zealand during COVID-19'. *Journal of Risk and Financial Management* 16, no. 2 (2023).

Yog Shah, Shalia, & Jost Pachaly. 'The Ukraine war: Perspectives and reactions in Asia'. *Heinrich Böll Foundation*, 19 May 2022, www.boell.de/en/2022/05/11/ukraine-war-perspectives-and-reactions-in-asia

Young, Audrey, & Claire Trevett. 'NZ wins seat on Security Council: Victory for the small states'. *New Zealand Herald*, 16 October 2014, www.nzherald.co.nz/nz/nz-wins-seat-on-security-council-victory-for-the-small-states/2AC43UL3YEWCZRAUFRBIAOZ3B4

Yurchenko, Yuliya. 'Fighting for Ukrainian self-determination'. *International Viewpoint,* 13 April 2023, https://internationalviewpoint.org/spip.php?article7611

Zabrodskyi, Mykhaylo, Jack Watling, Oleksandr V. Danylyuk & Nick Reynolds. *Preliminary Lessons in Conventional Warfighting from Russia's Invasion of Ukraine: February–July 2022.* London: Royal United Services Institute for Defence and Security Studies, 2022.

Zając, Justyna. 'International Roles of Medium-sized State: Theoretical aspects'. *National Studies* 10, no. 4 (2013): 15–27.

Zarate, Juan. *Treasury's War: The unleashing of a new era of financial warfare.* New York, Public Affairs, 2013.

Zhang, D. 'China's military engagement with Pacific Island countries'. Asia and the Pacific Policy Society Policy Forum, 17 August 2020, www.policyforum.net/chinas-military-engagement-with-pacific-island-countries

Zhou, Q. 'China's GDP grew by 3 percent in 2022, population declined 0.85 million'. *China Briefing*, 17 January 2023, accessed March 22, 2023, https://www.china-briefing.com/news/chinas-gdp-grew-by-3-percent-in-2022-population-declined-0-85-million/

Zhou, T., Y. Huang, C. Chen & Z. Xing, 'Exploring AI Ethics of ChatGPT: A diagnostic analysis'. arXiv:2301.12867v4 [cs.CL], 29 May 2023, https://arxiv.org/pdf/2301.12867.pdf

Zidan, K. 'Tara LaRosa: The worrying case of MMA's Proud Girl'. *The Guardian*, 21 January 2021, www.theguardian.com/sport/2021/jan/21/tara-larosa-mma-far-right-proud-boys

Zimmer, Zac. 'Bitcoin and Potosí Silver: Historical perspectives on cryptocurrency'. *Technology and Culture* 58, no. 2 (2017): 307–34.

About the contributors

José Miguel Alonso-Trabanco was born in Mexico and is an international relations professional. He holds a master's degree in national security and strategic intelligence and is pursuing a PhD in defence and security studies at Massey University, New Zealand. His doctoral research project seeks to scrutinise the geopolitical dimension of digital currencies and their implications for security. Alonso-Trabanco has been an analyst, researcher, advisor, consultant, professor, lecturer and author of scholarly papers. His work is regularly featured in the Canadian intelligence platform *Geopolitical Monitor*. His expertise includes geopolitics, geoeconomics, security, statecraft, foreign policy, the changing nature of national power, international rivalries, conflict, economic warfare, hegemony, grand strategy, new arenas of strategic competition and the increasing significance of financial and monetary matters for geopolitical realities in the twenty-first century. He is a member of the executive board of the New Zealand Institute of International Affairs (Auckland branch).

Rouben Azizian is a professor at Massey University's Centre for Defence and Security Studies. His major areas of expertise are Asia-Pacific security environment and architecture, diplomacy and conflict resolution, security sector governance and post-Soviet politics. Professor Azizian is the editor-in-chief of the *National Security Journal* and a member of the editorial boards of various international academic journals. Previously he taught at the Asia-Pacific Center for Security Studies in Honolulu (2002–15) and the Department of Political Studies at the University of Auckland (1994–2001). Prior to becoming a full-time academic, Azizian had an extensive career in the Soviet and later Russian Foreign Service, which included assignments in Nepal (1972–78), Sri Lanka (1980–85) and New Zealand (1991–94). He has published several books as well as numerous book chapters, journal articles and working papers on Asia-Pacific security issues and post-Soviet policies and politics.

Dr John Battersby is a senior fellow at the Centre for Defence and Security Studies (CDSS), Massey University, and lectures in intelligence and counterterrorism. He joined the New Zealand Police in 2005 and served in a range of frontline, prosecution and training roles. In 2016 Battersby was the inaugural New Zealand Police Research Fellow at the Centre for Strategic Studies, Victoria University, Wellington, commencing research into the impact of terrorism on New Zealand. He joined CDSS as a teaching fellow in 2016. He has published on New Zealand wars, United Nations, terrorism and intelligence topics and is the managing editor of the *National Security Journal*.

Donna Carson is a PhD candidate at the Centre for Defence and Security Studies, Massey University. With several years as a security and intelligence practitioner in both public and private capacities, she now consults in criminal and security settings. Carson holds a bachelor's degree in psychology with a criminal/forensic focus and a master's in defence and security. Her research thesis, 'Breaking the Masculine Looking Glass: Women as co-founders, nurturers, and executors of extremism in New Zealand', offers an innovative perspective on gender and extremism.

Dr Jodie Chapell is an analyst in biosecurity New Zealand. Her research interests explore the importance of connection and mobility in the creation of knowledge and artefacts. Areas of interest include bioproperty, access and benefit sharing, indigenous people's knowledges and the sociology of scientific knowledge. Her influences include Michel Foucault, Marilyn Strathern, Anna Lowenhaupt-Tsing and Bruno Latour. Her doctoral research, 'Biopiracy in Peru: Tracing biopiracies, theft, loss and traditional knowledge', involved ethnographic research in Peru and Brazil and was completed at the University of Lancaster in 2011. She graduated with a BSc in social anthropology and communications from Brunel University in 2004. She lives in Eastbourne, Lower Hutt.

Dr Justyna Eska-Mikołajewska holds a PhD in social sciences in the field of political science from the Jagiellonian University in Krakow, Poland, and works as an assistant professor at the Department of Political Studies at the Krakow University of Economics. Previously she was a senior lecturer at the University of Bydgoszcz. She is a member of the Australia, New Zealand and Oceania Research Association, the Polish Economic Society and the editorial board of academic journal *SN Social Sciences*. Her research interests include political systems, human rights and security policies of Anglo-Saxon countries, especially in the Australia and Oceania region. She was a visiting scholar at Massey University,

Wellington, where she worked on the co-authored book *Statehood, Economy and Security of New Zealand: History and the present.* Her current projects focus on changes in national security of New Zealand and Australia and the post-Brexit UK relations to the Pacific countries.

Thomas Graydon-Guy is technical officer at Massey University's SHORE & Whāriki Research Centre. He works on research projects as a programmer, primarily in the area of data collection.

Dr Nina Harding is a lecturer in anthropology at Massey University. Her research is based on ethnographic fieldwork with the New Zealand Army Ngāti Tūmatauenga and focuses on the intersections of soldier and national identity. She has published her work in *Critical Military Studies* and in edited volumes with Routledge and Massey University Press.

Associate Professor Stephen Hoadley is a senior academic at the University of Auckland, New Zealand, and an international politics analyst, media commentator and public speaker. He is an honorary professor of the New Zealand Defence Force Command and Staff College and an honorary captain in the Royal New Zealand Navy.

Phil Holdstock is an aviation fuel specialist in the New Zealand Defence Force. He recently earned a master's in international security with merit in intelligence and a graduate diploma in environmental health from Massey University. He also holds a Bachelor of Health Science (Paramedic) from Whitireia Community Polytechnic and an advanced international diploma in emergency medical dispatch. He has a varied background encompassing the theatre and music industry as a stage technician and in IT as a Cisco and Novell network engineer. He has held pre-hospital medical roles as an ambulance officer and is currently a registered paramedic. His interests span military intelligence, tactical medicine, space exploration, and communication networks. He unwinds by collecting New Zealand military memorabilia and crafting model aircraft and ships.

Associate Professor William Hoverd is the director of the Centre for Defence and Security Studies (CDSS) at Massey University. CDSS teaches New Zealand's only qualifications in defence studies, security studies, border and biosecurity, and intelligence. Wil is resident on the Wellington Pukeahu campus, from where he regularly engages with the government security sector. This is his second edited volume on New Zealand National Security with Massey University Press and his fourth book.

Terry Johanson is a lecturer at the Massey University's Centre for Defence and Security Studies. Since 2011 he has educated military professionals at the Command and Staff College programmes of the Canadian Armed Forces, Royal Brunei Armed Forces and New Zealand Defence Force, as well as the Royal New Zealand Air Force commissioning course. Prior to joining Massey University, Johanson served 17 years as an artillery officer in the New Zealand Army, during which he conducted operational tours to East Timor and Afghanistan, as well as overseas training in Europe, Southeast Asia and North America. He is also a graduate of the US Army Command and General Staff College and UK Royal School of Artillery.

Marcin Lasoń is an associate professor of international relations and national security at A.F. Modrzewski Krakow University. He has published around 100 publications, including books, articles and chapters, on these issues. In 2017 he completed a research fellowship at the National Center for Peace and Conflict Studies, Otago University, New Zealand. Since 2019 he has been a visiting professor at the University of Silesia in Katowice and from 2016 he has been a subject editor of the well-regarded Polish journal *Security – Theory and Practice*. His knowledge is used by Polish Armed Forces and he cooperates with the Special Forces Command and the Territorial Forces Command. He is a member of the foundation council SPRZYMIERZENI z GROM.

Madeline Marshall is an analyst with biosecurity intelligence at New Zealand's Ministry for Primary Industries. She has previously completed a PhD in ecology at Lincoln University, Christchurch, and a Master of Biology at the University of Texas – Rio Grande Valley. Before working for MPI, she worked with the United States Department of Agriculture's *Arundo donax* biological control program in south Texas. She currently lives in Christchurch and when not working can likely be found at a café, a bookshop, building a garden bed she doesn't need, or enmeshed in a board game battle against her husband.

Deidre Ann McDonald is a teaching fellow at Massey University's Centre for Defence and Security Studies. Prior to teaching, Dee had a legal career — mostly working in the government sector. She now coordinates

Massey University's Diploma and Certificate in Border and Biosecurity and teaches biosecurity from a social science perspective. Dee has recently submitted her PhD on Aotearoa's Mycoplasma bovis incursion.

John Moremon is a senior lecturer in defence studies at Massey University. He has taught in the areas of defence force operations, military technology, history of warfare, and war and society. He graduated from the University of New England (BA) and the University of New South Wales (PhD) prior to moving to New Zealand, and has since also completed postgraduate studies in higher education and museum studies at Massey University. His diverse research interests relate mainly to Australian and New Zealand military history, armed forces and society, and regional air power.

Dr Germana Nicklin is an honorary research associate in the School of People, Environment and Planning, Massey University. From 2016 to February 2023 she was a senior lecturer at the Centre for Defence and Security Studies at Massey University. She researches and teaches border concepts, border security and maritime security. She has published on Indo-Pacific maritime security, Australian and New Zealand border practices, Antarctic borders and policy performance. She holds a PhD in public policy for which she received a Dean's Award, a post-graduate diploma in strategic studies, and a master's in public policy (with distinction), all from Te Herenga Waka Victoria University of Wellington. Prior to joining Massey University, Nicklin worked in the New Zealand and Australian public services for over 30 years, including 17 years in the New Zealand Customs Service.

Damien Rogers is associate professor of international relations and security studies at Massey University, Auckland. His research concerns the ways in which political actors — intelligence and security professionals, governments and the wider international community — respond to various forms of political violence, including armed conflict, terrorism and mass atrocity.

Dr Jose Romeo is a senior research officer and statistician at Massey University's SHORE & Whāriki Research Centre. He specialises in multivariate survival analysis and is interested in applying statistical models for decision-making in public health and social sciences.

Dr Marta Rychert is a senior researcher at Massey University's SHORE & Whāriki Research Centre. Her research work lies at the intersection of public policy, law and health, with particular focus on cannabis legalisation, drug harm reduction, cannabis consumption trends and commercial determinants of health. She has analysed implementation of drug policy reforms in Europe, New Zealand, Canada and the Caribbean. Prior to her academic appointments in New Zealand she worked in the European Union Drugs Agency (EMCDDA) in Portugal. She is a co-editor-in-chief of the international journal *Drugs, Habits and Social Policy*.

Dr Reuben Steff is a senior lecturer of international relations and global security at the University of Waikato, New Zealand. His research encompasses US-China Great-Power Competition, the implications of artificial intelligence for international security, nuclear deterrence theory, and New Zealand's geopolitics. He has published in multiple journals, regularly participates in policy development processes, and is the author of four books, including *Emerging Technologies and International Security: Machines, the State and war* (Routledge, 2020). His forthcoming book is *Indo-Pacific Geopolitics in an Era of Intensifying Great Power Competition: A New Zealand security strategy perspective* (Palgrave Macmillan, 2024).

Robin van der Sanden is a PhD student at Massey University's SHORE & Whāriki Research Centre. Her doctoral thesis explores the use of social media and messaging apps for drug trading in New Zealand. She has published work in *The International Journal of Drug Policy, Contemporary Drug Problems* and *Drugs: Education, Prevention and Policy*.

Associate Professor Chris Wilkins is leader of the drug research team at Massey University. Chris has expertise in drug trends, drug markets and drug policy and evaluation. Over the past 20 years, he has completed a range of studies with particular focus on methamphetamine, cannabis, NPS, ecstasy, and organised crime and drug market structure. He has published over a hundred academic articles on a range of topics related to drug use, drug harms and policy response, including recently co-editing an international book evaluating cannabis legalisation reforms: *Legalizing Cannabis: Experiences, Lessons and Scenarios*, with Professors Tom Decorte and Simon Lenton.

Acknowledgements

This book could not have happened without the support of various groups and people along the way. The book was financially supported by the Centre for the Defence and Security Studies (CDSS) strategic advisory board. Specific thanks go to our board chair, Tony Lynch, for his foreword and his ongoing support. Working alongside the Massey University Press team has improved the book in so many little ways. We specifically thank the chapter contributors for their labour, ideas and contributions. Vanessa Bramwell and Imogen Coxhead delivered detailed work with the text at various stages. Thanks also go to long-serving CDSS administrator Tania Lasenby for all her support.

The book is indebted to all the students and staff at the CDSS. CDSS sits within the School of People, Environment and Planning in the College of Humanities and Social Sciences. The book is both informed by and informs all our discussions about security. We want to acknowledge our past and present CDSS colleagues. A particular mention goes to Professor Rouben Azizian, whose leadership of CDSS between 2015 and 2021 implicitly informs this work in so many ways and leaves him deservedly having the last chapter in the book.

Wil would like to thank Deidre McDonald for all her mahi, patience and excellent eye for detail as a co-editor. He would also like to acknowledge Kosal, Cassandra, Barbara and Alan for their patience, love and support.

Deidre would like to thank her chapter co-author, Dr Jodie Chapell, for her insights about the nature and meaning of security, and for her willingness to contribute to the collective and multiple discussions contained in this book. Her gratitude also goes to Dr Wil Hoverd, who suggested she might like to co-edit a book on security, for his expert guidance and leadership during this endeavour. On a personal note, a final thank-you to Gina, who has been very supportive of yet another writing project.

Index

5G internet networks 38
9/11 terrorist attacks 36, 76, 177
'501 deportees' 15, 113

academic experts 13
'accelerationism' 187
accountability *see* public accountability
adversarial idea acceptance 21
Afghanistan 15, 36, 46, 65, 156, 177, 223
Ainsworth, Kathy 191
air defence systems 46–47, 50, 51
Al Qaeda 17, 181
Alduino, Erica 191–92
algorithms 136, 141, 142, 143–44, 145, 212
All-Red Line cable network 99
'Ananda Marga four' 175
Antarctic Treaty 77
Antarctica 219
    Chinese research stations 74
anti-access area denial (A2/AD) concept
    56, 57
ANZUS Treaty 35
Aqua Link network 101
Aramoana, mass shooting 176, 177, 181, 182
Ardern, Dame Jacinda 12, 17, 20, 161, 163,
    165, 169–71, 172, 182, 208
armed neutrality 42, 44, 219
Armenia 238–39
Arms Act 1983 179
Arnold, Sir Terence 157
artificial intelligence (AI) 136
artificial intelligence use in biosecurity
    134–35, 136–37, 139–40
    applications 136
    biases and gaps in datasets 139–42,
        143–44
    limitations on assessment of threats
        138–39, 140, 143–45
    predictive analytics 136, 142–44
Asia, New Zealand's relations 204, 205–06
Asian Infrastructure Investment Bank
    (AIIB) 219
Asia-Pacific region 100, 104, 105, 106
    separatist movements 234–35
Association of Southeast Asian Nations
    (ASEAN) 235
Atlantic Council report (2023) 236
AUKUS agreement 23
    New Zealand as a Pillar 2 member
        23, 43, 143
Australia
    '501 deportees' 15, 113
    defence of Taiwan 37
    implications of China–US GPC 43
    implications of Chinese influence in the
        Pacific 40
    New Zealand's security and military
        relationship 33, 43–44, 77, 227
    and Russian-Ukrainian war 199

South Pacific Nuclear Free Zone (SPNFZ)
    Treaty 205
trade with China 21, 43, 73
Australian Maritime Safety Authority 79
authoritarianism 13, 23, 29, 34, 201, 206,
    209, 229, 230, 236, 239, 242, 243
Azerbaijan 234, 238, 239

Babbitt, Ashli 192
Belt and Road Initiative 73, 102
bin Laden, Osama 177
biosecurity 135–36, 244
    assemblages, assessment of threats 138–
        40, 141, 142
    classification of organisms 13
    dataset interpretation 140–41
    human values in decision-making 137–38,
        139, 145
    scenario-based predictions 143
    see also artificial intelligence use in
        biosecurity
Biosecurity Act 1993 103
Biosecurity Intelligence team (BSI)
    surveillance 124, 132–33
    adaptation of intelligence
        methodology 127
    analysis and assessment 130–31
    driver- and indicator-led approach 125–
        26, 127
    environment scan 128
    identifying indicators 128–29, 133
    monitoring indicators 129–30
    reporting 131–32
Biosecurity New Zealand 124
biosecurity operations 80, 122–23, 132–33,
    135, 164
    border management 123
    post-border management 123
    pre-border activity 123, 133
    prevention 123
    review and adaptability 124
    see also artificial intelligence use in
        biosecurity
Bitcoin 212, 214, 215
blockchain 212, 216, 217, 218–19
Boe Declaration on regional security 102–03
bombings 175–76
border closures, Covid-19 pandemic 18, 21,
    87, 92
border security and controls 85, 89, 123,
    129, 130, 136, 138, 145, 166; *see also* New
    Zealand Customs Service
Boswell, John 62–63, 68
Brentonettes 191
Brexit 21
BRICS countries 216
brown marmorated stinkbug (BMSB) 127,
    128, 129, 130, 131, 132, 140

Cabinet 150, 151, 152, 156, 159
  National Security Committee 162
cables 97–98; *see also* submarine cables
cannabis 112, 115, 120
  regions with highest proportion of
    purchasing 115–16, 118
central bank digital currencies (CBDCs) 212,
  214, 219–20
Central Intelligence Agency (US) 156
chemicals for improvising explosives 183
China
  concerns about invasion of Taiwan
    22–23, 37, 74, 203, 238, 243
  countries hosting China's investments in
    seaports 74
  Covid-19 border closure 21
  Covid-19 impact on trade 88
  de-dollarisation campaign 215, 216
  economy 37
  influence in the Pacific region 23–24
  maritime trade 73–74
  militarisation and military
    modernisation 22–23, 36–37
  near-alliance with Russia and Iran 37, 56
  North Korean treaty 39
  nuclear weapons 37
  Russian relations 22, 23, 39–40, 203, 237–38
  Solomon Islands base 24
  South Pacific interests 15
  spheres of influence 40, 41
  state-run capitalist model 40
  tacit support for Russia's invasion of
    Ukraine 23
  trade 14, 43, 73, 88 (*see also* maritime
    trade, above)
  trade with New Zealand 23, 33, 41, 43, 73,
    86, 241
  views on AUKUS 23–24
  Xinjiang region 241
China–United States relations
  differences between Cold War and current
    GPC 39–40
  GDP and defence budget growth
    1991–2022 37
  great-power competition 33–34, 37, 41–42,
    43, 45, 203
  technology 38–39, 41, 43–44
  threat of war between US and China
    39, 43, 55–56
  trade 21, 38
  US neo-containment strategy against
    China 38
  see also great-power competition (GPC)
China–United States relations: implications
  for New Zealand 33, 40, 41, 42, 45, 209,
  216, 217
  armed neutrality option 44–45
  asymmetric hedging option 42–43,
    205–06
  tight US alignment option 43–44
Christchurch Call 17, 170, 172, 182
Christchurch terror attack (2019) 12, 16–18,
  152, 163, 165, 172, 174, 178, 180–82, 244; *see
  also* Royal Commission of Inquiry into the
  Terrorist Attack on Christchurch Mosques
  on 15 March 2019

Civil Defence mechanisms 164
classified information 12, 160, 161, 171, 218
climate change 16, 36, 84, 86, 92, 170, 244
  global cooperation 42
  South Pacific impacts 15, 16, 44, 102–03, 108
  species habitat and fitness impacts 124
  threats to submarine cables 102–03,
    107, 108
cocaine 80, 120
co-governance, New Zealand 240
Cold War (1945–91) 34–35, 36, 38, 104, 126,
  177, 200–01, 202, 203, 224, 226, 232
community security
  gang influence 109, 110, 112–13, 116–18
  safety 118–20
conspiracy theories 20
container ports 71
container shipping 72
Convention for the Protection of Submarine
  Telegraph Cables (1884) 99, 103–04
Convention for the Safety of Life at Sea
  (SOLAS, 1914) 76
Convention on the International Regulations
  for Preventing Collisions at Sea
  (COLREGS) 76
conventional warfare 47–48, 51, 54
  aim 47
  applications of armed force 48, 54
  industrial demand 51, 53–54, 57
  manoeuvre operations 52, 53
  New Zealand's position 55–58
  potential characteristics of future
    conflict 55–58
  see also Russian-Ukrainian war
Corrections 109
cost-of-living concerns 45
counterterrorism activities 17, 152, 155, 157,
  164, 165, 166, 170, 177, 181, 183–84, 244
Covid-19 pandemic 16, 18–19, 42, 62, 68,
  80–81, 82, 88–89, 135, 163, 165
  link to rise in extremism 193
  lockdowns 18, 21, 87, 89
  see also border closures, Covid-19
    pandemic; managed isolation and
    quarantine (MIQ) facilities; supply
    chain disruptions during Covid-19
Crimea 37, 46, 50–51, 105, 199, 202, 207, 221,
  222, 233
Crimes Act 1961 166, 167
crisis response system 163–64, 172
cryptocurrencies 212, 213, 217
  decentralised environment 217–18
cryptocurrency mining 217–18
Cuban Missile Crisis (1962) 35
Cullen Reddy report 162
Cullen, Sir Michael 157
cybercurrencies *see* digital currencies
cyberthreats 15, 164, 165, 170, 182, 213,
  214, 244
  to submarine cables 104–05, 106, 108
Cyclone Gabrielle 19, 62, 68, 106–07

Davidson, Marama 232
'debt trap diplomacy' 24
Deep South Te Kōmata o te Tonga National
  Science Challenge 92

317

Index

Defence Assessment (Ministry of Defence, 2014) 207
Defence Policy and Strategy Statement (Ministry of Defence, 2023) 40
defence spending 227–28
  New Zealand 45, 58, 227, 244, 245
  Poland 223–24, 225
Defence White Paper (Ministry of Defence, 2016) 207, 222
democratic principles 201, 206, 227, 230, 238, 240
democratic principles, New Zealand 12, 14, 20, 35–36, 83, 166, 168, 208, 209, 246
  secret intelligence activities 149–50, 155–60
Department of Homeland Security (US) 104–05
Department of Prime Minister and Cabinet (DPMC) 12, 16, 90, 163, 167, 169, 172
digital currencies 211–12
  alternatives to the American dollar 215–16
  New Zealand's experience 213–15, 216–20, 246
  non-state cybercurrencies 215–16, 217, 218
Digital Economy Partnership Agreement 219
digital engagement, New Zealand 114
diplomacy 24, 45, 76, 202, 205, 206, 207–08, 209–10, 238, 245
dis- and misinformation 11, 20, 21, 145, 166, 170, 201, 246
disaster relief 48, 59, 62, 82
'Dissent Homeschool' 190–91
Donbas 50, 54, 232, 233
Dotcom, Kim 154, 162
drones 183
drug markets
  gang involvement 109, 110, 111–17, 120–21, 214
  smuggling 80, 214
Drug Use Monitoring in Australia 114

e-CNY 216
economy, New Zealand 41, 42, 44, 45, 65, 123, 137, 203, 214, 218, 244
ecstasy (MDMA) 115, 120
electromagnetic spectrum 52, 56
electronic warfare assets and systems 51–52, 53, 56
Elizabeth II, Queen, attempted shooting 175
English, Bill 161
environmental disasters 76, 164, 166
European Bank of Reconstruction and Development (EBRD) 199
European Union (EU) 14, 21, 199
exclusive economic zones (EEZs) 59, 74, 75
exotic plant and animal species 122; *see also* biosecurity operations
extremism, violent 8, 17, 21, 157, 166, 168, 169, 170, 179, 180, 182; *see also* right-wing extremism

Facebook 114
fake news 11
Faucheux, Bre 189, 190–91
feminism, views of right-wing extremists 187, 189–90, 194
Fiji 15

financial intelligence (FININT) 216–17
Finlayson, Chris 162
firearms 17, 178, 180, 184, 191
  gang-related offences 113
  mass killings 176–77, 179, 181
  regulation 180, 181–82, 183
Five Eyes (FVEY) relationships 12, 23, 24, 41, 42, 43, 44, 104, 106, 209
foot-and-mouth disease (FMD) 135, 136, 137
foreign interference 166–67, 171
foreign policy, New Zealand 200, 203–04, 225
  Asian direction 204, 205–06
  bilateral and multilateral cooperation 35, 41, 203, 204, 205, 206, 207, 208–09, 210
  independence in security matters 43, 45, 200, 205, 206, 209, 210
  see also China–United States relations: implications for New Zealand; national security, New Zealand; nuclear-free policy; and under names of countries and regions
free market 87–88, 243
freedom of speech 20, 188, 245, 246

Gang Harm Insights Centre (GHIC) 111
gangs *see* motorcycle gangs
geopolitical tensions 24, 29, 36, 42, 131, 166, 202, 206, 208, 219, 233, 234–35, 240–41, 242, 246
Georgia 37, 202, 222, 223, 234, 239
Gerasimov, Valery 50
global financial crisis (2018) 212
global security *see* international security
'Global War on Terror' 36
globalisation 22, 39, 70, 243
Government Communications Security Bureau (GCSB) 15, 104, 105, 150, 151–54, 156, 159–60, 162
great-power competition (GPC) 16, 19, 22, 37, 84, 108, 200, 215–16, 226
  definition 34
  see also China–United States relations
Grotius, Hugo 76
Gulf War (1991) 51
Gwyn, Cheryl 154–55, 157

hate speech and crime 17, 155, 186, 194, 245; *see also* Christchurch terror attack (2019)
Hawaiki Cable spur 102
He Whenua Taurikura (Hui, and National Centre of Research Excellence) 169, 170
Hipkins, Chris 161, 165, 167
homeschooling 190–91
housing crisis 21, 22
Huawei 38
human rights 35–36, 158, 160, 188, 203, 239, 241
humanitarian emergencies 36, 44, 48, 59, 62, 224–25

Illicit Drugs Monitoring System (Australia) 114
import health standards (IHS) 123, 124
Independent Police Complaints Authority 155
indicators in a warning system 125–26
  biosecurity threat assessment 126

Indonesia 233, 235, 241
Indo-Pacific region 33–34, 37, 45, 101, 209
  map 38
  militarisation and possibility of
    conflict 33, 37, 39, 47, 56
  minor regional reserve currency 219
  see also Asia-Pacific region; Pacific region
Industrial Revolution, Fourth 212
inflation 22, 82, 243
information warfare 47, 49
Inspector-General of Defence 160, 165
Inspector-General of Intelligence and
  Security 153–55, 156, 159
integrity mandates 157–58
Intelligence and Security Act 2017 17, 152,
  154, 162, 165, 167, 172
Intelligence and Security Committee 149,
  152–53, 154, 156–57, 159, 162
intelligence collection and networks 12, 44,
  45, 51–52, 53, 56, 57, 124, 244
  4i mode of intelligence-led operations 125
  financial intelligence (FININT) 216–17
  intelligence on gangs 109–10
  maritime security intelligence 77, 81
  use of submarine cables 104, 105
  see also Biosecurity Intelligence team
    (BSI) surveillance; secret intelligence
    activities; surveillance activities
interest rates 22, 82
International Cable Protection
  Committee 101
International Criminal Court 208
International Maritime Organization 76, 77, 79
International Monetary Fund 35, 199
international rules-based order 35–36, 39,
  41, 44, 59, 76, 88, 166, 200, 206, 207, 208,
  209, 221, 226, 229, 243
  maritime rules-based order 76, 77
international security 11, 59, 201–02
  New Zealand's role 203–04
  see also great-power competition (GPC)
International Ship and Port Facility Security
  (ISPS) Code 76, 78
International Terrorism (Emergency Powers)
  Act 1987 176
internet accessibility 97, 100, 107
introduced plant and animal species see
  exotic plant and animal species
Iran 37, 56, 215
Iraq 36, 46, 168
  Camp Taji 15
  US invasion (2003) 51, 55
Islamic State of Iraq and the Levant
  (ISIL) 14–15, 17, 36, 167–69, 172

James, Wolfie (Anna Vuckovic) 188
Japan 37, 40

Key, Sir John 151–52, 161, 162, 163, 165,
  167–69, 172
Kitteridge, Rebecca 167
Kitteridge Report (2012) 162
'Ko Tātou This is Us' biosecurity
  campaign 144
Ko tō tātou kāinga tēnei 152, 155, 157
Komorowski Doctrine 222–23

LaRosa, Tara 191
Lawrence, Katja 190–91
Lewis, Chris 175
Little, Andrew 15, 23, 62, 162
Lokteff, Lana 185, 188, 189, 190, 191
London Convention on the Prevention of
  Marine Pollution (MARPOL) 76
long-range precision weapons 51, 52–53,
  56, 57
LSD 115, 120
LynnMall terrorist attack (2021) 18, 156

Mahuika, Matanuku 157
Mahuta, Nanaia 232
managed isolation and quarantine (MIQ)
  facilities 18, 19, 62, 63, 68, 69; see also
  Operation Protect
Manus Island 15
Māori 13, 60, 91, 114, 115, 118, 120, 232,
  239–40, 241–42
Māori honey business, reciprocal
  relationships 91
Maritime New Zealand 79, 81, 82
  Rescue Coordination Centre 79
maritime patrol 77, 78
Maritime Security Act 2004
Maritime Security Oversight Committee
  (MSOC) 79, 82
Maritime Security Strategy 2020 (Ministry
  of Transport) 75–76, 77–78, 82, 83
maritime trade 70
  carrier mergers and acquisitions 72
  Chinese predominance 73
  Covid-19 impacts in New Zealand 80–81
  environmental aspects 78, 81
  merchant ship fleets, 1 January 2015 73
  potential threats to New Zealand
    trade 82–83
  rise in global maritime trade 71
  security 70, 75, 78, 79, 82–83, 166
  statistics 70–71
  terminal operations and logistics
    services 72
  threats from Russia's invasions of
    Ukraine 74–75
methamphetamine 109, 111–12, 113, 115, 120
  gang selling in small towns and rural
    areas 112, 120
  prices 112, 120–21
  regions with highest proportion of
    purchasing 115, 116, 118
military forces
  non-state 46, 48–49
  state 46, 48
military technologies 43, 47, 48, 51–52, 54, 57
Minister for National Security and
  Intelligence 12, 161, 167, 171–73
  public governance speeches 167–71
  purposes of creating the portfolio 162
  role and responsibilities 162–65
ministerial responsibility 150–53, 159
Ministry for Primary Industries 80, 81, 90,
  123, 124, 135
  Emerging Risks System 126
Ministry of Business, Innovation and
  Employment 90

Ministry of Defence 40, 207, 222
Ministry of Foreign Affairs and Trade 79, 240
Ministry of Health 89
    National Crisis Management Centre 90
Ministry of Transport 75, 76, 77, 79, 80–81, 82, 90
Minsk II agreements 49
misogyny 20, 21, 245
Moldova 234
monetary policy, New Zealand 215
    and fragmentation of global financial and monetary system 216
motorcycle gangs
    community impact 109, 110, 112–13, 116–20
    crime 109, 110, 214
    firearms offences 113
    illegal drug market involvement 109, 110, 111–17, 120–21, 214
    intelligence sources 109–10, 111
    membership numbers 109, 111, 115, 120
    patch wearing and tattoos 111, 117, 119
    regional variations and associations 110, 111, 115, 116, 118, 121
    violence 15, 109, 110, 113, 120, 121
munitions strikes 51, 52, 54, 57
Muslim community 17
Myanmar 234–35, 238
Mycoplasma bovis 16, 135

National Cyber Security Centre 213
National Gang List (NGL) 111
national identity 198, 210, 225, 245
National Security Agency (US) 104
National Security Conference, Massey University (2018) 179
national security, New Zealand 11–13, 59, 61, 63, 64, 67, 68–69, 162, 245–46
    bipartisan policy 12
    blockchain applications 218–19
    definitions 15–16, 161, 163–64, 165, 166–67, 171, 172
    threat environment, 2018–23 14–24, 244
    threats and risks 163–64, 165–71, 172–73, 214–15, 220, 222, 243–44
    see also foreign policy, New Zealand; Intelligence and Security Committee; Minister for National Security and Intelligence; secret intelligence activities
National Security Strategy (2023) 12–13, 16, 22, 165, 167, 170, 171, 173
NATO 23, 44, 54, 55, 200, 222, 243
natural disasters 15–16, 59, 70, 82, 85, 164, 170
    submarine cable damage 106–07
naval warfare 47, 53, 56, 57, 58
navies, size 71
    China 36–37, 74
neoliberal societies and values 60, 61, 63, 65, 67–68, 69, 87
New Caledonia 241
New Zealand Army 60
    attrition rate 60, 61–62, 63
    punishment 64
    reasons for joining and leaving 61, 62, 63, 65–67, 68

salaries 61, 62, 63, 67
self-development 61, 62, 63–64, 65–66, 67–68, 69
New Zealand Arrestee Drug Use Monitoring 114
New Zealand Customs Service 78, 80, 89, 90, 109
New Zealand Defence Force (NZDF) 15, 16, 19, 23, 58, 169, 229, 244, 245
    accountability 155
    Capability and Readiness update (2022) 62
    conventional warfare contribution 47, 55–58
    future force planning 57–58
    personnel shortages 58, 59, 60, 61, 62–63, 67, 68–69, 244
    roles 59, 61, 68–69, 78, 82
    support of international order based on law 225–27
New Zealand Drugs Trends Survey (NZDTS) 110, 113–18
New Zealand National Front 192
New Zealand Nuclear Free Zone, Disarmament, and Arms Control Act 1987 205
New Zealand Police 18, 19, 20, 65, 78, 80, 109, 111, 113, 115, 214, 2244
    anti-terrorist activities 174, 176, 177–78, 180–81
    Computer Centre bombing (1982) 175
    Te Urewera armed raids 155
New Zealand Security Intelligence Service (NZSIS) 15, 150, 151–54, 156, 159–60, 162, 176, 181
New Zealand Special Air Service (SAS) 15, 155, 156
New Zealand's Covid-19 Trade Recovery Strategy 88
nuclear-free policy 14, 35, 205, 206, 210
nuclear war threat 23, 200, 201, 210, 237

Officials Committee for Domestic and External Security Coordination 164, 165
online environment 20, 21, 170, 246
online purchasing 89
Operation Burnham Inquiry 165
Operation Eight 181
Operation Protect 18, 19; *see also* managed isolation and quarantine (MIQ) facilities
Optional Protocol to the Convention against Torture 158

Pacific Islands Forum 77, 102, 239
    Biketawa Declaration 239
Pacific Ocean 56
Pacific region 15
    China's influence 23–24
    conflict scenario 57, 58
    New Zealand relations 77–78, 166
    organisations, programmes and groups
    security 103, 166
    see also Asia-Pacific region; Indo-Pacific region; South Pacific
Pacific Reset Policy 15
pandemics 25, 85, 170, 244; *see also* Covid-19 pandemic

Papua New Guinea 39; *see also* West Papua
Parliament grounds protest (2022) 13, 18, 19–21, 87, 188, 244
peacekeeping 59, 177, 223
Pelosi, Nancy 22
people-centric warfare 54–55, 56
People's Republic of China *see* China
Philippines 39
piracy 70, 75, 85
platform-centric warfare 56
Poland
  aid for Ukraine 224–25, 230
  defence spending 223–24, 225
  NATO member 223
  response to Russian-Ukrainian war 221, 222–25, 227, 230
  security and defence policy 222–24
Polish Armed Forces 223, 224
Port Arthur, Tasmania 176, 177
ports 71, 75
  Chinese port facilities 73, 74, 81
  electronic systems 78
  New Zealand 78, 79, 80
prime minister 149, 151–52, 153, 154, 156, 159, 160, 161, 162, 163, 166, 172–73; *see also* Minister for National Security and Intelligence
privacy rights 158–59, 160
Productivity Commission 92
Proud Boys 191
Proud Girls 191
public accountability 149–50, 153, 155–60
  ministerial responsibility 150–53
public engagement with national security 13–14, 154, 156–57, 159, 160, 165, 167–71, 244, 246
Putin, Vladimir 23, 222, 232, 235, 236

radicalisation 179
Rainbow Warrior bombing (1985) 175–76
ransomware 213
rapid antigen tests (RATs) 89
recession
  global recession 16, 22, 85
  New Zealand 18, 22
Reddy, Dame Patsy 157
refugees
  assistance and processing systems 78
  New Zealand quotas 15
Regional Assistance Mission to the Solomon Islands (RAMSI) 60, 66, 240
Regional Comprehensive Economic Partnership 219
regional security 15, 66, 102–03, 203, 204, 205; *see also* Asia-Pacific region; Indo-Pacific region; Pacific region; South Pacific
Rena sinking 164, 166
renminbi internationalisation 216
Reserve Bank of New Zealand 214, 219–20
right-wing extremism 176, 178, 180
  ideological variations 186–87
right-wing extremism, women's involvement 185–86, 191–92, 193–94
  anti-feminism 187, 189–90, 194
  ideologies 187–88
  New Zealand 192–93

traditional wives (Trad Wives) 190–91, 193, 194
Ring of Fire, Pacific region 106, 108
Royal Commission of Inquiry into the Terrorist Attack on Christchurch Mosques on 15 March 2019 152, 155, 157, 165, 167, 182–83
Royal New Zealand Infantry Regiment 60
Royal New Zealand Navy 58, 80
  personnel shortages 82
rule of law 219, 246; *see also* international rules-based order
Russia
  break-up of the Federation 236–37
  de-dollarisation campaign 215–16
  Federal Security Service (FSB) 49–50
  hybrid warfare model
  imperial heritage 202
  near-alliance with China and Iran 37, 56
  New Zealand's relations 206–07, 230
  relations with China 22, 23, 39–40, 203, 237–38
  resurgence into former Soviet areas 37, 201, 222, 234, 235–36, 238
  sanctions 21, 40, 202–03, 207, 208, 210
  South Pacific interests 15
  spheres of influence 202
  trade 14, 203
  see also Soviet Union
Russia Sanctions Act 2022 207
Russian-Ukrainian war 21, 22, 23, 37, 39–40, 46–47, 48–49, 54–55, 199–203, 231, 243
  Chinese plan for political settlement 237–38
  dispersed operations 52–53, 57
  effect on sovereignty and territorial integrity principles 231, 232–33, 234–39, 242
  implications for New Zealand 55–58, 82, 207–09, 210, 221, 222, 226, 229–30
  land and air force experiences 53
  maritime threats 53, 74–75
  new technologies 48, 51–52, 54, 57, 183
  people-centric warfare 54–55
  Polish response 221, 222–25, 227, 230
  Russian propaganda 229
  Russia's invasion plan 50–51
  Russia's military build-up 49–50, 202
  social and mass media use 48
  support for Ukraine 202–03, 207, 210, 224–25, 226, 232, 243

Safe Goods group 90
Sambom, Sebby 233
Samsudeen, Ahamed Aathil Mohamed 18, 156
sanctions 75, 208–09, 238, 243
  New Zealand's regime 206, 207, 208, 209
  against Russia 21, 40, 202–03, 207, 208, 210
satellite communications 75, 100, 107
  low-orbit satellites 101, 107
search and rescue 59, 75, 79, 82
Search and Surveillance Act 2012 169
Second World War (1939–45) 40
secret intelligence activities 149
  democratic control 149–50, 155–60
  ministerial responsibility 150–53, 159
  oversight measures 153–55, 156, 158–59

see also Government Communications Security Bureau (GCSB); New Zealand Security Intelligence Service (NZSIS)
Seed, Chris 231–32
self-determination 233–34, 234–37, 242
  New Zealand's obligations 239–42
Short, Kevin 19, 62
Singapore, trade with New Zealand 91
small and medium enterprises (SMEs) 91
Snowden, Edward 104
Snyder, Timothy 229
social cohesion 17, 18, 20
social licence 87, 88, 145
social media 48, 56, 97, 129, 182, 189, 191, 192, 218; *see also* Facebook
social values 91, 245, 246
Society for Worldwide Interbank Financial Telecommunication (SWIFT) 102, 219
socioeconomic gaps 245
Solomon Islands
  Chinese base and influence 24, 41, 241
  see also Regional Assistance Mission to the Solomon Islands (RAMSI)
South China Sea 36, 41, 56
  Chinese artificial islets 74
South Pacific 39, 40
  climate change impacts 15, 16, 44, 102–03, 108
  communications networks 105
  implications of Chinese influence 40–41, 209
  New Zealand relations 77–78, 82, 163, 166, 204, 209, 226, 230, 245
  New Zealand's role in mitigating conflicts 240–42
  submarine cables 106, 108
  see also Pacific region
South Pacific Nuclear Free Zone (SPNFZ) Treaty 205
Southeast Asia Treaty Organization (SEATO) 204
Southern Cross Cable 101–02
Southern, Lauren 189, 191
sovereign states 233, 235, 242
Soviet Union 34–35, 36, 177, 201, 202, 237; *see also* Cold War (1945–91); Russia
space 42, 166, 200
Speargun metadata collection programme 104
Springbok Tour (1981) 175
'stablecoins' 212
standard of living, New Zealand 82, 227
Starlink satellite network 101
stewardship role of government 87, 151
Strategic Framework for Preventing and Countering Violent Extremism 170
submarine cables 97
  Cable Protection Areas, New Zealand 103
  Chinese companies 101, 102, 106
  coaxial telephone cables 100
  communications and content companies 101
  cyberattacks 104–05, 106, 108
  damage 98, 103–04, 105, 106–08
  high-bandwidth fibre-optic cables 100, 101–02, 104

history 98–100
  intelligence gathering use 104, 105
  military use 103–04
  natural disaster impacts 106–07
  New Zealand 98, 99–100, 101–02, 106–07, 108
  protection and response protocols 108
  Russian aggression 105
  security 75, 98, 102–08
  strategic importance 99, 100, 108
  'triple invisibility' 97–98
Submarine Cables and Pipelines Protection Act 1996 103
Suez Canal blockage by *Ever Given* 85
Sunak, Rishi 98
  Undersea Cables 105
supply chain disruptions 85–86, 243
  causes 21, 74, 75
  global trade impacts
  multiplier effect 86
  ripple effect 89
  societal assumptions 87–89, 92–93
  unpredictability and uncertainty 85, 86
supply chain disruptions during Covid-19 80–81, 84, 91
  border closures 18
  impact on small and medium enterprises 91
  industry groups 89, 90
  relationships between government officials 90–91
  working groups 90
Supply Chain Ministers Forum 81
supply chains 85
  community connections 89, 91, 93
  connections with government and society 85, 89
  free-market environment 87–88
  institutional relationships and personal connections 89–90, 91, 92, 93
  interconnected economic supply chains 39, 86
  international relationships 91, 92
  local government relationships 91, 92
  multiple agencies involved 89, 90
  pause points 85
  resilience 87, 88, 89, 92, 93, 166, 243
  security 18, 92
surveillance activities 39, 40, 52, 56, 77, 82, 104, 142–43, 144, 145, 154, 169, 178–80, 245
  digital surveillance 158
Switzerland 44–45
Syria 36, 46, 168

Taiwan 73, 106
  concerns about Chinese invasion 22–23, 37, 74, 203, 238, 243
Taiwan Strait, Chinese inspection of commercial ships 74
Tarrant, Brenton 178, 180, 181, 183, 191
Tasman Global Access Cable 102
Te Urewera armed raids 155
technology
  China and United States influence 38–39, 41
  new technologies in warfare 43, 47, 48, 51–52, 54

terrorism
global terrorism 15, 85, 168, 177, 179–80, 182
Islamic jihadi terrorism 17
mass-killing based 176–77, 179, 180
'self-initiated terrorists' 18
submarine cable attack potential 104, 108
see also 9/11 terrorist attacks; extremism;
'Global War on Terror'
terrorism, New Zealand 174–75, 184, 244
legislation 174, 175, 176, 177–78, 179
risks, past, present and future 15–16, 17–18,
174–78, 179–80, 181, 182–84, 186, 194
see also Christchurch terror attack (2019);
counterterrorism activities
Terrorism Suppression Act (2002) 177–78
'The Great Replacement' (TGR) 187, 191
Thorp Report (1997) 176–77, 181
Tokelau 240
trade 14, 70, 88, 243
Covid-19 impacts 88–89
erosion of trust in international trade
rules 88
global trade and supply chains 85
implications of Russian-Ukrainian war on
New Zealand trade 200
implications of US–China conflict on
New Zealand trade 43
New Zealand trade with China 23, 33, 41,
43, 73, 86, 241
New Zealand trade with Singapore 91
see also maritime trade; supply chains
Trade Recovery Strategy 88–89
Trades Hall bombing (1984) 175
transnational organised crime 15, 59, 104,
108, 166
use of unofficial cybercurrencies 214–15
Treaty of Waitangi 239
Trojan horse campaigns 188
Tusk, Donald 222

Ukraine 48–49, 50, 75, 105, 221, 222
sovereignty and territorial integrity 231,
232–33
see also Russian-Ukrainian war
uncertainties 85, 86, 140, 142
deep uncertainty 86–87, 93
Unite the Right rally, Charlottesville
(2017) 192
United Liberation Movement of West
Papua 233
United Nations 35, 77, 179, 201, 229
Charter 233, 239, 240
General Assembly 208
General Assembly emergency session on
Ukraine (2022) 238
Human Rights Council 208
Security Council 23, 177, 207, 208
United Nations Act 1946 206
United Nations Conference on Trade and
Development (UNCTAD) 71, 73, 75
United Nations Convention on the Law of
the Sea (UNCLOS) 76, 101
United Nations Declaration on the Rights of
Indigenous Peoples (2007) 239–40
United Nations Environment
Programme 101

United States
alternatives to the American dollar 215–16
commitment to Taiwan 23
Covid-19 impact on trade 88
GDP and defence budget growth
1991–2022 37
global primacy 36, 201, 203
internet 100
invasion of Iraq (2003) 51, 55
National Security Strategy (2017) 37
New Zealand's relationship 33, 35, 41,
42–44, 204, 206, 226, 227, 230
submarine cable monitoring 106
trade 14, 88
weaponisation of the American dollar 216
see also China–United States relations;
Cold War (1945–91); great-power
competition (GPC)
United States Coast Guard 79
United States Navy 71, 72
University of Waikato 100
unmanned aircraft systems (UAS) 51–52, 56
Uppsala Conflict Data Program 234, 241

vaccine mandates 18, 19, 21, 87
violence 12, 13, 17, 18, 20, 21, 149, 177–78,
179, 180, 183, 186, 187, 188, 192, 194, 244,
245; *see also* extremism, violent; and
under motorcycle gangs
Volitich, Dayanna 191

Waikato District Health Board
cyberattack 213
war crimes 208
warfare
character of warfare 47
hybrid warfare 23, 46, 105, 108
information warfare 47, 49
intra-state and state-to-state conflicts 234
nature of war 47
new technologies 43, 47, 48, 51–52, 54
see also conventional warfare; Russian-
Ukrainian war; China–United States
relations; Taiwan
Warkworth Satellite Earth Station 100
Weaver, Vicky 191
welfare state 64–65
Wenda, Benny 233
West Papua 233, 235, 241; *see also* Papua
New Guinea
Western Operation Against ISIL 15
Whakaari White Island eruption (2019) 16, 165
white nationalism 187–88, 189–90, 191,
192–93
World Bank 199
World Conservation Monitoring Centre 101
World Organisation for Animal Health 137
World Peace Council (WPC) 201
World Trade Organization 35

First published in 2023 by Massey University Press
Private Bag 102904, North Shore Mail Centre
Auckland 0745, New Zealand
www.masseypress.ac.nz

Text copyright © individual contributors, 2023

Design by Megan van Staden
Cover images by Stuff Media Ltd

The moral rights of the authors have been asserted

All rights reserved. Except as provided by the Copyright Act 1994, no part of this book may be reproduced, stored in or introduced into a retrieval system or transmitted in any form or by any means (electronic, mechanical, photocopying, recording or otherwise) without the prior written permission of both the copyright owner(s) and the publisher.

A catalogue record for this book is available from the National Library of New Zealand

Printed and bound in New Zealand by Bluestar

ISBN: 978-1-99-101652-2
eISBN: 978-1-99-101663-8